Engage Students to Embrace Civility

Embrace Civility
(Second Edition)

NANCY WILLARD, M.S., J.D.

ENGAGE STUDENTS TO EMBRACE CIVILITY

(Second Edition)

Nancy Willard, M.S., J.D. Embrace Civility LLC

The Appendices for this book are available online on the Embrace Civility LLC website at http://embracecivility.org.

ISBN: 978-0-9724236-8-7

Imprint: Independently published by Embrace Civility LLC

Attention school districts: Quantity discounts are available on bulk purchases.

Praise for Engage Students to Embrace Civility

Nancy's approach is centered on using young people as agents of change who can powerfully transform their communities by modeling and sharing positive behaviors marked by kindness, civility, respect, inclusion, and meaningful resolution of hurtful situations. Nancy has painstakingly reviewed the relevant research and distilled the implications to a manageable and understandable set of guidelines that professionals working in schools can incorporate into their activities. *Engage Students to Embrace Civility* provides excellent insight to help support a positive school climate, to empower young people to reduce hurtful behavior and build positive relationships, and to improve the responses of principals in serious situations.

- Sameer Hinduja. Ph.D. and Justin W. Patchin, Ph.D. are co-directors of the Cyberbullying Research Center co-director of the Cyberbullying Research Center, co-author of *Bullying Today: Bullet Points and Best Practices, Bullying Beyond the Schoolyard: Preventing and Responding to Cyberbullying (2nd edition), Words Wound: Delete Cyberbullying and Make Kindness Go Viral.*

Nancy Willard has integrated and translated the current research and knowledge on effective bullying prevention into a set of very useful and practical tools. *Engage Students to Embrace Civility* will help schools transform the problem of bullying into an opportunity for creating and sustaining a safer and more supportive learning environment for students, parents and staff.

- James Dillon, Director, The Center for Leadership and Bullying Prevention, author of *Reframing Bullying Prevention to Build Stronger School Communities.*

Nancy Willard's new book, *Engage Students to Embrace Civility*, stands out as highly relevant, comprehensive, and evidence-based. This book results from decades of research, practical experience, and personal passion. Unlike many others, Nancy's program is solution-focused, using young peoples' strengths as a real opportunity to make a difference while also building critical knowledge and skills. This book is a unique intersection of education, character development, school policy, and common sense. Nancy's challenges to the status quo are timely and welcomed. *Engage Students to Embrace Civility* is a must-read for anyone who works with youth and wants to engage and empower them to embrace civility more effectively.

- Dr. Russell A. Sabella is currently a Professor in the College of Education, Florida Gulf Coast University, and President of Sabella & Associates. He has published articles, magazine columns, and a book focusing on helping kids with their digital reputations and cyberbullying. Russ has also presented to students, school staff, and parents/caretakers throughout the country. He is Past President of the American Association of School Counselors.

Nancy Willard is a knowledgeable, caring and tough – in the best sense of the word! – advocate for all children. Combining educational and legal understandings, Nancy is an important leader in supporting and furthering practically important school improvement efforts. *Engage Students to Embrace Civility* provides helpful research-based insight and practical guidance for school leaders to establish a more positive school climate and respond effectively to the more serious hurtful situations in a manner that is in accord with civil rights regulations.

- Jonathan Cohen, Ph.D., Co-president, International Observatory for School Climate and Violence Prevention; Adjunct Professor in Psychology and Education, Teachers College, Columbia University; President Emeritus and co-founder, National School Climate Center.

Nancy combines a genuine passion for justice for kids with an equal desire to help schools cope with the challenges they face and shift to a more positive approach. In *Engage Students to Embrace Civility* Nancy goes beyond the standard guidance provided to school leaders to address these concerns. Her insights, thoroughly backed by current research, show schools how to effectively engage students in leadership roles and foster a more positive school climate.

- Stuart Green, DMH, LCSW, Founding Board Member, Alliance for Social Emotional Learning in NJ; Associate Director, Overlook Family Medicine Residency Program; Clinical Assistant Professor of Family Medicine, Sidney Kimmel Medical College of Thomas Jefferson University.

Contents

Introduction

Introducing Me

I thought I would introduce myself and tell you a bit about my background. In this way you will understand the driving motivations in my life and my underlying perspectives.

"Weirdo Willard" was my name throughout junior high school in the 60's in southeast Idaho. My mother, a graduate in chemical engineering in Philadelphia, was promoting woman's liberation—on local talk radio. This did not go over well in this conservative community. From my mother, I learned about the importance of speaking up and supporting those who are more marginalized. My sister, who is highly intelligent, had dyslexia. She was constantly bullied by her teachers—which, of course, led to her experiencing even more profound bullying than I did.

You will see evidence of this driving motivation in this book. I learned of the pain that can be caused by being bullied both by students, as well as by school staff.

We moved to Idaho because my father had invented the process to make potato flakes while working in a government laboratory in Philadelphia. He helped to set up the first potato flake processing plant. He went on to invent many more food products. From my father I learned the importance of learning from failure. All inventors fail much more than they succeed.

He was able to invent the process of of making potato flakes by evaluating why the prior process, potato granules, resulted in a glob of inedible starch. By studying the underlying nature of potato starch, he was able to create a new way to dry it, grounded in research of the underlying nature of potato starch—which could be successfully reconstituted.

What schools are currently doing to try to address bullying is failing. While increased efforts to address bullying were launched in 2010, there is zero evidence of effectiveness. The harmful impact of the pandemic, which had a devastating impact on more marginalized communities, as well as the controversies associated with emerging demands for greater equity and inclusion, has led to increased disruption in our schools.

When school leaders continue to use the same approaches, that have no evidence of effectiveness, they should be mindful of what Einstein reportedly said about this. (Apparently, Einstein did not say this.[1])

> Insanity Is Doing the Same Thing Over and Over Again
> and Expecting Different Results.

I became a special education teacher of students with emotional challenges, burned out, went to law school, and became involved with software companies. I shifted to educational technology planning. Then the Internet came into schools—and there was a need for someone who understood student behavior, legal issues, and technology in schools.

Through this, I became a recognized authority on digital safety. I testified before a Congressional Commission and for a National Academy of Sciences committee which prepared a report on digital safety.[2] In this era, the primary approach to protection was filtering software. Oh, and some members of Congress were going to make cyberbullying a federal crime.

I read to them from Dr. Seuss's *Oh, the Places, You'll Go.*

> *You'll look up and down streets. Look 'em over with care.*
> *About some you will say, "I don't choose to go there."*
> *With your head full of brains and shoes full of feet.*
> *You're too smart to go down those not-so-good streets.*

So this brings us to a discussion on the first two words of the title of this book "engage students." Why engage students? Several reasons. As they become teens, adults are often not present. Rules and policies are obviously not working. The accepted social norms of the students have far greater influence. If the students in your school who are considered "popular" and "cool" are modeling that it is okay to treat those "weirdos" or "misfits" in your school badly, school staff are not going to be successful in changing these behaviors.

Along with engagement comes "empowerment." Many students will face no ongoing challenges being treated badly. However, others will continue to have such challenges. These are students who are "misfits"—frequently members of identity groups that are more marginalized in our society. They will always face the potential that someone will be hurtful to them. It is not possible to "protect them." We have to empower them.

We have to help them gain those heads full of brains and shoes full of feet so they can reduce the potential of being treated badly, effectively respond when they are, and have the support systems in place so that they are not unduly harmed by the hurtful acts of others. They need to know that while they cannot control what might happen to them, they do have the ability to control how they feel about themselves and respond.

The initial concerns related to the Internet were porn and predators. However, as social media emerged, first open a site called MySpace, and young people flocked to this, the concern of cyberbullying arose. I wrote the first book ever published on cyberbullying, *Cyberbullying and CyberThreats: Responding to the Challenge of Online Social Cruelty, Threats, and Distress.* I self-published in 2006 and then my book was picked up by an academic publisher. Facebook opened from a college site to the general public in fall of 2006.

I have always maintained a strong focus on the research. So I focused on the existing research on bullying. Thereupon, I discovered two concerns:

The description of those who engage in bullying did not fit with the students who I saw engaging in cyberbullying. This also did not match the description of those who bullied me back in the 60's. This included the description that was on the website of United States (US) Health Resources and Services Administration (USHRSA), Substance Abuse and Mental Health Services Administration (SAMHSA), then called Stop Bullying Now.[3] The more recent research that demonstrates that I was correct in my understanding is set forth in Chapter 2.

The recommended approach to address bullying was not going to work in cyberspace. This recommended approach was to have a policy against bullying, supervise, tell students to report, investigate, and punish the wrongdoer. How was this going to work in an environment where schools are not making the rules, adults are not present, students are not reporting because they know that adults will overreact and make things worse, principals do not have the skills to investigate, and punishment can lead to uncontrollable digital retaliation? Based on survey data here in the US, which has been measuring bullying since 2009, this approach does not appear of have resulted in a reduction of in-person bullying either.

In 2010, I shifted my focus to all forms of bullying and hurtful behavior. It is not possible to address cyberbullying as some kind of separate phenomenon. Also in this year, the Obama Administration launched significant efforts to better address bullying. With the passage of the *Every Student Succeeds Act (ESSA)*, most attention to bullying in schools vanished. The reason for this is explained in Chapter 3.

Those of us in this field have not achieved any significant success in seeking to provide guidance to schools on more effective approaches to address bullying since the passage of *ESSA*. It is my hope that the increased level of concerns subsequent to the pandemic have provided the incentive to consider alternative approaches to address these challenges.

INTRODUCTION OF BOOK

Engage Students to Embrace Civility provides schools leaders and mental health professionals with guidance—grounded in academic research and legal principles—to fully engage students to maintain positive relationships and effectively respond when hurtful behavior occurs, either within your school environment or between students online. This includes the objectives of both reducing the instances of such hurtful behavior and responding in a way that stops and remedies the harm. Civility means being kind and respectful, even if you disagree.

The term "school leaders" should be read to incorporate district and building leadership, as well as mental health professionals.

The title of this book is *Engage Students to Embrace Civility*. The title of the companion student program is *Empowered to Embrace Civility*. So what is "civility?" I totally embrace this definition from The Institute for Civility in Government:

> *What is Civility?*
>
> *Civility is claiming and caring for one's identity, needs and beliefs without degrading someone else's in the process. ...*
>
> *Civility is about more than just politeness, although politeness is a necessary first step. It is about disagreeing without disrespect, seeking common ground as a starting point for dialogue about differences, listening past one's preconceptions, and teaching others to do the same. Civility is the hard work of staying present even with those with whom we have deep-rooted and fierce disagreements. It is political in the sense that it is a necessary prerequisite for civic action. But it is political, too, in the sense that it is about negotiating interpersonal power such that everyone's voice is heard, and nobody's is ignored.*
>
> *And civility begins with us.*[4]

My shortened definition is: Being kind and respectful to others—even if you disagree or think they are "different."

Key Components of Engage Students to Embrace Civility

The key components of engaging students to embrace civility are:

- **Engage Students.** Empower students in efforts to maintain positive relationships and respond effectively when hurtful incidents occur. Students are the ones who are interacting with each other—in positive or negative ways. Students are the ones who either support or encourage hurtful behavior. When students express their disapproval, hurtful behavior most often stops. When students support those who are treated badly, the distress is better resolved. Adults are not in control. We must empower students to maintain positive relationships.

- **Focus on Civility**. Focus on "embracing civility," rather than "anti-bullying." This is a shift from the negative to the positive. This focus on civility also seeks to avoid a focus on identity groups and identity politics—focusing on the goals of unity along with respect for diversity, where every student feels safe, welcomes, and respected.

- **Collaboratively Build a Positive School Climate.** Build a school climate that will foster positive relationships—rather than relying on adult control "rules and punishment" approaches. Shift from an authoritarian approach to an authoritative approach that maintains a strong focus on maintaining positive values, not domination to ensure compliance. Ensure the voices of students, parents or caregivers, and community partners are collaboratively engaged. Focus on community developed standards and values that support positive relationships and will create an environment where everyone feels welcomed and supported.

- **Address all Forms of Hurtful Behavior.** Focus on reducing all forms of hurtful behavior. Do not focus solely on what is called "bullying"—which has too many conflicting definitions. Hurtful incidents that do not meet the various definitions of "bullying" can also disrupt the school community and cause students to experience emotional distress. This includes hurtful acts directed at students because of their identity, persistent but more minor hurtful acts, pervasive hurtful acts, retaliation situations, and bi-directional hurtful acts. Strong school community norms against hurtful behavior, in all forms, will create an environment where all students are focused on maintaining positive relationships.

- **Empower Targeted Students.** Empower targeted students by supporting them to build their underlying self-confidence and social skills to reduce the likelihood of their being treated badly, effectively respond when they are, and to reduce the likelihood of emotional harm by maintaining support networks and a focus on their future. Assuming that "victimized" students will always require the assistance of adults to protect them will only result in the continuation of their victimization. These students cannot control what might happen to them. They can control how they feel about themselves and respond.

- **Address the Concerns of All Hurtful Students.** Address the concerns of the students who are the greatest source of hurtful behavior—the popular, "leadership" students who are hurtful to achieve dominance and social status. There are two kinds of students who engage in hurtful behavior. This includes the "at risk" students, who have both experienced adversities and are now being reactively aggressive. But socially-skilled popular students are the greatest source of hurtful behavior. As these students are generally compliant, staff may not recognize or acknowledge the hurtful behavior they direct at others. Risk prevention approaches will not achieve success in reducing this hurtful behavior. Shifting these students away from the path of being hurtful to others to achieve dominance will require a focus on positive social norms and elevating in status other kinds of leadership students in your school—those who are consistently kind and step in to help.

- **Address Staff Bullying of Students.** Ensure appropriate policies and practices are in place to prevent staff maltreatment of students. Unfortunately, staff maltreatment of students is a generally unrecognized concern. Further, there are generally no negative consequences when staff are hurtful to students. This must change. When staff consistently model kindness and respect for all students, the hurtful behavior of students can be significantly reduced.

- **Empower Compassionate Student Leaders.** Identify and empower a diverse group of students who are consistently kind and inclusive, who step in to help, and who have a natural drive for leadership to function as a student leadership team encouraging civility, positive relationships, and positive peer intervention. Make sure your empowered team of student leaders is diverse and represents all student groups within your school—except for those who are hurtful to achieve dominance. This is a way to communicate to all students which leadership approach is supported in your school.

- **Emphasize Positive Social Norms.** Recognize the vast majority of students do not like to see their peers be hurtful to others. Further, they strongly admire those who are kind and respectful, step in to help, respond to being treated badly in a positive manner, and stop themselves and say they are sorry if they were hurtful. It is possible to solicit these positive social norms via a local survey. Schools can then provide insight into these positive norms, along with insight into strategies students can use to better maintain positive relationships, through indirect instructional approaches that are coordinated by positive student leaders.

- **Reduce Impulsive Retaliation.** Reduce impulsive retaliation by supporting students in gaining increased self-regulation and personal power, knowing that others can change, having effective problem solving skills, and having positive connections with supportive peers and adults. Impulsive retaliation appears to be frequently implicated in hurtful situations.

- **Focus on Accountability.** Engage students who have been hurtful in a process that leads to acceptance of personal responsibility, efforts to remedy the harm, and a commitment not to engage in further hurtful acts. By treating hurtful situations as disciplinary matters, the school staff member usurps the position of the student who was treated badly, who deserve a remedy of the harm. The disciplinary approach turns the matter into a violation of a rule with a punishment that is imposed by the adult authority—and frequently leads to retaliation against the targeted student.

- **Provide Trauma and Resilience Informed Support.** Provide support for students who are persistently targeted, as well as those who have suffered adversities, are treated badly at school, and who are also being hurtful. These students should be supported to better maintain positive relationships, self-regulate, and achieve happiness.

- **Increase Positive Peer Interventions.** Increase positive peer intervention by students who witness hurtful incidents by empowering students to effectively step in to help, be supportive of those who are treated badly, encourage those who were hurtful to stop and remedy the harm, and report serious or unresolved situations to an adult who can help. This requires a focus on motivation, personal power, self-efficacy, school climate, the role of friends, and, most importantly, a focus on positive norms that support such positive intervention actions.

- **Support Staff to Effectively Intervene in Minor Incidents.** Support staff in gaining the skills to effectively intervene when they witness hurtful incidents. Research documents significant concerns regarding the effectiveness of school staff in responding to the hurtful incidents they witness. This is not surprising given that generally staff are only taught about the enforcement school rules and not how to help students resolve hurtful incidents. Staff must also identify when a more minor incident they witness is evidence of a more serious persistent hurtful situation.

- **Ensure Effective Interventions When Students Report.** Implement a diversionary restorative approach in more serious, persistent, or pervasive hurtful situations that holds those who are hurtful accountable, supports and empowers those who are treated badly, addresses any school environment concerns that are contributing to the situation, and monitors to ensure things have gotten better for all involved students. The majority of students do not report. Simply repeatedly telling students to "tell an adult" and setting up new digital reporting systems are not approaches that will lead to greater numbers of students reporting—if when they do so there is a significant likelihood that things will not get better.

STRUCTURE OF THIS BOOK

This book is set forth in four major parts, with eleven chapters:

Part 1. The Harmed, the Harms, the Hurtful, and What is Not Working

- **Chapter 1. Being Bullied and Harms.** This Chapter outlines what this book focuses on—specifically "hurtful behavior." The term "bullying" has a multitude of definitions, which is part of the problem. This Chapter addresses the two kinds of targets of hurtful behavior. This includes students who have experienced significant adversities, who are also being hurtful. The term "bully/victim" is generally applied to these students. This is backwards—these are students who have experienced adversities in numerous ways, who are now also being hurtful. This also includes those students who are targeted, many of whom are considered to be "social misfits." This Chapter addresses Identity-Based Bullying. The numerous harms from being bullied are also set forth, including the overall harmful impact, as well as concerns associated with suicidal and violent behavior.

- **Chapter 2. The Nature of Hurtful Behavior.** This Chapter addresses two critical issues of those who engage in hurtful behavior, both of which are very frequently not accurately addressed. The greatest source of hurtful behavior are not the "at risk" students who are also being hurtful, who are addressed in Chapter 1. The greatest source of bullying are students who are socially skilled and generally compliant to staff—who are being hurtful to achieve dominance and social status. Risk prevention approaches will have no positive effect in stopping this hurtful behavior. The other issue that is rarely addressed is bullying of students by staff. Bullying of students by staff is almost entirely ignored in the research literature. When staff are hurtful to students, even in more minor ways that suggest this student is a "misfit," this can significantly increase the potential that the targeted student will also be treated badly by students.

- **Chapter 3. Anti-Bullying Activities Effectiveness Concerns.** This Chapter will address the concerns associated with the rules and punishment thinking that underlies most bullying prevention guidance and statutory directives. There is zero evidence that this approach is achieving any success. The vast majority of students do not report. When they do, this most often does not resolve the situation and too often makes things worse. Of significant concern in the US, is an additional requirement that schools report the number of bullying incidents that have been alleged to the federal government. This requirement of schools appears to be having a profoundly negative impact on the willingness of schools to engage in effective efforts to respond to any reported incidents. This Chapter also addresses the concerns associated with Positive Behavior Interventions and Supports and Restorative Practices, as well as Institutional Betrayal.

Part II. Research that Supports an Effective Approach

- **Chapter 4. Positive School Climate.** This Chapter will present the research upon which the recommendations in this book for reducing hurtful behavior are grounded. As is clearly evident in Chapter 3, what schools are currently doing is not working effectively. New approaches are needed. It is important that these approaches are grounded in research. The research-based approaches presented in this Chapter focus on the overall school climate issues. This includes Framework for Success, Continuous Improvement, Likelihood of Success, Authoritative School Management, Trauma and Resilience Practices, Self Determination Theory, Authentic Student Voice, Prestige Leaders, Social Emotional Growth Mindset, Positive Psychology, Character Strengths, Positive Social Norms, Principles of Influence, and Reflective Listening.

- **Chapter 5. Teen Development.** This Chapter addresses developmental factors that impact approaches that will be successful in addressing hurtful behavior in secondary schools, brain development, including the key areas of the brain that are involved in self-regulation, decision making and distress, moral development, identity development, trauma, and neuroplasticity. Understanding these factors will lay the groundwork for an understanding of strategies set forth in Chapters 6, 7, and 8, to support students in becoming empowered and resilient, accepting personal responsibility, and stepping in to help.

- **Chapter 6. Positively Powerful—Empowerment of Students.** This Chapter addresses issues that are of specific importance to supporting students who are more frequently targeted, including those who are both targeted and are being hurtful. The insight presented in this Chapter can also support all students in becoming more personally empowered. This is especially helpful as a way to increase the personal power of students to step into hurtful situations to help achieve a resolution. The Chapter then presents seven powerful strategies that are grounded in resilience and Positive

Psychology insight that can support all students in becoming more resilient and positively empowered.

- **Chapter 7. Accountability and Remedy.** This Chapter presents the research that is specifically focused on how to influence hurtful students to accept personal responsibility for their actions, develop a plan to remedy the harm, and discontinue being hurtful or supporting someone who is being hurtful in the future. This is especially focused on strategies to implement with those students who are being hurtful to achieve dominance, as well as their supporters.

- **Chapter 8. Positive Peer Intervention.** This Chapter presents a research-based approach to influence and empower students who are witnesses of hurtful incidents to step in to help. When students witness someone being hurtful they have a choice. They can be a hurtful supporter, a passive observer, or a helpful ally. There appear to be three personal factors that are implicated in a decision to step in to help. These include personal values, personal power, and self-efficacy. There also appears to be three environmental factors—friendships, the school climate, and the perception of the norms. There are also barriers that interfere with stepping in to help.

Part III. Legal Issues

- **Chapter 9. Civil Rights and Free Speech.** This Chapter presents insight into the requirements under the US civil rights regulations. These requirements include responding in a manner that is reasonably directed at stopping the hurtful behavior, remedying the harm to the target, correcting aspects of the environment that appear to be contributing to the hurtful situation, and monitoring to ensure the hurtful situation has stopped. This is the foundation of the approach that should underly a resolution for all students, not only those who are considered to be a Protected Class under the civil rights laws. This Chapter also addresses free speech laws, including how to address the distinctions of free speech versus hurtful speech and how to respond to hurtful online speech.

Part IV. Instruction and Intervention Strategies

- **Chapter 10. *Empowered to Embrace Civility*.** This Chapter provides recommendations on strategies to more fully engage students in maintaining positive relationships and civility. This Chapter provides insight on the establishment of a Student Leadership Team and insight into the implementation of an indirect instruction strategy to transmit information about the Positive Social Norms of a school, as well as personal relationship skills. The approach and objectives of the companion *Empowered to, Embrace Civility* are addressed in this Chapter.

- **Chapter 11. Intervention and Empowerment.** This Chapter provides guidance on how school leaders and staff can positively intervene in hurtful incidents. There are two objectives of this intervention approach. One is to stop the hurtful behavior, remedy the harm to the target, and correct the Hostile Environment. The second underlying objective is, through this process, to impart insight and skills to students to more effectively resolve hurtful incidents in the future.

Appendices

The Appendices for this book are provided on the Embrace Civility LLC website. They can be downloaded in 8 1/2 x 11 page format and reproduced.

EMPOWERED TO EMBRACE CIVILITY STUDENT PROGRAM

A student empowerment program, *Embrace Civility*, is provided as a supplement to this book. More information about this program is available on the Embrace Civility LLC website at http://embracecivility.org. This program uses an indirect instructional approach, with active student leadership. More information is included in Chapter 10. This program is provided at a low price based on the average number of students in a school.

EMBRACE CIVILITY STUDENT SURVEY

In October, 2015, I conducted a national survey of 1,549 secondary students on bullying and hurtful behavior. The insight from this survey was used to inform the development of the *Engage Students to Embrace Civility* approach. Students were asked questions about hurtful incidents. "Hurtful" was defined for them as including what is typically called "bullying," but also including other hurtful interactions. This was an intentionally broad definition.

Students were asked how frequently in the last 30 days they experienced someone being hurtful to them, how frequently they were hurtful, how frequently they witnessed a student be hurtful to another, and how frequently they had witnessed a school staff member be hurtful to a student. If students reported someone had been hurtful, they were asked how upset they were and how effective they felt in responding. If they had been hurtful, they were asked what they were thinking at the time.

An analysis was done to identify the "more vulnerable" students. Those who had been treated badly once or twice a week or almost daily, were upset or very upset, and who felt it was very difficult or impossible to get this to stop. Nine percent (9%) of the students were considered to be "more vulnerable" based on this criteria. Based on other survey data I have seen, I think this figure is closer to accurate in terms of the percentage of students who are being seriously harmed through the experience of someone being hurtful to them at school.

Students who reported that someone was hurtful to them or that they were hurtful were also asked whether staff was present and, if so, how effectively the staff member responded. Students who reported that someone was hurtful to them were also asked if they reported this to the school, if so, how effectively the school responded, and, if not, why not.

Students were asked numerous other questions to identify their norms and values related to being hurtful or witnessing hurtful situations. Insight from this survey will be discussed throughout this book.

A new version of this survey is included as an Appendix to this book. This *Embrace Civility Student Survey* is also a key component of the *Empowered to Embrace Civility* student program.

TERMINOLOGY

The term "bully" and "victim" will only appear in this book on a few occasions. This terminology is harmful. To call students these terms is a form of name calling. When children are labeled as "bullies" or "victims" this can send a Fixed Mindset message that this is who they are and that their attitudes and behavior cannot change. We must take a Social Emotional Growth Mindset perspective that their attitudes, behavior, and situations can change.

I will use the term "bullying" in the context of a discussion of the research, as this is all framed in the context of the use of his term. I will use the term "harassment" in the context of a discussion of legal issues. In other sections, I will seek to avoid the use of these terms unless necessary to the context. I suggest it would be helpful, as best as possible, to avoid the use of the terms "bullying" or "anti-bullying" and seek to shift the discussion to address all forms of "hurtful behavior." More on this definition issue in in Chapter 1.

The terms "racist," "homophobic," "transphobic," "ableist" also will not appear in this book. It is my perspective that use of these Fixed Mindset terms is also harmful name calling. Acts associated with these terms are also behavior—not who these people are. These are people who are engaging in unacceptable discrimination and bias based on the identity of others. Hopefully, these are also attitudes and behavior we can change to create a society that is more inclusive.

The National Institutes of Health started an office in 2015 called the Sexual & Gender Minority Research Office.[5] I prefer this term to LGBTQ+ and variations.

The terms "he" and "she" will not appear. Fortunately, the battles with grammarians over the use of "they" as a singular third-person pronoun have been finally won.

The term "incidents" is used in most chapters to describe hurtful incidents. However, as discussed in 11, when intervening in these situations it is necessary to distinguish between more minor "incidents" from the more serious, persistent, or pervasive situations. In this Chapter, the terms "Incidents" and "Situations" are used to make this distinction.

Proper grammarians would insist my use of prepositions at the end of a sentence or question is wrong. "Who did you have a positive connection with?" It should be written, "With whom…

Sorry grammarians. Nobody talks this way. Especially, students do not talk this way. If there is a suggestion they use the "with whom" language, they will feel that some old adult is dictating how they should think and act. I have chosen to violate the rules of grammar in this regard.

Empowerment of "Misfits"

Finally, some words about misfits. Thornberg reviewed qualitative studies of students, that asked them to describe attributes of those who are victimized by bullying[6]

> Research has shown that a common explanation among students as to why bullying occurs is that the victim is different or deviant in some way, such as having different clothes, appearance, behaviour or way of speaking. The victim is seen as a person who does not fit in.

Among the words describing those who are targets of bullying in this article were: " deviant and marginal," "unpopular and socially rejected," "deviant student," "odd student who deserved to be treated with hostility," "'little bit different," "odd," "weird" "student who did not behave as he or she should have," "deviant students disturb the existing order and threaten the status quo— and its demands on conformity."

I do use the term "misfit" sometimes in this article. My use of this term is in praise, in similar manner to this statement:

> *Here's to the crazy ones. The misfits. The rebels. The troublemakers. The round pegs in the square holes. The ones who see things differently. They're not fond of rules. And they have no respect for the status quo. You can quote them, disagree with them, glorify or vilify them. About the only thing you can't do is ignore them. Because they change things. They push the human race forward. And while some may see them as the crazy ones, we see genius. Because the people who are crazy enough to think they can change the world, are the ones who do.* — Rob Siltanen[7]

Being a bullied "misfit" I have great love and respect for all "misfits." Who in the world would want to be "normal?"

However, for "misfits" to accomplish positive change in this world, they need to become empowered. There are too many disempowered "misfits" walking around schools with the ever present fears they will be treated badly—experiences that have undermined their success and happiness for the rest of their lives. This must change.

AVOIDANCE OF TOXIC IDENTITY POLITICS

The underlying focus in this book is to ensure that all students feel safe, welcomed, and respected in school and in society.

PART I
The Harmed, the Harms, the Hurtful, and What is Not Working and Why

Chapter 1.
Being Bullied and Harms

HIGHLIGHTS

The Highlights from this Chapter include:

- **Definition of Bullying**. There are too many confusing definitions of "bullying." The academic definition incorporates the concepts of intent to inflict harm, repetition, and imbalance of power. Various statutory definitions often include both "bullying" and "harassment." In the US, there are 50 different state definitions. The definition of "discriminatory harassment" is grounded in civil rights laws. Internationally, these terms are defined in different ways by different countries. The term "bullying" is also used in surveys. These generally ask about hurtful acts, which does not meet the definition of "bullying." The approach taken in this book is to assist schools in empowering students to maintain positive relationships and effectively reduce and respond to all forms of hurtful behavior.

- **Students at Greatest Risk**. There are two kinds of students who are at greatest risk of long lasting harms from hurtful behavior inflicted on them by students or school staff.

  - **Marginalized Hurtful Students.** These are students who have often experienced adversities at home and who have been treated badly and excluded at school—who are now engaging in hurtful behavior. These students are generally called "bully/victims." These terms are backwards. These students have been harmed and are now being hurtful. These students engage in what is called "Reactive Aggression." They are at highest risk of significant lifelong negative outcomes. The harm that is being inflicted upon them needs to be stopped. They require assistance in recovery from this harm. They also need to be held accountable for the harm they do to others.

  - **Targeted Students.** Targeted Students are those who are seriously or persistently treated badly by peers. Frequently, these students are targeted based on their identity. Research has consistently shown that students who are more frequently targeted are often perceived as less powerful. It is not possible to "protect" these students through a disciplinary code approach. Unfortunately, these students will likely always face the potential of being treated badly. We must empower them to reduce the potential they will be treated badly, ensure they have the ability to respond effectively, and have the supports to reduce the harmful impact.

- **Survey Data.** Over the last decade, there has been an increase in the use of surveys to measure bullying. Since the early 2010's in the US there has been no decline in the rate at which students report being bullied. Surveys also document that bullying occurs in areas of the school where it should be noticed and stopped—but most often it is not. Internationally, there are expanded efforts to assess the amount of bullying through surveys. These surveys document that being bullied is a global concern.

  - **Survey Language Concerns.** A challenge with many surveys is use of language that asks whether someone has been hurtful to them, which could include minor incidents, and fail to assess seriousness or frequency. When the reported results are that a large percentage of students are bullied, this could lead some to dismiss the concerns because this is then considered to be typical youth behavior. The Program for International Student Assessment (PISA) identifies students who are "frequently bullied." Internationally, 8% of students report being "frequently bullied."

- **Identity-Based Bullying**. Identity-Based Bullying is biased-based bullying that occurs because of the student's actual or perceived "identity" within a group of people who are marginalized within our society. Identity groups include those who receive protection under most civil rights laws. However, students within other identity groups, such as overweight or low income, also experience Identity-Based Bullying. Identity-Based Bullying may be serious incidents, persistent more minor incidents directed at one student, or pervasive targeting of all or most students within the entire identity group. Identity-Based Bullying causes greater harm than more general bullying. Many students also have a history of transgenerational trauma.

- **Cyberbullying Insight.** During the pandemic, when students were in lock down or restricted environments, there was a reduction in reported bullying. There was not, however, a significant increase in cyberbullying. This appears to support the understanding that most cyberbullying is closely connected to hurtful incidents that are happening between students while they are at school.

- **Life-Long Harmful Consequences.** Being bullied can have life-long harmful consequences. Being bullied can result in stress-related physical and mental health symptoms.

  - **Trauma.** Bullying is a form of trauma. There is a high incidence of Post Traumatic Stress Disorder (PTSD) symptoms, as well as depression and anxiety, among students who reported they were bullied and a strong association between frequency of exposure to bullying and such symptoms. Those students with the worst mental health symptoms are Marginalized Hurtful Students.

  - **Academic Performance.** Being bullied leads to lower academic performance and increased absences and drop outs. Schools with higher levels of bullying have lower academic scores, even after accounting for such factors as poverty, enrollment, and the like.

  - **Suicide.** There is a clear connection between bullying and suicide. Persistent experience of being bullied, combined with ineffective intervention by the school, can lead to feelings of hopelessness and helplessness that can result in suicidal thinking or behaviors. A serious incident of bullying may act as a trigger. Bullying is also associated with self-harming behaviors.

  - **School Violence.** There is a clearly established connection between being bullied, school violence, school shootings, and bringing weapons to school. When students do not feel that they can safely report being bullied to school officials, bringing a weapon to defend themselves may follow. In association with the concerns of school violence are also concerns of hate group recruitment. Being bullied and not having any friends at school are vulnerabilities that hate group recruiters look for.

WHAT IS "BULLYING?"

What is bullying? Unfortunately, the answer is not at all that clear. This lack of clarity presents a significant problem for school leaders.

Once I reviewed a guide provided to educators in a state in the US on bullying prevention. On the first page, this guide provided the academic definition. On the second page the guide provided the state statutory definition for that state, which included both the terms "bullying" and harassment." There was no discussion about the difference between the academic definition and the statutory definition. There was no presentation of the standards for discriminatory harassment under US civil rights laws. Then, in the appendix, was a model survey that asked students about experiencing someone being hurtful. Educators are clearly not at fault for being confused.

The traditional academic definition of bullying is grounded in the work of Dr. Olweus, an early researcher in this field from Norway.[8] His definition included the concepts of intention to inflict harm, repetition, and imbalance of power. There is general agreement with the understanding that bullying behaviors include these components and can involve physical aggression, verbal aggression, and relational aggression or social exclusion.[9]

However, even these components raise questions. Is something posted once on the Internet, that is then generally available or has been shared by others, considered "repeated?" School leaders may have difficulties interpreting the concept of "imbalance of power." If the student being hurtful is larger and stronger than the other student, but the targeted student has a higher social status or vise versa, how is an "imbalance of power" to be assessed? How is imbalance of power to be assessed online?

In the US, the Centers for Disease Control and Prevention (CDC), US Department of Education (USDOE), and USHRSA more recently partnered with bullying experts to develop a uniform definition of bullying.[10] In January 2014, the definition that was released was:

> *Bullying is any unwanted aggressive behavior(s) by another youth or group of youths who are not siblings or current dating partners that involves an observed or perceived power imbalance and is repeated multiple times or is highly likely to be repeated. Bullying may inflict harm or distress on the targeted youth including physical, psychological, social, or educational harm.*[11]

However, a review of the surveys compiled by CDC, entitled *Measuring Bullying Victimization, Perpetration, and Bystander Experiences: A Compendium of Assessment Tools*, reveals that most surveys assess bullying by providing youth with a list of hurtful behaviors and asking if they have experienced any of these actions.[12] Thus, these surveys essentially define bullying as "hurtful acts."

Some more recent surveys seek to measure students experiences with bullying based on the new definition. This approach presumes that students are able to effectively sort out issues of "imbalance of power," which, based on research, is doubtful.[13] A study that asked students about bullying in a variety of ways, including a format similar to that described differences in power or strength, then asked a follow-up question whether this involved someone with greater power or strength. Only fifty-nine percent (59%) of the students who said they were bullied based on a definition that included these terms, then indicated this involved someone with greater power or strength.

There are also the legal or statutory definitions of bullying to consider. Many, if not most, countries have enacted laws directing schools to address bullying.

In the US, federal civil rights laws protect students against discriminatory harassment based on race, color, native origin, sexual orientation or identity, disability, sex, and religion if this is grounded in native origin.[14] Although defined with slightly different terminology in various federal publications, a Hostile Environment exists when unwelcome hurtful conduct directed at a student who is considered within a Protected Class becomes so severe, persistent, or pervasive that it creates an intimidating, threatening, or abusive environment that affects a student's ability to participate in or benefit from an educational program or activity.[15] The US civil rights laws are discussed extensively in Chapter 9.

Complicating matters further in the US is that there are fifty different state statutory definitions of what is called bullying or harassment or other related terms.[16] These definitions provide the basis upon which schools are required to enforce disciplinary policies.

A 2011 USDOE report, *Analysis of State Bullying Laws and Policies*, noted that the lack of consistency in use of terms in these statutes "contributes to confusion over how a specific incident should be treated."[17] In the US there are additional complications related to the use of terms such as "bullying" or "harassment" that are related to state or federal reporting requirements. This is discussed in Chapter 3.

Expanding this discussion to an international focus will result in the question of definition becoming even more complicated. The definition used by researchers internationally appears to still focus on the three components of intent to harm, repetition, and imbalance of power.[18] There also is a common understanding of the negative consequences of bullying behavior, however defined, on academic performance and social-emotional well-being.[19]

However, there are cross-cultural differences in how hurtful behavior is expressed in different countries. There are differences in perspectives associated with physical aggression, verbal aggression, and relational aggression or social exclusion.[20] It appears that there is more emphasis on social exclusion in Eastern countries, as compared to Western countries.

Focus on Hurtful Behavior

In this book, I have implemented a different approach and manner of thinking. Rather than a limiting focus on "bullying," by whatever definitions are followed, it is my perspective that we need to to shift to a focus on empowering students to maintain positive relationships, reducing all forms of hurtful behavior, and ensuring school staff respond effectively to all incidents that involve hurtful behavior.

All of these hurtful incidents cause some level of harm and can disrupt the environment. If a student is experiencing someone being hurtful to them, they are unable to independently get this to stop, should it really matter whether whether the hurtful acts meet your district's policy on "bullying?" If two students are in a conflict situation, should they not have skills necessary to resolve such conflict, shouldn't their friends know how to help them resolve this conflict, and shouldn't there be a mechanism within your school to assist these students if they and their friends have not been successful?

In the chapters in Part I, and some other areas of the book I will use the term "bullying" because the focus is on the research—and that is the most common term used. In the parts that set forth recommendations for how to address these concerns, I will shift to the term "hurtful behavior." The kinds of hurtful behavior I suggest should be addressed by schools includes:

- **Bullying.** Serious, persistent, or pervasive hurtful acts directed at a student that have caused the student to feel distressed and which has resulted in an interference with their ability to engage in learning or participate in school activities. Note this definition is based on the concept of Hostile Environment under US civil rights laws, however bullying is not limited to students within defined protected classes. This incorporates the concept of intent to cause harm as serious, persistent, or pervasive hurtful acts are not engaged in by accident.

- **Discriminatory Harassment or Harassment.** Bullying, based on the above definition, directed towards another student that is based on their membership in a class that is considered protected under civil rights laws or human rights laws of the country or other jurisdiction.

- **Identity-Based Bullying, Hate Speech, and Bias Incidents.** Identity-Biased Bullying is Bullying or Harassment that occurs because of the student's actual or perceived "identity" within a group or class of people who are more marginalized within our society.

Hate speech is pejorative or bias-based language or other acts such as graffiti, that negatively refers to a person or a group based on their membership in a marginalized identity group which could include classes of people protected by civil rights laws and other marginalized groups.[21]

- **Microaggressions.** Verbal, nonverbal, and environmental slights, snubs, or insults, whether intentional or unintentional, that communicate hostile, derogatory, or negative messages that target students. Frequently, these could also be considered bias incidents.[22] A challenge in referring to these as "microaggressions" is that this term appears to be used both for intentional and unintentional statements of comments. Obviously, a response must be sensitive to this difference.

- **Sexual Assault or Harassment.** Unwelcome sexual comments, gestures, or touching. Sexual harassment could constitute discriminatory harassment under civil rights laws.[23]

- **Relational Aggression or Exclusion**. A type of aggression in which harm is caused by damaging someone's relationships or social status, including excluding others from social activities; damaging victim's reputations with others by spreading rumors, gossiping, or humiliating them in front of others; or withdrawing attention and friendship. However, students should have the ability to engage in social activities with peers of their own choosing, so a situation that is reported as exclusion requires a careful assessment.

- **Drama.** Two-way interpersonal social conflict, that is dramatic in nature and most involves active and engaged supporters on both sides. Often, drama situations involve intimate romantic relationships in one way or another. In these situations, the level of power and involvement is generally relatively equivalent.

- **Conflict or Bi-Directional Hurtful Behavior.** Two-way interpersonal social conflict involving students with a roughy equivalent level of personal power. Conflict is usually more private, at a lower level of dramatics, and generally also does not involve active supporters.

- **Retaliation.** When a student who has been treated badly engages in aggression as a response or to try to get this to stop. This is Reactive Aggression. Retaliation must be distinguished from conflict by paying attention to the initial act of harm.

- **Mobbing.** When a group of students are engaging in hurtful conduct directed at one or several students. Usually in mobbing situations there is a student leading the attack who is skillfully bringing in lots of other participants. Mobbing frequently occurs in online environments.

- **Physical Violence or Threat.** Physical assault, destruction of property, or a threat to do so.

- **Dating Abuse, Hurtful Break-ups of Intimate Partner Relationships, Sextortion.** Being hurtful, controlling, or abusive to someone within a romantic relationship or who they were in a, intimate romantic relationship with. Sextortion is the abusive and controlling use of digital intimate images that were sent under the expectation of privacy.

- **Hazing or Hurtful Behavior Involving Athletics.** Being hurtful to new or younger members of a team or group as a form of initiation or intimidation of team members.

- **Hurtful by Mistake.** Jokes or pranks that weren't meant to be hurtful but were, or impulsive, angry outbursts followed immediately by remorse.

- **Cyberbullying** Cyberbullying is all of the above hurtful behavior that is accomplished using digital technologies and social media. Because there is such a clear overlap between face-to-face bullying while students are at school and cyberbullying, it is recommended that the focus be on the hurtful behavior, not the means by which it is perpetuated.

STUDENTS AT RISK

Marginalized Hurtful Students

Marginalized Hurtful Students are those who have both been targeted and are being hurtful. They are at a highest risk.[24] Sometimes, these students are called "bully/victims." This is backwards. The saying "hurt people hurt people" fully applies to these students. They are "victims" who are now "bullies." It is imperative to address how these students are being targeted to stop their hurtful behavior.

These students have generally been repeatedly denigrated and excluded at school. They also often come from homes that have a high level of violence, thus they enter school having experienced adversities at home. This has impacted their ability to self-regulate. These students tend to be aggressive, easily angered, low on popularity, frequently bullied by their siblings.

Because of their behavioral challenges, these students generally have challenging relationships with their peers. They are very low on the school's social ladder—the most ostracized by peers.[25] They may appear to be loners because they often have few, if any, friends.[26]

These students may engage in behavior that encourages other students to be hurtful to them. They are generally impulsive and poor in regulating their emotions.[27] Because they lack self-regulation, other students can subtly pick on them until they trigger and become disruptive. Then, these students are the ones who are disciplined, when the students who subtly picked on them are not even noticed. Issues related to this phenomenon were described by Green:

> *What seems to be missing, however, is the ability to recognize when behavioral issues become bullying incidents. To be able to do this, teachers may need to be attuned to the behaviors that proceed bullying incidents. If they are inclined to ignore most instances of misbehavior (as per standard behavior management principles), then it is likely they are not seeing or recognizing the verbal and relational bullying that is happening in the peer group. For example, a child may be continuously taunted and excluded until they "snap" and only then does the child physically lash out at the provocateurs. However, it is only at this point that the teacher steps in to admonish the child who engaged in the physical act. The relational and verbal bullying that preceded this incident remains unseen and is therefore not addressed so as to prevent escalation. Without a good understanding of peer group dynamics, the physical incidents might also be treated in isolation as one-off acts of misbehavior, rather than as a pattern of behavior that warrants a systematic intervention approach.[28]*

Reactive or Proactive Aggression

Researchers investigating aggression have identified two forms of aggression: Reactive Aggression and Proactive Aggression.[29] Reactive Aggression is characterized by high emotionality, which makes the person prone to impulsive reactions after provocation. These students impulsively react badly in response to something harmful that has happened to them. They have become dysregulated.

By comparison, Proactive Aggression is evidenced by lack of emotional arousal, intentionality, and high levels of social effectiveness to obtain benefits and rewards from their hurtful actions. Proactive Aggression occurs in the absence of provocation.

Marginalized Hurtful Students most often engage in Reactive Aggression. When a Marginalized Hurtful Student also is demonstrating Proactive Aggression, this may reflect an even more serious concern that this student is on a life path of harmful aggression.

Evidence of Significant Harms

Marginalized Hurtful Students display the highest levels of physical and psychosomatic health consequences and demonstrate the poorest outcomes associated with mental health, economic adaptation, and social relationships.[30] An international survey of 11- to 15-year olds found that those who are both victimized and are hurtful experienced worse emotional adjustment in all 25 countries surveyed.[31] They suffer higher levels of depression, anxiety, eating disorders, substance abuse, and suicidal behavior.[32]

These students show poor school adjustment and report more negative perceptions of the school climate.[33] They are low achievers and are less successful academically.[34] These are the students who are more likely to carry weapons to school to protect themselves.[35] They are less likely to graduate.[36] They have the highest rates of self-harm, plans for suicide, and attempted suicide.[37] When older, they also have higher rates of serious criminal charges in young adulthood.[38]

These students most often function at a high level of traumatic distress.[39] They have learned that their environments are unsafe. This likely includes both home and school. Their Amygdala, the threat sensor, is always functioning on "on"—they are easily aroused and engage in reactive behavior. As a result, they are more likely to trigger to situations that, from the outside perspective, appear to be relatively minor.

Targeted Students

Targeted Students are those who are seriously or persistently treated badly by their peers. Research has consistently also shown that targeted students are often perceived as less powerful. They are considered to be weak and unable to defend themselves.[40] They may be depressed, anxious, or have low self-esteem which may both lead to their being targeted or be the result thereof. They are more often less popular than others, do not get along well with others, and have few friends. Further, sometimes, they are seen as annoying or provoking, or they antagonize others for attention.

In focus group studies, students frequently refer to Targeted Students in a negative way.[41] They are the deviant student, the 'odd student', who deserved to be treated in a hurtful manner. These are students who are on the lower end of the school's social ladder. When students talk about reasons for bullying they talked about the Targeted Student as a "little bit different," "odd," or "weird,"—who is not behaving as they should. These "misfit" students disturb the existing order and threaten the status quo, which demands conformity to "normal." Their lack of conformity to "normal" then justifies how they are treated.

Many studies have found that Targeted Students often tend to be unpopular and disliked by their peers.[42] There appears to be two-way factors involved. Students who are targeted are more likely to be disliked and students who are disliked are more likely to be targeted.[43] Those who engage in bullying strategically target students who others do not support, because this is less risky for them. Students may not step in to help these targets, because this could raise the risk of being targeted themselves.

However, this is not always the case. The traditional view that targets of bullying have significant challenges and have been rejected by their peers has recently been challenged by findings showing that sometimes, especially in the teen years, students at higher levels of the social hierarchy can also be targeted.[44] Their risk of being targeted may be higher than for average-status peers. This relates to the issues of bullying by students who are being hurtful to obtain dominance and social status, which will be discussed more fully in Chapter 2. Students who are hurtful to achieve dominance may target those with lower social power. However, they may also target those who are rivals or potential rivals who are at a relatively equivalent level of the school's social ladder.

Identity-Based Bullying

Identity-Based Bullying is biased-based bullying that occurs because of the student's actual or perceived "identity" within a group or class of people who are more marginalized within our society.[45] Marginalized identity groups include those who are considered Protected Class under most civil rights laws. This generally includes race, color, national origin, religion, disabilities, and sexual or gender minority.

However, students within other identity groups are also the subject of Identity-Based Bullying. This includes students who are overweight or obese, low income, on in foster care. Identity-Based Bullying may be serious or may be persistent more minor incidents. These serious or persistent hurtful acts may be directed at one student. However, this pattern also includes the pervasive targeting of all or most students within the entire identity group.

Identity-Based Bullying may be in the form of persistent micro aggressions or bias incidents. These persistent hurtful acts may be directed at one student. However, this pattern also includes the pervasive targeting of most students within the entire identity group in a school.

The US Office of Juvenile Justice and Delinquency Prevention (OJJDP) has launched a comprehensive national initiative to prevent youth hate crimes and identity-based bullying.[46] In October 2021, OJJDP hosted a two day *Virtual Symposium: Understanding and Preventing Youth Hate Crimes and Identity-Based Bullying.* Further virtual workshops are provided and additional resources are under development.

The United Nations Educational, Scientific and Cultural Organization (UNESCO) released an excellent report, *School Violence and Bullying: Global Status Report* about bullying from an international perspective.[47] This report noted that the primary drivers of bullying are disability, gender, poverty or social status, ethnic, linguistic, or cultural differences, physical appearance, sexual orientation, gender identity and expression. This report noted that in a 2016 the United Nations Children's Fund (UNICEF) report a survey of 100,000 young people in 18 countries identified that 25% reported that they had been bullied because of their physical appearance, 25% because of their gender or sexual orientation and 25% because of their ethnicity or national origin.

Minority Stress Theory, Intergenerational Trauma, Intersectionality

Identity-Based Bullying is recognized as causing greater harm than more general bullying.[48] The Minority Stress Theory explains the increased concerns of the health, psychosocial, and academic disparities among youth in marginalized groups in society who are bullied.[49] Minority Stress processes are related to stigma and prejudice that are experienced. This includes actual experiences, as well as the continued expectations of prejudice and discrimination. For sexual and gender minorities, the stress may also include the need for concealment within their family, school, and/or community.

There are also issues related to intergenerational trauma to be considered.[50] Children of trauma survivors have higher levels of evidence of the experience of trauma. The experiences of trauma are heightened within those groups within society that are marginalized.

Intergenerational trauma can be imparted through the pregnancy health of the mother, gene expression, and messages received from family members. The messages parents or caregivers provide to their children related to the dangers they will encounter in the world impacts how the child experiences the world. This, in turn, can be anticipated to impact how they respond when treated badly and whether they will feel comfortable reporting to an authority to gain assistance.

Intersectionality refers to concerns associated with students' membership in more than one marginalized identity group.[51] Youth with multiple marginalized identities experience even greater bullying victimization and significantly increased stress as a result.

Identity-Based Bullying and Hate Crimes

There is an overlap between Identity-Based Bullying and hate crimes.[52] A hate crime is a criminal offense against a person or property motivated in whole or in part by an offender's bias against someone based on their race, ethnicity, national origin, religion, disability, sexual orientation or gender identity.[53]

Hate crimes perpetrated by young people look similar to adult hate crimes.[54] Most juvenile hate crimes are motivated by bias based on race or ethnicity. The vast majority of these are anti-Black crimes. Juvenile hate crimes frequently involve written comments or graffiti. However, about a quarter involve assault. Almost half of the hate crime cases involving juvenile suspects are incidents that happened at school or on school grounds.

A key question for school leaders related to hate crimes is whether these situations should be handled as a disciplinary matter or whether law enforcement should be involved. There are benefits to young people who have been victimized in having the situation be recognized and treated as a hate crime. However, the down side is the school-to-prison pathway for the student who engaged in the hurtful action.

Societal Values of the Local Community

There are very likely regional differences in how these factors manifest in schools related to the societal values held by local community residents. In regions where there is more support for societal values of non-acceptance of various minorities, it is likely that students who hold more prejudicial attitudes towards minority students are in a majority within their school. Their quest for dominance and social status in these schools will likely be demonstrated through harassment of these minority students.

Recently in the US, intense battles have emerged in many states the increased efforts of schools to achieve greater diversity, equity, and inclusion and have incorporated these objectives into social emotional learning. These initiatives are under attack with by state legislation. Battles over these issues are raging in some communities, with angry parents accosting board members, school leaders, and teachers. These parents have children who are attending school in these communities.

In these regions, students likely have increased concerns that a report they are being treated badly to a school leader will not result in a positive outcome. In regions where any identity group is under more general attack, especially if some local political leaders have expressing opinions against such identity group, Targeted Students who are members of these groups may fear that their school's leadership holds the same views as the local elected leaders.

Likewise, the degree to which students who engage in Identity-Based Bullying are accepted or not will likely also be shaped by the societal values of the community. In non-accepting communities, it is probable that those students who engage in Identity-Based Bullying will receive support from their peers. In more accepting communities, peer disapproval of Identity-Based Bullying is more likely.

Identities

Based on Race, Ethnicity, Religion, National Origin

Data related to the concern of race, ethnicity, or religious based bullying can be complicated. It is possible to look at data from a larger national perspective, however, the basis and level of bullying of racial or religious minorities will likely be different depending on the racial or religious make-up of the school and community.[55] In schools where students of what would be considered a marginalized minority population are in the majority within that school, the dynamics of Identity-Based Bullying are likely to be different.

Within the context of ethnicity-based bullying, it is important to also consider the situation of students who have newly immigrated.[56] These students most likely experienced profound trauma that led to their relocation, which could contribute to their behavior. These students are also more likely not to feel comfortable reporting this to the school due to their lack of comfort in their new community and school.

In the US, most often concerns associated with bullying of students of color focus on the concerns of students who are Black or Latino.[57] Often left out of the discussion is the bullying experienced by Native American students.[58] Campbell and Smalling found US Native American students had both the highest rates of experiencing victimization in the form of threats or physical violence and the highest dropout rates when compared to other racial groups. More than half of all Native American students in the study experienced physical violence or threatening at school and nearly a quarter of them students experienced both. A comprehensive study of crimes involving Native Americans found that they are far more likely to be the victims of violent crime than members of any other racial group.[59] Moreover, 70% of violent crimes against Native Americans are committed by members of other racial groups, primarily by Whites. In other countries, these hurtful dynamics between the majority society and indigenous peoples also appear evident.[60]

The bullying of Asian American students in the US is also frequently not as well-noticed. Act To Change is a nonprofit working to end bullying among Asian American and Pacific Islander youth.[61] In a 2021 survey, they found that eighty percent (80%) of Asian Americans teens had experienced bullying, both in-person or online, and that Asian American teens are significantly less likely to report bullying to an adult than non-Asian American teens. This was considered potentially due to cultural barriers and lack of trust in adults and schools. There also was a surge of cyberbullying in 2020. This was apparently exacerbated by COVID-19 fueled racism.

Religious minorities also experience Identity-Based Bullying. In the US, this includes members of minority religions such as Muslims, Sikhs, Hindus, and Jews. In a study conducted by the Institute for Social Policy and Understanding (ISPU) of a nationally representative sample of US families, 42% of Muslims, 23% of Jews, and 6% of Catholics reported that at least one of their children had been bullied in the past year because of their religion.[62] Of significant concern is that in 25% of the cases involving Muslim students, a teacher or administrator at their school was identifying as the one who engaged the bullying.

Hinduja and Patchin, of the Cyberbully Research Center, conducted a study that focused on religious based bullying and cyberbullying using a nationally representative sample of 5,000 middle and high schoolers in the US.[63] Based on their data, students of various faiths appear to be bullied at school relatively equally. However, more Muslim youth said they were cyberbullied than those of other faiths. Their data demonstrated that 34.3% of Muslim students, 25% of Jewish students, and 23.1% of Hindu students reported they had been targeted at school because of their faith the last 30 days.

Based on Disabilities

A new report from UNESCO, *Violence and Bullying in Educational Settings: The Experience of Children and Young People with Disabilities*, noted that little is known about the nature of violence and bullying experienced by young people with disabilities in schools, as global surveys do not collect specific data on these students.[64] Further, the academic literature makes it difficult to compare findings or draw conclusions because different definitions of violence and bullying and of disability have been used. There is also little information about characteristics that, together with disability, may influence vulnerability to violence and bullying. This may include gender, sexual identity or gender orientation, race, color, national origin, and socio-economic status.

The UNESCO assessment concluded that young people with disabilities are three to four times more likely to be victims of any type of violence in all settings. This includes the home and in the community as well as in school. Within education systems throughout the world, students with disabilities have been found to experience substantially higher rates of peer bullying than those without disabilities. Students with emotional and behavioral challenges are more likely to be victimized than those with other disabilities. Students with disabilities also experience higher rates of physical violence at the hands of teachers, are more likely to be physically restrained or confined, and are also subjected to greater emotional and psychological violence from teachers than students without disabilities.

Based on Sexual or Gender Minority Status

Sexual and gender minority students are extremely vulnerable to being bullied.[65] Although there have been improvements as a whole in societies in the way sexual identity and gender orientation differences are acknowledged, sexual and gender minority people are particularly high at risk of being bullied throughout their lifetime. Ultraconservative political environments throughout the world represent a clear hazard.

In the US, while there is protection for sexual and gender minority students at the federal level under *Title IX*, there are concerted efforts in many states to place restrictions on the full participation and welcome of sexual and gender minority in schools.[66] These legislative actions include demanding the removal of books that reflective of their lives and preventing discussion issues of sexual orientation or identity in class, because this may make heterosexual students of a particular religious background feel "uncomfortable."

Violence against sexual and gender minorities contributes to high levels of feelings of insecurity, as sexual and gender minority students can expect to be assaulted in one way or another at any time.[67] Further, these students may be living in families where their sexual or gender minority status will not be accepted. They risk being thrown out of their homes. These students often must hide their sexual identity or gender orientation to avoid negative reactions and bad treatments from peers, school staff, and their families. Further, they cannot risk reporting any concerns of being treated badly to school leaders. These leaders could also be biased against them or could "out" them in a way that will lead to family problems, homelessness, and retaliation.

Groups That Do Not Receive Civil Rights Protections

Students in all of the above sections are considered Protected Class Students under US civil rights laws. It is essential to recognize that these laws likely do not provide protections for all students who may experience Identity Based Bullying. This includes students who are overweight, obese or have some other undesirable physical appearance; students who are in foster care; and lower income students, especially those who are experiencing significant home adversities such as parents who are incarcerated or engaged in drug or alcohol abuse.[68]

In a study of students in middle and high school, both overweight and obese students were at increased risk of experiencing bullying. They also were more likely to experience increased distress than other normal weight victimized students.[69] Overweight students appear to have reduced internal protective factors, such as self-esteem. They may also experience where school staff might at some level blame them for being targeted.[70]

Under US civil rights regulations, if a Protected Class student is experiencing a Hostile Environment as a consequence of discriminatory harassment, one of the requirements is that the school take steps to remedy the harm to this student. Students who have experienced a Hostile Environment who are not a member of a Protected Class also deserve attention to remedy the harms they have experienced.

Survey Data on Bullying

The historical data over the last decade comes from the US As noted, significant international efforts have more recently been launched under the leadership UNESCO to better address bullying. In the US, significant efforts were launched by the Obama Administration in 2011.[71] The focus on what has happened in the US will hopefully assist in informing international efforts. As will become readily evident in this data, the efforts over the last decade in the US have not achieved any reduction in the rate at which US students report bullying.

Concerns Associated with Surveys

An analysis of the surveys reveals some significant concerns. Some ask about the experience of bullying in a year. Others limit the time frame to the last month. Surveys often do not ask about frequency. Many use terms such as "teasing," "made fun of you," "excluded you from activities" that possibly could be implicated in more serious situations, but raises the potential that students may identify more typical youth relationship challenges as "bullying."

What this survey data often does not identify is the percentage of students who were treated badly on a very frequent basis, felt emotionally distressed by this, and were unable to get this to stop. These are the students who are at greatest risk.

These national and international surveys are also not going to inform school leaders what is happening at the local level—in your school. Therefore, I strongly conducting an annual local survey. A recommended survey, which does seek insight into degree of distress and ability to effectively respond is included as an Appendix on the Embrace Civility website and is a key component of the *Empowered to Embrace Civility* student program.

A recent UNESCO survey report demonstrates the concerns of bullying questions that are too broad. The UNESCO report documented that almost one-third of young teens worldwide have recently experienced bullying.[72] This conclusion was based on-school surveys that track the physical and emotional health of youth, the Global School Health Survey (GSHS), which focuses on children aged 13 to 17 years in low-income regions, and the Health Behavior in School-Age Children (HBSAC) which targets young people aged 11 to 15 years in 42 countries, primarily in Europe and North America.[73]

Data that indicates that large percentages of students are bullied is of concern. One unfortunate interpretation of a large incident rate could be that being bullied is a normal occurrence for young people, thus should not be considered a serious concern. The GSHA survey question was:

> *Bullying occurs when one or more students or other people about your age say or do hurtful or mean things. Bullying can occur when someone teases, threatens, ignores, spreads rumors about, calls someone a bad name, makes sexual remarks, or hits, shoves, or hurts another person over and over again. It is not bullying when two people of about the same strength or power argue or fight or tease each other in a friendly way. During the past 12 months, were you bullied on school property? Yes. No. During the past 12 months, were you bullied when you were not on school property? Yes. No.[74]*

Let's consider this question from the perspective of a student. "In the last year, did someone tease you, call you a bad name, or make sexual remarks to you?" It is actually surprising that only a third of youth responded to this question in the positive. Is this "bullying" based on any definition?

US Data

Youth Risk Behavior Survey

The following is the history from the US efforts, which will hopefully be informative for those in other countries. The CDC's Youth Risk Behavior Survey (YRSB), added a question related to bullying in 2009.[75] There are language concerns about the YRBS question similar to the GSHA question. It reads:

> *Bullying is when 1 or more students tease, threaten, spread rumors about, hit, shove, or hurt another student over and over again. It is not bullying when 2 students of about the same strength or power argue or fight or tease each other in a friendly way. During the past 12 months, have you ever been bullied on school*

property? Yes. No. During the past 12 months, have you ever been electronically bullied? Yes. No.[76]

Again, there are the same concerns over the length of time and what what behavior is being asked about. This raises the question of whether all of the positive responses to this question constituted serious or persistent "bullying."

However, because the YRSB is delivered to students biannually, it is possible to track trends. The trends data is very helpful, but disappointing. Based on survey data in the US, there has been no decline in the rate at which students report being bullied at school. This is the data from 2009 until 2019:[77]

The percentage of high school students who	2009	2011	2013	2015	2017	2019
Were bullied at school	19.9	20.1	19.6	20.2	19.0	19.5

National Crime Victimization Survey - School Crime Supplement

The National Crime Victimization Survey - School Crime Supplement (NCVS-SCS) a joint effort of USDOE and the US Department of Justice (USDOJ) also has a question on bullying.[78] This question read as follows:

Now I have some questions about what students do at school that make you feel bad or are hurtful to you. We often refer to this as being bullied. You may include events you told me about already. During this school year, has any student bullied you? That is, has another student...a. Made fun of you, called you names, or insulted you, in a hurtful way? b. Spread rumors about you or tried to make others dislike you? c. Threatened you with harm? d. Pushed you, shoved you, tripped you, or spit on you? e. Tried to make you do things you did not want to do, for example, give them money or other things? f. Excluded you from activities on purpose? g. Destroyed your property on purpose?[79]

This question asks about the entire school year and, again, the terms could apply to less Hurtful Student interactions—"made fun of you." Again, there is the concern about what kinds of hurtful behavior students are reporting.

In the reports about these survey results, there is a consistent statement that "between 2009 and 2019, the percentage of students ages 12–18 who reported being bullied at school during the school year decreased from 28 to 22%."[80] However, the data shows virtually no change from 2013 and 2019. In 2013, 21.5% of students said they had been bullied.[81] In 2019,

22% reported they had been bullied.[82] Note that the significant efforts to address bullying were initiated in the US in 2010.

There is helpful data from 2019 NCVS-SCS survey. The largest percentages of students reported that the manner in which they were bullied was being the subject of rumors (15%) and being made fun of, called names, or insulted (14%). These are forms of verbal aggression which are less likely to be considered to have created a "substantial disruption"—which is the general guiding principal for when a principal will implement a disciplinary action. Only 5% reported being physically abused.

A helpful comparison of student bullying by grade level shows that the percentages of students who reported being bullied at school in 2019 were far higher for 6th, 7th, and 8th graders (ranging from 27% to 28%) than for 9th, 10th, 11th, and 12th graders (ranging from 16% to 22%). Clearly, the middle school years present the greatest concerns.

Of students who reported being bullied at school, 47% reported being bullied inside the classroom, 39% reported being bullied in the hallway or stairwell at school, 26% reported being bullied in the cafeteria, 20% reported being bullied outside on school grounds, 16% reported being bullied online or by text, 11% reported being bullied in the bathroom or locker room, 10% reported being bullied on the way to or from school, and 3% reported being bullied somewhere else in the school building. The vast majority of bullying appears to be occurring in places where staff should be expected to be more present, which should have reduced the hurtful behavior.

The NCVS-SCS does ask about frequency. It is significant to note that about 32% of students who reported that they had been bullied, indicated that they were bullied one day in the school year, 20% indicated that they were bullied two days, 29 percent indicated that they were bullied three to ten days, and 19% indicated that they were bullied on more than ten days. This latter group of students are the ones we should be most concerned about. This is around 4% of all students. Given the definition of "bullying provided to the students, should being bullied one, two, or even three to ten days in a school year be considered "bullying?"

Lastly, the NCVS-SCS survey asked students who reported being bullied at school whether or not they notified an adult at school. Only about 46% reported notifying an adult at school about the incident. The percentage of students who reported notifying an adult at school after being bullied was higher for 6th, 7th, and 8th graders (ranging from 49% to 57%) than for 12th-graders (28%). About 60% of students who reported being bullied on more than ten days in the school year reported notifying an adult at school after being bullied, compared with 43% for those who were bullied on two days in the school year and 35% for those who were bullied on one day in the school year. A student who was treated badly on only one or two days likely effectively responded and did not need to obtain assistance from the school.

US General Office of Accounting Report

In November 2021, the US General Office of Accounting (GAO) provided a report to the Chairman of the Committee on Education and Labor, House of Representatives, entitled *K-12 Education: Students' Experiences with Bullying, Hate Speech, Hate Crimes, and Victimization in Schools*.[83] For this study, numerous US surveys were relied on, including the YRBS and NCVS-SCS.

A concerning finding in this report was the survey finding that school officials indicated they were aware of students being bullied "regularly" in only about 30% of schools and "occasionally" in about 64% of schools. The fact that only 30% of school officials thought students in their schools were being regularly bullied is a disturbing finding. This appears to reflect a lack of recognition of what is happening to their students.

International Data

Program for International Student Assessment (PISA)

PISA is an international assessment that measures 15-year-old students' reading, mathematics, and science literacy every three years.[84] PISA is coordinated by the Organization for Economic Cooperation and Development (OECD), an intergovernmental organization of 38 industrialized countries. The PISA survey assessed students in over 80 countries. Starting in 2015, PISA has been asking questions about bullying. The PISA 2018 Results, *What School Life Means for Student Lives,* contained a chapter that reported findings on bullying.[85]

PISA 2018 asks about three distinct types of bullying including physical, relational and verbal, with a number of listed hurtful acts for these types. Students are asked about frequency. They are asked how often they had experienced this, including the responses of "never or almost never", "a few times a year", "a few times a month", "once a week or more." This approach to asking about experience of bullying will generate more helpful information about the extent to which students are experiencing persistent bullying.

On average across OECD countries, 23% of students reported being bullied at least a few times a month; 8% were classified as being frequently bullied. There were large between-country differences in students' reported exposure to bullying. The PISA 2018 data for the US indicated that 26% of students reported being bullied at least a few times a month, with 10% reporting frequent bullying.

The prevalence of bullying varied substantially, depending on the student's age, the country and the culture. However, verbal and relational bullying were the most common types of bullying and physical bullying was less prevalent. Previous research has shown that the prevalence of bullying peaks in lower secondary school years and declines over upper secondary school years. This was also observed on PISA 2018.

The PISA 2018 study indicated that boys were more likely than girls to report being bullied in all forms at least a few times a month. However, when it came relational aggression, the difference between boys and girls was relatively small. Being bullied was associated with students' socio-economic status. A larger share of disadvantaged students reported being bullied at least a few times a month. However, there were differences between countries. In some Asian countries, advantaged students reported higher levels of bullying.

Internationally, the issue of immigration is a concern as more countries are experiencing increased levels of immigration more recently. On the average, the difference between the numbers of immigrant or non-immigrant students who reported being bullied at least a few times a month was not large. But there was a difference in some countries.

On PISA 2018, a larger share of low-achieving than high-achieving students reported having been bullied at least a few times a month. PISA 2018 data also demonstrated that a greater exposure to bullying was associated with lower performance in reading. The findings suggest that that physical bullying is more strongly associated with lower academic performance than verbal bullying.

PISA 2018 asked school principals to describe the extent to which learning is hindered by students intimidating or bullying other students. There were also significant differences across countries. On average, 24% of students attended schools whose principals reported that learning is "not at all" hindered, 64% of students were in schools whose principals reported that learning is hindered "very little", and 12% of students were in schools whose principals reported that learning is hindered to "some extent" or "a lot" by students intimidating or bullying other students. Note the similarity in the findings identified in the US related to the lack to which school leaders perceive there to be significant concerns associated with bullying. The lack of recognition that bullying is occurring appears to be an international concern.

The PISA 2018 survey included helpful social norms data. The survey asked students about five forms of bullying-related attitudes. The responses indicated that an overwhelming percentage of students hold very positive norms against bullying. These findings are discussed more in depth in Chapter 4. The *Empowered to Embrace Civility* student program uses social norms data such as this to influence students to engage in behave in kind, respectful, and inclusive ways.

PISA 2018 data show that frequently bullied students were more likely to feel sad, scared and not satisfied with their lives than students who were characterized as not frequently bullied. Frequently bullied students were also less likely to feel happy and have the self-belief to get through hard times. This difference holds for virtually all participating countries/ economies with available data, after accounting for student and school characteristics. Students in schools with a high prevalence of bullying were more likely to report a weaker sense of belonging at school, a poorer disciplinary climate and less co-operation amongst their schoolmates than students in schools with a low prevalence of bullying.

Pandemic Data

Bullying and Cyberbullying

Preliminary data related to what happened during the pandemic appears to demonstrate the interrelationship between bullying and cyberbullying. Given most students were in remote learning, it was reasonable to predict a decrease in in-person bullying and an increase in cyberbullying. This prediction is,, not in line with what other research has suggested, which is that cyberbullying is strongly associated with in-person bullying.[86]

Bacher-Hicks and colleagues conducted a study in an innovative manner.[87] They assessed Google Internet searches for bullying and cyberbullying. Their prior research had documented that Internet searches provided useful information about actual bullying behavior. Searches for terms associated with bullying decline during the summer months and are higher in the states with higher levels of reported bullying on YRBS.

During the pandemic, they found that searches for both "bullying" and "cyberbullying" dropped 30-40% when schools went to remote learning in the spring of 2020. This reduced level of searching continued into the 2020-2021 school year, but began to increase once schools began to shifted back to in-person learning in the spring of 2021. This data provides an indication that the decreases in online searches for "bullying" and "cyberbullying" were correlated with reductions in the both forms of harmful behaviors.

Patchin and Hinduja of the Cyberbullying Research Center have been regularly collecting data on bullying and cyberbullying in the US since 2004.[88] They conducted studies using nationally-representative samples collected in 2016, 2019, and 2021. These studies used the same methodology and an identical instrument. This allowed them to evaluate the trends in bullying and cyberbullying behaviors during the pandemic. In addition to asking adolescents in their 2021 study to report if they had been bullied or cyberbullied in the last 30 days, they also asked whether they had been bullied or had bullied others at school or online more or less since the start of the COVID-19 pandemic.[89]

Students overwhelmingly said that they had been bullied less at school since the start of the pandemic, as could logically be assumed because many times they were not in school or if they were, their environments were severely restricted. When it came to cyberbullying, most said they had been bullied online less or about the same as before. However, about a quarter did report more cyberbullying during the pandemic. The vast majority of students also said they bullied or cyberbullied others less since the start of the pandemic.

As is clear from both of these studies, cyberbullying did not surge the way some had expected. This data appears to provide support for the hypothesis that most cyberbullying is closely associated with in-person bullying. These are related events, not isolated incidents.

Concerns After Pandemic

As of the writing of this book, there is no data related to bullying or other school violence in the 2021-22 school year. However, news reports in the US document that there has been an increase in hurtful behavior, disruption, and violence.[90]

Unfortunately in the US, it appears that radical public advocacy groups and parents protesting everything from masks, to vaccines, to Critical Race Theory and school efforts to address racism and increase equity and inclusion has led to significant threats of violence against school boards and school staff.[91] Given that a fight has emerged over school efforts to increase inclusion and address racism and discrimination within schools and this has apparently become an election strategy, improvement in addressing the concerns of school climate is a more significant challenge.[92]

The parent protests in the US appear to be generated by a lack of comfort about "other." What appears to create greatest lack of comfort are people of different religions, nationalities, or colors and sexual and gender minorities. Of greater concern, it appears also that white wing extremism networks are growing throughout the world, building international networks to spread their violent ideology.[93]

THE HARMS OF BULLYING

The harms caused by being bullied have been extensively and well documented. A recent commentary in *Pediatrics*, outlined these harms:

> *Bullying can have life-long health consequences. It has been associated with stress-related physical and mental health symptoms, including depression, anxiety, post traumatic stress, and suicidal ideation. When bullying is motivated by discrimination or an attack on someone's core identity (eg, their sexual orientation), it can have especially harmful health consequences. The effects of bullying are not limited to the bullied. Bystanders who witness bullying may experience mental health consequences (eg, distress) as well.*[94]

A report by the American Educational Research Association, entitled *Prevention of Bullying in Schools, Colleges, and Universities: Research Report and Recommendations,* also provided an overview of concerns:

> 1. *Bullied students experience higher rates of anxiety, depression, physical health problems, and social adjustment problems. These problems can persist into adulthood.*
>
> 2. *Bullying students become less engaged in school, and their grades and test scores decline.*
>
> 3. *In high schools where bullying and teasing are prevalent, the student body is less involved in school activities, performs lower on standardized tests, and has a lower graduation rate.*
>
> 4. *Students who engage in bullying are at elevated risk for poor school adjustment and delinquency. They are at increased risk for higher rates of criminal behavior and social maladjustment in adulthood.*
>
> 5. *Students who are bullied but also engage in bullying have more negative outcomes than students in bully-only or victim-only groups. ...*
>
> 6. *Cyberbullied students experience negative outcomes similar to those experienced by their traditional counterparts, including depression, poor academic performance, and problem behavior. ...*[95]

A significant aspect related to the harms experienced by those who are bullied depends on the extent to which those targeted are defended by their peers. If they are defended by at least one classmate, targets have higher levels of self-esteem and are more popular and liked.[96] Their adjustment is also related to their relationships with other students who are also targeted. It appears that they are less likely to blame themselves if there are others, especially friends, who are also targeted.[97]

The well-being of those targeted may also depend on the overall level of to which students are bullied. In classrooms or schools where bullying is less prevalent or is more focused on a few specific targets, the negative consequences of bullying on the targets are exacerbated. Targets of bullying were found to have lower self esteem, to be more depressed and to be even more disliked in classrooms in which bullying was less common.[98] This is an aspect that clearly presents a conundrum is that in school environments where there is less bullying, those few remaining targets can be even more negatively impacted.[99]

Trauma

It is also essential to "connect the dots" between experiencing being bullied and trauma. Both Targeted Students and Marginalized Hurtful Students demonstrate evidence of having experiencing trauma.

The Adverse Childhood Experiences (ACE) study documents the profound, long lasting harm of experiencing childhood adversities.[100] Unfortunately, the participants in the original study ACE study were middle class white adults. The sole focus was on adversities that had occurred within the family. The study showed that the family-based adversities these participants experienced had significantly harmful physical and behavioral consequences.

The original study did not address the far more significant adversities experienced by the minority children who are subjugated in our society or lower income children. The ACE study also did not incorporate adversities children experience while at school. Most significantly this study did not inquire about being bullied or harassed, or frequently suspended, or other adversities students face while in school. Further studies have documented the extensive experience of additional adversities.[101] Compelling research is also focusing on concerns of intergenerational transmission of trauma.

A study by Idsoe and colleagues, revealed a high incidence of PTSD symptoms among students who reported they were bullied and a strong association between frequency of exposure to bullying and such symptoms.[102] Further, those students with the worst PTSD symptoms were the students who both engaged in and were bullied. The association between bullying and PTSD was described as follows:

> *People who have experienced events of an interpersonal nature show significantly higher levels of PTSD symptoms than those who have experienced other types of events. Bullying is an interpersonal event, and there are many salient aspects of children's development that may make repeated bullying experiences especially harmful. Bullying happens at a time when the brain is undergoing development in several bio-psycho-social systems that regulate behavior. During childhood and adolescence there is a gradual development and strengthening of brain systems involving a variety of cognitive, emotional and behavioral systems, from self-regulation and emotional processing to executive functions, from social connectivity to perception of threat. In adolescence, bullying might affect the development of*

executive functioning, including attention, response inhibition, organization and planning. The effects of bullying on the development of these biopsychosocial systems are not known, but a developmental perspective on trauma is needed both for understanding how the diagnosis of PTSD can be applied to this population, as well as for how potential traumatic effects can be reduced.[103]

Additional research is increasing the understanding of the connections between bullying and trauma disorders. Vaillancourt and colleagues have outlined how the experience of being bullied by peers becomes biologically embedded in the physiology of the developing child, which in turn impacts their health and behavior.[104]

The National Child Traumatic Stress Network (NCTSN) describes two forms of traumatic distress.[105]

- Acute traumatic events involve experiencing, witnessing, or a threat of a serious injury to yourself or another.

- Chronic traumatic situations that occur repeatedly over periods of time and result in feelings of fear, loss of trust in others, decreased sense of safety, guilt, and shame.

Bullying situations could involve acute trauma, chronic trauma, or both.

The standards for PTSD under the new American Psychiatric Association's *Diagnostic and Statistical Manual of Mental Disorders, Fifth Edition (DSM-5)* focus on major traumatic events, unfortunately not chronic or complex traumatic situations.[106] However, the four diagnostic symptom clusters include:

Re-experiencing covers spontaneous memories of the traumatic event, recurrent dreams related to it, flashbacks or other intense or prolonged psychological distress. Avoidance refers to distressing memories, thoughts, feelings or external reminders of the event.

Negative cognitions and mood represents myriad feelings, from a persistent and distorted sense of blame of self or others, to estrangement from others or markedly diminished interest in activities, to an inability to remember key aspects of the event.

Finally, arousal is marked by aggressive, reckless or self-destructive behavior, sleep disturbances, hyper-vigilance or related problems.[107]

The PTSD symptoms outlined in *DSM-5* closely match the reported symptoms of young people who are bullied, as well as those who both are bullied and engage in bullying.

Academic Performance and Absences

Clearly, maintaining a positive school climate is widely recognized as a critical component for supporting student academic achievement.[108] School climate is a particularly important factor in supporting academic success for students who are at greater risk for lower achievement. Pervasive school bullying creates a "noxious school climate the induces school avoidance, disengagement, and poorer academic performance."[109]

Schools where students perceived greater prevalence of bullying have lower achievement scores. Students' perceptions of the level of bullying were significant predictors even after accounting for student poverty, school size/enrollment, and the racial make-up of the school populations.

Persistent absenteeism is also a major concern associated with student success. When students do not experience a positive experience at school because of bullying there is a significant risk that they will withdraw or be absent from school.[110] An assessment of student absence data may provide insight into the level of bullying that is occurring in your school.

A study by Steiner and Rasberry using YRBS data that compared the responses on being bullied and data on missing school because of feeling of lack of safety.[111] This study demonstrated that students who were bullied in either at school of electronically were more likely to miss school. Those who were bullied in both venues had the highest risk of missing school. A study by Vidourek and colleagues examined the impact that bullying had on fear of attending school and school avoidance. Bullied students were six times more likely to report fear at school and school avoidance when compared to their non-bullied peers.[112]

Suicide and Self Harm

There is a a clear association between bullying and suicide and self harm.[113] It is known that suicide is multidimensional, involving many factors, at many levels of influence. Persistent bullying can create higher risk of suicide thoughts and behavior. A serious or significant bullying incident can trigger suicide behavior.

A recent study by Plemmons and colleagues, released in *Pediatrics* found that youth suicides are most prevalent during the school year.[114] A news story announcing these findings was sobering:

> *It's no secret the school year can bring students plenty of stress and other problems. But a study published Wednesday in the journal Pediatrics indicates the school year also corresponds with an increase in hospital visits for suicide attempts and serious suicidal thoughts among America's youth.*

"We noticed that anecdotally here in our own hospital over the last several years, we would have a fairly quiet summer as far as kids coming in for mental health issues, then right about four to six weeks after school started, we became inundated," says Dr. Greg Plemmons, the study's lead author ... "We found it really is consistent across all regions of the country."[115]

Hinduja and Patchin of the Cyberbullying Research Center released a comprehensive study on bullying, cyberbullying, and suicide in 2018.[116] Middle and high school students were asked about their experiences with bullying at school or cyberbullying in the last 30 days. They were also asked about the seriousness of the event and whether this impacted their ability to learn and feel safe at school. These findings were reported in a blog on their site:

We ... examined the relationship between school bullying and cyberbullying on suicidal ideation. Students who experienced only school bullying or only cyberbullying were about 1.6x significantly more likely (for each) to report suicidal ideation. Students who experienced both forms of bullying, however, were more than 5x as likely to report suicidal ideation compared to those who had not been bullied or cyberbullied.

Interestingly, those who experienced only school bullying or only cyberbullying were at no greater risk for attempted suicide, while those who experienced both forms of bullying were more than 11 times as likely to attempt suicide compared to those who had not been bullied.

Finally, we looked at the impact of serious bullying on suicidal thoughts and attempts among subsamples of those who had been bullied only at school or only online. As expected, even among those who had been bullied, the more serious incidents of bullying or cyberbullying all had a significant and positive association with suicidal ideation and suicide attempts. Specifically, students who ranked their experience with school bullying or cyberbullying as 6 or higher on a scale that ranged from 0 to 10, or indicated that the experience seriously affected them at school, were more than 3x as likely to report suicidal ideation compared to those who had relatively less serious experiences with school bullying and cyberbullying.

Finally, students who reported that their experience with school bullying or cyberbullying affected them at school were at the highest risk for suicidal ideation and attempted suicide.[117]

A meta-analysis by Holt and colleagues assessed 47 studies found that being targeted by bullying, engaging in bullying and both being targeted and hurtful were all associated with increased experiences of suicidal thoughts and suicidal behavior.[118] Those who are both targeted and hurtful have the greatest risk for suicidal thoughts and behaviors.

Self-harming behavior, which is also referred to as non-suicidal self-injury, is when individuals are intentionally engaging in harmful self-directed behavior when the immediate objective is not to lead to death.[119] Such self-harming behavior is linked to various mental health concerns, including an increased risk of suicidal ideation and behavior.[120] Engagement in bullying situations, as the target or the one being hurtful increases the risk of teens and young adults engaging in self-harming behaviors.[121]

While being bullied is a well-documented factor in youth suicide, students who have engaged in bullying should never be blamed for the decisions of other students.[122] Blaming tragic incidents on students who engaged in bullying ignores the multiple factors, can increase copy-cat behavior, and unfairly blames students for what are overall school climate concerns. What should be considered, however, is whether school leaders knew of the fact that persistent bullying of the student who took their life was occurring and whether they failed to effectively intervene. The feelings of hopelessness and helplessness of students, who are forced to be in a hostile school environment, who are experiencing persistent bullying, and who know from experience that there is no way to get this stopped must be profound. Institutional Betrayal is discussed in Chapter 3.

Of significant importance to the discussion of suicide and self-harm behavior is the willingness of students to report regarding concerns they are having. Data on reporting from the NCVC-SCS was reported earlier. This concern will be more fully discussed in Chapter 3. In brief, the data consistently indicates that only a minority of students who are bullied and feeling distressed report to the school and, in general, students do not perceive reporting concerns to the school is effective. There is clearly not a high level of trust that schools will respond in an effective manner.

To effectively address the concerns of student suicide and self-harm behavior it is essential that schools diligently address the reticence that students have regarding reporting concerns they are feeling or the concerns they have regarding the well-being of others.

School Violence

There is a clearly established connection between being bullied and bringing weapons to school, or engaging in a school shooting. When students do not feel that they can safely report being bullied to school officials, bringing a weapon to defend themselves may follow. Like suicide, engaging in school violence is multidimensional, involving many factors, at many levels of influence.

School shootings, although significantly tragic, remain exceptionally rare. This is a problem that is much more significant risk in the US, where gun ownership is more heavily supported. Of significant concern is that the reported rate of shootings occurring on school campus exploded after return to school following the pandemic.

As there is no formal collection of such data, the Washington Post keeps track of reported school shootings in the US.[123] They recently reported that at least 42 acts of gun violence committed on K-12 campuses during regular hours in 2021. Most of these shootings have been since students returned to campus Fall 2021. This was the most during any year since at least 1999. More than 285,000 students have experienced gun violence at school since Columbine. About 34,000 students were exposed to gun violence in the US 2021.[124]

Across the US, state or district school safety teams are releasing new "school safety plans." Too often, these plans are focused on technical security and increased law enforcement presence.[125] This is the so-called "hardening of schools." There is no evidence of the effectiveness of this approach.[126]

The recent massive school shooting in is a case in point. As well expressed by a Texas newspaper, "Texas already "hardened" schools. It didn't save Uvalde."[127] As noted in this article, the majority of public schools in the US already implement the security measures that are most often promoted by public officials. This includes locked doors to the outside and in classrooms, active-shooter plans, and security cameras.

Bullying Associated with School Shootings

A comprehensive study of school shootings by the US Secret Service (USSS) and USDOE, demonstrated that bullying is associated with shootings.[128] Almost three-quarters of the attackers felt persecuted, bullied, threatened, attacked or injured by others prior to the incident. In some of these cases, being bullied appeared to have a significant impact on the shooter and appeared to have been a factor in his decision to attack at the school.[129]

Students who engage in school shootings or other forms of violence or who attempt suicide do not fit into one singular profile.[130] There are always multiple factors involved in these situations. Most attackers engaged in behaviors prior to the incident that caused others concern or indicated a need for help. Most attackers had difficulty coping with significant losses or personal failures. Moreover, many had attempted suicide.

A comprehensive analysis of mass school shooters by Langman set forth a complex bio-psycho-social model. As this was described:

> *Mass violence is a complex phenomenon that defies simplistic explanations. This article proposes a bio-psycho-social model to account for the many factors that contribute to rampage school shootings. Biological factors include those related to health, appearance, and ability. The psychological domain includes three types of perpetrators: psychopathic, psychotic, and traumatized. The social factors include*

family patterns, multiple types of failures, and external influences. In addition, there are issues that cut across the bio-psycho-social domains, such as masculine identity. The sense of damaged masculinity is common to many shooters and often involves failures and inadequacies in more than one domain.[131]

The importance of addressing bullying was reinforced by the USSS document *Enhancing School Safety Using a Threat Assessment Model: An Operational Guide for Preventing Targeted School Violence.*[132]

All students face stressors such as setbacks, losses, and other challenges as part of their lives. … Stressors can occur in all areas of a student's life, including at school with coursework, friendships, romantic relationships, or teammates; or outside of school with parents, siblings, or at jobs. Many students can experience bullying, a stressor which can take place in person at school or online at home. Teams should intervene and prevent bullying and cyberbullying of a student who has been brought to their attention. More broadly, administrators should work to address any concerns regarding bullying school-wide and ensure their school has a safe climate for all students.[133]

Based on an analysis of the 2015 CDC's YRBS data, students who are bullied were twice as likely to bring weapons to school.[134] However, the researchers in this study looked more deeply. They found that the victims of bullying were more likely to bring weapons if they had also been in a fight, been threatened or injured at school, or skipped school out of fear for their safety. Each additional risk factor increased the likelihood of bringing a weapon to school.

Student Reporting of Concerns

The concerns regarding student reporting discussed in the section on Suicide and Self-Harm Behavior also relate to concerns regarding student reporting of concerns. The USSS and USDOE report documented that attackers were found to have demonstrated concerning behavior 93% of the time; at least one adult was concerned by the student's behavior 88% of the time; and at least three people were concerned by the student's behavior 76% of the time.[135] To prevent these incidents requires that reporting becomes the norm instead of an anomaly.

The US Federal Bureau of Investigation (FBI) created a guide *Making Prevention a Reality: Identifying, Assessing, and Managing the Threat of Targeted Attacks to Help Communities Assess and Manage Possible Threats* to help communities recognize threats and act accordingly.[136] The guide identified at the importance of reporting mechanisms, information sharing within the confines of the law, and encouragement for reporting. This report emphasized a need for "upstander" versus "bystander" behavior—that is, creating norms and opportunities for others to be able to report concerns.

Many states have implemented digital tip lines to seek to increase reporting. Unfortunately, research on the effectiveness of such tip lines is very limited. One recent study by RTI International noted that very little is known about how widely they have been implemented and what their characteristics are.[137] This study involved a survey a nationally representative sample of 1,226 school principals. The principals reported that principals perceive tip lines are an effective school safety strategy, that addressed multiple threats. The data indicated these perspectives of principals:

- *Seventy-seven percent (77%) percent believed that their tip lines made them more aware of safety issues at their school.*

- *Over 50% said that their schools' tip lines had prevented violent incidents.*

- *Two-thirds believed that their tiplines allowed their schools to respond more effectively to bullying.*

- *Seventy-three percent (73%) reported that their tip lines had prevented incidents of self-harm or suicide.[138]*

However, the most common challenges to operating a tip line included:

- *Receiving tips with insufficient information to act on.*

- *Raising student awareness and getting students to submit tips.*

- *Identifying false or bogus submissions.*

- *Receiving tips for situations that are considered out of scope.*

- *Raising community awareness.[139]*

It was noted that concerns of school violence or suicide are by far not the most frequent. Evidence from Oregon's SafeOregon state tip line program demonstrated that concerns of bullying were far in excess of other reported concerns. Thirty-four percent (34%) of the reports were associated with bullying, as compared to 11% reporting that another student was engaging in suicide behavior and 6% reporting a planned school attack. It is unknown whether the report of bullying was by the student being bullied or a Witness.

More helpful insight on the effectiveness of digital tip lines will hopefully emerge in the future. Stein-Seroussi and colleagues have implemented a comprehensive study of the effectiveness of the Nevada Tip Line. [140] However, this study is in early stages.

As will be discussed in Chapter 3, many students do not trust that schools will respond well to reports of concerns regarding bullying. The same lack of reporting is clearly evident in situations of threats to school safety. This reticence to report serious situations to schools is of significant concern.

Hate Crimes and Recruitment

Organizations, such as in the US the Southern Poverty Law Clinic (SPLC) and the Anti Defamation League (ADL), that track hate groups and their activities, have documented a more recent increase in white nationalistic activities.[141] These organizations have also documented for many years, the efforts these white nationalist groups make in recruiting teens.[142]

There are concerns about the algorithms that Meta uses to direct users to information they may find of interest on Facebook and Instagram. Clear evidence was recently submitted to the US Congress on the way in which Meta is driving users to view hate messages.[143] Reportedly, content that stirs anger and outrage is of higher value for attention getting. Attention getting translates to advertising dollars.

The SPLC and the Polarization and Extremism Research and Innovation Lab have developed resources to assist in building community resilience against extremism. The primary resource is a document entitled *Building Resilience & Confronting Risk: A Parents and Caregivers Guide to Online Youth Radicalization.*[144] The following is brief insight from this document.

The key pathways to recruitment include online content "rabbit holes" and filter bubbles, where young people are constantly being presented with hate and bias information. This may start to occur because they initiated an action that expressed some interest. Recruitment may also occur through peer sharing or direct online contact with extremists. A significant level of recruitment occurs within online gaming sites. During the pandemic, teens increased their engagement in activities on such gaming sites—known online places for recruitment activities.

There are some key indicators can identify that a student may be exposed to radicalized material. It will be helpful for teachers to recognize these signs that may become evident in class discussions or conversations.

- *Fear of a "Great Replacement" or "White Genocide" in which a white minority is politically oppressed by a non- white majority.*
- *Belief in antisemitic conspiracy theories.*
- *Belief in the necessity of violent insurrections, honoring those involved in past insurrections, planning for a future of necessary violence.*
- *Belief in male supremacy or expressions of misogyny, including the policing of the behavior of females.*
- *Belief in the necessity of violence to suppress the movements against racial injustice and police brutality.*
- *Sharing concepts associated with scientific racism. Using language of genetics, evolution, and psychology to support racist stereotypes and justify racial hierarchies.*

- *Blaming immigrants for societal shortcomings.*
- *Looking forward to societal chaos or collapse and a desire for complete societal breakdown.*

It is exceptionally important for educators, as well as parents or caregivers, to recognize and address the vulnerabilities that make students more susceptible to extremist recruitment. There is no single reason why one person will be drawn to extremist groups and another one will not. However, most young people who are recruited have experienced some combination of the following:

- **Trauma, Disruption, and Loss.** *Sudden unwanted changes can leave young people feeling powerless, which makes them more vulnerable to radicalization.*

- **Confusion and Uncertainty.** *Extremists offer simple, false solutions to complex problems.*

- **Anger and Betrayal.** *When young people feel something has unjustly been taken from them, they may turn to extremists for easy answers and a scapegoat to blame.*

- **Rebellion and Status.** *Rebellion increasingly occurs online, such as by sharing provocative content with both friends and strangers.*

- **Desire for Love and Friendship.** *Strange as it sounds, many extremists embrace hate hoping it will bring them closer with someone they love such as a family member or a friend.*

- **Isolation and Lack of Belonging.** *Feeling isolated and a lack of belonging is the major driver towards extremist groups. All humans have a strong desire for connections with others. When those connections are lacking either in the family or at school, young people are at higher risk of being recruited into a community they feel supports them.*

- **Curiosity.** *Boredom and idleness can help spread conspiracies or lead people to adopt radical ideologies.*

Unfortunately, the SPLC guidance provided for educators does not adequately address how schools can intervene and inoculate students so they are not vulnerable to such recruitment. Most of the above vulnerabilities can be counteracted in a school that focuses strongly on ensuring that all students feel safe, included, and respected. This is why it is so important to address the concerns of all students experiencing bullying in an effective manner.

Chapter 2.
The Nature of Hurtful Behavior

HIGHLIGHTS

- **Who Bullies?** Most insight provided to educators casts those students who engage in bullying as having significant other challenges —"maladjusted youth." This is an inaccurate stereotype. The greatest source of bullying is socially competent students who are often perceived by school staff to be "leaders," who are being hurtful to achieve dominance and social status. There are also significant concerns associated with school staff who are hurtful to students.

- **Quest for Dominance and Social Status.** The greatest source of bullying behavior in schools is students who are hurtful to establish dominance and social status, Dominance Motivated Hurtful Students.

  - **Public Stereotype.** A report from the National Academy of Sciences noted concerns about the unfortunate "public stereotype" of those who bully that ignores students who bully others who are high-status perpetrators perceived by peers as being popular, socially skilled, and leaders. One key source of this "public stereotype" is the information that is on stopbullying.gov, the US website that provides information about bullying.

  - **Ethological Basis.** Aggression is a strategy in most animal groups to achieve dominance, which supports the acquisition of territory, resources, and mates. Bullying behavior of students is for the same purpose. Bullying behavior is seen in all cultures, although the way it manifests is different. These students target both those who are considered "misfits" as well as rivals, especially rivals for mates.

  - **Motivations for Bullying.** Motivations for engaging in bullying include: dominance, status and popularity, resources, revenge or retaliation, justice, belonging, romance, identity, well-being, and entertainment. Revenge or retaliation is a form of Reactive Aggression. The other are examples of Proactive Aggression.

- **Significant Rewards.** Dominance Motivated Hurtful Students achieve significant rewards from their hurtful behavior. They experience earlier ages of dating and first sexual intercourse, greater dating and sexual relations, are more likely to be dating, and have a significantly greater number of sexual partners. They also achieve the ability to dictate social interactions, become leading players on athletic teams, obtain admission to a high ranking university, and obtain a dynamite job where they can rise in status within a hierarchal corporation, and gain wealth.

- **Situational Dynamics.** Dominance Motivated Hurtful Students are perceived as leaders by many school staff members. When they are hurtful, they do not display outbursts. They engage in persistent hurtful acts, which cause profound harm to the target—but these single acts are often not perceived as of significant concern. Especially if they target "misfits," these students may have engaged in concerning behavior. When these Targeted Students report they are being trotted badly by a Dominance Motivated Hurtful Student, this often does not lead to a positive intervention by the school.

- **Social Dominance Theory.** Social dominance theory studies group-based social hierarchies that legitimize social inequality and mistreatment of marginalized social groups. People differ in their "social dominance orientation"—the degree to which they support these inequities. One study determined that college students who had high social dominance orientation reported significantly greater involvement in bullying while in secondary school.

- **Dominance or Prestige Leaders.** Other researchers have focused on two strategies to achieve leadership positions. Dominance Leaders gain and maintain social rank by using coercion and intimidation. Prestige Leaders gain and maintain social status by displaying valued knowledge and skills that support the community's well-being. This research has also not been integrated into bullying. The Prestige Leaders in your school hold the key to shifting the school climate away from supporting Dominance Motivated Hurtful Students. (Discussed in Chapter 4.)

• **Bi-Directional Hurtful Behavior or Impulsive Retaliation.** Hurtful behavior that would likely not be considered "bullying" is a significant source of disruption in schools. These are situations of either bi-directional hurtful behavior or impulsive retaliation.

- **Bi-Directional Hurtful Behavior.** These are situations where both students are being hurtful to each other. The involved students are roughly equivalent in social status. These may be situations of true conflict where both students have been equally involved or where one student instigated hurtful actions that targeted a rival. This is often called "drama" by students.

- **Impulsive Retaliation.** This is a form of Reactive Aggression. The Targeted Student has become dysregulated and impulsively responds in an aggressive retaliatory manner. Students who are not able to self-regulate are more likely to engage in impulsive retaliation. However, retaliation when one has been treated badly is well-supported by many in our society.

• **Hurtful Staff.** Staff who are hurtful to students is a highly significant concern that is not at all well addressed. Staff bullying is an abuse of power that tends to be persistent and involves degrading a student, often in front of other students.

  - **Social Cognition Theory.** A person's behavior can be directly related to what they have learned by observing others. The manner in which school staff treat students models guidelines on how students should treat others.

  - **Concern is Ignored.** There are significant examples of how this concern is ignored, in professional studies, on websites addressing bullying, and in academic studies.

  - **What We Do Know.** The issue of staff who bully students is a known concern, that is discussed privately, if at all. When this issue becomes a labor conflict, an adversarial dynamic is established.

    ‣ There are two kinds of teachers who engage in bullying: Those seen as intentionally humiliating students. Those seen as being overwhelmed by situations, including a lack of support from the administration and lack of training in effective classroom management, and classes that were too large.

    ‣ There are usually no negative consequences for staff who engage in bullying. Students who are targeted often are vulnerable, have some devalued personal attribute, are unable to stand up for themselves, and others will not defend them.

    ‣ Teachers may view their actions as an appropriate disciplinary response or good classroom management.

    ‣ The students who are reportedly being bullied by teachers are the ones who are at highest risk of being bullied by students and experiencing long lasting harm.

- **Identity-Based Staff Bullying**. Staff bullying of sexual and gender minority students, students with disabilities, overweight students, and religious minority students are documented concerns.

- *Embrace Civility Student Survey.* On the *Embrace Civility Student Survey,* the results were significant. Those students who had "ever" witnessed staff be hurtful to a student were significantly more likely to report witnessing, engaging in, or being targeted by hurtful behavior. These findings indicate that dramatic declines could be achieved in reducing hurtful student behavior by reducing staff hurtful behavior directed at students.

- **Students Hurtful to Staff.** Students who are hurtful to staff must be held accountable in the manner outlined in Chapter 11. Of significant importance is assessing whether these students engaged in Reactive Aggression because the staff member was hurtful to them or Proactive Aggression against a staff member because of their membership in an identity group.

- **Staff Hurtful to Staff**. This is an additional concern that must be addressed, but is beyond the scope of this book.

THE QUEST FOR DOMINANCE AND SOCIAL STATUS

The depiction of "bullies," as maladjusted youth, is highly common. This description is, unfortunately, inaccurate or at the very least incomplete. Marginalized Hurtful Students are present in schools and can indeed be aggressive to other students. However, they are not the greatest source of bullying behavior. The greatest source of bullying behavior is students who are hurtful to establish dominance and social status, Dominance Motivated Hurtful Students.

The late Dr. Phil Rodkin should be credited for tireless work in presenting insight on the characteristics of the two primary groups of youth who engage in bullying.[145] Please realize that these are the "primary" groups. There may be various permutations with individual students. The following description of these two primary groups is from a paper that was published shortly after his untimely death:

> *Some youth who bully are well-integrated into their peer culture and do not lack for peer social support; they have surprisingly high levels of popularity among their peers. These youth are relatively evenly split between boys and girls. They have a variety of friends that engage in varying degrees of bullying and possess strengths that are easy to recognize, including social skills, athleticism, and/or*

attractiveness. These youth tend to use proactive and goal-directed aggression. Some incorporate prosocial strategies into their behavioral repertoire, for example reconciling with their targets after conflict, or becoming less aggressive once a clear dominance relationship has been established. They may have lower physiological reactivity to stressful situations than aggressive children who are less well integrated in the social sphere. Socially integrated bullies are both underrecognized as seriously aggressive, and popularized in the media. Vaillancourt (and colleagues) go so far as to call these socially connected youth "Machiavellian": "popular, socially skilled and competent . . . [with] high self-esteem . . . low on psychopathology . . . [and] many assets". Hawley ... seems to suggest that bistrategic controllers (who employ both prosocial and coercive strategies to gain resources) are aggressive, but may not be bullies given that they aggress upon their "inner circle" more than they aggress upon low status peers.

However, not all youth who bully are socially integrated; instead, some are socially marginalized. For these children, the source of their power is more difficult to identify. It may come from their unsuccessful attempts to raise their own social status or to attempt to dominate others through coercive strategies. It may also come from their efforts in bringing together a small group of equally marginalized youth to support their attacks. A peer rejection framework is a compelling explanatory framework for marginalized youth who bully, who are in conflict with others in the world. These children, mostly boys, tend to be characterized by a clear pattern of deficits in broad domains of developmental functioning. Their aggression is impulsive and overly reactive to real or perceived slights; they are consistently identified as "at-risk" students. Cook (and colleagues) meta-analysis concluded that this type of bully "has comorbid externalizing and internalizing problems, holds significantly negative attitudes and beliefs about himself or herself and others, is low in social competence, does not have adequate social problem-solving skills, performs poorly academically, and is not only rejected and isolated by peers but also negatively influenced by the peers with whom he or she interacts". ... Farmer (and colleagues) reported that marginalized, unpopular youth who bully, whether girls or boys, are often shunted into peer groups with other bullies, and sometimes even with the children they harass. In sum, marginalized bully victims have a host of problems of which bullying behavior is but one manifestation. Their bullying might stem from an inability to control their hostile actions, or from a desire to gain a preferred status that generally eludes them. These youth would benefit from services that go beyond bullying-reduction programs such as more general aggression reduction therapies and social skills training.[146]

As will be discussed below, the description of those who engage in bullying, that is using old terminology of "bullies," which you are encouraged not to use, should be used to apply to only the kinds of students described in the first paragraph above. Some researchers have begun to refer to these students as "pure bullies."

The students who are described in the second paragraph may more appropriately be considered "bully-victims," using old terminology as was discussed in Chapter 1. These Marginalized Hurtful Students have been victimized and their hurtful behavior is associated with this victimization. Their Reactive Aggression is vastly different from the hurtful behavior of those engaging in hurtful behavior to achieve dominance and social status, who engage in Proactive Aggression. Proactive Aggression is characterized by lack of emotional arousal, intentionality, and the use of effective strategies to gain desired outcomes.

Public Stereotypes About Those who Bully

The public stereotype about those who engage in bullying as maladjusted students is strong. The following helpful insight has been provided by the US National Academies of Sciences, Engineering, and Medicine (NAS) in a 2016 report entitled, *Preventing Bullying Through Science, Policy, and Practice.*[147] Very important insight from this publication is the following:

> There is evidence that supports a finding that individuals who bully others have contradictory attributes. Research suggests that there are children and adolescents who bully others because they have some form of maladjustment or ... are motivated by establishing their status in a social network. Consequently, the relation between bullying, being bullied, acceptance, and rejection is complex. **This complexity is also linked to a stereotype held by the general public about individuals who bully. This stereotype casts children and youth who bully others as being high on psychopathology, low on social skills, and possessing few assets and competencies that the peer group values.** Although some occurrence of this "stereotypical bully" or "classic bully" is supported by research, when researchers consider social status in relation to perpetration of bullying behavior, a different profile emerges. These studies suggest that most children and youth who bully others wield considerable power within their peer network and that high-status perpetrators tend to be perceived by peers as being popular, socially skilled, and leaders. High-status bullies have also been found to rank high on assets and competencies that the peer group values such as being attractive or being good athletes; they have also been found to rank low on psychopathology and to use aggression instrumentally to achieve and maintain hegemony. Considering these findings of contrasting characteristics of perpetrators of bullying behavior, it makes sense that the research on outcomes of perpetrating is mixed. Unfortunately, most research on the short- and long-term outcomes of perpetrating bullying behavior has not taken into account this heterogeneity when considering the impact to children and youth who have bullied their peers.[148]

Note the key statement that is emphasized. It is not hard to find the source of this public stereotype. The Federal Partners in Bullying

Prevention StopBullying.Gov website is a source of this public stereotype. This is the current information provided on one page on the website:

Children More Likely to Bully Others

There are two types of kids who are more likely to bully others:

- *Some are well-connected to their peers, have social power, are overly concerned about their popularity, and like to dominate or be in charge of others.*

- *Others are more isolated from their peers and may be depressed or anxious, have low self esteem, be less involved in school, be easily pressured by peers, or not identify with the emotions or feelings of others.*

Children who have these factors are also more likely to bully others;

- *Are aggressive or easily frustrated.*

- *Have less parental involvement or having issues at home.*

- *Think badly of others.*

- *Have difficulty following rules.*

- *View violence in a positive way.*

- *Have friends who bully others.*[149]

Note that while the first bullet does appear to address the two sources of bullying, as outlined by Rodkin. However, the overall characteristics presented are still in accord with the "unfortunate stereotype held by the general public." Further, there is no reference to the fact that the youth described in all but the first bullet very likely should be considered to be "bully-victims"—both being targeted and hurtful. Of even greater concern is text from another page currently on the website:

Why Some Youth Bully

Children and teenagers who feel secure and supported by their family, school, and peers are less likely to bully. However, some youth do not have these types of support. Every individual is unique and there are many factors that can contribute to bullying behavior. A youth who bullies may experience one, several, or none of these contributing factors.

Peer factors. *Some youth bully:*

- *to attain or maintain social power or to elevate their status in their peer group.*

- *to show their allegiance to and fit in with their peer group.*

- *to exclude others from their peer group, to show who is and is not part of the group.*

- *to control the behavior of their peers.*

Family factors. *Some youth who bully:*

- *come from families where there is bullying, aggression, or violence at home*

- *may have parents and caregivers that do not provide emotional support or communication.*

- *may have parents or caregivers who respond in an authoritarian or reactive way.*

- *may come from families where the adults are overly lenient or where there is low parental involvement in their lives.*

Emotional factors. *Some youth who bully:*

- *may have been bullied in the past or currently.*

- *have feelings of insecurity and low self-esteem, so they bully to make themselves feel more powerful.*

- *do not understand other's emotions.*

- *don't know how to control their emotions, so they take out their feelings on other people.*

- *may not have skills for handling social situations in healthy, positive ways.*

School factors. *Some youth who bully:*

- *may be in schools where conduct problems and bullying are not properly addressed.*

- *may experience being excluded, not accepted, or stigmatized at school.*[150]

A very important and critical question must be asked why this public stereotype has been perpetuated for so long—by the Federal Partners in Bullying Prevention.[151]

Efforts to address the concerns of Marginalized Hurtful Students are obviously highly critical. These students are at profound risk. However, efforts to reduce bullying by those Dominance Motivated Hurtful Students who are popular and are receiving significant rewards within their school community for engaging in such hurtful behavior will require an approach that is vastly different from the "risk prevention" and "trauma informed" practices schools also need to implement.

It is exceptionally important to recognize that recommendations on strategies to address bullying are highly unlikely to be effective—when the underlying perspective of those who engage in bullying is so inaccurate.

Being Hurtful to Achieve Dominance

This section will provide more extended insight into the behavior of Dominance Motivated Hurtful Students. Insight on the motivations and behaviors of these students has clearly not been well-articulated for educators. Faris and Felmlee explained the nature of hurtful behavior:

Clearly it is the strong who do the attacking: recent scholarship has debunked the traditional view of aggressive youth as socially marginal and psychologically troubled. Indeed, aggressors often possess strong social skills and harass their peers, not to reenact their own troubled home lives, but to gain status. ...

[A]ggression is highly related to dominance and territoriality. Most adolescents desire status, albeit to varying degrees, and this desire motivates much aggressive behavior: the more adolescents—or their friends—care about being popular, the more aggressive they become over time. Bullies appear to pursue status, as well as affection, as goals.

Popularity is associated with increased physical and relational aggression, behavior used to maintain social dominance. As social status increases, aggressive behavior escalates—at least until youth approach the pinnacle of the school hierarchy, when such actions are no longer required and aggression again declines. ...

The adaptive bullying of pure bullies represents aggressive, dominance-seeking behaviors, therefore giving rise to the understanding of bullying as adaptive in the first place. In contrast, the bullying of bully-victims is characterized by the risky, impulsive, and hostile behavior typically described by the developmental psychopathological approach to bullying. This kind of behavior may be better explained by the social learning, maladaptive cognition, and impoverished environmental theories described previously. An important distinction between bullies and bully-victims lie in the associated outcomes as well. Bully-victims do not experience positive outcomes in terms of social dominance or intrasexual competition, indicating that the types of bullying employed by bully-victims are not adaptive strategies. In addition to failing to benefit from their bullying behavior, bully-victims also experience high levels of depression when compared to pure bullies, victims, and uninvolved individuals.[152]

Ethological Basis of Behavior

Juvonen identified that students who were named by peers as the "coolest" were also often named the most hurtful and the ones engaging in spreading of rumors.[153] This insight from Juvonen explains the ethological basis for this hurtful behavior:

Ethological research suggests that aggression is a strategy to establish a dominant position within a group. Among a number of species (e.g., various non-human primates), physical aggression enables attainment of a dominant position, such that the most powerful fighter (typically male) acquires a top position within a group and therefore gains access to valued resources. Within human youth, aggression can be considered a strategic behavior that serves similar social dominance functions.[154]

An ethological framework is based on the foundation of natural and sexual selection.[155] Natural selection favors traits that enhances an an organism's ability to survive, secure resources, and provide for offspring.

Sexual selection favors traits that enhance an organism's ability to attract mates and reproduce.[156] Considering bullying in the context of an evolutionary theory would suggest that bullying may be an adaptation that provides benefits that support the survival of an organism, in this case, young people.

There are some other factors to consider. Bullying has been observed in every modern country on the planet.[157] This suggests that bullying is not associated with specific cultural factors.[158] Bullying has been ubiquitous across all recorded history. For adolescents in isolated hunter-gatherer communities, bullying has been noted to serve reliable, functional purposes associated with mating. This bullying behavior tend to be more relational in nature, as many groups have strong social sanctions against displays of anger or violence and close genetic ties exist between members of the group.

Consider the social behavior of animals. Bullying is apparent in most animal communities. The functions of bullying may vary depending on the species. However, bullying is primarily focused on competition over mates, food, and territory. There is even potential evidence that older or more established trees might bully other trees.[159]

In this regard, I have personal experience. I own donkeys, goats, chickens, and ducks. Anyone who owns livestock understands these dynamics. If a baby chick or duckling is sick, the other chickens or ducks will peck at it until it dies. If I were to put several donkeys who had not had an established connection with each other, newly into a pasture, bullying in the form of head lowering, kicking, and biting would occur. Even with a well-established herd, when hay is placed in the barn, my dominant jenny will put back her ears and look like she is going to kick to get the first bite and my lowest ranked jenny stays back to make sure she can safely approach the food. If I were to keep two baby boy goats to use as bucks for breeding, they would be the best of friends—until puberty. Then, there would be lots of head butting until dominance had been established.

Does any of this reflect on what you see happening in your school's classrooms, hallways, and other places? Are you seeing students pick on the "weak chicks" and also against "rivals?" Are you seeing students treated badly based on identity as they are not desired members of the "herd" or "pack?" Are you seeing aggression in the context of athletics or other activities such as place on a team, playing time, position on the field, starring role in a play, or first seat in the orchestra? Is aggression associated with personal relationships—who is allowed to date or be seem with whom? Are you seeing those students who are being hurtful gaining significant rewards from their behavior?

Motivations for Bullying

Considering the motives of students who engage in bullying is helpful. Asking what students who are hurtful what they are trying to accomplish can provide a better understanding of the needs they try to fulfill and the goals they try to achieve.[160] If we use a goal-oriented, motivation focused approach to consider student behavior, this can better help to identify more positive alternatives to achieve the same goals.[161] It is exceptionally important to distinguish between Reactive Aggression and Proactive Aggression in this analysis of motivation.

An excellent article by Sanders and colleagues, entitled Why Do Bullies Bully? Motives for Bullying, provided a discussion on the identified motivations of those who are hurtful.[162] It was noted that the developmental age of the student, as well as the social norms of the school community should also be considered in the context of motivations. This analysis did not reference the differences between Reactive and Proactive Aggression. The motivations Sanders and colleagues identified in the research literature include:

- **Dominance.** Social dominance and power within a group is a clearly recognized goal of students who are hurtful. Dominance motivated students who bully are hurtful to demonstrate control over others or over desired resources or opportunities.[163] Many of the other motivations can accurately be phrased "dominance and ...."

- **Status and Popularity.** Status refers to a student's social standing and position within the school's social hierarchy. Status motivations work in two directions. Students may bully others to reduce the social status of those they are hurtful to or to increase their own social standing.[164] Status is clearly associated with dominance. Status goals appear to be most active in the teen years.[165] Status goals are also strong when there is a school level transition. The transition from elementary to middle school, as well as into high school level is a time where their perceived place on the school's social status "ladder" is important to many students.

- **Resources.** In modern society, aggression to achieve resources necessary for survival is no longer a predominant goal. Aggression to achieve resources has been noted in sibling aggression situation, as well as in the work place and in prison.[166] Consider the resources that secondary students, especially might consider important. A high priority for most teens is romantic partners. Other resource priorities may vary and could include a student body position, a desired position on the field on an athletic team, or a leading role in a play or seat in the band.

- **Revenge or Retaliation.** Revenge or retaliation is another commonly cited motive that those who bully provide when asked to explain their motives.[167] Those who bully often justify their actions as having resulted from being justifiable because they were provoked and the need to retaliate against the wrong doing of the one they were hurtful to.[168]

- **Justice.** Some students may be hurtful out of a sense of their position to correct a student who has acted outside of the social or cultural peer norms of the school.[169] The objective is to demonstrate to the target and the peer group which norms will be tolerated or not. This motivation is involved in Identity-Based Bullying—targeting a student who is perceived to be a "misfit."

- **Belonging.** Bullying can be a strategy used to be accepted in a group or to acquire or maintain friends. Students may engage in bullying to fit in, gain peer acceptance, and avoid rejection.[170] These behaviors may be evident in the behavior of students who are often Hurtful Supporters.

- **Romance.** Especially during the teen years, dominance and status is often likely sought to achieve the end goal of obtaining romantic relationships.[171] Students may engage in bullying to show their sexual interest or deal with competitors.[172] They may also be hurtful to those who have spurned their attentions or who they have had a break-up with.

- **Identity.** Bullying may be used by a student as a way to boost their positive self-image.[173] This motivation for engaging in bullying appears to be closely linked to revenge. Students may be hurtful in retaliation for actions of another that attacked their identity.

- **Well-being.** This factor has not been extensively studied. However, in conversations with students who admitted to being hurtful, the reasons provided included to avoid being in a situation where others were hurtful to them, a distraction from their own negative feelings.[174]

- **Entertainment.** Bullying for entertainment or excitement. "Because one is bored," is frequently mentioned as a motive by students.[175]

Note that most of these motivations would fall under the description of Proactive Aggression. However, the motivation of Revenge or Retaliation would more likely fall under the category of Reactive Aggression.

Successful Outcomes of Proactive Aggression

The Proactive Aggression of Dominance Motivated Hurtful Students is positively associated with a number of positive benefits. They experience earlier ages of dating and first sexual intercourse, report greater dating and sexual relations opportunities, are more likely to be in a dating relationship, and report a significantly greater number of sexual partners.[176] Indeed, when one considers the sexual relationship objectives of most teens, bullying can be considered to be a highly effective "head butting" strategy to achieve these objectives.

Dominance Motivated Hurtful Students are also focused on other status goals, including the ability to dictate what is happening in social interactions, becoming leading players on athletic teams, obtaining admission to a high ranking university, and obtaining a a dynamite job where they can rise in status within a hierarchal corporation, and gain wealth.[177] Being willing and able to use power aggressively is supported by many in our society.

Now contrast this to what is happening with your students who are both being treated badly and are aggressive.[178] Marginalized Hurtful Students do not achieve such beneficial outcomes from their hurtful acts. They generally experience high levels of depression. When they are physically aggressive, this has a significant social cost. Other students do not want to be associated with them.

Being considered popular is positively correlated with Proactive Aggression and negatively correlated with Reactive Aggression.[179] In one study, students who were consistently considered to be popular showed the highest levels of Proactive Aggression, whereas those who were consistently unpopular showed the highest levels of Reactive Aggression.

Dominance Motivated Hurtful Students frequently appear to have a sense of entitlement grounded in privilege. They may feel they are entitled to determine who is to be considered "deviant" or "weird"— and thus deserve to be "put in their place." They may not recognize or be willing to admit their actions are hurtful. They are just reinforcing a natural social order, which has them on top. Throughout their schooling, they have likely experienced environments where their drive for dominance has been valued, such as in athletics or receiving "token rewards" for their compliance with school expectations. They are often well behaved in front of staff and are not considered "problem students."

Dominance Motivated Hurtful Students very likely have socially prominent parents or caregivers. This creates challenges in a disciplinary context. Having a disciplinary record of engaging in bullying, would have a negative impact on their ability to gain admission to a top level university. They are not headed to prison. They are headed to leadership positions in society. Obviously, society would be greatly benefitted by helping these students change their approach to leadership.

Situation Dynamics

The dynamics of this situation must be more fully considered, especially in situations where socially skilled, students who are perceived by staff to be compliant, competent students have been hurtful to students who have greater challenges—the "social misfits." The hurtful actions of Dominance Motivated Hurtful Students are likely to be sophisticatedly cruel, but largely invisible to any staff member. They engage in subtle verbal and relational aggression, not physically aggressive hurtful acts.

If the Targeted Student is a "misfit," they likely have had more challenges in managing their behavior in school. This likely has resulted in disciplinary actions.

If a Targeted Student reports they are being bullied, the principal may view the situation based on what they think about the differences in the degree to which both students are compliant to school staff. The principal may not to think that the compliant student Dominance Motivated Hurtful Student was really all that hurtful. These are also often minor incidents, that by themselves would not meet the statutory definition of "bullying" or warrant a suspension.

Experiencing the persistent harm and realizing that the school will do nothing to stop this, also likely increases the risk that the Targeted Student will trigger and have a more visible, emotionally aggressive outburst that is more visible—and more likely to be considered a violation of the disciplinary code. Even if these students protest that their aggressive outburst was in response to being treated badly, these statements will likely be disregarded and a suspension will ensue.

The Targeted Student has learned a huge lesson that they cannot trust that the principal or any other school staff will care about their well-being or will step in to help. The Dominance Motivated Hurtful Student has learn that they can be slyly hurtful to a "misfit" and there will be no negative consequences.

Another social dynamic may be present if a Dominance Motivated Hurtful Student is being hurtful to a student they perceive to be a rival. The Targeted Student may be a relationship rival or a rival for some other resource. The standard academic definition of bullying includes the concept of "imbalance of power." This imbalance will not be present. However, the dynamics of this situation should not be considered to be "conflict" if one student is engaging in hurtful behavior and the other student is trying to respond in a way to get this to stop. Yet another situation may involve two Dominance Motivated Hurtful Students who are both being equally hurtful.

These kinds of situations very likely cause the higher social status Targeted Students to experience significant distress. These situations can also generate significant peer involvement. Students most often refer to these situations as "drama."

Social Dominance Theory

More recent research is drawing a connection between bullying behavior and social dominance theory.[180] Social dominance theory is a social psychological theory of group-based social hierarchies and how these hierarchies remain stable and perpetuate themselves. This theory examines how societies develop ideologies to legitimize social inequality and mistreatment of marginalized social groups based on different traits, including gender, race, age, economic status, and other characteristics.

The Social Dominance Theory has outlined that human social groups consist of distinctly different group-based social hierarchies. These hierarchies are based on:

- **Age.** Recognizing that adults have more power and higher status than children.

- **Gender.** Recognizing that in most societies men have more power and higher status than women.

- **Arbitrary.** Group-based hierarchies that are culturally defined and do not necessarily exist in all societies. These can include ethnicity, religion, nationality, or similar categories.

Within this theory is the concept of a "social dominance orientation." Those who maintain a social dominance orientation demonstrate greater support for group-based dominance and opposition to equality, regardless of their position in the power structure. People who believe in the natural inequity of social groups support dominance over the lower status groups, even though they themselves may be of lower social status.

A scale has been developed to assess individual's social dominance orientation, the SDO scale.[181] A higher SDO correlates with prejudicial attitudes, maintaining greater social distance from members of other groups, and less helping of out-group members. A recent study of college students measured their SDO and asked them to report on their bullying activities while in middle and high school.[182] The researchers found positive associations between beliefs in social inequity and reported engagement in bullying, especially for male students.

This theory can also help to explain Identity-Based Bullying.[183] Students may have a social dominance orientation that reflects the perspective that members of their "in-group" are superior to and should have more social power than members of the "out-group." This could manifest in hurtful behavior by those who identify themselves as white and/or heterosexual —who will justify their socially dominance status in your school.

It is known that the rate of bullying is higher in classrooms where there is a strong social status hierarchy—authoritarian environments.[184] In environments with such hierarchy, the environment will be more supportive of competition for such status seeking. In school environments with strong social status hierarchies, aggressive students have been found to be more popular and better liked.[185]

Dominance and Prestige Leaders

Other researchers in the field of social hierarchies have focused on two strategies to achieve leadership positions in society or in the workplace. These two different strategies are called dominance or prestige.[186] This is a helpful description:

> *Dominance and prestige represent evolved strategies used to navigate social hierarchies. Dominance is a strategy through which people gain and maintain social rank by using coercion, intimidation, and power. Prestige is a strategy through which people gain and maintain social rank by displaying valued knowledge and skills and earning respect.[187]*

This exceptionally important insight will be discussed more in Chapter 4. Understanding the differences between two kinds of students who are engaged in leadership activities in schools is key to the development of a more effective strategy to foster more positive relationships.

In most social groups in every school, there are students who seek leadership positions by displaying valued knowledge and skills and earning respect. These powerful and positive Prestige Leader students should be identified and engaged to provide the leadership within the school to support positive relationships.

Thinking in Terms of Intervention

Strategies to address the concerns of Proactive Aggression by Dominance Motivated Hurtful Students will necessarily be dramatically different from the strategies used to address the concerns of Reactive Aggression of Marginalized Hurtful Students.

It is also important to consider this insight in the context of Multiple Tier System of Supports (MTSS).[188] Because of the inaccurate description of students who engage in bullying that has so predominated, school leaders may be inclined to enunciate strategies to respond to hurtful conduct by any student in line with MTSS, with interventions at Tier II or Tier III.

Students who are considered to be at a Tier II or III level may engage in aggression. This fits within the description of the Marginalized Hurtful Student. However, it is highly improbable that the concerns of Dominance Motivated Hurtful Students would ever be considered appropriate to address as a Tier II or III concern.

BI-DIRECTIONAL HURTFUL BEHAVIOR AND IMPULSIVE RETALIATION

Not all incidents of hurtful behavior are one directional. Sometimes students are engaged in mutual hurtful treatment of each other. Sometimes, these situations are indeed "conflict." However, school leaders would make a mistake to conclude that all situations that involve students who are each or all being hurtful to each other is "conflict." Conflict involves situations where all parties have a relatively equivalent social status level, and equivalent levels of hurtful behavior.

Revenge or Retaliation was noted above as one of the motivations for being hurtful. Retaliation is a specific behavioral response that children can and do use to cope with being bullied. Retaliation is not an effective strategy, however, it is a very common strategy.[189] Retaliation is also a strategy recommended by many parents, caregivers, and society. Students are told that if they are bullied they should fight back and that this is the only way to get the bullying to stop.

Research has documented that students' emotional responses are linked to their selection of response strategies.[190] Students who felt angry were less likely to seek help and more likely to seek revenge. Revenge seeking was associated with a greater risk for additional victimization, which then, was associated with greater distress.

Retaliation situations may involve a student who was bullied by a more socially powerful student, who has responding in an aggressive manner. Such response is likely impulsive. It is also necessary to identify those situations that involve students of a similar level of social status, but the hurtful situation was started by one student against a perceived rival, and the other student is mostly trying to get the hurtful situation to stop.

The *Embrace Civility Student Survey* results revealed a significant amount of bidirectional hurtful behavior. Students who indicated they had been hurtful to another student in the last month were asked what they were thinking at the time. The two key reasons students provided for when they were hurtful were:

- "I acted too fast when I was angry and really did not think"—47%.

- "This student had been hurtful to me or a friend of mine"—44%.

Clearly, reducing impulsive retaliation must be a high priority for schools to achieve a more positive school climate. A research-based strategy to reduce Impulsive Retaliation is set forth in Chapter 7.

HARMFUL IMPACT OF STAFF BULLYING

A factor that has not received sufficient attention is the hurtful treatment of students by staff. Staff bullying is an abuse of power that tends to be persistent and involves degrading a student, often in front of other students.[191] When students are denigrated by staff, frequently in front of other students, this has a profoundly negative impact on their well-being. While the research has focused on "teachers," it is probable the concerns relate to all staff.

Social Cognition Theory

The concerns associated with how students might treat a student who they witness being treated badly by a school staff member can be explained by Social Cognition Theory. Bandura is a leading researcher in this field.[192]

Under this theory a person's behavior can be directly related to what they have learned by observing others. This includes social interactions, experiences, and outside media influences. Under this theory, when people observe a model performing a behavior and the consequences of that behavior, they remember the sequence of events and use this information to guide their subsequent behaviors. People do not learn new behaviors solely by trying them and either succeeding or failing. They copy of the actions of others.

Bandura's famous experiment was the 1961 Bobo Doll study, with additional follow-up studies.[193] Bandura made a video in which an adult woman was shown being aggressive to a Bobo doll. She was hitting and shouting aggressive words. This video was shown to children.

Then, the children were allowed to play in the room with the same doll. They imitated the model that had been shown to them by beating up the doll. They used similar, aggressive words. The children had received no encouragement or incentives to beat up the doll. They imitated the behavior they had observed.

It is exceptionally important that school staff consistently model the behavior they desire of students. The manner in which school leaders treat and interact with staff also communicates to students guidelines on how they should treat others.

Examples of Insufficient Attention

Some disturbing examples of how the concern of staff hurtful treatment of students does not receive sufficient attention include:

- In April, 2014, the NAS Board on Children, Youth, and Families of the Institute of Medicine and the National Research Council held a 2-day workshop and published a report entitled *Building Capacity to Reduce Bullying and Its Impact on Youth.* [194] The last session of this workshop included a panel of students who had been present throughout the presentations. The students were asked to identify issues that had not been raised by the professionals.

  - The key issue raised by the students was "Teachers and Adults as Bullies." Student comments included: "Teachers can be bullies too." "If teachers are giving the impression that this kind of behavior is okay, the kids are going to think this kind of behavior is okay." "We cannot be having teachers and coaches being okay with bullying kids in addition to the students who are doing so."[195]

  - Unfortunately, the resulting NAS report, *Preventing Bullying Through Science, Policy, and Practice*, published in 2016, totally omitted any reference to this strongly expressed student concern—despite an entire section on the school climate which focused on student-staff relationships.[196]

- The StopBullying.Gov website, coordinated by the Federal Partners in Bullying Prevention, is a key resource on issues related to bullying in the US.[197] There is no insight presented on this site on the concerns of school staff who bully students.

- The recently published *Wiley Blackwell Handbook of Bullying: A Comprehensive and International Review of Research and Intervention* is quite comprehensive. Unfortunately, none of the 74 articles, written by academic researchers from 30 countries across the world, addressed the concern of staff bullying of students.

As discussed in Chapter 1, the new UNESCO report, *Violence and Bullying in Educational Settings: The Experience of Children and Young People with Disabilities*, is notable in that it honestly addressed the concern that students with disabilities experience higher rates of physical violence at the hands of teachers, are more likely to be physically restrained or confined, and are also subjected to greater emotional and psychological violence from teachers than students without disabilities.[198] From this report:

> Learners with disabilities are also subjected to psychological violence from teachers. …Young people with disabilities participating in focus group discussions in a range of countries also described being humiliated, mocked and picked on by teachers and suggested that abuse by teachers can encourage violence and bullying by other students. …
>
> Teacher violence is linked to lack of understanding and negative attitudes towards disability. Young people participating in focus groups commented that teachers have low expectations of learners with disabilities – reflecting negative attitudes in wider society about disability and the capabilities of people with disabilities – and do not pay equal attention to their education. They described teachers lacking patience with learners with disabilities, ignoring them, telling them that they cannot do well in their studies, and voicing concerns that they will adversely affect the overall performance of the class.[199]

To the best of my knowledge, this UNESCO report is the first significant government report that accurately and extensively addressed this concern. It is hoped that this positive step by UNESCO will lead to improvement in the focus on these concerns.

Limited Research Insight

There is some research insight into the concern of staff being hurtful to students, albeit limited. The term "teacher" will be used in this discussion because this is what the research focused on.

In an early study by Twemlow and colleagues, the researchers discussed some of the concerns.[200] They noted the concerns that arose from discussions with principals in many parts of the US. Based on these discussions, the issue of teachers who bully students was known to many. However, the discussions revealed that no clear way had been found to handle or even assess the prevalence of such a problem.

Most public school teachers in the US are part of collective bargaining groups that represent the teachers on labor issues. When the issue of teachers who engage in bullying becomes a labor conflict, then an adversarial teacher-administrator dynamic is set up. The labor group often then acts to protect the bullying teacher, to the serious disadvantage of the bullied student.

In Twemlow's study, teachers in elementary schools completed an anonymous questionnaire. The results revealed there was evidence that the teachers recognized the problem, but felt it was isolated. However, the data demonstrated that around 32% of teachers reported knowing one or more teachers who bullied students in the past year. In addition, 45% of the teachers indicated that they themselves had bullied a student. Some were angry at being asked these questions.

The teachers identified two kinds of teachers who engage in bullying:

- Those seen as intentionally humiliating students. This appears to be Proactive Aggression.

- Those seen as being overwhelmed by situations, including a lack of support from the administration, lack of training in effective classroom management, and classes that were too large. This appears to be Reactive Aggression.

McEvoy is a researcher who has focused attention to this concern. McEvoy collected information from 236 public and parochial high school and college students. Of these student respondents, 93% identified teachers who bullied students in their schools, with 47% identifying 3 or more teachers.

McEvoy's research indicates that there are usually no negative consequences for staff who engage in bullying.[201] Students who are targeted often are vulnerable, have some devalued personal attribute, are unable to stand up for themselves, and others will not defend them. Frequently, there are references to how this student differs from other students who are more capable or valued. As a result, the student may also become a target by peers. As explained:

Students who are bullied by teachers typically experience confusion, anger, fear, self-doubt, and profound concerns about their academic and social competencies. Not knowing why he or she has been targeted, or what one must do to end the bullying, may well be among the most personally distressing aspects of being singled out and treated unfairly. Over time, especially if no one in authority intervenes, the target may come to blame him or her self for the abuse and thus feel a pervasive sense of helplessness and worthlessness.[202]

In a survey study of 50 alternative education students by Whitted & Dupper, 86% of students reported physical maltreatment, and 88% reported psychological maltreatment, by an adult in the school.[203] More than 64% indicated that their worst school experience involved maltreatment by an adult. Students perceived bullying by school staff as more distressing than bullying by a peer. (, 2008).

Sylvester has suggested that teachers may not recognize their behavior as bullying.[204] The four common ways teachers may unintentionally bully students: sarcasm, name-calling, denying work, and humiliation, may not be perceived by the teacher as bullying because their motivation was to achieve a positive response from the student. Teachers may also view their actions as an appropriate disciplinary response, or good classroom management.

A study of elementary and middle school teachers by Wilson on positive and negative classroom management techniques used in the classroom found that 74.6% of teachers used separation as a disciplinary consequence, 62% yelled or shouted, and 50.4% used sarcasm.[205] Male teachers reported using negative techniques more frequently.

A very excellent doctoral dissertation by Kim involved structured discussions with six principals about teacher to student bullying.[206] These were her conclusions:

> Despite the evidence that teacher to student bullying is a pervasive problem in education, few principals purported it was an existing issue at their school sites, however, the sensitivity of the topic matter did not prevent them from conceding that it occurs frequently and under the radar of most people. This lack of awareness regarding the pervasiveness of bullying, as exemplified by the incongruence of their statements, suggests a lack of awareness of what constitutes bullying behavior. Principals provided divergent definitions of bullying based on intentionality and frequency as the most referenced caveats. They did, however, allude more generally to bullying as the assertion or reassertion of power, hierarchy, or dominance. These descriptions of bullying as "put-downs" or delineations of order in dyadic interchanges prove problematic when considering the hierarchical nature of most human organizations, whether they are classrooms led by teachers, or schools led by principals. At the same time, perceptions of superiority and inferiority were described as ideological precursors to bullying behavior.
>
> Teachers' awareness, or lack thereof, of their own behaviors, was found to be the most referenced characteristic when describing incidents of teacher to student bullying. Principals reported that teachers would relegate responsibility to students and lacked the skills to reflect upon themselves and their impact on the behavior of those around them, citing significant disparities in teacher education that would promote reflective practices and self-accountability. However, their acknowledgements of teacher education programs that pay little attention to conscious discipline were not met with attempts to address the disparity in the provision of teacher development opportunities.
>
> The findings, while preliminary, suggest that principals needed additional support in the area of preventive and responsive action for teacher to student bullying. The majority of principals cited "high expectations" as their primary preventive measure, implying the existence of consequences for negative actions toward stakeholders. However, this data, in tandem with the findings on awareness, lead to questions about whether or not subtly implying teacher to student conduct without explicit examples of appropriate and inappropriate behavior is an effectual preventive measure.
>
> The study also found that responsive support was not being provided to students after victimization, sometimes for periods of an entire year, or not at all. Three of the principals mentioned similar steps were taken after official complaints were submitted, including a meeting with the student as a means of rebuilding trust

and communicative pathways, and moving the student out of the classroom. No further actions were taken to support students who were victims of teacher to student bullying in the study. Additional measures were deemphasized by principals as unnecessary or superfluous based on observations of students' apparent tolerance to such behaviors due to the ubiquity of verbal abuse by parents and family members.

As thorough as this conclusion is, it is my perspective that the conclusion left out the very serious issues related to responsiveness of the principals to known concerns.

McEvoy conducted an online survey of 1,067 educators during July 2017.[207] In the survey, the following key questions were asked:

- How often have you seen a teacher displaying an extreme emotional outburst to a student? Never: 20%, 1-2 times 27%, 3-4 times 22%, 5-9 times 13%, 10 or more times 18%.

- How often have you observed a teacher unnecessarily embarrassing a student in front of other students or teachers? Never: 16%, 1-2 times 26%, 3-4 times 22%, 5-9 times 18%, 10 or more times 17%.

- How often have you observed a teacher publicly suggesting a student is stupid? Never: 50%, 1-2 times 24%, 3-4 times 13%, 5-9 times 6%, 10 or more times 7%.[208]

When asked to specify what percentage of teachers in their school bully students, 65% of respondents indicated "less than 10%," and just under 14% indicated "none." Thus, this is a concern reflecting the harmful behavior of just a minority of staff. However, the impact of this conduct can be profound.

The teachers identified low-achieving students and students with behavioral disorders as the most targeted by their peers, followed by students with poor attendance. However, this question also included "other" as a category. The responses on this indicate that students of color and students from other minority groups, such as LGBT students and English language learners, are often targets of staff bullying. Open-ended comments also indicated that teachers often feel frustrated when dealing with students who misbehave, who lack motivation, or who seem poorly prepared for school.

Note that the students who are reportedly being bullied by teachers are the ones who are at highest risk of academic failure and school drop-out. The responses by teachers related to the kinds of students who are most often bullied are many of the ones whose behavior causes concern. This appears to validate Twenlow's findings that one of the reasons for this hurtful behavior is lack of effective behavior management skills of teachers, especially in working with students with more behavior challenges. The "other" category appeared to reflect instances of Identity-Based Bullying.

Schools often do not have effective policies or processes in place to address these concerns. Two-thirds of the teaching staff did not have a clear understanding of where to report—or if they even should report. Less than 13% of respondents could say, unequivocally, their school's policy indicates that bullying could involve teachers as well as students. The vast majority of teachers reported that there had been no professional development addressing this issue.

A study by Datta and colleagues compared the prevalence and school adjustment of students bullied by teachers or staff, students bullied by peers, and students who were not bullied.[209] The sample consisted of 56,508 students in Grades 7 and 8 who completed a statewide school climate survey. Students were classified into four groups:

- Those who had not been bullied—87.2 percent.
- Those bullied only by peers—9.3 percent.
- Those bullied only by teachers or staff—1.2 percent.
- Those bullied by both peers and teachers or staff—1.5 percent.

In comparison to students who reported no bullying, students bullied by teachers and other school staff were significantly more likely to report lower school engagement and self-reported grades and more negative perceptions of school climate.

The insight suggests that hurtful educators are in the minority, but appear to be present in most schools. Addressing this concern raises complications due to labor relationships. There are usually no negative consequences for staff members who are hurtful. There are frequently no policies or procedures to follow when other staff members witness these hurtful acts.

Identity-Based Staff Bullying

The following evidence of staff bullying of students is from the US, with the exception of the excellent report on bullying of students experiencing disabilities from UNESCO.

Sexual and Gender Minority Students

The Gay Lesbian Straight Education Network (GLSEN) study *2011 National School Climate Survey* found that 56.9% of sexual minority students heard teachers or other staff make homophobic comments or negative comments about a student's gender expression at school and when school staff were present, less than a fifth of the students reported that staff frequently intervened.

A 2016 GLSEN study, *From Teasing to Torment: School Climate Revisited, A Survey of US Secondary School Students and Teachers* asked students whether they had heard biased comments from teachers and other staff members.[210] The survey participants included all students, not just those who identified as LGBT. Students reported teachers and other staff had:

- Made negative remarks about how "masculine" or "feminine" students are—26%.
- Made comments about students' academic ability—23%.
- Made sexist remarks—21%.
- Use the expression "that's so gay" or "you're so gay"—16%.
- Made racist comments—14%.
- Made negative religious remarks—14%.
- Made anti-transgender comments—13%.[211]

Students With Disabilities

What is most striking related to this issue is the lack of academic studies investigating staff bullying of students with disabilities. As noted, the recent UNESCO report discussed the concern of teachers bullying students with disabilities.[212]

A recent report issued by the Council of Parent Attorneys and Advocates in the US documented reports of children with disabilities who were subjected to abuse by school staff.[213] A webpage by WrightsLaw, an information service related to the legal rights of students with disabilities in the US, has extensive information of successful lawsuits against school districts for egregious actions taken by staff against students with disabilities.[214]

A news story in Pacific Standard, recently reviewed three state level reports that focused on harsh treatment of students with disabilities by school staff.[215] News reports cover situations where these students are handcuffed, placed in restraints, placed in time out rooms for hours at a time and ridiculed or shamed by school staff.

As discussed in the most recent report by McEvoy, students who are bullied by school staff are very often students who have greater difficulties maintaining their behavior in accord with expectations. One of the challenges of many of the students with disabilities is difficulty controlling themselves. Many neurodiverse students, such as those on the autism spectrum or with hyperactivity move around a lot and find it difficult to focus their attention on tasks. As a result, teachers find these kids to be disruptive.

The classes in which these students receive special services are taught by teachers who are have special training in dealing with these types of students. However, to minimize the stigma of being in a separate type of class, these students are often mainstreamed into general classes. These teachers have a much larger number of students to attend to and may lack effective skills in supporting students with disabilities.

Students with Weight Concerns

In a survey conducted of students with obesity or weight problems who were attending a weight loss camp, 42% of these students reported being bullied by physical education teachers or sport coaches and 27% reported being bullied by teachers.[216] Note that these students are not considered to be in a Protected Class.

Religious Minority Students

As noted earlier, in a study conducted by ISPU of a nationally representative sample of US families, many religious minority students reported their child had been bullied in the past year because of their religion.[217] Importantly with respect to staff bullying, in 25% of the cases involving Muslim students, a teacher or administrator at school was identifying as the one who engaged the bullying.

Racial Minority Students

While there is a focus of research on inequities in disciplinary actions, there appears to be no substantive research that inquires into the experiences of racial minority students in the context of school staff bullying. Certainly, there is significant evidence of bias and maltreatment of minority students in US schools.

The National Clearinghouse on Supportive School Discipline has outlined the concerns of harsh and exclusionary disciplinary policies and practices have been applied disproportionately to members of specific demographic groups, such as racial and ethnic minorities, males, and students with disabilities.[218]

A study of preschool teachers conducted by the Yale Child Study Center found signs of implicit bias in administering discipline. The researchers used eye-tracking technology and found that preschool teachers "show a tendency to more closely observe black students, and especially boys, when they were directed to watch for challenging behaviors.[219]

Embrace Civility Student Survey

On the earlier version *Embrace Civility Student Survey* that was used in 2015 students were asked about student-student hurtful acts. They were also asked how frequently in the last month, they had witnessed a school staff member be hurtful to a student. Student responses were:

- Almost every day—9%.
- Once or twice a week—12%.
- Once or twice a month—21%.
- Never—58%.

The results on questions about student-on-student hurtful behavior were analyzed based on the student response to the question about witnessing staff being hurtful to students.[220] Students were classified as "ever" or "never" having witnessed staff being hurtful to a student. "Ever" included those who witnessed such hurtful behavior once or twice a month, once or twice a week, or almost daily. The results were significant.

Those students who had "ever" witnessed staff be hurtful to a student were significantly more likely to report witnessing, engaging in, or being targeted by hurtful behavior.

- Students who witnessed hurtful behavior:
  - Students who "ever" witnessed a staff member be hurtful to a student who reported they had also witnessed a student being hurtful to a student—85%.
  - Students who "never" witnessed a staff member be hurtful to a student who reported they also had witnessed a student being hurtful to another student—56%.[221]
- Students who engaged in hurtful behavior:
  - Students who "ever" witnessed a staff member be hurtful to a student who reported they had been hurtful to another student—50%.
  - Students who "never" witnessed a staff member be hurtful to a student who reported they had been hurtful to another student—13%.[222]
- Students who were targeted by hurtful behavior:
  - Students who "ever" witnessed a staff member be hurtful to a student who reported someone had been hurtful to them—73%.
  - Students who "never" witnessed a staff member be hurtful to a student who reported someone had been hurtful to them—36%.[223]

The issue of staff being hurtful to students appears to be enormously important. It appears that in schools where staff treat students in hurtful ways, this results in significantly higher levels of student hurtful behavior directed at peers and significantly lower levels of assistance provided to students.

An alternative perspective to consider these research findings is to consider the dramatic declines that could be achieved in reducing hurtful student behavior by reducing staff hurtful behavior directed at students.

Students Hurtful to Staff

There are also situations where students are hurtful to staff. The critical first question in these situations is whether these are situations of Reactive Aggression or Proactive Aggression. Is the Hurtful Student emotionally distressed, dysregulated, and lashing out or if this hurtful behavior intentional and planned, based on some level of bias against the teacher or other staff member?

If this is a Reactive Aggression situation the critically important question must be, what led to this. What caused this student to become emotionally distressed and dysregulated? If the manner in which this student was treated by this staff member or by someone else in a recent timeframe, that is the source of the concern. Did this student treat this staff member badly because they triggered because of something that happened to them in the past?

The student who was hurtful must be held accountable, as discussed in Chapter 11. However, if the staff member was hurtful to this student, that staff member must also be held accountable. Underlying factors that are leading this student to treat others badly must be addressed.

If the student is being Proactively Aggressive, this is highly likely that this is a situation that is grounded in deep-seated identity based bias. Complicating matters, this may be identity bias that is shared by this student's family. Resolving these situations may be possible with some cultural competence efforts. A "no contact" order may be necessary.

Staff Hurtful to Staff

The issue of workplace bullying in schools is beyond the scope of this book, as the focus is on strategies to engage students to embrace civility. However, just as staff bullying of students is generally not a recognized concern, staff bullying of staff is an equally ignored concern. Kleinhekse, and Geisel conducted a study that assessed such workplace bullying.[224] Close to 28% of school staff respondents indicated they were bullied on an infrequent to daily rate during the first seven months of the 2016-2017 school year.

The highest level of kinds of hurtful acts reported were: being exposed to an unmanageable workload, having opinions or views ignored, feeling ignored or excluded, having someone withhold information which affects their performance, and believing they are given tasks with unreasonable deadlines. Thirty-three percent (33%) of the bullying was from someone the respondent considered to be a supervisor, 28% was from a same level colleague, 4% was from a support person, and 57% was from "other," which included responses like department chair, board member, union official, student, parent, grandparent of a student, and the like. Teporting the incidents did not resolve the problem in almost 40% of incidents, and over 65% of respondents indicated their K-12 schools have never addressed adult bullying.

Chapter 3.
Anti-Bullying Activities Effectiveness Concerns

HIGHLIGHTS

- **Effectiveness of Anti-Bullying Approaches**. Schools are advised or required to have anti-bullying policies, to implement a bullying prevention program, and to tell students to report. There are significant concerns regarding the effectiveness of these approaches.

  - **Effectiveness of Policies**. A meta-analysis of the effectiveness of policies concluded that while educators tend to perceive policies are effective, most studies have found no positive associations.

  - **International Studies.** A recent international meta analysis of evaluation studies suggested that anti-bullying programs can reduce bullying at a very modest level. The rate of effectiveness varied greatly across studies. Most studies used self-report measurements, which may not measure actual behavioral change. It is also challenging to determine what aspects of such programs resulted in the modest level of effectiveness.

  - **Competing Demands in the US.** In the US, competing demands on student and teacher time for standardized testing is a considered a limitation. Programs showing effectiveness in some countries may not be effective in other countries.

  - **Developmental Differences**. A recent meta-analysis demonstrated zero effectiveness of such programs for students in eighth grade and beyond.

- **Student Perspectives of Staff Effectiveness.** Research suggests that staff overwhelmingly think they have effective strategies and respond effectively to the bullying incidents they witness or are reported. The student perspective is that staff are not doing enough, ignore the hurtful incidents they witness, and generally make things worse when they respond.

- **Effectiveness of the "Tell an Adult" Approach.** It is well established that the majority of secondary students do not report hurtful incidents. When students either do not report or do not report again if things became worse, school leaders may mistakenly believe that bullying is not a significant concern in their school, despite student reporting data indicating otherwise.

- **Student Willingness to Report.** Students' lack of willingness to report to school staff appears to be because most students believe that school staff will make the situation worse if they intervene or that staff are not interested in taking any actions against bullying.

- **Reporting Concerns.** Students perceive numerous barriers that prevent them from obtaining help from adults at school. Students will calculated whether the risks outweighed the benefits. The risks include public disclosure, fear of ridicule, retaliation, and the lack of effectiveness of a possible adult interventions. Sexual and gender minority students may fear disclosure to parents.

- **Effectiveness of School Response After Report**. Educators often appear to think that they are effectively responding to incidents that are reported to them—which is not the case. The vast majority of students do not report. When students do report, if this has not resolved the situation or has made things worse, students are less likely to report continuing or new concerns.

  - ‣ **Not Effective.** Several studies have shown that when students do report, the situation is likely to stay the same or get worse. If one considers the percentage of students who do report and for what percentage things get better, the level of success oof the "tell an adult" approach appears to be around 10%.

- **Statutes and Directives.** This section on statutes and directives is based solely on US laws. In the US, there are no federal statutes that address "bullying." There are federal civil rights laws that address discriminatory harassment of Protected Class students. There are anti-bullying statutes in every state. There is profound confusion between requirements under state statutes and civil rights regulations.

  - **Key Components in State Statutes.** In December 2010, USDOE released a document entitled *Key Components for State Anti-Bullying Laws*. This guidance encouraged states to enact more comprehensive bullying prevention statutes and districts to address bullying as a disciplinary code violation. The guidance is based on the perception that students will readily report to the school if they are being bullied and that the intervention by the school will effectively resolve the problem.

- **Rules and Punishment.** When school staff use authoritarian practices to address student misbehavior, this results in an increase in bullying and aggression and reinforces the idea that those who have power are able to dominate others. "Punishment by authority" models bullying to achieve dominance. Punitive responses often cause problem behaviors to increase rather than diminish. This approach turns the situation from a harmful offense that should require remedy, to an investigation of an alleged violation of a school rule.

- **Confusion between State Statutes and Civil Rights Regulations.** The inclusion of enumeration of specific populations in statutes has caused profound confusion. The requirements under civil rights regulations are more stringent.

- **Substantial Disruption.** Student misbehavior generally must meet the standard of causing a "substantial disruption" to warrant any disciplinary consequence. The situation of students who are targeted in a persistent manner—in a series of ongoing, but more minor, incidents—does not meet this standard. These incidents, individually, are generally not sufficiently severe to warrant a disciplinary consequence—but cause profound emotional harm.

- **Requirements to Reduce Exclusionary Discipline**. In 2010, USDOE advised schools to respond to bullying by imposing a disciplinary consequence. In 2014, schools were directed to avoid imposing exclusionary discipline. The concerns of exclusionary discipline relate to the discriminatory impact on racial minority students and students with disabilities—students who are being bullied. School leaders were told: "Apply disciplinary consequences to stop bullying." Then, they were told: "Don't use disciplinary consequences."

• *Every Student Succeeds Act.* Under *ESSA*, states, districts, and schools must describe their plans and provide data related to school climate and discipline in their annual district and school report cards. This includes measures of school climate, rate of exclusionary disciplinary actions, rates of absenteeism, and incidences of violence, including bullying and harassment.

- **Required Public Bullying Reports**. Note above that the 2010 *Key Components* guidance advised states to enact a state statutory provision to require schools to make annual public reports on the number of bullying incidents. In states that have made this a statutory requirement, the rates of bullying reported by the schools are very low. However, the rate at which students report being bullied on surveys has remained constant or has increased.

- *Dignity Act* **Example.** An analysis of what has happened in New York (NY) after 2011 the passage of the *Dignity Act for All Students* (DASA) statute is helpful. DASA requires that all schools make an annual report of bullying incidents. A 2017 report analyzed this report data from the 2013-14 school year and found that 71% of New York City schools reported zero incidents of bullying of students for that entire year.

- **Avoid "Black Marks."** What appears to be happening is that schools want to avoid "black marks." Principals who admit to problems of bullying in their schools may be seen as ineffective leaders. As principals are the ones who decide whether a reported incident meets the policy definition, they can control such reports.

- *ESSA* **Accountability.** A similar annual reporting of incidents was incorporated into *ESSA*. A review of the data for any district on the USDOE site will reveal an exceptionally low level of reports.

• **Alternatives to Exclusionary Discipline.** Schools have been advised by USDOE to use PBIS and Restorative Practices as an alternatives to exclusionary discipline. Both of these programs have many positive benefits. However, both also have components or have been implemented in ways that are counter productive in the context of the challenges associated with bullying and hurtful behavior

- **Positive Behavior Interventions and Support.** The behavioristic authoritarian manner in which PBIS is implemented presents concerns. Schools that function in an authoritarian manner have higher levels of bullying behavior.

  ‣ **Behaviorism Concerns.** The underlying foundation of PBIS is grounded in behaviorism and operant conditioning. Research on behaviorism predated the research on the impact of trauma or neurodiversity on student behavior. Rewards cannot result in students behaving in a way they do not have the ability to do.

  ‣ **PBIS and Bullying Concerns**. These are the concerns:

    - **Shaming and Exclusion.** Students who have challenges in maintaining their behavior repeatedly experience the situation of failing to meet expectations and, thus, often feel shamed and excluded in front of their peers.

    - **Decrease of Intrinsic Motivation.** Use of tangible rewards has been found to decrease intrinsic motivation, which is essential for students to maintain positive relationships.

- **Discriminatory Impact.** When schools use token rewards, it becomes very apparent that some students are identified by school staff as "good" and others are "bad."

- **Models Relational Aggression.** The PBIS rewards approach models relational aggression.

- **Labeling and Stigmatization.** Approaches that publicly identify to all students the teacher's assessment of each student's behavior contributes to labeling and stigmatization.

- **Restorative Practices.** The underlying principles and objectives of Restorative Practices are excellent. There are concerns related to the current implementation approaches. There is confusion about what Restorative Practices are and no consensus about the best way to implement such practices.

- **Mediation or Conflict Resolution.** These practices can be useful if there is an equivalent level of wrongdoing by both parties and an equivalent level of personal power.—but can be dangerous in situations where there is an imbalance of power between students.

- **Logical Consequences.** Logical consequences is a superior approach to punishment. Logical consequences are still a consequence that is being imposed by an authority that may or may not remedy the harm.

- **Restorative Circles.** Circles should never be used to discuss misbehavior of an individual member of the class, especially if hurtful hurtful conduct has been directed at another student.

- **Indigenous Foundation.** In the Restorative Practices approach, wrongdoing is viewed as a violation of relationships and people. The source for this perspective is from indigenous peoples—who have a strong focus on supporting the well-being of their community.

• **Institutional Betrayal.** Institutional Betrayal occurs when an "institution" fails to respond in an effective manner when it knows or should know of the harmful treatment being experienced by a target of hurtful conduct. When those who are victimized reach out for help, they must place a great deal of trust in the institution from which they are seeking help. When the institution does not respond in an effective manner to such reports of abuse, this is associated with a significant increase in trauma-related outcomes.

- **Institutional Courage.** Institutional Courage requires a commitment to respond in an effective manner to address concerns that are reported.

LACK OF EFFECTIVENESS OF ANTI-BULLYING APPROACHES

Schools are advised or required to have anti-bullying policies, to implement a bullying prevention program, and to tell students to report. It is necessary to consider how effective these approaches are in reducing and responding to bullying.

Effectiveness of Policies

The primary way that schools seek to manage bullying concerns is through the use of anti-bullying policies. On the Federal Partners in Bullying Prevention StopBullying.Gov website, the following is the guidance on school strategies to prevent bullying.

> *What Schools Can Do. School staff can help prevent bullying by establishing and enforcing rules and policies that clearly describe how students are to treat each other.*[225]
>
> *Staff Training on Bullying Prevention. To ensure that bullying prevention efforts are successful, all school staff need to be trained on what bullying is, what the school's policies and rules are, and how to enforce the rules.*[226]

Thus, an initial question must be asked about the effectiveness of this policy based approach.

A meta-analysis conducted by Hall of the effectiveness of anti-bullying policies concluded that while educators tend to perceive that policies are effective and several studies showed that the presence or quality of policies was associated with lower rates of bullying among students, other studies found no such associations.[227] Findings were mixed regarding the relationship between having an anti-bullying policy and educators' responsiveness to general bullying. Hall concluded:

> *(O)ne may conclude from these findings that the presence of bullying policies does not influence bullying among students; however, the presence of a policy is necessary but is not sufficient to affect student behavior. Indeed, after a policy has been adopted, it must be put into practice. The mere adoption or presence of a policy does not mean that it will be immediately and consistently put into practice exactly as intended. The implementation of a policy is a complex, dynamic, and ongoing process involving a vast assortment of people, resources, organizational structures, and actions. No study that examined the implementation of school bullying policies found that the policies were being implemented precisely as intended.*[228]

It has been found that schools with anti-bullying policies that enumerated protections based on sexual and gender minorities were associated with better protections of these students, as reported by these students.

This, however, may be a "chicken and egg issue." Which came first? Schools that are more accepting of students who are sexual and gender minorities, likely have included express provisions in their policies to indicate the importance of protection for these students. Forced inclusion of these terms may not achieve the same positive results.

Effectiveness of Prevention Programs

Some studies that have evaluated the effectiveness of bullying prevention programs have documented a modest reduction in rates of bullying.[229] However, there are significant concerns regarding the level of effectiveness demonstrated through research analysis and it is challenging to determine what aspects of such implementations resulted in the reported modest level of effectiveness.

A recent international meta analysis of evaluation studies of bullying prevention programs by Gaffney and colleagues documented that the implementation of such programs did result in a modest reduction in reported bullying perpetration and bullying victimization. These results suggested that anti-bullying programs reduced school-bullying perpetration by approximately 19–20% and school-bullying victimization by approximately 15–16%.

However, rate of effectiveness varied greatly across studies. The report noted that the impact of evaluation methodology did not adequately explain the significant differences between the studies. The report also noted noted that reliance of self-reported measurements may suggest the change is in reports of perpetration or victimization and not actual behavioral change.

Most of these evaluation studies were conducted by the creators of the programs, which could have introduced bias into the studies. Unfortunately, the designs of the studies did not allow the researchers to identify which program elements accounted for any identified impacts. It is also important to consider whether a program that has appeared to show some effectiveness in a country such as Finland will be effective in schools in other countries.

The aforementioned NAS *Preventing Bullying* report in the US noted that despite this growing interest in and demand for bullying prevention programs, there have been relatively few randomized controlled trials that tested the effectiveness of programs specifically designed to reduce or prevent bullying or offset its harmful impact on students.[230] Some studies have demonstrated a modest reduction in the student reported rate of bullying and victimization. However, NAS noted that it is necessary to both implement a more universal approach for all students, along with more targeted interventions for those bullied and engaging in bullying. Relatively few studies have examined this.

Further, this NAS study is the one that noted the concerning public stereotype about those who engage in bullying. Programs that have been designed to address concerns of bullying by "at risk" students will not incorporate approaches to influence the behavior of Dominance Motivated Hurtful Students.

The NAS study also noted a concern that has also been found in international meta-analyses, which is that programs appear to be more effective in countries other than the US. As described:

Competing demands on student and teacher time, such as standardized testing, also limit US teachers' perceived ability to focus on social-emotional and behavioral activities, as compared with traditional academic content. The challenges in designing and delivering effective bullying prevention programs in the US may also include the greater social and economic complexities of US school populations, including greater income disparities and racial/ethnic heterogeneity.[231]

The NAS report also noted the challenges of evaluating studies of approaches that are implemented at different school levels due to developmental issues. A recent meta-analysis examining developmental differences in the effectiveness of anti-bullying programs demonstrated significant declines in program effectiveness for students in eighth grade and beyond.[232]

Helpful insight into these concerns emerged in research related to the KiVa Antibullying Program, which was developed in Finland.[233] This program was implemented in both grades 1-3 and 7-9. An earlier implementation was evaluated in grades 4-6. In both grades 1-3 and 4-6, the program showed signs of effectiveness. Note that "effective" is determined by a modest reported reduction in hurtful behaviors and an increase in positive behaviors. However, at the grade 7-9 level, the results were mixed. In fact, this program, which was designed to increase positive peer intervention actually resulted in students in the intervention schools defending the victims less. The researchers suggested that this was a "surprising finding."

When viewed in terms of teen development and the factors related to which kinds of students are engaging in bullying, this should not be considered surprising. In adolescence, the Dominance Motivated Hurtful Students are the greater source of bullying. Challenging this hurtful behavior is exceptionally challenging if the concerned students is not at a similar level of personal power. These factors are addressed in Chapter 7.

Student Perspectives of Staff Effectiveness

Research suggests that staff overwhelmingly think that they have effective strategies and respond effectively to the bullying incidents they witness or are reported. The student perspective is that staff are not doing enough, ignore the hurtful incidents they witness, and generally make things worse when they respond.

A study by Bradshaw and colleagues demonstrated the following the concerns between staff perspectives and student perspectives.[234] This study found:

- While 87% of school staff thought they had effective strategies for handling bullying, 58% of middle and 66% of high school students believed adults at school were not doing enough to stop or prevent bullying.

- While only 7% of school staff thought they made things worse when they intervened in bullying situations, 61% of middle school students and 59% of high school students reported that staff who tried to stop bullying only made things worse.

- While 97% of school staff said they would intervene if they saw bullying, 43% of middle school students and 54% of high school students reported they had seen adults at school watching bullying and doing nothing.

A study by Thompson and Gunter found that students overwhelmingly believed that most teachers ignored or did not recognize such hurtful activities, were not prepared to intervene if asked, and were incapable of doing anything effective if they took actions.[235]

A recent study by Perkins and colleagues in middle schools found that the highest reported prevalence rates of bullying was in classrooms, hallways, and lunchrooms.[236] These are the places where presumably staff supervision should be the highest. The fact that these incidents were witnessed by staff and continued to occur increased the distress of the students.

Interviews with bullied students have suggested they believe that their teachers ignore bullying, despite being aware of it, or that they downplay the situation or blame the victim.[237] An extensive Australian study found that approximately 40% of students did not think their teachers cared enough to take action against bullying and approximately 20% thought that if their teachers became involved, this would would make things worse.[238]

Effectiveness of "Tell an Adult"

The primary approach schools are directed to take to address bullying is tell students to "tell an adult." It is well established that the majority of secondary students do not report hurtful incidents.[239] Of concern is that when students either do not report or do not report again if things became worse after the first report, school leaders may mistakenly believe that bullying is not a significant concern in their school, despite data indicating otherwise.

Student Willingness to Report

Students' lack of willingness to report to school staff that they are being bullied appears to be grounded in the fact that most students believe that school staff will make the situation worse if they intervene or that staff are not interested in taking any actions against bullying.[240]

MacDonald and Swart in a study at the elementary school level found that there was a perception among the students that the school tolerated bullying because nothing was ever done and, therefore, it was a waste of time to report.[241] A study of secondary students by Garpelin revealed that students did not report their situation to teachers or other adults for fear of being viewed as a "squealer," belief that the school staff would act in a way that would make their situation worse, and they did not trust school staff to keep secrets told to them in confidence.[242] In study conducted by Oliver and Candappa, students associated telling a teacher with a double jeopardy: they might not be believed and telling might result in retaliation.[243]

One interesting study that interviewed students who had been bullied sought to identify teacher characteristics that resulted in effective intervention when bullying had been reported. The researchers ran into a difficulty. When describing how the bullying stopped, none of the students described their class teacher being directly involved in stopping the harmful behavior.[244]

Research exploring reasons why students do not report bullying has suggested a sense of helplessness or uselessness of reporting for some students. Students described their bullying experiences as "not serious enough" to report or that if the bullying was severe, they felt there was nothing that anybody could do about it. Before reporting bullying to anybody, targets consider the risks associated with reporting, including whether they will be believed, as well as possible retaliation. Students appear to be fearful that adults will make a fuss, punish those being hurtful, talk openly about their situation, or call their parents or caregivers. They feel the need for confidentiality, especially if the bullying is related in any way to sexuality or romantic relationships.

One possible reason students do not report they are being bullied, that has not been fully explored, is likely related to the personal power within the school environment of those students who are most frequently hurtful, as compared to those who have been targeted, as was discussed in Chapter 2. The risks of reporting bullying by a Dominance Motivated Hurtful Student, who are perceived to be leaders and are generally compliant to school staff, are likely quite profound.

As was discussed in Chapter 1, students who are bullied frequently are considered "social misfits."[245] These students are also likely not to be looked upon well by staff. Some teachers tend to blame the target for provoking bullying or for being unable to respond to bullying. They recognize the bullied students as the quiet and physically weak, and with a low school achievement. This may result in a tendency to blame the target for being victimized. This could contribute to students' reluctance to disclose bullying.

A factor that has not been explored in research may be the images of bullying victims that are often displayed to students. Do a search on the term "bullying" and then look at "images." Look specifically at the images of those being bullied. Do the terms "wimp" or "helpless" come to mind. To report that you are being bullied is likely, in the eyes of many students, a confession that they are a "helpless wimp."

It appears that many students think that "official channels" for reporting may be risky because this would lead to public disclosure that they had reported.[246] They may not trust the digital reporting systems because they do not know who might receive the report or how this would be handled.

A helpful study by Lai and Koa examined the ethnic and gender differences in high school students reporting of bullying.[247] They found that compared to White and female students, minority students, and male students reported comparable or greater experiences of being bullied. However, the minority and male students were much less likely to report to the school that they had been bullied. Their findings point raise concerns that reporting may carry a a stigma of "weakness," especially for minority and male students.

Students absolutely want the bullying to stop.[248] But they perceive numerous barriers that prevent them from obtaining help from adults at school. Students will think carefully about both the situation and the people involved. It appears they will calculated whether the risks outweighed the benefits, where the risks concerned confidentiality, fear of ridicule, retaliation, or losing face, and the effectiveness of a possible adult interventions.

Teens generally expect that they are becoming independently effective, including in managing their own personal relationships. To report to an adult that they are being bullied and cannot get this to stop is, essentially, reporting that they are failing in the task of managing their life.

Effectiveness of School Response After Report

Educators often appear to think that they are effectively responding to the hurtful incidents that are reported to them.[249] Research documents that this is not the case.

One reason for this misperception is that the vast majority of students do not report—even the more serious or persistent situations that are causing them significant distress. Additionally, when students do report, if reporting has not resolved the situation or has made things worse, students are less likely to report continuing or new concerns.

To assess the effectiveness of school staff after students did report, the Youth Voice Project asked students who were repeatedly bullied and felt distressed whether they reported to an adult at school and, if so, whether things got better, stayed the same, or got worse.[250] The findings indicated:

- Elementary (grade 5) students—46% did not tell an adult, 29% told and things got better, 17% told and things stayed the same, 11% told and things got worse.

- Middle school (grades 6 to 8) students—68% did not tell an adult at school, 12% told and things got better, 8% told and things stayed the same, 12% told and things got worse.

- High school (grades 9 to 12) students—76% did not tell an adult at school, 7% told and things got better, 8% told and things stayed the same, 9% told and things got worse.

A study in the Netherlands found that only 53% of 9- to 11-year-old students reported bullying to their teachers.[251] Note that this age range is of students more equivalent to grades 5 and 6 in relation to the Youth Voice Project study. Younger students appear to be more likely to report these concerns to teachers. The reported level of success was:

- They didn't know I was bullied—34%
- No, they did not try to stop it—8%
- Yes, they tried to stop it, but it stayed the same—20%.
- Yes, they tried to stop it, but it got worse—10%.
- Yes, they tried to stop it, and it stayed decreased—28%.

Rigby and Johnson conducted an extensive study of the effectiveness of anti-bullying efforts in Australia.[252] They asked students in graded 5 to 10 about asking for help. Only 38% of students reported asking for help a teacher or school counsellor. The reported outcomes after telling a teacher or school counselor were:

- Stopped—29%
- Reduced—40%.
- Same—24%.
- Worse—8%.

In this study, the reasons why bullied students did not tell a teacher or counselor included:

- The bullying was not severe enough to justify telling a teacher.
- There were other preferred options of getting help: parents, friends, outside counseling service.
- Uncertainty about the teacher/counselors' role.
- Having to disclose a personal matter to someone who they do not have a trusting personal relationship with.
- Negative views about the help that would be offered.
- Fear of repercussions.
- A sense of personal inadequacy.

A study conducted in 2021 by Act To Change, ADMERASIA, and NextShark of Asian American teens found that only 38% of bullied teens told an adult.[253] Of those who did not tell an adult:

- Believed that doing so would not make a difference—39%.
- Reported they did not want to worry people—20%.
- Were afraid telling would make things worse—15%.
- Said an adult would not care—10%.

Of those who reported to an adult, which was either at school or other adult, the adult took action only 68% of the time. Only 14% of the time, did the action the adult take make things better and 33% of the time this made things somewhat better. Sadly, 53% of the time telling an adult made no difference.

Embrace Civility Student Survey

On the *Embrace Civility Student Survey*, students who were treated badly were also asked if they told school staff and, if so, whether things got better, stayed the same, or got worse. If they did not tell a school staff member, they were asked why they did not do so. Overall, only 32% of all students told a school staff member. Only 36% of the "more vulnerable" students told a staff member. For all targeted students who told a school staff member, after they told, the reported impact was:

- Things got better—48%.
- Stayed the same—39%
- Things got worse—15%

However, after "more vulnerable" students told, the reported impact was:

- Things got better—30%
- Things stayed the same—45%.
- Things got worse—25%.

Thus, looking at these findings from an overall perspective, the current level of the "tell an adult" approach to bullying for "more vulnerable" students was:

- Did not tell a staff member—64%.
- Told a staff member and things got better—11%.
- Told a staff member and things stayed the same—16%.
- Told a staff member and things got worse—9%.

The reasons given by the "more vulnerable" students for not telling, in order of prevalence, were:

- Did not think a school staff member would do anything to help.
- Thought that a school staff member might make things worse.
- Thought I would be blamed.
- I probably deserved it.
- The student being hurtful would likely have retaliated.

The *Youth Voice Project*, studies in the Netherlands and Australia, the study of Asian American teens and *Embrace Civility Student Survey* were conducted in different ways and yielded very consistent results. Overall, the level of effectiveness of the "tell an adult" approach, if one considers what percentage of students actually reported and for what percentage things got better, appears to be around 10%.

STATUTES AND DIRECTIVES

This following section is based solely on US laws. However, the insight will hopefully be of assistance to readers in other countries related to what to look for in their statutes. In the US, there are no federal statutes that address "bullying." There are federal civil rights laws that address discriminatory harassment of Protected Class students.[254] These laws are discussed more extensively in Chapter 9. The federal civil rights laws require that public schools respond to situations that have created a Hostile Environment for a student based on race, color, native origin, religion if grounded native origin, gender identity or sexual orientation, sex, or disabilities.

Ineffective Disciplinary Code Approach

In the US, there are anti-bullying statutes in every state. In December 2010, USDOE released a document entitled *Key Components for State Anti-Bullying Laws*.[255] This guidance encouraged states to enact more comprehensive bullying prevention statutes and districts to address bullying as a disciplinary code violation. Included in the recommendations for state statutes were provisions addressing:

1. **Purpose Statement.** *Outlines the range of detrimental effects bullying has on students, including impacts on student learning, school safety, student engagement, and the school environment. Declares that any form, type, or level of bullying is unacceptable, and that every incident needs to be taken seriously by school administrators, school staff (including teachers), students, and students' families.*

2. **Statement of Scope.** *Covers conduct that occurs on the school campus, at school-sponsored activities or events (regardless of the location), on school-provided transportation, or through school-owned technology or that otherwise creates a significant disruption to the school environment.*

3. **Specification of Prohibited Conduct.** *Provides a specific definition of bullying that includes a clear definition of cyberbullying. The definition of bullying includes a non-exclusive list of specific behaviors that constitute bullying, and specifies that bullying includes intentional efforts to harm one or more individuals, may be direct or indirect, is not limited to behaviors that cause physical harm, and may be verbal (including oral and written language) or non-verbal. The definition of bullying can be easily understood and interpreted by school boards, policymakers, school administrators, school staff, students, students' families, and the community. Is consistent with other federal, state and local laws.*

4. **Enumeration of Specific Characteristics.** *Explains that bullying may include, but is not limited to, acts based on actual or perceived characteristics of students who have historically been targets of bullying, and provides examples of such characteristics. Makes clear that bullying does not have to be based on any particular characteristic.*

5. **Development and Implementation of LEA Policies.** *Directs every Local Educational Agency (LEA) to develop and implement a policy prohibiting bullying, through a collaborative process with all interested stakeholders, including school administrators, staff, students, students' families, and the community, in order to best address local conditions.*

6. Components of LEA Policies

A. **Definitions.** *Includes a definition of bullying consistent with the definitions specified in state law.*

B. **Reporting Bullying** *Includes a procedure for students, students' families, staff, and others to report incidents of bullying, including a process to submit such information anonymously and with protection from retaliation. The procedure identifies and provides contact information for the appropriate school personnel responsible for receiving the report and investigating the incident. Requires that school personnel report, in a timely and responsive manner, incidents they witness or are aware of to a designated official.*

C. **Investigating and Responding to Bullying.** *Includes a procedure for promptly investigating and responding to any report of an incident of bullying, including immediate intervention strategies for protecting the victim from additional bullying or retaliation, and includes notification to parents of the victim, or reported victim, of bullying and the parents of the alleged perpetrator, and, if appropriate, notification to law enforcement officials.*

D. **Written Records.** *Includes a procedure for maintaining written records of all incidents of bullying and their resolution.*

E. **Sanctions.** *Includes a detailed description of a graduated range of consequences and sanctions for bullying.*

F. **Referrals.** *Includes a procedure for referring the victim, perpetrator and others to counseling and mental and other health services, as appropriate.*

7. Review of Local Policies. *Includes a provision for the state to review local policies on a regular basis to ensure the goals of the state statute are met.*

8. Communication Plan. *Includes a plan for notifying students, students' families, and staff of policies related to bullying, including the consequences for engaging in bullying.*

Training and Preventive Education. *Includes a provision for school districts to provide training for all school staff, including, but not limited to, teachers, aides, support staff, and school bus drivers, on preventing, identifying, and responding to bullying. Encourages school districts to implement age-appropriate school- and community-wide bullying prevention programs.*

9. Transparency and Monitoring. *Includes a provision for LEAs to report annually to the state on the number of reported bullying incidents, and any responsive actions taken. Includes a provision for LEAs to make data regarding bullying incidence publicly available in aggregate with appropriate privacy protections to ensure students are protected.*

10. Statement of Rights to Other Legal Recourse. *Includes a statement that the policy does not preclude victims from seeking other legal remedies.*

Rules and Punishment Approach

Note that the entire focus of this statutory approach is based on the perception that students will readily report to the school if they are being bullied, that the intervention by the school will effectively resolve the problem, and that sanctions will be effective in stopping the hurtful behavior.

Research makes it clear punishing students is ineffective in changing behavior.[256] When school staff use authoritarian practices to address student misbehavior, this results in an increase in bullying and other forms of aggression.[257] Use of authoritarian power over students who have engaged in misbehavior reinforces the idea that those who have power are able to dominate others and cause them to suffer.[258] Punitive sanctions often cause problem behaviors to increase, not diminish.[259]

This approach turns the situation from a harmful offense that should require remedy, to an investigation of an alleged violation of a school rule. A disciplinary consequence response generally ignores the concerns of the Targeted Student. Because of privacy restrictions, the consequence imposed on the Hurtful Student cannot even be disclosed.[260] Instead of responding in a way to best support this harmed student, the attention of the principal often shifts away from the target and focuses solely on a determination of whether the accused student has violated the district policy. Further, Dominance Motivated Hurtful Students are generally compliant to staff and, therefore, are rarely punished.

Confusion Between State Statutes and Civil Rights Regulations

Enumeration of Specific Characteristics

The recommendation that state statutes enumerate specific characteristics relates to Identity-Based Bullying. The inclusion of these provisions in state statutes has caused significant confusion over whether policies implemented pursuant to statutes, are consistent with the requirements of schools to respond to discriminatory harassment under civil rights laws.

Many school leaders appear to assume that having a anti-bullying policy, reporting mechanism, and engaging in an investigation, and imposition of consequence are a sufficient response. The requirements to respond to a hostile environment under civil rights laws, discussed fully in Chapter 9, are far more stringent than the investigate and impose sanctions response under state statutes and district policies.

If serious or persistent hurtful acts have caused a significant interference in the ability of a student to learn and participate, a school is required to take steps reasonable calculated to stop the harassment (which is more than punishment), remedy the harm to the targeted student, correct any aspects of the school environment that are supporting the hurtful behavior, and monitor to ensure effectiveness.

The "Substantial Disruption" Standard

From a disciplinary perspective, the misbehavior of a student generally must meet the standard of causing a "substantial disruption" to warrant any disciplinary consequence.[261] Because of this there is often a lack of attention paid to the concerns of students who are being targeted in a persistent manner—in a series of ongoing, but more minor incidents. These incidents, individually, are generally not sufficiently severe in the eyes of a principal to warrant a disciplinary consequence.

In many statutes, this persistent hurtful behavior will not even fit the statutory definition of "bullying." The statutes and resulting policies, often focus on "an act" of hurtful behavior. Often, students experiencing such persistent harm will not even report, because they do not think the principal will do anything about such minor incidents. Or, if they do report, the principal tells them "this is not bullying because the hurtful act was insufficiently serious, so there is nothing I can do." See Chapter 4 for a discussion about mechanisms of moral disengagement.

These persistent hurtful incidents can cause profound emotional harm. Such persistent hurtful acts have created a chronic situation of toxic stress. Every day, they must face coming to a school environment where the odds are someone will be hurtful to them.

Further, under civil rights laws, a "Hostile Environment" can be created created by persistent or pervasive, but more minor, hurtful acts.

Reduce Exclusionary Discipline

Schools in the US have also been provided with additional conflicting guidance. Schools have been directed to apply disciplinary sanctions to those who are hurtful. Schools have also been directed not to apply disciplinary sanctions in response to student misbehavior.

Rethinking School Discipline

As noted in 2010, USDOE OCR issued a *Dear Colleague Letter (DCL)* where schools were told that to address bullying, they should implement policies, set up reporting systems, and impose sanctions if a student engages in bullying—essentially impose a disciplinary consequence.[262]

Then, in early 2014, USDOJ and USDOE jointly released a *DCL* that directed schools to identify, avoid, and remedy discriminatory discipline.[263] In 2015, they released an associated resource package, *Rethinking School Discipline Guidance.*

This *DCL* and associated resources raised attention to the serious concerns that exclusionary discipline policies more often remove racial minority students from the classroom and are having a negative impact on student achievement and well-being.[264] This includes behavior problems, lower achievement, disengagement from school and increased risk of dropping out. The 2014 *DCL* was rescinded in December of 2018.[265] This decision was reached as a product of the Federal Commission on School Safety, headed by Secretary of Education DeVoss. As of writing this book, the *DCL* is "under review."

These requirements have created an even more confusing situation. Note that the intent of these new disciplinary requirements was especially to protect the rights of students of color and those experiencing disabilities. These are the students who are more likely to be bullied. There is absolutely zero evidence that Dominance Motivated Hurtful Students were or are being subjected to the "school-to-prison pipeline." These students are in the "school to high positions of power pipeline."

All of these actions have created a situation of confusion for school leaders. In 2010, state legislatures and school leaders were told: "Apply disciplinary consequences to stop bullying." Then, in 2014 and 2015, they were told: "Don't use disciplinary consequences."

Every Student Succeeds Act

The *Every Student Succeeds Act* (*ESSA*) was signed into law in 2015.[266] *ESSA* requires that states support school districts in reducing the overuse of exclusionary discipline policies. State educational agencies must described their plans to address this requirement in the *ESSA* State Plan and provide data related to school climate and discipline in the annual state report card.[267]

In lieu of exclusionary disciplinary actions, schools have been advised to implement Positive Behavior Interventions and Supports (PBIS) and Restorative Practices. Issues related to these effectiveness of these approaches are discussed later in this Chapter.

Under *ESSA*, schools must also describe their plans and provide data related to school climate and discipline in the annual district and school report card. These measures must include:

- Measures of school quality, climate, and safety.

- Rates of in-school suspensions, out-of-school suspensions, expulsions, school-related arrests, and referrals to law enforcement.

- Rates of chronic absenteeism (including both excused and unexcused absences).

- Incidences of violence, including bullying and harassment.[268]

Required Public Bullying Reports

Note above that in its 2010 *Key Components* guidance to schools on bullying statutes, USDOE advised states to increase Transparency and Monitoring by enacting a state statutory provision to require schools to make annual public reports on the number of bullying incidents—that is the number of incidents that met the statutory definition and resulted in the imposition of a disciplinary consequence.

In states that have made this a statutory requirement, the rates of bullying reported by the school have plummeted, while the rate at which students report being bullied on surveys has remained constant or increased.

An analysis of what has happened in the state of New York after 2011 the passage of the *Dignity Act for All Students (DASA)* statute is helpful. *DASA* requires that all schools make an annual report of bullying incidents.[269]

A 2017 report by the State Comptroller was entitled, *Some NY Schools Not Reporting Bullying or Harassment.* [270] An analysis of data from the 2013-14 school year that found that 71% of New York City schools reported zero incidents of harassment, bullying or discrimination of students for that entire year.[271] Similar concerns about reporting throughout the state were found. By comparison, the rate at which students report being bullied on the New York YRBS has steadily increased since 2011 from 17.7% in 2011 to 20% in 2019.[272]

Similar reports of low levels of bullying incidents by schools are evident in other states with this annual state statute reporting requirement. These are some news story headlines:

- Vermont: "Data indicates schools are likely underreporting bullying."[273]

- Florida: "Florida schools say bullying is down, but are kids afraid to report it?"[274]

- Indiana: "Despite law, Indiana schools are misreporting their bullying data, Call 6 Investigation finds."[275]

So what likely has happened? Schools want to avoid such "black mark" reports. Principals who admit to problems of bullying in their schools may be seen as ineffective leaders. This very likely influences them to provide socially desirable responses—"there is no bullying occurring in my school." As principals have total control of the determination of whether a reported incident meets the policy definition, they have the ability to control the number of reports.

As a result of this statutory provision, some states or districts created complicated decision grids for principals to determine whether the reported incident meets the statutory definition.[276] As a result, reported incidents often are determined to not constitute "bullying"—not to violate the disciplinary code. Thus, the school does not have to report this "black mark."

This annual reporting of incidents to achieve accountability approach was incorporated into the *ESSA*.[277] At the federal level, the reporting requirement is only of allegations of harassment based on Protected Class under the federal civil rights statutes. The bullying and harassment data from each school and district is reported directly to the USDOE Office for Civil Rights (OCR). Data for individual districts and schools can be viewed on this website: https://ocrdata.ed.gov/.

A review of the data for any district will likely reveal an exceptionally low level of reports. For example, in 2017, New York City Public Schools our nation's largest district, with 1603 schools and 966,510 students reported 4,915 allegations of harassment (.005%), with 1,887 students disciplined (.002%).[278] At Los Angeles Unified, our nation's second largest district, with 1041 schools and 511,610 students, reported 426 allegations of harassment (.0008%), with 94 students disciplined (.0002%).[279] There is, quite obviously, a significant discrepancy between these reported allegations and student reports of being bullied on surveys.

The reporting requirements under these state statutes and *ESSA* were intended to support greater transparency and accountability. Based on the data, most school leaders appear to not classify most student reported concern as "bullying" or "harassment." This allows them to avoid having to make a report. Most of the research into the perceptions of students regarding the effectiveness of the "report to the school" approach predated these current requirements. It would be helpful to have more current research of the impact of this transparency and accountability approach.

A strategy that seeks to ensure effective resolution of hurtful incidents and avoid such required reporting is set forth in Chapter 11.

ALTERNATIVES TO EXCLUSIONARY DISCIPLINE

As noted earlier, schools have been advised by USDOE that they should use PBIS and Restorative Practices as an alternatives to exclusionary discipline.[280] Both of these programs have many positive benefits. However, both also have components or have been implemented in ways that are counter productive in the context of the challenges associated with hurtful behavior.

Positive Behavior Interventions and Support

The authoritarian manner in which PBIS is implemented presents concerns. Schools that function in an authoritarian manner have higher levels of bullying behavior. In addition, the use of extrinsic rewards that are provided to students who are acting in compliance, to modify the behavior of those who are not models the thinking and behavior of Dominance Motivated Hurtful Students—"if you do not act in accord with our expectations, we will denigrate and exclude you."

PBIS is grounded in behavioristic research dating from the early 1960's.[281] Positive behavioral supports is an approach that was included in the 1997 reauthorization of the *Individuals with Disabilities Education Act (IDEA)*.[282] The PBIS program has received federal funding to provide technical assistance to schools on implementing a positive behavioral supports approach to behavior management.

The PBIS framework and current guidance incorporate excellent core features that are important for school behavior management planning. The effort of PBIS to focus on positive, rather than negative is certainly excellent. However, the continued reliance on behaviorist principles that are currently incorporated into PBIS extrinsic rewards approach requires rethinking.

Behaviorism Concerns

The underlying foundation of PBIS is grounded on B.F. Skinner's research in operant conditioning.[283] As is clear, the research on behaviorism has predated the research on the impact of trauma or neurodiversity on student behavior. The concept of shifting to positive approaches to seek to influence appropriate student behavior is clearly superior to the use of negative approaches and punishment. Behavioral practices are effective. They are a foundation of strategies to teach animals like dogs and dolphins to perform complex actions.

Behaviorism and operant conditioning support the idea that animal or human behavior is learned, can be changed, and is controlled by external environmental factors. Behaviorism emphasizes the importance of investigating the function of behavior, changing the environment, teaching new skills, and removing rewards that maintain negative behaviors. The goal of PBIS is to use positive reinforcement and consequences in order to decrease the likelihood of negative behaviors while increasing the likelihood of positive behaviors in the school setting. A very recent article published on the PBISApps website that addressed student misbehavior illustrates the concern with behavioristic thinking.

> *A student's reasons for acting out are rooted in one of two motivations: getting something or avoiding something, specifically activities, attention, or stimulus.*[284]

Note from this article the concerns of the experience of trauma or issues related to neurodiversity are entirely absent. Is the only reason your students are misbehaving because they want attention or want to avoid something? The wide acceptance of an approach that is grounded in this simplistic misunderstanding of human behavior is of concern.

The damaging impact of behavioral thinking has been explained by Pollastri and colleagues, who promote the use of the Collaborative Problem Solving approach:

> *While behavioral methods are useful in some cases, problems arise when attempting to use these operant approaches with children who know what is expected of them and who are motivated to do well, but who lack skills to do so due to deficits in impulse control, frustration tolerance, flexibility, problem solving, or other adaptive skills. For children who are aware of the consequences of their maladaptive behaviors but who lack the skills to inhibit these behaviors, the operant approach falls short. In fact, these approaches can sometimes do more harm than good: first, by increasing behavioral performance only in response to promise of reward; second, by negatively affecting the self-esteem of children who want to do well but lack the skills to do so, and who are told repeatedly that they are failing to meet expectations because they are not trying hard enough; and third, by increasing power struggles between adults and children that can be detrimental to the relationship. In sum, through increase of motivation, operant approaches can make the possible more probable, but they simply cannot make the impossible possible.*[285]

Cohen and colleagues, note that the PBIS program is implemented in disempowering authoritarian fashion, rather than democratically and collaboratively.[286] Cohen is the founder of the National School Climate Center. Espelage, the second author, is a world renowned bullying prevention researcher. Cohen and colleagues further explained the differences between a focus on positive school climate and PBIS as follows:

There is confusion about how these two improvement efforts, Positive Behavioral Intervention and Support (PBIS) and school climate reform, are similar and/or different. Some State DOE's suggest that they are one and the same. And, the recent US DOE announcement also confuses rather than clarifies this issue. As my colleagues ... and I have recently written, PBIS and school climate reform are similar in a number of ways: (i) they are school wide efforts; (ii) they are focused on supporting positive change; (iii) they support student learning; (iv) they support student-family-school personnel and community partnerships; (v) they are data driven; (vi) they appreciate that adult behavior and "adult modeling" matters; and, (vii) they are both focused on advancing policies and procedures that support effective practice.

However, we suggest that they are actually much more different than they are similar:

First, the goals are different: As noted above, the goals for school climate improvement efforts are to support students, parents/guardians, school personnel and even community members learning and working together in a democratically informed manner to foster safe supportive, engaging and flourishing schools that support school—and life—success. This is a much broader, positively stated and collaborative set of goals than the PBIS goal to "prevent the development of problem behaviors and maximize academic success for all students."

Second, school climate reform uses a different data set to support learning and guide action planning student, parent/guardian, school personnel and even community member perceptions of how safe the school is (e.g., rules and norms as well as how safe people feel socially and physically), relationship patterns (e.g., respect for diversity, social support), teaching and learning (e.g., support for learning and prosocial education) as well as the environment. PBIS, on the other hand, focuses on individual student disciplinary related data e.g., disciplinary referral, suspensions, expulsion rates), which is aggregated and analyzed to determine effectiveness.

Third, PBIS is based on a behaviorally informed model that is narrowly focused on providing supports to prevent, teach, and reinforce desirable behavior. We appreciate that PBIS also strives to consider how to modify the environment and adult behavior (adult modeling) in helpful ways. However, we are concerned that it does so in a disempowering authoritarian fashion rather than democratically and collaboratively. On the other hand, school climate reform supports the development of social emotional learning and intrinsic motivation through engaging community members to be co-learners and co-leaders who consider and work on the three essential questions noted above.

Fourth, rather than being an adult driven or "top down" effort school climate reform is a much broader, systemic effort grounded in a democratically informed process of engaging students, parents/guardians, school personnel and even community members in being co-learners and co-leaders (under the leadership of the principal).

Fifth, school climate reform not only recognizes that adult modeling "counts" but also explicitly focuses on and supports adult learning as a foundational element of effective school reform. Adult learning and professional learning communities is an explicit and foundational dimension of an effective school climate reform process.

*Sixth, PBIS's policy efforts focus on supporting the design and implementation of effective interventions to change student behavior. School climate reform, on the other hand, is focused on supporting policies that shape systems – the school community – and using data as a "flashlight," not a "hammer." School climate reform promotes school connectedness and prevents bully-victim-bystander behavior because it is a powerful, effective strategy that engages youth to be co-learners and co-leaders together with school personnel. PBIS is a top down, behaviorist model that rests on extrinsic motivation and is not an effective engagement strategy. PBIS uses a systems approach to shape individual (student) behavior, whereas, school climate reform uses a systems approach to shape systems as well as instructional and one-on-one processes. Nonetheless, I believe that PBIS and school climate improvement are not "either/or": when PBIS is well implemented, I believe that it can support positive school cli*mate improvement efforts. But, it is not the same as school climate reform.

PBIS and Bullying Concerns

From the perspective of strategies to foster positive relations and reduce bullying, there are significant concerns the PBIS approach.

Marginalized Hurtful Students

A significant problem emerges when students have challenges in maintaining their behavior so because they lack the skills, have neurological challenges, or have experienced trauma.[287] These students repeatedly experience the situation of failing to meet expectations and, thus, often feel shamed and excluded in front of their peers.

These students also match the description of some of the students who engage in bullying, Marginalized Hurtful Students.

Students who lack impulse control because of the trauma they have experienced or their neurodiversity and who have become discouraged because of the punitive nature of the behaviorist system, as applied to them, may also be much more likely to engage in aggression towards their peers—either because they feel so bad about themselves or in response to being treated badly or excluded by their peers.

Decrease of Intrinsic Motivation

Use of tokens that seek to increase positive behavior may actually decrease such positive behavior, especially when students are outside of the view of an adult. Use of tangible rewards has been found to decrease intrinsic motivation. A meta-analysis of 128 studies on the effects of rewards by Deci and colleagues concluded that:

> *(T)angible rewards tend to have a substantially negative effect on intrinsic motivation (...) Even when tangible rewards are offered as indicators of good performance, they typically decrease intrinsic motivation for interesting activities.*[288]

Consider this insight in the context of those students who are known to be the greatest source of bullying behavior. Some students may at a younger age be highly motivated to receive extrinsic rewards from adults. However, when these extrinsically motivated students become teens, their desire for external reinforcement from adults will wane. Their desire for external reinforcement from peers will likely significantly increase. Being hurtful to others to gain dominance and social status is behavior that is clearly motivated by the extrinsic rewards of attention and power.

Students who are intrinsically motivated to be kind and compassionate to others will be less likely to be eager to receive rewards at any age. When they become teens, their intrinsic motivation to engage in compassionate behavior can be expected to continue—whether or not they are being directly supervised by school staff or expect to receive rewards.

Students who have disabilities, including behavior challenges, are among those who most often experience being bullied. Students who engage in bullying to gain dominance are likely to be hurtful to those who have greater challenges. Consider how this dynamic may play out when a student who is known to have behavior challenges reports to the principal that a student who is known to always receive rewards is the one being hurtful.

Discriminatory Impact

When a school implements token rewards, gives Self Manager buttons, or requires the certain students to carry behavior cards, it generally becomes very apparent that some students are identified as the "good" students and other students are the "bad" students.

It is possible that implicit bias also plays a role in who does or does not receive rewards, as bias has been found to play a role in many ways in which teachers treat students.[289] Some schools take the "good" students on field trips or allow them to engage in other fun activities. A visit to the school while these "good" students are away will readily reveal that the majority of students who were excluded from these fun activities, the "bad" students are those who came from families living in poverty, are a students of color, or have disabilities—all students who are experiencing higher levels of toxic stress—on top of which they have been cast as less desirable and worthy by their school.[290] These are also the students who are more frequently bullied—by the Dominance Motivated Hurtful Students who are compliant to adults and have been rewarded.

Models Relational Aggression

Relational aggression is a type of aggression in which harm is caused by damaging someone's relationships or social status.[291] Manifestations of relational aggression include:

- Excluding others from social activities.
- Damaging victim's reputations with others by spreading rumors and gossiping about the victim, or humiliating him/her in front of others.
- Withdrawing attention and friendship.[292]

The public designation of those students who are in the "green zone" and those who are not essentially creates a "PBIS caste system" in the school. Staff are modeling that it is acceptable to look down on some students and exclude them from groups and activities. School staff are engaging in shaming and exclusion that models relational aggression.

Labeling and Stigmatization

Public behavior charts, behavior cards, or other approaches that publicly identify to all students the teacher's assessment of each student's behavior —frequently with green yellow, or red, cards or indicators—are present in many classrooms. The use of public behavior charts, which is not an approved PBIS practice, was just appropriately criticized in an article by the PBIS OSEP Technical Assistance Center.[293] The concerns included:

- Ineffective in changing behavior class-wide or the behavior of those students who have the most challenges.
- Contribute to labeling and stigmatization because students who are regularly publicly clipped are identified by peers as troublemakers.
- Intensify anxious behavior and decrease engagement.
- Don't teach the right way, because misbehavior comes from skill deficits and clip charts do not address those missing skills.

The concern set forth in this article are identical to the Check In-Check Out (CI-CO) approach that requires certain students to carry "behavior cards" with them wherever they go in school to have their compliance regularly assessed by staff. These students must carry their behavior cards throughout the school day. Other students know that these students must have staff regularly record their behavior, and know that this is because these students engage in "bad" behavior. This can stigmatize these students—this is shaming.

Consider the increased anxiety and demoralization of students who know someone will mark their behavior as "good" or "bad" in frequent time periods throughout the day. Behavior cards that focus solely on compliance are not an effective approach to address skills deficits.

Actual Data

I used to live in Eugene, Oregon. My children went to school there. Eugene is home of the University of Oregon (UO), birthplace of PBIS. PBIS is used in schools throughout the region. The nearby school district, Springfield Public Schools, is a model PBIS district. Most of the educators in the region received their education at the UO. The UO authorities on PBIS are close by for consulting. If PBIS is effective in reducing bullying at any location, it would be effective in the schools in this region.

Several years ago, I asked for more specific data from these two districts. The student reported rate of bullying in Eugene 4J School District on the state's youth risk survey was close to the average for the state. The student reported rate in Springfield, the model PBIS district, was several percentage points higher. The extensive use of PBIS in these schools has shown no evidence in reducing bullying.

What I saw repeatedly in schools in this region were examples of situations where students with greater challenges—including lower income students, students of color, and students with disabilities—who were repeatedly excluded from fun reward activities. These non-rewarded students were also consistently bullied by the students who did not have challenges, who were always rewarded for their compliance. Examples are in the footnotes.[294]

Updating PBIS

PBIS does provide a valuable framework for assisting school personnel in adopting and organizing evidence-based interventions into an integrated continuum to support positive student behavior.[295] PBIS can and should be updated to incorporate greater insight into cultural competence, trauma informed practices, resilience, and to address concerns of students who are neurodiverse—all insight that has emerged subsequent to the era when B.F. Skinner first conducted his research.

Restorative Practices

While there is generally support for the underlying principles and objectives of Restorative Practices, there are some concerns related to the current implementation approaches. The International Institute for

Restorative Practices (IIRP) has been providing leadership in the efforts to support expanded use of Restorative Practices.[296]

The WestEd Regional Educational Laboratory Justice & Prevention Research Center has been focusing on what they refer to as restorative justice (RJ) as an alternative to traditional responses to student misbehavior has issued a number of excellent reports.[297] Recent findings from their research review are:

> *The literature underscores the many challenges confronted when implementing RJ in the schools. For example, there is confusion about what RJ is and no consensus about the best way to implement it. RJ also requires staff time and buy-in, training, and resources that traditional sanctions such as suspension do not impose on the school. With RJ, teachers are often required to perform duties traditionally outside of their job description, such as attending RJ trainings, conducting circles during instruction time, and spending more time one-on-one talking with students. Some educators and other stakeholders are resistant to RJ because it is sometimes perceived as being "too soft" on student offenses. Finally, while RJ programs will certainly vary by the size of the school and scope of the program, some researchers suggest that a shift in attitudes toward punishment may take one to three years, and the deep shift to a restorative-oriented school climate might take up to three to five years. This timing assumes that the program will also be sustained financially, which underscores the importance of considering what resources will be needed and for how long to introduce RJ in a school or district.[298]*

A study in Hong Kong did find that the implementation of a very comprehensive approach to restorative practices that focused primarily on the school climate did result in a significant reduction in reported bullying. A focus of this program was on building strong relationships among all members of the school community.[299]

The Practices of Restorative Practices

It is necessary to dig deeper to identify the reasons why schools in the US, and likely in other countries, have had significant challenges integrating concepts of Restorative Practices.

It appears that a foundational problem in the US is that school leaders have been told to stop suspending students and instead use Restorative Practices. However, it also appears that there has been insufficient or ineffective guidance on how to accomplish this—and, as WestEd has noted, there is there is no consensus on what Restorative Practices is, much less on how best to implement these practices.

It appears that what many principals are trying to implement, under the guise of Restorative Practices, are two strategies: mediation and alternative or logical consequences. In addition, restorative circles are used in a variety of ways.

Mediation or Conflict Resolution

Mediation or conflict resolution may be a helpful practice, if, and only if, there is an equivalent level of wrongdoing by both parties and an equivalent level of personal power. Mediation can be exceptionally dangerous in situations where there is an imbalance of power between the students or in a situation where one student has harmed another.

A document on StopBullying.Gov, *Misdirections in Bullying Prevention and Intervention,* wisely warns against use of mediation or conflict resolution in situations of bullying due to the imbalance of power between the participants.[300] In a study of the effectiveness of bullying prevention programs by Farrington and Ttofi, it was found that as peer-mediation or peer-led conflict resolution resulted in increased victimization.[301]

Amstutz and Mullet have noted that the students harmed by bullying may not wish to face the person who harmed them because they fear further victimization.[302] Face-to-face mediation can be easily manipulated by a Dominance Motivated Hurtful Student and harmful to a Targeted Student who lacks self-confidence and is, therefore, unable to be effectively assertive. Forced apologies are entirely ineffective. Forced acceptance of what the Targeted Student knows to be a forced apology is exceptionally disempowering.

There is a clear risk that mediation will lead to retaliation, because the Dominance Motivated Hurtful Student realizes they will not suffer any significant consequences. The Targeted Student will likely not report this retaliation, because the forced mediation experience has increased their distrust.

Further, if any student who is involved in the hurtful situation—either the one engaging in hurtful behavior or the student who is being targeted— has other challenges, neither mediation nor other Restorative Practices are designed to address these concerns. In situations involving a Marginalized Hurtful Student, the student who is engaging in hurtful behavior has significantly greater concerns. These must be addressed specifically and privately.

Logical Consequences

Another strategy principals appear to be using, would more appropriately be called "alternative consequences" or "logical consequences." Dreikurs should be noted as introducing the concept of logical consequences as an alternative to punishment.[303] This concept can be capsulated by the statement "let the punishment fit the crime." Rather than a punishment, like suspension, which is totally unrelated to the wrongdoing, the consequence should be logically related to the wrongdoing.

The logical consequences approach is clearly preferable to punishment. However, the logical consequences approach is not a Restorative Practice. It is still a consequence that is being imposed by an authority. To implement a Restorative Practices requires different thinking and engaging the student who has engaged in wrongdoing in the process of identifying and executing a remedy of the harm to anyone who was harmed by their actions.

Restorative Circles

Another common practice in schools that is incorporated into Restorative Practices is the concept of a Restorative Circle. Community Circles provide an excellent environment to engage in problem solving about general classroom concerns. This approach is highly encouraged. This is an excellent way that schools can engage with students to build a common understanding and commitment to the well-being of their school community.

However, Circles should never be used to discuss misbehavior of an individual member of the class, especially if hurtful hurtful conduct has been directed at another student. The imbalance of power between a Dominance Motivated Hurtful Student and the Targeted Student would not allow for a positive resolution. Further, the likelihood that other class members would fear retaliation from the Dominance Motivated Hurtful Student would totally undermine the effectiveness of such efforts. The concerns of a Marginalized Hurtful Student should be addressed privately.

There is one place where I would make an exception to this guidance. As is discussed in Chapter 9, complaints are being field against schools that establish Affinity Groups to support marginalized students that are limiting membership to only those students who are within that marginalized group. This is a violation of civil rights laws. These groups must be opened to students within marginalized groups and their allies.

This presents a situation where a student who participates in this group then engaged in hurtful behavior directed towards another group member, based on what should have been maintained as confidential information that was shared. One important strategy is the establishment of Group Agreements. However, of someone breaks that agreement, the Restorative Circle approach could be highly effective. Note in this case, a smaller community that has expressed shared values has been established. Therefore, the Restorative Practices approach has a much greater potential of achieving success.

Indigenous Foundation

There is an underlying reason why schools have had difficulties in implementing Restorative Practices in many regions of the world. Understanding this reason requires an understanding of the underlying philosophical and research foundation of Restorative Practices.

Zehr is a leading researcher who articulated a comprehensive theory of Restorative Practices. His book *Changing Lenses—A New Focus for Crime and Justice*, was first published in 1990.[304] In this book, he set forth the guidance of the need to shift from a focus on retribution, where crime is viewed as an offense against the state, to a focus on restoration, where crime is viewed as a violation of relationships and people. The source for this perspective is from indigenous peoples. As Zehr noted:

> *Two people have made very specific and profound contributions to practices in the field – the First Nations people of Canada and the US, and the Maori of New Zealand... [I]n many ways, restorative justice represents a validation of values and practices that were characteristic of many indigenous groups," whose traditions were "often discounted and repressed by western colonial powers".[305]*

Prior to European contact and continuing today, indigenous peoples throughout the world focused greatly on social stability and the responsibilities of members of the group to support the well-being of their community. In many parts of the world, our schools and our society lack the underlying community philosophy and practices to support full effectiveness. Moving in this direction is definitely recommended.

Despite these foundational challenges, efforts to effectively resolve Hurtful Incidents of Situations must fully integrate Restorative Practices. However, as will be discussed in Chapter 11, it essential that other insight into how to influence positive behavior of those students who have been hurtful accept accountability. Chapter 11 will set forth recommendations for an intervention approach to be used in situations of hurtful Incidents or Situations that incorporates aspects of Restorative Practices, into an Accountability Process, with additional activities to increase effectiveness.

INSTITUTIONAL BETRAYAL

When schools do not respond effectively to bullying by students, especially upon a report to the school by the Targeted Student, the failure to effectively respond can cause profound harm. The research evidence reported earlier in this Chapter clearly demonstrates that far too many schools are betraying their obligations to ensure the safety and well-being of all students. When schools fail to effectively address the concerns of Targeted Students, who are required by law to be present in locations where they are the targets of persistent hurtful acts, they engage in Institutional Betrayal.

Institutional Betrayal occurs when the "institution," fails to respond in an effective manner when it knows or should know of the harmful treatment being experienced by a target of hurtful conduct. Please consider the research evidence in this section in the context of the evidence presented earlier on student reports on the lack of staff effectiveness in responding to hurtful incidents that are witnessed or reported.

The concept of Institutional Betrayal has not yet been integrated into bullying prevention field of research.[306] Significant leadership in exploring this concept in connection with university responses to sexual harassment and assault has been made by Freyd and colleagues.

The concept of Institutional Betrayal is grounded in an understanding of betrayal trauma. Betrayal trauma theory holds that abuse that occurs within close relationships is more harmful than abuse by strangers. This is because in addition to the abuse, there has been a violation of trust and the situation involves a continuation of the relationship.

Institutional Betrayal occurs when the person who has engaged in the abuse and the one victimized are associated within the same institution. This leads to the situation where the one victimized must reach out for help from the institution to get the abuse to stop.

When those who are victimized reach out for help, they must place a great deal of trust in the institution from which they are seeking help. When the institution does not respond in an effective manner to such reports of abuse, this is associated with a significant increase in trauma-related outcomes for the one who has already been victimized.

Institutional Betrayal is clearly associated with the profound challenges those who are sexually assaulted within an institutional setting. This includes sexual assault at universities, religious institutions, and athletic teams or other youth organizations. In significant recently reported situations, not only did the sexual assaults repeatedly occur, profound harm was caused by the institutions through their denial and cover-ups of what was known by leaders in the institution to be happening.

Smith and Freyd created the Institutional Betrayal Questionnaire (IBQ) for use in studies of students who had experienced sexual harassment or assault at the university level.[307] The questions on this survey are quite relevant to the challenges associated with addressing bullying and harassment in K-12 schools. The IBQ Version 2 questions are:

In thinking about the events described in the previous section, did an institution play a role by (check all that apply)...

1. Not taking proactive steps to prevent this type of experience?

2. *Creating an environment in which this type of experience seemed common or normal?*

3. *Creating an environment in which this experience seemed more likely to occur?*

4. *Making it difficult to report the experience?*

5. *Responding inadequately to the experience, if reported?*

6. *Mishandling your case, if disciplinary action was requested?*

7. *Covering up the experience?*

8. *Denying your experience in some way?*

9. *Punishing you in some way for reporting the experience (e.g., loss of privileges or status)?*

10. *Suggesting your experience might affect the reputation of the institution?*

11. *Creating an environment where you no longer felt like a valued member of the institution?*

12. *Creating an environment where continued membership was difficult for you?*

In the context of civil rights laws and regulations, the concept of a Hostile Environment is related. A Hostile Environment is an environment that appears to support the continuation of the hurtful behavior. This is discussed more fully in Chapter 9.

The IBQ questions clearly relate to the characteristics of a school that constitute a Hostile Environment. The lack of effectiveness of current approaches provides evidence of Institutional Betrayal.

The term DARVO, refers to a reaction those engaged in wrongdoing, may display in response to being accused of such behavior. As described:

> *DARVO refers to a reaction perpetrators of wrong doing, particularly sexual offenders, may display in response to being held accountable for their behavior. DARVO stands for "Deny, Attack, and Reverse Victim and Offender." The perpetrator or offender may Deny the behavior, Attack the individual doing the confronting, and Reverse the roles of Victim and Offender such that the perpetrator assumes the victim role and turns the true victim—or the whistle blower—into an alleged offender. This occurs, for instance, when an actually guilty perpetrator assumes the role of "falsely accused" and attacks the accuser's credibility and blames the accuser of being the perpetrator of a false accusation.[308]*

To remedy these concerns requires Institutional Courage. Having Institutional Courage requires a commitment to responding effectively and sensitively to reports, accepting responsibility taking steps to remedy the harm, encouraging witnesses to report, engaging in self-study through focus groups and by conducting surveys, ensuring that leadership has received effective professional development, being transparent about data and policy, using the power of your institution to address the larger issues, and committing resources to these actions.

PART II
Research that Supports an Effective Approach

Chapter 4.
Positive School Climate

HIGHLIGHTS

- **Social-Ecological Framework.** According to a social-ecological framework, bullying is understood as a social phenomenon that is established and perpetuated over time as the result of the complex interplay between individual and environmental factors. Hurtful incidents unfold in social contexts that not only involve the single individuals who are being treated badly and are hurtful, but also implicate the interactions of peers and adults, including parents, caregivers, school leaders, counsellors, teachers, and other staff.

- **School Climate—Framework for Success.** In 2013, the National Association of School Psychologists (NASP) in conjunction with other leading educational organizations in the US released *A Framework for Safe and Successful Schools*. The approach recommended by this *Framework* should be consider the foundational aspect of how a school or district is managed.

- **Continuous Improvement with a Likelihood of Success.** Under *ESSA*, the concept of "evidence-based" has been set forth in a manner that supports implementation of newly developed approaches that are logically grounded in research, when the implementation also includes an evaluation component. This is the "Demonstrates a Rationale" approach. The Demonstrates a Rationale category fully supports the concepts of Continuous Improvement by using approaches that have a Likelihood of Success, with a commitment to evaluation. The key to success is these six words: *"ongoing efforts to examine the effects."*

- **Likelihood of Success.** The now retired *Safe and Drug Free Schools and Communities Act (SDFSCA)*, provided block-grant funding to states and schools and required the use of evidence-based programs. However, a waiver from this requirement allowed for the use of innovative programs that demonstrated a Likelihood of Success. Engage Students to Embrace Civility is in compliance with these waiver guidelines.

- **Continuous Improvement Approach.** To implement a Continuous Improvement Approach: Ensure Representative Leadership. Gather Data. Assess Date. Develop Objectives. Identify and Implement Strategies. Evaluate.

• **Authoritative School Management.** Schools that adopt an authoritative approach to school management will have a more positive school climate, with less hurtful behavior. Schools that use a top-down hierarchal management approach will have greater difficulties.

• **Trauma and Resilience Informed Practice**s. Stopping and remedying the trauma that students are experiencing within the environment over which educators have the most control should have a high priority. Many schools are now integrating trauma informed practices.

- **Lack of Focus on Bullying.** A review of these trauma informed practices guidelines, reveals the lack of references to addressing the concerns of bullying—the most significant trauma to be occurring to students while they are in school. None of these strategies will address the challenge of stopping the hurtful behavior of Dominance Motivated Hurtful Students.

• **Self Determination Theory.** Students often interact in environments where no adults are present or the adults who are present do not recognize or respond to hurtful behavior. To reduce hurtful behavior in these environments requires that students have internalized values and intrinsic motivation to reduce the likelihood that they will be hurtful and increase the likelihood they will step in to help. The Self Determination Theory focuses on the natural tendencies of humans to behave in effective and healthy ways. The universal driving human desires that are the focus of Self Determination Theory are:

- **Connections.** The desire to interact with, be connected to, and experience caring for others.

- **Mastery or Competencies.** The desire to gain competence and understandings, control the outcome of experiences, and to experience mastery.

- **Autonomy or Control.** The universal urge to be causal agents of one's own life and act in harmony with one's integrated self.

• **Authentic Student Voice.** The best way to motivate students to foster a positive and inclusive school climate is to give them the responsibility to make things better—by giving them Authentic Student Voice.

• **Prestige Leaders.** All human social groups form a hierarchical structure. A small group of people at the top have the benefits of their high rank, whereas a much larger group at the bottom do not have such benefits. While there are students in your school who are hurtful to achieve dominance, there are also other very valuable kinds of student leaders. There are two leadership strategies:

- **Dominance Leaders.** Leaders high in dominance motivation— who seek to attain social rank through the use of coercion and intimidation—selfishly prioritize their social rank over the well-being of the group. They demonstrate arrogance and superiority.

- **Prestige Leaders.** Leaders high in prestige motivation are motivated by the desire for respect and admiration. They behave in ways that benefit the group and its members, because those behaviors are likely to foster feelings of respect and appreciation. Prestige leaders do not sacrifice the good of the group in favor of their own power. Prestige is defined in a highly consistent manner conferred respect, honor, esteem, and social regard. Prestige Leaders have feelings of achievement and authentic pride.

- **Applied to Hurtful Behavior.** The students who are most often engaged in a range of hurtful behavior are those who are Dominance Leaders. The students who will become a school's most effective allies in forming a positive social climate are the Prestige Leaders. These are the students who hold the key to effectively changing the social environment of the school.

- **Athletics Culture.** A school and/or community's sport culture may influence the prevalence and nature of bullying behaviors within your school. Being aggressive to achieve dominance may be considered to be part of the "game." However, there are clearly student athletes and coaches who demonstrate the positive prosocial traits of Prestige Leaders.

- **Is It Possible to Change from Dominance to Prestige?**
  Research in this area has not addressed the potential of influencing
  students who have a desire to be perceived as leaders to modify
  their leadership style. Evidence suggests that this may be possible.

- **Social Emotional Growth Mindset.** Students' implicit views of
  where their ability comes from and whether such abilities are fixed or
  can grow impacts their learning activities. Most attention has been
  directed towards improved academic performance. The term Social
  Emotional Growth Mindset is used to emphasize the important of
  incorporating this thinking into the social emotional arena. Students
  with a Social Emotional Growth Mindset know they can gain
  effective skills to maintain positive personal relationships.

  - **Targeted Students.** Targeted Students can hold onto the
    promise that things will get better and they can have a positive
    future and be willing to try strategies to assist them in becoming
    more resilient and empowered.

  - **Marginalized Hurtful Students.** These students are the least
    likely to have a Social Emotional Growth Mindset. If they can
    be encouraged to adopt such a mindset, they then will know that
    things can change for them in stopping the way in which they
    are treated—and they can also change their inappropriate
    reactive behavior.

  - **Dominance Motivated Hurtful Students.** These students
    should be encouraged to know that they can change and
    hopefully recognize that the prestige approach to leadership
    offers significant advantages.

  - **Witnesses.** Witnesses will know that they can get better in
    intervening in a positive manner and that their positive actions
    can foster growth for others.

  - **Supporting a Social Emotional Growth Mindset.** Create a
    Social Emotional Growth Mindset culture that provides the right
    kind of positive acknowledgement and encouragement. Directly
    teach students about how how their brain functions and what it
    means to adopt a Growth Mindset in the context of maintaining
    positive relationships.

- **Positive Psychology.** Positive Psychology is the scientific study of
  the strengths and virtues that enable individuals and communities to
  thrive. The field is founded on the belief that people want to lead
  meaningful and fulfilling lives, to cultivate what is best within
  themselves, and to enhance their experiences of love, work, and play.

- **Ten Building Blocks**. The Greater Good Science Center's ten building blocks of individual and community well-being include: altruism, awe, compassion, diversity, empathy, forgiveness, gratitude, happiness, mindfulness, and social connection.

- **Resilience.** The Center on the Developing Child at Harvard University has identified a common set of factors that predispose children to positive outcomes in the face of significant adversity, including: Facilitating supportive adult-child relationships. Building a sense of self-efficacy and perceived control. Providing opportunities to strengthen adaptive skills and self-regulatory capacities. Mobilizing sources of faith, hope, and cultural traditions.

- **Critical Factors.** The National Center for School Engagement identified three critical factors that increased the resilience of bullied students: A place of refuge where they could feel safe, appreciated, and challenged in a constructive way. Responsible adults who supported and sustained them and provided them examples of appropriate behavior. A sense of future possibility to persuade them that staying in school, despite the bullying, promised better things to come.

• **Character Strengths.** Character Strengths are the core capacities that lead to goodness in human beings across cultures, nations, and beliefs. Everyone has different Character Strengths. Intentionally using one's personal Character Strengths can result in increased happiness. Two researchers with the Positive Psychology Center led a team of 55 social scientists from around the world to identify and classify these core strengths that support goodness. These strengths can be integrated into social emotional learning activities.

- **Character Strengths**. The identified Character Strengths include: Wisdom and Knowledge. Creativity. Curiosity. Judgment. Love of Learning. Perspective. Courage. Bravery. Perseverance. Honesty. Zest. Humanity. Love. Kindness. Social Intelligence. Justice. Teamwork. Fairness. Leadership. Temperance. Forgiveness. Humility. Prudence. Self-Regulation. Transcendence. Appreciation of Beauty and Excellence. Gratitude. Hope. Humor. Spirituality.

• **Positive Social Norms.** When students learn about the actual positive norms of their peers related to disapproval of those who are hurtful and strong admiration of those who step in to help, they will be more willing to abide by those norms. In classrooms with stronger recognized norms against bullying, there are fewer bullying behaviors and greater support for targets by student witnesses.

- **Influences Behavior.** People misperceive the attitudes and behaviors of others and this influences their own actions. When people learn about the actual positive norms of their peer group, they are more willing to abide by those norms. Use of student's own data strongly reinforces their perception of the norms within their community. An indirect approach of displaying student's positive social norms on posters led to significant reductions peer bullying and pro-bullying attitudes. The perceived expectations of peers has also been identified as a critically important factor in influencing the willingness of students to step in to help if they witness hurtful incidents.

- **Principles of Influence.** The key premise of influence thinking is that as we live in a complex world, people tend to fall back on a decision making approach based on generalizations. These generalizations allow people to usually act in a correct manner. The primary principles of influence include:

  - **Reciprocity—the Golden Rule.** When someone does something for us or gives us something, we feel obliged to repay in kind.

  - **Commitment and Consistency.** Humans have a desire to be consistent with the commitments they have made. Schools are advised to ask students to create a Personal Relationships Commitments Statement that sets forth their personal commitments to maintain positive relationships.

  - **Social Proof.** (Positive Social norms) We assume that if lots of people are think a certain way, they must be correct.

  - **Liking.** Friendships and personal relationships can have a strong influence on someone's choices.

  - **Authority.** We feel an obligation to follow the leadership of those in positions of authority or who have earned our respect.

  - **Scarcity or Possible Loss.** Things are more attractive when their availability is limited, or when we stand to lose the opportunity to acquire them on favorable terms.

- **Reflective Listening.** When school leaders and staff engage in Reflective Listening, this will support students in knowing that they have been heard accurately and that they are supported. The use of Reflective Listening is especially important in any situation where the student is emotionally distressed or dysregulated as this will help them to self-regulate.

Social-Ecological Framework

According to a social-ecological framework, bullying is understood as a social phenomenon that is established and perpetuated over time as the result of the complex interplay between individual and environmental factors.[309] Hurtful incidents unfold in social contexts that not only involve the single individuals who are being treated badly and are hurtful, but also implicate the interactions of peers and adults, including parents, caregivers, school leaders, counsellors, teachers, and other staff.

Chapter 4 will outline the research insight that supports the *Engage Students to Embrace Civility* approach to make positive changes in the environment to support more positive relationships and reduce hurtful behavior.

Framework for Safe and Successful Schools

When considering the approaches necessary to improve school climate to better support students in maintaining positive relationships and improve the manner in which students and staff respond to hurtful incidents requires a strong focus on effectiveness. This requires implementing the specific strategies recommended in *Engage Students to Embrace Civility* into a larger Framework for Success. Please note that significant efforts to reduce bullying were initiated in the US in 2010.[310] Increased efforts to address these concerns have more recently been implemented internationally.[311] Despite a strong focus on these efforts in the US, there has been no decline in reported incidents of bullying as reflected on two youth wellness surveys in the US.

In 2013, the National Association of School Psychologists (NASP) in conjunction with other leading educational organizations in the US released *A Framework for Safe and Successful Schools*.[312] The *Framework* was released in response to calls for more armed personnel in schools to address school safety. The *Framework* set forth joint recommendations for improved school safety and access to mental health services for students. From the *Framework*:

> *Efforts to improve school climate, safety, and learning are not separate endeavors. They must be designed, funded, and implemented as a comprehensive school-wide approach that facilitates interdisciplinary collaboration and builds on a multitiered system of supports.*[313]

The approach recommended by this *Framework* should be consider the foundational aspect of how a school or district is managed. Fostering more positive relationships between students, as well as between staff and students, and responding effectively to the hurtful Incidents or Situations that arise are an important component of this work.

The NASP interdisciplinary *Framework* provided six policy recommendations and eight best practices for successful schools. The policy recommendations included:

1. *Allow for blended, flexible use of funding streams in education and mental health services;*

2. *Improve staffing ratios to allow for the delivery of a full range of services and effective school–community partnerships;*

3. *Develop evidence-based standards for district-level policies to promote effective school discipline and positive behavior;*

4. *Fund continuous and sustainable crisis and emergency preparedness, response, and recovery planning and training that uses evidence-based models;*

5. *Provide incentives for intra-and interagency collaboration; and*

6. *Support multitiered systems of support (MTSS).*[314]

The eight best practices that were recommended included:

1. *Fully integrate learning supports (e.g., behavioral, mental health, and social services), instruction, and school management within a comprehensive, cohesive approach that facilitates multidisciplinary collaboration.*

2. *Implement multitiered systems of support (MTSS) that encompass prevention, wellness promotion, and interventions that increase with intensity based on student need, and that promote close school–community collaboration.*

3. *Improve access to school-based mental health supports by ensuring adequate staffing levels in terms of school-employed mental health professionals who are trained to infuse prevention and intervention services into the learning process and to help integrate services provided through school–community partnerships into existing school initiatives.*

4. *Integrate ongoing positive climate and safety efforts with crisis prevention, preparedness, response, and recovery to ensure that crisis training and plans: (a) are relevant to the school context, (b) reinforce learning, (c) make maximum use of existing staff resources, (d) facilitate effective threat assessment, and (e) are consistently reviewed and practiced.*

5. *Balance physical and psychological safety to avoid overly restrictive measures (e.g., armed guards and metal detectors) that can undermine the learning environment and instead combine reasonable physical security measures (e.g., locked doors and monitored public spaces) with efforts to enhance school climate, build trusting relationships, and encourage students and adults to report potential threats. If a school determines the need for armed security, properly*

trained school resource officers (SROs) are the only school personnel of any type who should be armed.

6. *Employ effective, positive school discipline that: (a) functions in concert with efforts to address school safety and climate; (b) is not simply punitive (e.g., zero tolerance); (c) is clear, consistent, and equitable; and (d) reinforces positive behaviors. Using security personnel or SROs primarily as a substitute for effective discipline policies does not contribute to school safety and can perpetuate the school-to-prison pipeline.*

7. *Consider the context of each school and district and provide services that are most needed, appropriate, and culturally sensitive to a school's unique student populations and learning communities.*

8. *Acknowledge that sustainable and effective change takes time, and that individual schools will vary in their readiness to implement improvements and should be afforded the time and resources to sustain change over time.*

The *Framework* also included an information box entitled "Actions Principals can Take Now to Promote Safe and Successful Schools." From this information box:

- *Policies and funding that support comprehensive school safety and mental health efforts are critical to ensuring universal and long-term sustainability. However, school leaders can work toward more effective approaches now by taking the following actions.*

- *Establish a school leadership team that includes key personnel: principals, teachers, school-employed mental health professionals, instruction/curriculum professionals, school resource/safety officer, and a staff member skilled in data collection and analysis.*

- *Assess and identify needs, strengths, and gaps in existing services and supports (e.g., availability of school and community resources, unmet student mental health needs) that address the physical and psychological safety of the school community.*

- *Evaluate the safety of the school building and school grounds by examining the physical security features of the campus.*

- *Review how current resources are being applied, for example:*
  - *Are school employed mental health professionals providing training to teachers and support staff regarding resiliency and risk factors?*
  - *Do mental health staff participate in grade-level team meetings and provide ideas on how to effectively meet students' needs?*
  - *Is there redundancy in service delivery?*
  - *Are multiple overlapping initiatives occurring in different parts of the school or being applied to different sets of students?*

- *Implement an integrated approach that connects behavioral and mental health services and academic instruction and learning (e.g., are mental health interventions being integrated into an effective discipline or classroom management plan?).*

- *Provide adequate time for staff planning and problem solving via regular team meetings and professional learning communities. Identify existing and potential community partners, develop memoranda of understanding to clarify roles and responsibilities, and assign appropriate school staff to guide these partnerships, such as school-employed mental health professionals and principals.*

- *Provide professional development for school staff and community partners addressing school climate and safety, positive behavior, and crisis prevention, preparedness, and response.*

- *Engage students and families as partners in developing and implementing policies and practices that create and maintain a safe school environment.[315]*

All of these components are considered to be exceptionally important. *Engage Students to Embrace Civility* is a specific approach designed to increase positive relationships that should fit within this broader NASP *Framework*.

CONTINUOUS IMPROVEMENT WITH A LIKELIHOOD OF SUCCESS

The *Engage Students to Embrace Civility* approach is fully grounded in research. As of the publication of this book, this program has not been implemented in schools under evaluation protocol and deemed to be "effective." This approach incorporates practices that seek to achieve a Likelihood of Success.

Demonstrates a Rationale

Fortunately, under *ESSA*, the concept of "evidence-based" has been set forth in a manner that supports implementation of newly developed approaches that are logically grounded in research, when the implementation also includes an evaluation component.

ESSA set forth four evidence levels to guide schools in selecting evidence-based programs and approaches that have a Likelihood of Success. These included: "Strong," "Moderate," "Promising," and "Demonstrates a Rationale."[316] The *Engage Students to Embrace Civility* approach should be considered under the category of "Demonstrates a Rationale." This guidance was provided by USDOE.

Demonstrates a Rationale. *To demonstrate a rationale, the intervention should include:*

1) A well-specified logic model that is informed by research or an evaluation that suggests how the intervention is likely to improve relevant outcomes; and

2) An effort to study the effects of the intervention, ideally producing promising evidence or higher, that will happen as part of the intervention or is underway elsewhere (e.g., this could mean another SEA, LEA, or research organization is studying the intervention elsewhere), to inform stakeholders about the success of that intervention.[317]

In an excellent article explaining the significant benefit of this Demonstrates a Rationale category by the Brookings Institute, it was noted that the "evidentiary cupboard" is bare.[318] As was discussed in Chapter 3, this is absolutely the case in the area of bullying prevention. As was discussed in Chapter 3, current bullying prevention programs have only demonstrated modest effectiveness in some countries, with significant concerns about effectiveness at the secondary level.

Concerns about implementing only those programs that have been evaluated in randomized control or quasi-experimental studies are numerous. The time lag between collection of data and the publication of research works against this ideal programs, because there are often no programs available to meet the current concerns. To develop and evaluate a program based on today's research insight often takes so long that by the time the program is deemed "effective" in such experimental implementations, it may be out of date with new research insight.

Likelihood of Success

The Demonstrates a Rationale category fully supports the concepts of Continuous Improvement by using approaches that have a Likelihood of Success, with a commitment to evaluation. As the Brookings Institute article noted:

*Crucially, for many purposes the law also treats as evidence-based a fourth category comprising activities that have a research-based rationale but lack direct empirical support—provided, that is, that they are accompanied by **"ongoing efforts to examine the effects"** of the activity on important student outcomes. Those six words, if taken seriously and implemented with care, hold the potential to create and provide resources to sustain a new model for decision-making within state education agencies and school districts—a model that benefits students and taxpayers and, over time, enhances our knowledge of what works in education.*[319]

In developing an approach that has the highest Likelihood of Success, it is necessary to consider the underlying steps that are necessary to achieve such Likelihood of Success.

The now retired *Safe and Drug Free Schools and Communities Act (SDFSCA)*, provided block-grant funding to states and schools and required the use of evidence-based programs.[320] However, a waiver from this requirement allowed for the use of innovative programs that demonstrated a Likelihood of Success.[321] The following requirements were considered necessary to support a waiver:

- *A needs assessment based on objective data that described the problems or concerns currently faced by the school.*

- *A description of the performance measure or measures the program or activity would address.*

- *The rationale for the program or activity, including how it was designed and why it was expected to be successful in accomplishing the improvements described in the performance measures.*

- *A discussion of the most significant risk and protective factors the program or activity has been designed to target.*

- *A detailed description of the implementation plan, including a description of how the program or activity would be carried out, the personnel to be involved, the intended audience or target population, and the time frame for conducting the program or activity.*

- *An evaluation plan that addressed: the methods used to assess progress toward attaining goals and objectives; the personnel who would conduct the evaluation; the way the results of the evaluation would be used to refine, improve, and strengthen the district's comprehensive plan; and the way progress toward attaining objectives would be publicly reported.*

- *Evidence to support that the program or activity has a "substantial Likelihood of Success." This should include: a description of the prevention research and principles the program has been based upon; a description of the results achieved from previous implementation of the activity or program in a setting similar to the one the district was proposing or, if the program has not yet been rigorously evaluated, a description of the plan and timeline for doing so.[322]*

Continuous Improvement Approach

The requirements for a waiver under the former *SDFSCA* program provide an excellent guide. This thinking can be considered a Continuous Improvement Approach. Within a Continuous Improvement Approach, an ongoing assessment of effectiveness is considered essential.

It is recommended when implementing the recommendations set forth in *Engage Students to Embrace Civility* that the district or school proceed using a Continuous Improvement Approach as follows:

- **Ensure Representative Leadership.** It is assumed that schools have a Positive School Climate Committee. Ensure this committee includes administrative and staff representatives, as well as student and parent and caregiver representatives who are reporting back to and obtaining feedback from their respective communities.

- Leadership of this Committee should be well familiar with the strategies suggested in this book.

• **Gather and Assess Data.** All available data related to student well-being should be gathered and assessed. This includes the comprehensive school climate survey or student wellness surveys that hopefully schools are using.

- Districts should focus on school data that provides evidence of how safe, welcomed, and respected in school. This should include absences data—because excess unexcused absences and excess absences for psychosomatic illness, such as headaches or stomach aches, are an indication of concerns.

- Most student well-being surveys, like YRBS, ask questions about that are in three categories: student demographics, relationship issues such as experiencing bullying and hopefully relationships with school staff, and what I would classify as "outcomes" data—mental health, suicidal behavior, avoiding school because of fears of safety, bringing weapons to school. What is important with these surveys is to do further analysis. Disaggregate the data on demographics and relationships. Then, disaggregate based on responses to relationships questions and outcomes.

- A survey to assess Social Emotional Learning status has recently been released by Panorama.[323] The questions are research based. However, one aspect is, in my opinion, very dangerous. The surveys are not anonymous. They encourage allowing teachers to access each student's individualized data. I strongly advise against collecting and using this data in an individual student manner. Using this survey in anonymous mode could provide valuable insight. Repeat data could allow for assessment of progress.

- The *Embrace Civility Student Survey,* is provided in the online Appendix. Permission is given to use this survey even if the school does not choose to use the *Empowered to Embrace Civility* student program This survey will generate data that is not incorporated into any of these other surveys. This includes Positive Social Norms data, the importance of which is discussed in this Chapter. Survey questions also assess student perspectives of their effectiveness in maintaining positive relationships.

  ‣ Request that school staff leadership team and the Student Leadership Team (discussed in Chapter 8), review the *Embrace Civility Student Survey* data.

- The staff leadership team should be charged with specifically evaluating the data related to staff responsiveness and effectiveness, as well as the responses to questions that assessed school climate concerns.

- The Student Leadership Team should be charged with evaluating the data and creating objectives for improvement. This will send an important message: "The quality of student relationships with each other is not just a staff responsibility. This is also a student responsibility. If you really do not like to see students being hurtful to others, what are you going to do about this?"

- If either of these groups think that further insight may be helpful, focus groups could gain further insight.

- **Develop Objectives**. Based on an assessment of this data, both the staff team and Student Leadership Team should generate objectives for improvement.

  - The staff objectives will be focused on improvement of staff responses and the school climate.

  - The student objectives should be focused on decreasing the level of hurtful behavior and improving students' responses to this—as the targets, the ones who are hurtful, and witnesses.

  - There are no specific requirements for parents or caregivers to develop objectives. They may wish to do so. The parent and caregiver leadership team should be engaged in review and comment for both the staff and student teams.

- **Identify and Implement Strategies.** The Positive School Climate Committee should then identify strategies to achieve the objectives. This should be accomplished in a process that identifies strategies within the large committee, with return to the staff, student, and parent and caregiver groups for review and comment. This process could also integrate other issues raised by any other school climate surveys that are completed by the school.

- **Evaluate.** The administration of the *Embrace Civility Student Survey*, as well as other surveys, the following year will provide the opportunity for evaluation of effectiveness and revision of objectives and strategies.

AUTHORITATIVE SCHOOL MANAGEMENT

Schools that adopt an authoritative approach to school management will have a more positive school climate, with less hurtful behavior. Schools that use a top-down hierarchal management approach will have greater difficulties.

Thornberg and colleagues found that students in classrooms that maintained an Authoritative School Management approach were less likely to experience being bullied in school.[324] This study also found that an authoritative management environment appeared to be related to less reinforcement of hurtful actions by peers and a greater likelihood peers will step in to help.

What is meant by "Authoritative School Management?" The concept of an authoritative style is grounded in extensive research on parental styles by Baumrind.[325] The four styles of parenting identified by Baumrind are based on two dimensions—the degree of control and the degree of warmth. Control is demonstrated by enforcing demands for appropriate behavior. Warmth is demonstrated by supporting the child's agency and individuality, in addition to being sensitive and responding to the needs of the child. Authoritative parenting is high on warmth and high on control. Authoritarian parenting is low on warmth, but high on control. Indulgent parenting is high on warmth, but low on control. Neglectful parenting is low on warmth and low on control.

The authoritative–authoritarian approach to parenting has also been applied in the school management environment.[326] The differences are described as differences between an authoritative school environment or an authoritarian school environment.[327]

An authoritative school environment is an environment where school rules are perceived as strict, but are fairly enforced. Students perceive that their teachers and school staff members fully engaged with students, treat them with respect, and want them to be successful. Numerous studies have found that the authoritative school discipline approach, where students are aware of school rules, believe the rules are fair, and have positive relationships with their teachers, is associated with lowered levels of bullying.[328] A common question on school climate surveys is of critical importance in the assessment is this: 4-point Agree or Disagree. "School staff really care about me and want me to succeed."

Unfortunately, too many classrooms and school environments are coordinated in an authoritarian manner.[329] An authoritarian management style with too much control and too little warmth and support appears to increase the likelihood that students will model and establish their own hierarchical structure, which supports harm directed at those with lower social status.[330] The authoritarian management approach has been linked to higher levels of bullying and violence in schools.[331]

Cornell and colleagues have investigated Authoritative School Management extensively. Their studies have documented that an authoritative school climate is associated with lower levels of prevalence of teasing and bullying, bullying victimization, and general victimization. In such an environment, there are also lower levels of student aggression toward teachers, lower rates of school suspension, and and higher levels of student academic engagement, grades, and educational aspirations. They also found that authoritative school climate is associated with lower rates of school suspension and higher levels of student academic engagement, grades, and educational aspirations.

Cornell and colleagues developed the Authoritative School Climate Survey to measure the structure and supportiveness of a school from the perspectives of the students and school staff. This survey is available for use from the University of Virginia.[332] An excellent slideshow that demonstrates these concepts by Dr. Cornell is online.[333]

TRAUMA AND RESILIENCE INFORMED PRACTICES

Stopping and remedying the trauma that students are experiencing within the environment over which educators have the most control should have a high priority. Regardless of what might be happening to students in the outside world, knowing that they are safe and welcome in their school community will help students survive and thrive.

Chapter 5 will address the research insight into trauma related to specific strategies to assist students in gaining resilience and empowerment, that are addressed in Chapter 6. This section relates to the school environment itself—establishing a school environment that is trauma informed.

Research has validated the profoundly harmful impact of trauma on students, this includes the trauma of being persistently bullied, as well as the experience of other ACEs.[334] Trauma negatively impacts learning, behavior, and relationships at school. Students may respond with fear to people or situations because they do not trust that others care about them. Trauma also interferes with the ability of a student to manage their emotions and behavior.

Experiencing being bullied is experiencing trauma. Persistently Targeted Students, as well as those Marginalized Hurtful Students, demonstrate the symptoms associated with traumatic disorder.[335] If students are being persistently bullied while in school, by other students and especially by staff, they are experiencing trauma within the school building.

Implementation Strategy

Many schools are now integrating trauma informed practices. I prefer the term Trauma and Resilience Informed Practices. Key components of the most significant approaches in the US are set forth in the footnotes. The comprehensive strategies to establish a trauma informed school environment are beyond the coverage of this book. Some helpful sources of insight are provided.

- The National Center on Safe Supportive Learning Environments provides a resource entitled *Trauma-Sensitive Schools Training Package*.[336]

- The Massachusetts Advocates for Children Trauma and Learning Policy Initiative has distilled six core attributes of a Trauma Sensitive School in their resource, *Helping Traumatized Children Learn: Supportive School Environments.* for children traumatized by family violence.[337]

- The National Child Traumatic Stress Network (NCTSN) provides helpful resources, including their excellent document, *Creating, Supporting, and Sustaining Trauma-Informed Schools: A System Framework*.[338]

- A SAMHSA document, *SAMHSA's Concept of Trauma and Guidance for a Trauma-Informed Approach*, is an additional helpful resource.[339]

All of these resources provide similar guidance on the comprehensive steps necessary to establish a trauma informed school. The recommended actions are foundational for supporting more positive relationships in school. These efforts are all focused on addressing the concerns of students who have experienced trauma, which should include both students who are being bullied and those marginalized who are also being hurtful.

However, as you review these trauma informed practices guidelines, note the lack of references to addressing the concerns of bullying—the most significant trauma to be occurring to students while they are in school. When bullying is mentioned, the guidance is limited to ensuring a that a policy is in place and students know to report. No school should claim to be implementing trauma informed practices unless it it also assertively and effectively addressing the concerns of hurtful behavior between students.

Additionally, none of these trauma informed strategies will address the challenge of stopping the hurtful behavior of Dominance Motivated Hurtful Students. They will help to support those students who have experienced challenges, including Targeted Students and Marginalized Hurtful Students. The *Engage Students to Embrace Civility* approach is entirely in accord with these excellent foundational recommendations.

SELF DETERMINATION THEORY

Students often interact in environments where no adults are present or the adults who are present do not recognize or respond to hurtful behavior. To reduce hurtful behavior in these environments requires that students have internalized values and intrinsic motivation to reduce the likelihood that they will be hurtful and increase the likelihood they will step in to help. The Self Determination Theory provides insight into strategies to increase intrinsic motivation.

The ethological perspective on hurtful behavior was discussed in Chapter 2. There is also an ethological perspective on the development of compassion—an affective state that is oriented to enhancing the welfare of others.[340] Evolutionary analysis has offered key reasons why there has been an emergence of compassion as a trait in humans, as well as more sophisticated animal groups. Compassion enhances the care for and well-being of vulnerable offspring, is a desirable attribute in a mate, and enables cooperative relations with non-kin, which can ensure group survival.

The Self Determination Theory focuses on the natural tendencies of humans to behave in effective and healthy ways.[341] The theory was initially developed by Deci and Ryan of the Center for Self Determination Theory.[342] In a 1999 examination of 128 studies that investigated the effects of external rewards on intrinsic motivations, Deci and Ryan identified conclusive evidence that rewards have a negative effect on intrinsic motivation. Reliance on extrinsic rewards undermines people in taking responsibility for motivating or regulating themselves. Use of extrinsic rewards was found to actually decrease motivation for a task for which the student initially was motivated. This is why we need to stop seeking to manage student behaviors using extrinsic rewards.

Deci and Ryan describe the primary insight on motivating human behavior as follows:

> *Human beings can be proactive and engaged or, alternatively, passive and alienated, largely as a function of the social conditions in which they develop and function. Accordingly, research guided by self-determination theory has focused on the social-contextual conditions that facilitate versus forestall the natural processes*

of self-motivation and healthy psychological development. Specifically, factors have been examined that enhance versus undermine intrinsic motivation, self-regulation, and well-being. The findings have led to the postulate of three innate psychological needs—competence, autonomy, and relatedness—which when satisfied yield enhanced self-motivation and mental health and when thwarted lead to diminished motivation and well-being. Also considered is the significance of these psychological needs and processes within domains such as health care, education, work, sport, religion, and psychotherapy.[343]

The three universal driving human desires that are the focus of Self Determination Theory are described as follows:

- **Relatedness.** The desire to interact with, be connected to, and experience caring for others. The desire to act in ways that achieve a higher social purpose. Young people are naturally driven to reach out and connect with others. Students experience relatedness when they perceive that others are listening and responding to them.

- **Mastery.** The desire to gain competence and understandings, control the outcome of experiences, and to experience mastery. Students need to be engaged in authentic learning opportunities, challenged, and provided with effective feedback. The focus on high stakes tests and strictly scripted curriculum undermines the ability of students to gain mastery and competence. In appropriate learning environments, students will eagerly explore to better understand their world. If students are in a school environment where it is perceived that they require external rewards to remain attentive to the learning tasks, the source of the concern is the instructional environment.

- **Autonomy.** The universal urge to be causal agents of one's own life and act in harmony with one's integrated self. The desire to have personal control. "You are not the boss of me," the common statement of a toddler, provides evidence of the early emergence and strength of this desire. Students experience autonomy and personal control when they feel supported to independently explore and are supported in their independent efforts to develop and implement solutions for their problems.

Researchers in various field of social science are engaged in collaboration with Deci and Ryan to extend insight and application of this theory. More information and comprehensive research reports are available on the Self Determination Theory website.

Implementation Strategy

All actions that schools can and should take to improve school climate can be grounded in these three basic human desires (which I would suggest slightly renaming). Such actions include:

- **Ensure Effective Connections (Relatedness).** These actions include: ensuring positive connections with trusted adults in the schools environment, as well as fostering student friends; the use of Community Circles to build a sense of community in classrooms and the wider school community, all efforts to support cultural inclusion, initiatives to support kindness and compassion, the collaborative development of shared values within the school culture and personal commitments to those values, positive acknowledgements of positive behavior, and systems of holding students accountable that support connection to the community. Schools should consistently ask, "How does this approach increase positive connections within our school community?"

- **Focus on Increasing Student Competence (Mastery).** Efforts to increase student competence include: Social Emotional Learning, practices to support mindfulness and self-regulation, increasing the problem solving, goal setting, and action planning skills of students and staff. The *Empowered to Embrace Civility* student program specifically focuses on increasing students' competence in maintaining positive relationships. Schools should consistently ask, "How does this approach increase students' competencies?"

- **Ensure Student Voice and Personal Control (Autonomy).** Efforts to increase students' perspectives that they have personal control within the school community include ensuring Authentic Student Voice and engaging student leaders in all efforts related to school climate and personal relationships. The involvement of the Student Leadership Team in the Continuous Improvement process is one key way in which to increase the recognition of students that they are even placed into a situation where they have gained, and are expected to exert, personal control to maintain positive relationships in the school. The *Empowered to Embrace Civility* student program is an indirect instructional program that is managed (controlled) primarily by students. Schools should constantly ask, "How are we giving students authentic voice both in how the school is addressing these concerns and how the school is intervening in hurtful incidents?"

AUTHENTIC STUDENT VOICE

The title of this book basically sets forth the standard: "Engage Students." The best way to motivate students to foster a positive and inclusive school climate is to give them the responsibility to make things better—by giving them Authentic Student Voice. Unless and until students are motivated to address these challenges, nothing can be expected to change. Shifting responsibility to students requires giving them authentic voice in deciding what the school community should do to ensure a positive school climate for all students. Authentic Student Voice increases students feelings of "control," one of the key aspects of Self Determination Theory.

It is critically important to ensure Authentic Student Voice in relation to fostering positive relationships for these reasons:

- Hurtful Student behavior is most often for the purpose of achieving dominance and social status and, thus, this behavior appears to be supported by the social norms of the school.

- Students who are treated badly most often are students who are different who are cast as "misfits" by a powerful group of students, and sometimes by staff.

- Hurtful behavior often is not witnessed or detected by staff.

A commitment to Authentic Student Voice ensures meaningful student involvement. As described by Fletcher:

Meaningful student involvement is the process of engaging students as partners in every facet of school change for the purpose of strengthening their commitment to education, community and democracy. Instead of allowing adults to tokenize a contrived "student voice" by inviting one student to a meeting, meaningful student involvement continuously acknowledges the diversity of students by validating and authorizing them to represent their own ideas, opinions, knowledge, and experiences throughout education in order to improve our schools. ...

When is student involvement meaningful?

- *When students are allies and partners with adults in improving schools.*

- *When students have the training and authority to create real solutions to the challenges that schools face in learning, teaching, and leadership.*

- *When schools, including educators and administrators, are Accountable to the direct consumers of schools—students themselves.*

- *When student-adult partnerships are a major component of every sustainable, responsive, and systemic approach to transforming schools.[344]*

Implementation Strategy

Several organizations provide excellent guidance and resources on ensuring Authentic Student Voice.

* SoundOut School Consulting is a service initiated by Adam Fletcher who is an early pioneer in the promotion of Youth Voice.[345] The website contains many helpful free and low cost information resources.

* WestEd provides resources to assist in increasing student voice. They state: "Listening to student voice—that is, listening closely to what students say about their school experiences—can help educators understand topics or problems and rethink practices to inform school improvement efforts."[346]

* An excellent resource is the book *Student Voice: The Instrument of Change*. This book states: "When you take time to listen, you'll find that students' aspirations can drive your school toward exciting new goals. And when students know they're being heard, they develop self-worth, engage meaningfully in their own academic success, and become purposeful in their educations."[347]

* The Harvard Graduate School of Education's Usable Knowledge: Connecting Research to Practice article on Giving Students Voice recommends these important principles: "Regularly solicit student feedback. Engage students in studying and assessing their school. Include authentic student representation on leadership teams. Invite students to any discussion related to their own learning. Consider young people as stakeholders and partners in their schools.[348]

* An organization called Student Voice also provides excellent resources.[349] "Through our core initiatives, Student Voice aims to illustrate the state of schools today, as well as identify student-centric and student-created solutions to address the systemic inequity in the American education system. This inequity manifests itself as a disparity in access to opportunities and resources across schools nationwide, specifically as it relates to socioeconomically disadvantaged students and school districts. At Student Voice, we believe all students have the right to hold educational institutions accountable to them as partners in shaping their foundational experiences. Students must have a more powerful voice in order to combat the systemic inequity."

Chapter 11 sets forth recommended strategies to intervene in hurtful incidents situations. A core element of the recommended approaches is that all students who have been involved in a hurtful incident or situation are fully involved in the resolution of the situation. Thus, also in interventions, it is important to ensure Authentic Student Voice.

Targeted Students absolutely must be ensured Authentic Student Voice. These students' personal power has been challenged by the Hurtful Student. If a principal tells a Targeted Student, " I will deal with this," and does not involve the Targeted Student in the resolution, the principal also is taking this student's personal power. This is especially important at the secondary level. Teens are seeking independence. One reason they do not report concerns is this takes all power and control away from them.

In Chapter 11, an additional approach to more fully engage students in interventions in hurtful situations is set forth. This involves establishing a Peer Assistance and Accountability Team. Teens, especially, are far more concerned about peer approval, then approval of an adult. If a team of their peers in a formal setting essentially tells Hurtful Students, "You need to stop this behavior, own up to your responsibility, and make things better" it is presumed they will be more highly responsive and compliant to this Authentic Student Voice of their peers than to an adult voice.

PRESTIGE LEADERS

All human social groups form a hierarchical structure.[350] A small group of people at the top have the benefits of their high rank, whereas a much larger group at the bottom do not have such benefits. This hierarchal structure is present in our global society, the country and community, and in the social structure of the students in your school.

While there are students in your school who are hurtful to achieve dominance, there are also other very valuable kinds of student leaders. Research has distinguished between two strategies that those at the top use to achieve a high social status.[351] These are referred to as dominance and prestige. The Prestige Leaders in your school are the students who have significant influence and potential power to create a shift in your school environment. It should be noted that as of the writing of this book, I have not identified any academic papers that have applied the research on dominance and prestige leadership to bullying issues.

The identification of two different styles of leadership has primarily emerged in research that focuses on business leadership. This research is grounded in an evolutionary perspective. Under this perspective, it is assumed that people possess motivation systems that guide their behavior. These systems are designed to facilitate outcomes in mating, relationship maintenance, social hierarchy, affiliation, self-protection, disease avoidance, and care of offspring.[352]

These motivation systems incorporate specific mechanisms designed to promote positive outcomes for individuals living in highly interdependent social groups. Ultimately, these mechanisms are designed to increase an individual's mating success.

The objective of mating success is clearly evident in most secondary schools. However, students also have other outcome goals in schools. The motivation systems may foster cooperation and prosocial behavior, or in the alternative, they may promote aggression and the abuse of power.

Maner and Case have conducted extensive research on the differences between dominance leadership and prestige leadership.[353] Their insight is helpful in understanding the differences between these leadership styles and will hopefully assist school leaders in identifying the Prestige Leaders in their school.

> *Evolutionary theories that differentiate between dominance and prestige provide a useful conceptual framework for understanding when and why particular leaders behave in selfish ways that many would consider corrupt.*
>
> *Several studies suggest that leaders high in dominance motivation—those who seek to attain social rank through the use of coercion and intimidation—selfishly prioritize their social rank over the well-being of the group. Like dominant members of other nonhuman primate species, dominant people appear to care more about maintaining their social rank than about leading their group toward desired goals.*
>
> *Leaders high in prestige motivation, on the other hand, are motivated primarily by the desire for respect and admiration. They seek to attain high social rank that is freely conferred by others in the group. As a consequence, prestige-oriented individuals tend to behave in ways that benefit the group and its members, because those behaviors are likely to foster strong feelings of respect and appreciation. Indeed, participants high in prestige motivation did not sacrifice the good of the group in favor of their own power, as those high in dominance did. If anything, when confronted with threats to their social rank, they responded by increasing their tendency to support the group (eg, by encouraging connections between top-performing role models and other group members The motivations that drive people to attain social rank thus play a profound role in guiding their leadership behavior and the extent to which they prioritize the goals of the group over their own social rank.[354]*

As outlined in Chapter 2, the students who are most often engaged in a range of hurtful behavior are those who are being hurtful to achieve dominance. Under the terminology in this research area, these are the Dominance Leaders. The students who will become your most effective allies in forming a positive social climate are the Prestige Leaders. These are the students who hold the key to effectively changing the social environment of the school. These are the students who need to be identified and invited to participate on the Student Leadership Team, as discussed in Chapter 10.

The dominance leadership approach is quite evident in some animal groups, for example chimpanzees. The alpha or top-ranking group member, which is virtually always a male, dominates his subordinates through intimidation, coercion, and, as a last resort, direct aggression.

The prestige leadership approach originated in ancestral human groups that were small and had relatively flat hierarchies.[355] The evolutionary process favored mechanisms that led people to respond to and emulate what the highly successful group members were doing. Those members of the group who were successful and, therefore, emulated earned a higher social ranking via prestige—respect and admiration from group members. These cultures awarded respect to the individuals who meaningfully contributed to the good of their community.

As societies became more complex, the dominance strategy to leadership, became more prevalent. In today's society, it is quite easy to see public examples of both forms of leadership. A search on the terms "dominance leader, prestige leader, corporate" will yield ample articles demonstrating that these two different business leadership styles are under discussion within the business community.

Some argue this strategy is unique to humans.[356] However, this may not be the case.[357] For both African elephants and orca whales, the oldest females are considered the leaders. In some mammal communities, the members actively choose to follow an animal that has more knowledge and experience accumulated over its lifetime and knows how to help the group survive.

The status of Prestige Leader is conferred on those who display skills and knowledge that is valued by those in the group.[358] What is necessary to gains the status of a Prestige Leader will vary depending on the group. The competencies and skills valued by the group may differ. Competencies and skills including academic achievement, altruistic behaviors, as well as athletic, social, intellectual, and advice-giving abilities appear to be more valued by students in the educational environment.[359]

A student may become the Prestige Leader of an athletic team by both having physical expertise and by team building, so all can be successful in a game. A student may become the Prestige Leader of a drama group through both excellent acting skills and a focus on performance effectiveness of the group of players. A student may become the Prestige Leader of a Gay Straight Alliance group through both effective advocacy of their group's objectives and their kindness in reaching out to questioning students. Thus, the skills and knowledge set may differ based on the environment. Recognize that within your student community and also within the various subgroups within your student community, these leadership strategies are being used.

It has been found that people who gain leadership through prestige have many favorable personality traits.[360] They are generally high in self-esteem, agreeableness, need for affiliation, social monitoring, fear of negative evaluation, and conscientiousness. Across many different disciplines, prestige is defined in a highly consistent manner conferred respect, honor, esteem, and social regard.

While those who achieve social status through dominance demonstrate feelings of arrogance, superiority, and conceit, those who are are Prestige Leaders have feelings of achievement, authentic pride. This pride is not accompanied by a sense of superiority, arrogance, or hubris. Appreciative humility appears to be a trait of Prestige Leaders.[361] Appreciative humility and authentic pride is associated with personal success, as well as celebrating the success of others.

Athletics Culture

A discussion of athletics culture is within the scope of a discussion on dominance and prestige leadership, because it is within the athletics environment where a dominance approach to leadership is most likely to be reinforced in schools.

A fascinating study was conducted of members of four college athletic teams.[362] If was found those who were deemed to be Dominance Leaders were also considered to demonstrate narcissistic self-aggrandizement, aggression, extraversion, and disagreeableness. By contract, those who were considered to be Prestige Leaders demonstrated genuine self-esteem, social acceptance, and conscientiousness. Players perceived as prestigious were viewed as capable advice-providers, as well as intellectually, athletically, and socially competent. They were also viewed as altruistic, cooperative, helpful, ethical, and moral. In contrast, dominance was negatively related to all prosocial tendencies assessed. However, individuals high in dominance were perceived as athletically talented.

Research on bullying between athletes and fans in the sport environment is relatively new and there is a lack of extensive research about this topic.[363] Bullying is influenced by environmental factors, such as the athletic culture and social atmosphere—that often normalizes dominance-focused aggressive behaviors.

Your school and community's sport culture may influence the prevalence and nature of bullying behaviors within your school. Very often those students who are hurtful to achieve social dominance are athletes. Within the athletic environment, being aggressive to achieve dominance may be considered to be part of the "game." Fans and parents also may demonstrate aggressive behaviors. Aggression associated with athletics can permeate the school environment.

The sport culture is still strongly connected to the traditional the male stereotype, sometimes called "toxic masculinity"—which values characteristics such as power, dominance, and competitiveness.[364] Both in practice and in games or competitions toxic masculinity supports dominance-focused aggressive behaviors among athletes.[365]

Research suggests that aggressive behaviors are frequently normalized in sports settings.[366] Bullying in sport is often perceived as regular sport aggression and is not identified as bullying behavior. Furthermore, those athletes who are targeted tend to remain silent because of a tough culture existing in many sport domains. "What happens in the locker room, stays in the locker room," is a strong norm. Within the athletic environment, there is normalization and acceptance of several types of interpersonal violence as common practice.[367]

There are severe consequences for those who are targeted. In addition to the consequences of being bullied, such as increasing anxiety and social exclusion, the targets of bullying in sports also tend to dropout early from sports participation.[368] However, there are also very extreme severely negative consequences if an athlete reports such concerns.

Mendez-Baldwin and colleagues conducted a study of high school athletes' attitudes about bullying and hazing.[369] The number of participants were limited; there were 229 male high school athletes. Results on a survey demonstrated that athletes had mixed attitudes about sports hazing and bullying. While many believed that sports hazing can cause negative damage to an athlete, many also believed that a little hazing was okay, as long as no one gets hurts. The results also reveal that many behaviors and attitudes about sports bullying and hazing are related to the belief that hazing is a part of the sports culture.

However, it is important to reference the research noted earlier when discussing Prestige Leaders. There are clearly student athletes and coaches who demonstrate all of the positive prosocial traits of Prestige Leaders. Of significant question is whether and how these positive prosocial traits have been encouraged among athletes by coaches and parents or caregivers from the first time they step onto the football or soccer field, the basketball court, or into the baseball diamond.

The risk of being a victim of bullying in sport may vary considerably depending on the social group involved.[370] There appears to be a higher risk of being a target of bullying among those who have a disability, suffer from obesity, or otherwise vary from the norm in terms of weight, size, or body shape. Belonging to a different ethnic group or having a minority orientation or identity can result in more bullying. Seniority on the team, age, personality commitments, and work ethics are also possible factors that increase vulnerability to be targeted. Those who exhibit lower skill levels in sport or are a rookie have a higher risk of being bullied.

Within the athletic environment, there are concerns also associated with the behavior of the fans and parents watching from the stands.[371] There have been significant news reports of concerns of hate speech directed at player from the stands. The news stories often focus on based on racial harassment of players. Hurtful comments are also likely directed at those who are obese or appear to be less skilled.

Is It Possible to Change from Dominance to Prestige?

What the research in this area has not addressed is the potential of influencing students who have a desire to be perceived as leaders to modify their leadership style. Can those students who are Dominance Motivated Hurtful Students have a shift in their thinking to recognize that they can achieve their leadership desires through more respectful means?

Evidence suggests that this may be possible. Evidence suggests that dominance behavior occurs in environments where it is supported.[372] For example, in schools that maintain an authoritarian structure, dominance behavior is modeled by the school leadership and adopted by students. In schools with a more authoritative structure, prestige behavior is modeled by the school leadership and there are lower levels of dominance-based hurtful behavior.

My hypothesis is that the Positive Social Norms approach, that is discussed later in this Chapter, will also be effective in helping to shift those who may perceive dominance approaches as effective in achieving their objectives to use prestige strategies. My hypothesis is that if districts adopt the *Engage Students to Embrace Civility* approach through the grade levels, Prestige Leaders from the high schools will be influential at the middle school level and Prestige Leaders from the middle school will be effective at the elementary level. As students enter into puberty, in 4th through 6th grades, this is likely be an important time to focus on these distinctions in leadership style. It is also my hypothesis that the environment and philosophy of both the school and community athletic programs will be important aspects to consider. Athletic environments are discussed later in this Chapter.

Implementation Strategy

School leaders are advised to assess their personal leadership style and the structure of the school climate. Ensuring a school management structure that is authoritative in nature appears to reduce the tendency of students to behave in ways that seek dominance. Specific attention should be paid to the athletic environment. Coaches can become valuable allies if they focus on fully supporting those team members who demonstrate prestige leadership and are consistently acting in ways that benefit the team, not their individual performance.

Identifying students who are Prestige Leaders and engaging them on the Student Leadership Team will help to send a message of which leadership styles are being encouraged. The Positive Social Norms approach discussed later in this Chapter can also help to communicate student norms and values that promote prestige leadership.

School leaders must recognize the nature of the power dynamics that exist in athletic environments, in order to prevent bullying behaviors and to enhance the welfare of all student athletes. It is important to be exceptionally mindful of the manner in which their athletic departments are operating their programs.

In recent years, there has been an increasing number of funded projects and campaigns about the welfare of athletes.[373] Sport organizations and researchers have been working to make sports more inclusive and to protect athletes from violence in sport, including bullying.[374] The US Center for Safe Sports has a helpful document for coaches.[375]

SOCIAL EMOTIONAL GROWTH MINDSET

Encouraging a Social Emotional Growth Mindset is important for all students who are being treated badly, both Targeted Students and Marginalized Hurtful Students. Students who have a Growth Mindset are also less likely to engage in retaliation in response to being treated badly, because they know it is possible for the student who was hurtful to change.

One great example of a Growth Mindset is an organization called the It Gets Better Project.[376] The It Gets Better Project is a nonprofit organization with a mission to uplift, empower, and connect lesbian, gay, bisexual, transgender, and queer youth around the globe.

Consistently maintaining a Growth Mindset perspective in both instruction and intervention interactions with students will help to increase their effectiveness in maintaining positive relationships, becoming happier, and not engaging in retaliation if they are treated badly.

Growth Mindset

Dweck introduced the concept of Fixed Mindset and Growth Mindset to describe the underlying beliefs people have about learning and intelligence.[377] Students' implicit views of where their ability comes from and whether such abilities are fixed or can grow impacts their learning activities, especially their reaction to failure.

Most of the research and attention associated with Growth Mindset has been directed towards improved academic performance. However, this theory also has significant relevance in the area of social emotional learning, including how students engage in personal relationships with each other and respond when conflict or aggression occurs. In this book, the term Social Emotional Growth Mindset will be used to emphasize the important of expanding the original concept to matters beyond academic performance and intelligence.

Students who have a Growth Mindset believe that they and others can acquire any desired ability if they engage in the effort or study to do so. Students with a Social Emotional Growth Mindset know that they can gain effective skills to maintain positive personal relationships.

Students who have a Fixed Mindset believe that abilities are mostly innate. These students interpret failure of themselves or others as the lack of basic abilities. They deem intelligence as a factor that cannot be changed. Students with a Fixed Mindset ignore constructive feedback. They feel threatened by the success of their peers. They often blame outside factors for their failure. They tend to believe that their failure was not due to their lack of skill or determination, but rather the result of other people's actions.

Translate this Fixed Mindset thinking to personal relationships. Targeted Students with a Social Emotional Fixed Mindset are likely to believe that things will never change and their lives will never get better. Marginalized Hurtful Students with a Fixed Mindset will believe the same things—and also that they will not be able to change how they respond to these hurtful incidents. They will believe that when someone is hurtful to them, the only way they can respond is to retaliate.

Later in this Chapter will be a discussion of Mechanisms for Moral Disengagement. One of the rationalizations Hurtful Students frequently use is that the other student is a "loser" and deserves to be treated as such. Witnesses may also rationalize the failure to intervene based on Fixed Mindset thinking that even if they did, things would not get better.

Students who have a Growth Mindset believe that they and others can acquire any desired ability if they engage in the effort or study to do so. They are more likely to continue working or an academic project, even if they have experienced failure. Their perception is that failure to accomplish an objective is not an indication of their personal failure; rather this is viewed as motivation for them to try again so that they can continue to learn. They believe that everyone can get smarter if they work at it. Students with a Growth Mindset use constructive feedback to improve. They do not blame outside factors for their failures.

Social Emotional Growth Mindset

Translate this Growth Mindset perspective to personal relationships. Targeted Students with a Social Emotional Growth Mindset can hold onto the promise that things will get better and they can have a positive future. They will also be willing to try some of the strategies that will be suggested in Chapter 5, to assist them in becoming more resilient and empowered that will allow them to better maintain positive relationships, become happier, and self-regulate when things get tough.

Marginalized Hurtful Students the least likely to have a Social Emotional Growth Mindset. If they can be encouraged to adopt such a mindset, they then will know that things can change for them in stopping the way in which they are treated—and they can also change their inappropriate reactive behavior. Dominance Motivated Hurtful Students also should be encouraged to develop a Social Emotional Growth Mindset that they can change. As they have a desire for leadership, they can recognize that the prestige approach to leadership offers significant advantages. Witnesses who have a Social Emotional Growth Mindset will know that they can get better in intervening in a positiver manner and that their positive actions can foster growth for others.

To support students in adopting a Social Emotional Growth Mindset, schools must nurture this type of thinking. One way educators can do this is by creating a Social Emotional Growth Mindset culture that provides the right kind of positive acknowledgement and encouragement.[378] Students who are praised for their intelligence—"You must be smart at these problems"—develop a Fixed Mindset. Those positively acknowledged for their effort—"You must have worked hard at these problems"—develop a Growth Mindset.

However, note that these are academic and intelligence focused statements. Some Social Emotional Growth Mindset relationship statements could include: "I saw how helpful you were to …" "I know that what happened was upsetting to you. I could see that you were focused on remaining calm." "I know that what happened was upsetting to you. I could see that you were trying to remain calm and were able to for a while. It is okay that you were not totally successful. Trying and failing helps us learn how to do things better. What do you think you learned from this?"

In Practice Addressing Aggression

Yeager and colleagues, conducted a very noteworthy experiment that focused on increasing Social Emotional Growth Mindset.[379] This study applied the Growth Mindset research insight to teen aggressive behavior, with a specific focus on reducing retaliation. This was their premise:

> *We focus on implicit theories of personality—or beliefs about the potential to change personal characteristics—as a target for a new social-cognitive intervention. Adolescents' implicit theories of personality create a framework for their interpretations of setbacks, and have been shown to shape their vengeful and punitive versus prosocial and resilient reactions to conflicts, social failures, or a peer's wrongdoing. Specifically, some adolescents hold more of an entity theory of personality, which is the belief that people's traits are fixed. They believe that people who are "bullies" or "victims," "winners" or "losers," cannot change. From this perspective, victimization or exclusion may be seen as done by and to people who cannot change—for example, by a "bully" to someone who is considered a "loser." Under these conditions, harming the transgressor may seem satisfying. On the other hand, some adolescents hold more of an incremental theory of personality, believing that people have the capacity for change. Seen from this perspective, victimization may be thought of as done by and to people who can change over time. This may reduce aggressive retaliation by allowing students to see their future as more hopeful and by creating a greater desire to understand or perhaps influence transgressors.[380]*

The researchers hypothesized that an intervention that taught adolescents the Growth Mindset (incremental theory), and how to apply it to interpersonal situations this would reduce aggressive retaliation. The researchers also noted that students who are victimized exhibit more depressive symptoms. If one holds a Fixed Mindset, this may lead to the conclusion that one's own social labels as a "loser" or a "bully" and the associated difficulties cannot be improved. This can lead to feelings of hopelessness.

The second hypothesis was that teaching about about the Growth Mindset (incremental theory), and the idea that "bullies" and "victims" can change might also reduce depression, as well as retaliatory aggression. (Note, the labels of "bullies" and "victims" are damaging evidence of a Fixed Mindset.)

The research study had one control group that received no instruction. Another control group received extended and engaging instruction in coping skills that explicitly taught skills for thinking positively and coping productively in the face of victimization or exclusion. The Growth Mindset discussions taught the idea that people have the potential for change, especially in the context of victimization or exclusion, but did not teach any specific actions to take following conflict or aggression. The facilitators told students:

Scientists have discovered that people do things mainly because of the thoughts and feelings that they have—thoughts and feelings that live in the brain and that can be changed. When you have a thought or a feeling, the pathways in your brain send signals to other parts of your brain that lead you to do one thing or another. … By changing their brain's pathways or their thoughts and feelings, people can actually change and improve how they behave after challenges and setbacks. So it's not that some people are "rejects" or that other people are "bad." Everyone's brain is a "work in progress."[381]

The study found that found the instruction in Growth Mindset was successful in reducing levels of aggression, conduct problems, depression, and truancy for racially and socioeconomically diverse students. Specifically, they found that students who learned about Growth Mindset:

- Demonstrated reduced aggressive retaliation and increased prosocial behavior after a controlled provocation.

- Were more likely to be nominated by their teachers for reductions in conduct problems, such as aggression and acting out in class, relative to victimized students in the combined control groups.

- Reported fewer depressive symptoms and improved attendance compared with adolescents who received no treatment. The group that learned coping skills also reported fewer depressive symptoms, however, this group did not change their aggressive or prosocial reactions to exclusion, improve their classroom behavior, or attendance.

Implementation Strategy

There are many excellent resources for educators on encouraging a Growth Mindset. Dweck's website, Mindset Works is a good place to start.[382] Posters in the staff room and throughout the school can remind staff and students to use Social Emotional Growth Mindset language. Unfortunately, most of the posters that are commercially available have language focusing on intelligence and academics. Changing the "mindset" that "growth mindset" is about intelligence and academics will require a sustained intentional growth focus.

The *Empowered to Embrace Civility* student program features slideshow slides that can be turned into posters that have Social Emotional Growth Mindset language related to maintaining positive relationships, becoming happier, and self-regulating when things get tough.

In staff meetings, the staff could be invited to go around the room and provide personal relationship Social Emotional Growth Mindset statements regarding their favorite Social Emotional Growth Mindset personal relationships example from their students.

POSITIVE PSYCHOLOGY

Supporting all students in gaining resilience and personal empowerment will assist students who are being treated badly achieve greater resilience, support those students who are engaging in hurtful behavior to stop themselves and make things right, and empower those who are witnesses to step in to help. Research in the field of Positive Psychology provides insight to support these objectives.

This Chapter introduces the importance of the integration of principles of Positive Psychology into an approach to support students in maintaining positive relationships. As these strategies are directly related to increasing student resilience and empowerment, they are more expansively addressed in Chapter 6.

The Positive Psychology Center at the University of Pennsylvania provides this definition of Positive Psychology:

> *Positive Psychology is the scientific study of the strengths and virtues that enable individuals and communities to thrive. The field is founded on the belief that people want to lead meaningful and fulfilling lives, to cultivate what is best within themselves, and to enhance their experiences of love, work, and play.*[383]

The Greater Good Science Center studies the psychology, sociology, and neuroscience of well-being, and teaches skills that foster a thriving, resilient, and compassionate society.[384] Greater Good's ten building blocks of individual and community well-being—the behaviors that research suggests will support your health and happiness, and foster positive connections with other people include: altruism, awe, compassion, diversity, empathy, forgiveness, gratitude, happiness, mindfulness, and social connection.

The Center on the Developing Child at Harvard University has excellent resources addressing increasing resilience, that are grounded in Positive Psychology.[385] They say:

> **Research has identified a common set of factors that predispose children to positive outcomes in the face of significant adversity.** *Individuals who demonstrate resilience in response to one form of adversity may not necessarily do so in response to another. Yet when these positive influences are operating effectively, they "stack the scale" with positive weight and optimize resilience across multiple contexts. These counterbalancing factors include*
>
> *1. facilitating supportive adult-child relationships;*
>
> *2. building a sense of self-efficacy and perceived control;*
>
> *3. providing opportunities to strengthen adaptive skills and self-regulatory capacities; and*

4. mobilizing sources of faith, hope, and cultural traditions.[386]

The National Center for School Engagement conducted a study of high school students who had been bullied in elementary school.[387] The researchers identified three critical factors, that are all components of Positive Psychology that increased the resilience of these students and led to a successful outcome, despite the face they were being bullied:

- A place of refuge where they could feel safe, appreciated, and challenged in a constructive way.

- Responsible adults who supported and sustained them and provided them examples of appropriate behavior.

- A sense of future possibility to persuade them that staying in school, despite the bullying, promised better things to come. (Note the Growth Mindset nature of this factor.)

Research into factors that promote resilience to bullying victimization is still in its infancy. However, a recent study by Hinduja and Patchin of the Cyberbullying Research Center explored the relationship between resilience and experience with bullying and cyberbullying.[388] The results demonstrated that resilience is a potent protective factor, both in preventing experience with bullying and mitigating its harmful effects.

Implementation Strategy

The Greater Good Science Center maintains an excellent website with very accessible information.[389] They also provide a newsletter and books that can support educators in increasing their focus on strategies to foster a thriving, resilient, and compassionate school community.

The Greater Good Science Center newsletter can be distributed to staff, with a suggestion to discuss these issues with students. The Student Leadership Team could focus on Greater Good Science Center's ten building blocks and create a school program each month that focuses on one of these building blocks. Newsletters sent to parents or caregivers, and posts on school social media can highlight and provide brief information on the different aspects of Positive Psychology.

CHARACTER STRENGTHS

Character strengths are the core capacities that lead to goodness in human beings across cultures, nations, and beliefs. Everyone has different Character Strengths. Intentionally using one's personal Character Strengths can result in increased happiness.

Two researchers with the Positive Psychology Center, Peterson and Seligman, led a team of 55 social scientists from around the world to identify and classify these core strengths that support goodness.[390] The VIA Institute on Character has extensive research on their site that documents on how this strengths-based focus can improve people's lives in many ways—including increasing student well-being and academic success.[391]

This is the VIA Classification of Character Strengths:

1. ***Wisdom and Knowledge**—Cognitive strengths that entail the acquisition and use of knowledge.*

    - ***Creativity [originality, ingenuity]:*** *Thinking of novel and productive ways to conceptualize and do things; includes artistic achievement but is not limited to it.*

    - ***Curiosity [interest, novelty-seeking, openness to experience]:*** *Taking an interest in ongoing experience for its own sake; finding subjects and topics fascinating; exploring and discovering.*

    - ***Judgment [critical thinking]:*** *Thinking things through and examining them from all sides; not jumping to conclusions; being able to change one's mind in light of evidence; weighing all evidence fairly.*

    - ***Love of Learning:*** *Mastering new skills, topics, and bodies of knowledge, whether on one's own or formally; obviously related to the strength of curiosity but goes beyond it to describe the tendency to add systematic ally to what one knows.*

    - ***Perspective [wisdom]:*** *Being able to provide wise counsel to others; having ways of looking at the world that make sense to oneself and to other people.*

2. ***Courage**—Emotional strengths that involve the exercise of will to accomplish goals in the face of opposition, external or internal.*

    - ***Bravery [valor]:*** *Not shrinking from threat, challenge, difficulty, or pain; speaking up for what is right even if there is opposition; acting on convictions even if unpopular; includes physical bravery but is not limited to it.*

    - ***Perseverance [persistence, industriousness]:*** *Finishing what one starts; persisting in a course of action in spite of obstacles; "getting it out the door"; taking pleasure in completing tasks.*

    - ***Honesty [authenticity, integrity]:*** *Speaking the truth but more broadly presenting oneself in a genuine way and acting in a sincere way; being without pretense; taking responsibility for one's feelings and actions.*

    - ***Zest [vitality, enthusiasm, vigor, energy]:*** *Approaching life with excitement and energy; not doing things halfway or halfheartedly; living life as an adventure; feeling alive and activated.*

3. **Humanity**—*Interpersonal strengths that involve tending and befriending others.*

- **Love**: *Valuing close relations with others, in particular those in which sharing and caring are reciprocated; being close to people.*

- **Kindness [generosity, nurturance, care, compassion, altruistic love, "niceness"]**: *Doing favors and good deeds for others; helping them; taking care of them.*

- **Social Intelligence [emotional intelligence, personal intelligence]**: *Being aware of the motives and feelings of other people and oneself; knowing what to do to fit into different social situations; knowing what makes other people tick.*

4. **Justice**—*Civic strengths that underlie healthy community life.*

- **Teamwork [citizenship, social responsibility, loyalty]**: *Working well as a member of a group or team; being loyal to the group; doing one's share.*

- **Fairness:** *Treating all people the same according to notions of fairness and justice; not letting personal feelings bias decisions about others; giving everyone a fair chance.*

- **Leadership:** *Encouraging a group of which one is a member to get things done and at the time maintain time good relations within the group; organizing group activities and seeing that they happen.*

5. **Temperance**—*Strengths that protect against excess.*

- **Forgiveness:** *Forgiving those who have done wrong; accepting the shortcomings of others; giving people a second chance; not being vengeful.*

- **Humility**: *Letting one's accomplishments speak for themselves; not regarding oneself as more special than one is.*

- **Prudence:** *Being careful about one's choices; not taking undue risks; not saying or doing things that might later be regretted.*

- **Self-Regulation [self-control]:** *Regulating what one feels and does; being disciplined; controlling one's appetites and emotions.*

6. **Transcendence**—*Strengths that forge connections to the larger universe and provide meaning.*

- **Appreciation of Beauty and Excellence [awe, wonder, elevation]**: *Noticing and appreciating beauty, excellence, and/or skilled performance in various domains of life, from nature to art to mathematics to science to everyday experience.*

- **Gratitude:** *Being aware of and thankful for the good things that happen; taking time to express thanks.*

- **Hope [optimism, future - mindedness, future orientation]:** *Expecting the best in the future and working to achieve it; believing that a good future is something that can be brought about.*

- **Humor [playfulness]:** *Liking to laugh and tease; bringing smiles to other people; seeing the light side; making (not necessarily telling) jokes.*

- **Spirituality [faith, purpose]:** *Having coherent beliefs about the higher purpose and meaning of the universe; knowing where one fits within the larger scheme; having beliefs about the meaning of life that shape conduct and provide comfort.[392]*

Implementation Strategy

The VIA Institute on Character has free Character Strengths Inventories for adults and teens on their website. Both staff and secondary students can complete these surveys. A brief version, developed with their permission, is provided as an Appendix on the Embrace Civility website. Any of these surveys will help staff and students to identify top Character Strengths.

Also on the VIA Institute for Character website is guidance on strategies people can use to build every one of these Character Strengths. In addition to other social emotional learning programs, schools can rely on these resources. The Student Leadership Team could also be involved in these activities. Some suggestions:

- Encourage all students and staff to complete the Character Strengths Inventory to identity their strengths. Then, everyone should create a graphic image or collage that sets forth their greatest strengths. Following this, students could be encouraged to engage in a "Character Strengths scavenger hunt" to find other students or staff who have similar Character Strengths. This is a great way to achieve greater unity. "Hey, that kid does not look like me or hang out doing the same things I do, but we share a character strength."

- Identify a character strength for the school to focus on each week. Encourage students to strive to learn about and practice this strength during the week. Have this Character Strengths show up on their log in computer screen during the week. Also, encourage them to submit examples they have seen of people demonstrating this specific strength. This could be focused on examples they have seen at school by students or staff, examples from history or literature, or examples from contemporary news. Members of the Student Leadership Team could read some of these examples in morning announcements.

- Engage students to create posters that illustrate each of the Character Strengths to be hung on the walls or to show up on the computer log in screen.

- In Community Circle discussions of concerns, students can engage in problem solving to first identify what has happened and what their goal is. (More on problem solving in Chapter 6.) Then, the discussion could shift to the identification of strategies to resolve the problem that use different Character Strengths. The teacher could have cards that have each character strength noted and randomly pull 5 cards. Then ask the students to brainstorm a strategy to respond that uses this character strength.

- In an intervention with any student who is dealing with any kind of a challenge or problem, they can be asked to identify their greatest Character Strengths. Then, in participatory problem solving, they can develop a plan of action to resolve the situation using strategies that are grounded in their particular strengths.

POSITIVE SOCIAL NORMS

When students learn about the actual positive norms of their peers related to disapproval of those who are hurtful and strong admiration of those who step in to help, they will be more willing to abide by those norms.

The *Embrace Civility Student Survey* contains questions that focus on soliciting data grounded in Positive Social Norms. Based on prior use as well as the PISA 2018 results on attitude questions, this survey will identify that students do not like to see students being hurtful to others. This will also identify that students strongly admire those who are consistently kind and compassionate, step in to help others who are being treated badly, respond in a positive manner if they are treated badly, and say they are sorry if they made a mistake and were hurtful.

From a young age, children appear to recognize that bullying and social exclusion is wrong and harmful. In classrooms with stronger recognized norms against bullying, there are fewer bullying behaviors and greater support for targets by student witnesses. As children grow, they appear to become increasingly aware of the importance of behaving in accord with the norms of the peer group.[393] That is, they gain an understanding peer group "norms" or expectations, express group loyalty, and often demonstrate bias towards the what they perceive to be the norms of their peers both in terms of being hurtful and stepping in to help. "Perceive" is the key word in this sentence.

The association between group norms with bullying behaviors appear to be even stronger as students grow older.[394] As they become teens, with expanded social cognition and increased experience with peer groups, they learn that in order to fit in with a group they must follow the "norms" of their group. This is necessary to avoid negative perspectives of their peers or possible social repercussions themselves. They begin to base their reasoning about bullying and social exclusion based on their group identity and group status.

Social Norms Theory

The social norms theory suggests that people misperceive the attitudes and behaviors of others and this influences their own actions.[395] When people learn about the actual positive norms of their peer group, they are more willing to abide by those norms. Ensuring accurate understanding of the disapproval of hurtful behavior and admiration of those who are kind, respectful, and inclusive is a core component of an approach to foster positive relations. Use of student's own data strongly reinforces their perception of the norms within their community.

As the National Social Norms Center has explained:

> *Instead of using scare tactics or stigmatizing messages, the social norms approach steers people towards healthy behavior by letting them know it's the normal thing to do.[396]*

The National Social Norms Center, Youth Health and Safety Project made effective use of local surveys to reduce bullying behavior.[397] This project collected school-based data about students' perspectives on bullying at a school in five diverse schools.

This data was used to create colorful posters that demonstrated the actual school's norms, with messages such as: "80% of (name of school) students say students should not tease in a mean way, call others hurtful names, or spread unkind stories about other students." "85% of use feel that it is not cool to spread rumors." "We strongly agree that it is not okay to shove, kick, or hit other students." "81% of us would tell a teacher or counselor if we were being bullied."

An evaluation of the results revealed significant reductions overall in perceptions of peer bullying and pro-bullying attitudes. Reports of personal bullying of others and victimization were also reduced. In addition, support for reporting bullying to adults at school and in one's family increased. The only intervention was the use of posters demonstrating the social norms of the school, as identified by the local survey.

The perceived expectations of peers has also been identified as a critically important factor in influencing the willingness of students to step in to help if they witness hurtful incidents.[398] What students think other students think about those who are hurtful, those who support those being hurtful, and those who step in to help appears to be highly influential.[399]

> *Whether someone intervenes is ... influenced by the extent to which they feel that others in their immediate environment share their concerns and will support their efforts.*[400]

The issue of Positive Social Norms is also related to the very serious concern of whether students will report to the school if they witness that there is a knife or gun at school.[401] A study conducted in the UK explored whether students misperceive peer norms about support for telling adults about seeing weapons at school. Students were asked both about their own personal support for reporting weapons to adults and whether they perceived most other students at their school to support reporting weapons to adults in each category.

While most students, 64–78% on average, personally thought that students should report seeing a weapon at school to an adult either at school or at home, 34–44% of students erroneously thought that the majority of their peers did not support reporting to these adults. These misperceptions about reporting may contribute to a less safe environment.

As was discussed in Chapter 2, especially at the secondary level, most students who engage in hurtful behavior are doing so to gain dominance and social status. If the perceived social norms of the school are such that humiliating peers is an effective strategy to gain higher social status and be considered "popular," then the hurtful behavior of some students is highly unlikely to stop.

However, if the actual known Positive Social Norms are that the majority of students do not like to see their peers being treated badly, truly admire those who step in to help and do not admire those who are hurtful or support those being hurtful and admire those who respond to being treated badly in a positive manner, and those who, if they have been hurtful, stop themselves and make things right, a recognition of these actual positive norms of the majority of the students should help to influence those who are being hurtful to change their behavior.

Positive Norms Reflected on the PISA 2018 Survey

Students often assume their peers are more likely to support aggression than they personally are. Many students think that other students think that those who are hurtful are "cool," but they themselves do not like to see these hurtful acts.[402] Ensuring accurate understanding of the disapproval of hurtful behavior by their peers and admiration of those who step in to help is imperative.

The PISA 2018 survey, discussed in Chapter 1, included very helpful social norms data.[403] The survey asked students five bullying-related attitudes. These questions asked students whether they agreed or disagreed on a 4-point scale on five questions that asked about bullying-related attitudes.

PISA asked students whether they "strongly disagree", "disagree", "agree", or "strongly agree" with the following statements, with the following results:

- *It irritates me when nobody defends bullied students*—81% agreed or strongly agreed.
- *It is a good thing to help students who can't defend themselves*—88% agreed or strongly agreed.
- *It is a wrong thing to join in bullying*—88% agreed or strongly agreed.
- *I feel bad seeing other students bullied*—87% agreed or strongly agreed.
- *I like it when someone stands up for other students who are being bullied*—90% agreed or strongly agreed.

On average across OECD countries, girls had more negative attitudes towards bullying than boys. Advantaged students were also more likely than disadvantaged students to report anti-bullying attitudes. PISA 2018 showed that a prevalence of anti-bullying attitudes in schools is related to experience of bullying by students.

In schools with the highest percentage of students who agreed or strongly agreed with the statement "I feel bad seeing other students bullied," the reported level of bullying was lower than in schools with the lowest percentage of students who agreed with this statement. Students were experienced less bullying when they attended schools where their schoolmates were more likely to agree with this statement—even after accounting for students' and schools' socio-economic profile.

Embrace Civility Student Survey

What do you think the response of students in your school would be if the same or similar questions were asked of them? The *Embrace Civility Student Survey* is provided on the Embrace Civility website. This survey includes questions that are similar to the ones that were asked in a prior version that was use in 2015. The earlier *Embrace Civility Student Survey* asked all students questions about hurtful behavior and received these responses.

Question: What is your normal reaction if you see a student being hurtful to another?

- I really do not like to see this happen—89%.
- Don't care one way or the other—5%.
- This happens all he time, so it is no big deal—4%.
- The person probably deserves it—2%.

Based on an analysis of the "other reasons" it is clear that one of the answer options on this question should be "how I would make the other person feel." This answer option has been added in the updated and expanded version of the *Embrace Civility Student Survey*.

Question: What words would you use to describe a person who steps in to help when he or she sees someone being hurtful to another?

The most frequent words used, listed in order of prevalence were: Brave, Kind, Hero, Nice, Caring, Courageous, Admirable, Amazing, Awesome, Strong, Friend, Leader, Confident, Responsible, Respectful, Smart.

Question: People act in different ways. You might form opinions about them based on how they have acted. What do you think of these actions?

- A: Admire.
- NO: No opinion one way or the other. (This has been changed to "Mixed Feelings.")
- NA: Do not admire.

Action	A	NO	NA
Are respectful and kind to others.	88%	10%	1%
Reach out to help someone who is treated badly.	86%	12%	3%
Tell someone who is being hurtful to stop.	81%	15%	3%
Help someone who was hurtful decide to make things right.	71%	25%	4%
Were treated badly and responded in a positive way.	65%	25%	11%
Report serious concerns to an adult.	61%	32%	7%
Were hurtful, but stopped and made things right.	60%	32%	8%
Were treated badly and retaliated.	18%	52%	30%
Ignore hurtful situations involving others.	11%	34%	56%
Laugh when seeing that someone is being treated badly.	5%	13%	82%
Create hurtful "drama" to get attention.	4%	11%	84%
Think it is "cool" to be disrespectful to others.	4%	11%	84%

As is quite obvious, the vast majority of students hold negative views about students being hurtful to others, as well as those who support those being hurtful. Students hold very positive views about their peers who are kind and respectful step in to help those who are treated badly, as well as those who take steps to remedy situations if they were hurtful.

These questions solicit what researchers would call "socially desirable responses." The reason for these is instructional. This data is not for "research purposes," where the concern of social desirability response bias would be present. This data is for instructional purposes—to help students learn about the positive norms of their peers. This is in accord with the social norms approach to youth risk prevention.

A significant finding emerged that should be noted. This is in response to the answer option "Were treated badly and retaliated." Note that 52% of the students had mixed feelings about this and 30% thought this was something to admire. As was identified in another question asked of those who reported they had been hurtful, retaliation appears to have played a significant role in their decision to be hurtful. The fact that their peers also have mixed feelings about the appropriateness of retaliation is very significant. Note, as discussed above, having a Social Emotional Growth Mindset and knowing that others can change can reduce the potential of engaging in retaliation.

Implementation Strategy

The ways to increase students' understanding of actual Positive Social Norms in their school are:

- Conduct a survey that identifies students' actual norms and provide the data to students in presentations and posters. The *Embrace Civility Student Survey* contain social norms questions.

- Establish a diverse Student Leadership Team, discussed in Chapter 10, with Prestige Leader students who will engage in ongoing activities to communicate the Positive Social Norms of the school community.

- Engage the Student Leadership Team students, with staff mentor support as appropriate based on age, in the presentation of the school survey results that identify the Positive Social Norms to the students. Schools will find that students are exceptionally interested in what their data says about what they think about how they treat each other.

- Create posters and log on screen displays that display the schools' Positive Social Norms. The *Empowered to Embrace Civility* student program offers these images.

- Refer to the identified Positive Social Norms of their school community in efforts by staff when intervening with students who have engaged in hurtful behavior. This approach is incorporated into the recommendations in Chapter 11.

PRINCIPLES OF INFLUENCE

Research in the field of social influence is a study of the ways in which people might change their behavior to meet the demands of a social environment. Insight from this research can be integrated into many of the approaches to support students in maintaining positive relationships.

Cialidini's book, *Influence: The Psychology of Persuasion*, set forth an examination of the primary ways people can be more easily influenced.[404] The key premise of such influence thinking is that as we live in a complex world, people tend to fall back on a decision making approach based on generalizations. These generalizations develop because they allow people to usually act in a correct manner, with a limited amount of thought and time dedicated to this effort.

Cialdini has identified six primary Principles of Influence—ways in which people or organizations can influence the behavior of others. These are thoroughly research based principles that can be integrated into efforts to foster positive relationships. The primary principles include the following:

- **Reciprocity—the Golden Rule.** When someone does something for us or gives us something, we feel obliged to repay in kind. We generally try to return favors, pay back debts, and treat others as they treat us—or as we want them to treat us. The reciprocity principle facilitates sharing and cooperation which supports mankind's social advancement. Reciprocity is a vital part of how human society functions. This is the basis of the "golden rule," which is present in all of the global religions and spiritual practices.

- **Commitment and Consistency.** Humans have a desire to be consistent with the commitments they have made. Once we take a stand or make a choice, we feel compelled to behave consistently with our earlier commitment and to use this commitment to justify our own decisions. For this principle to be most powerful, a real commitment must be made. This is most likely to happen when someone has actively done something in support of their commitment, has put some effort into their commitment, or when their commitment has been made publicly.

- **Social Proof.** We assume that if lots of people are doing something or think a certain way, they must be correct. This is the social norms approach that was discussed above. It is necessary to ensure that students have an accurate understanding of the actual norms.

- **Liking.** Friendships and personal relationships can have a strong influence on someone's choices. People are more likely to follow the lead of those they know and respect. Generally, people are more likely to agree to someone's request if they know and like the person.

- **Authority.** We all, go varying degrees, feel an obligation to follow the leadership of those in positions of authority or who have earned our respect.

- **Scarcity or Possible Loss**. Things are more attractive when their availability is limited, or when we stand to lose the opportunity to acquire them on favorable terms. The "Limited offer! Buy now!" marketing approach is grounded in this principle. Obviously, the potential of punishment is a possible loss. However, when one has been hurtful, another possible loss is that of damage to their reputation or friendships.

Embrace Civility Student Survey

A question on the 2015 *Embrace Civility Student Survey* asked students why they would not be hurtful to others.

Question: What are the three most important reasons you would not be hurtful to another?

- How I would feel if someone did this to me—78%. (Reciprocity.)
- How I would feel about myself—50%. (Commitment and Consistency.)
- What my parents would think—36%. (Authority.)
- That I might hurt my future opportunities—33%. (Scarcity or Possible Loss.)
- That I might get into trouble—29%. (Scarcity or Possible Loss.)
- What this would do to my reputation—19%. (Social Proof and Scarcity or Possible Loss.)
- What my friends would think— 14%. (Liking and Social Proof.)
- Other reason that is important to you—9% (The most frequent other reason was "how I would make the other student feel," which is also Reciprocity.)

Implementation Strategy

The key principles of the Principles of Influence can be used in following ways to foster positive relationships:

- **Reciprocity.** Obviously, if you ask students why they would not be hurtful to others, a significant number of them will explain this in the context of how they would want to be treated. However, some students are likely to respond to a direct question of "How would you feel if someone treated you like this?" with a responses that indicates that they would not care. A slight change in the question is recommended. "How would you feel if someone treated a good friend of yours like this?"

- **Commitment and Consistency.** If a student has made a commitment, then they will likely be more inclined to follow through on this commitment. It is highly recommended to use this principle in a very strategic manner. Following a presentation by the Student Leadership Team of the survey results on the school's *Embrace Civility Student Survey*, ask students to create a Personal Relationships Commitments Statement that sets forth their personal commitments. The Personal Relationships Commitments Statement should ask students to complete the following:

  - I commit to treat other students in the following way:
  - If I witness someone being hurtful to another student, I will:
  - If I make a mistake and am hurtful to someone, I will:

- If a friend of mine is hurtful to another student, I will:

- If someone is hurtful to me, I will:

This Personal Relationships Commitments Statement should be completed in a digital format. Then, at any time when a school leader is intervening with a Hurtful Student or Supporter, this Commitment statement can be accessed. Questions like these can be asked: "I see that the commitment you made to how you intended to treat others was …. How would you judge your behavior in the context of this commitment that you made?" "I also see that you indicated that if you made a mistake and were hurtful, you would …. How might you go about doing this?" "I see that you made a commitment that if a friend of yours was hurtful, you would …. How have you acted on this commitment? What do you think you could do at this time?"

A school staff member likely will not have ready access to this Personal Relationships Commitments Statement. However, they could ask questions such as: "What commitments did you make about how you intended to treat others and what you were going to do if you made a mistake and were hurtful?" "What commitments did you make about how you would respond if a friend of yours was hurtful?"

- **Social Proof.** The strategies to implement a Positive Social Norms approach were addressed in the previous section. Asking students to complete a Personal Relationships Commitments Statement shortly after seeing the local school's Positive Social Norms data can combine the effectiveness of these two approaches.

- **Liking.** This principle provides a strong rationale for the establishment of a diverse Student Leadership Team that is viewed all students as providing inspirational leadership. This principle can also support the encouragement of Hurtful Supporters of the Hurtful Student to step in to tell their friend to stop.

- **Authority.** Under this principle, school staff must make a strong commitment to treat all students with respect. This specifically includes not establish a behavior management approach that publicly shames and excludes certain students. This principle provides support for one of the questions asked of students who have been hurtful in seeking to assist them in accepting personal responsibility. "What would your mom or dad or other adult who you respect think about how you acted?"

- **Scarcity or Loss.** Unfortunately, in too many schools, students who are hurtful are rewarded by their perception that others think they are cool. As the Positive Social Norms approach will reveal the actual accurate thinking of others, the possible loss of reputation or friendships with other students if a more potent principle of influence. A disciplinary action would also constitute for some students, a loss. However, the approach set forth in Chapter 11 seeks to avoid a disciplinary consequence.

REFLECTIVE LISTENING

When school leaders and staff engage in Reflective Listening, this will support students in knowing that they have been heard accurately and that they are supported.

Reflect on the insight from Chapter 3 in the Section on Student Perspectives of Staff Effectiveness and Effectiveness of the "Tell an Adult" Strategy. The overwhelming message from this research is that students do not trust that school staff will provide them with assistance in resolving relationship concerns. The use of Reflective Listening is a very simply approach that will likely result in a significant increase in students perceiving that leadership and staff truly care about their well-being.

A 1994 document entitled *Reflective Listening* by Katz and McNulty, which is available online, provides very excellent guidance on the practice of Reflective Listening.[405] From the Introduction:

> *Listening is following the thoughts and feelings of another and understanding what the other is saying from his or her perspective. Reflective listening is a special type of listening that involves paying respectful attention to the content and feeling expressed in another persons' communication. Reflective listening is hearing and understanding, and then letting the other know that he or she is being heard and understood. It requires responding actively to another while keeping your attention focused completely on the speaker. In Reflective Listening, you do not offer your perspective by carefully keep the focus on the other's need or problem. Thus Reflective Listening consists of a step beyond what is normally thought of as listening:*
>
> 1. *Hearing and understanding what the other person is communicating through words and "body language" to the best of your ability.*
>
> 2. *Responding to the other person by reflecting the thoughts and feelings you heard in his or her words, tone of voice, body posture, and gestures.[406]*

The benefits of Reflective Listening were presented as the following:

1. *It lets the speaker know that (they have) been heard, understood, cared for, and supported.*

2. *It gives the other feedback on what (they) said and how it came across.*

3. *It allows you to check your own accuracy in hearing what the other has said.*

4. *It avoids the illusion of understanding.*

5. *It helps prevent the "mental vacation" in which you are inattentive during the conversation.*

6. *It helps the other focus on self, vent, sort out issues, express feeling, and deal more effectively with emotions.*

7. *It allows the other to move to deeper levels of expression at (their) own pace.*

8. *It helps the other to think and articulate more clearly.*

9. *It helps the other arrive at a solution to their own problem.*

10. *It helps you clarify what you are expected to do.*

11. *It helps you deal effectively with the issue, problem and/or needs the other raised.[407]*

There are also many excellent instructional videos online that provide raining in this practice.

Implementation Strategy

When school leaders or staff are responding to hurtful incidents, the initial response should be to respond using Reflective Listening practices. Maintaining a strict focus on Reflective Listening until the student has reached the point of clarity in their thoughts and emotions will, most importantly, support the student in knowing that they have been truly heard.

The use of Reflective Listening is especially important in any situation where the Targeted Student, the Hurtful Student, a Hurtful Supporter, or a Witness are emotionally distressed or dysregulated. Reflective listening is the best approach to help them to self-regulate.

Chapter 5.
Teen Development

HIGHLIGHTS

- **Development Factors and Hurtful Behavior.** A meta-analysis of bullying prevention programs at the secondary level demonstrated zero effectiveness. The reasons include: developmental changes in the content of bullying, the characteristics of those who bully, the underlying psychological causes of bullying, and finally an overall increase in reactance against controlling adults among adolescents.

- **Teen Brain Development.** The teenage years are the time when young people start to explore and learn about the world. Their brain is still "under development." Challenges can arise in their decision-making—even when they are intent on making good decisions. Key parts of the brain include:

  - **Prefrontal Cortex**. The "thinking center" supports complex decision-making. When this area of the brain is fully functioning, they are able to think clearly, be aware of themself and others, evaluate situations, engage in effective problem solving, and make good decisions. This is the last region of the brain to fully develop.

  - **Anterior Cingulate Cortex**. When the "emotional regulation center" is working well, they are able to manage difficult emotions without being totally overwhelmed. This supports their ability to evaluate situations and make effective decisions.

  - **Hippocampus**. The "memory center" is part of the limbic system which is focused on what is necessary for physical survival. The Hippocampus retains memories so we can learn from experiences. A sad or distressful memory can cause an overreaction to a similar situation.

- **Amygdala.** The job of the "threat response center" is to receive all incoming information—that is everything they see, hear, touch, smell, and taste—and answer one question: "Is this a threat?" When the Amygdala is fully in charge, the thinking center can shut down and become disconnected from the emotional regulation center. It is not possible for students to manage their emotions and engage in effective problem solving.

- **Neurons—the Connections.** Neurons form connections with other neurons called "neural pathways." Neural pathways guide what we think about and how we respond. Experiences guide how our neural pathways are established. If students have more consistent negative experiences, their neural pathways will focus on those negative experiences—undermine happiness and success.

- **Challenges in Thinking and Problem Solving.** The ability of young people to think and solve problems improves with age because the neural pathways that support this are being strengthened. During the teen years, their developing brain can lead to some actions that could raise concerns, including:

  › **Act Without Thinking**. One of the greatest challenge students face is acting without thinking. They are at much greater risk of engaging in impulsive actions if they are upset.

  › **Fail to Predict Consequences of Their Actions**. Teen may fail to predict or recognize the consequences of their actions on others. They may truly believe that they know what someone else is thinking or or how they are feeling—only to find out later that they were wrong.

  › **Susceptible to Peer Influence.** Their focus is much more on how they are perceived by their peers so, they can very susceptible to peer influence.

  › **Follow the Leader.** Teens are highly motivated to gain peer acceptance and not be excluded. This may lead them to think it is necessary to go along with what someone who appears to be a "leader" does—even if this is against their personal values.

- **Identity Development.** The major task in the teen years is the development of a strong and stable sense of self — answering the question "Who am I?" One's identity includes two components: Self-identity—how teens define themselves. Social identity—how teens constructed themselves in reference to others. Intersectionality refers to identification in more than one identity group.

  - **Four Developmental Statuses.** Identity Diffusion —the status of teens or adults who have not made a commitment to a particular identity. Identity Foreclosure—committing to an identity prematurely, without time taken for exploration or choice. Identity Moratorium—a stage of active exploration coupled with low commitment to any particular identity. Identity Achievement— when the teen, having had the opportunity to closely explore an identity, chooses that identity with a high degree of commitment.

- **Identity Development of Students from Marginalized Groups.** Students who are from marginalized groups will have greater challenges in the identity development process. Not only do they have to figure out who they are, they have to figure out who they are in the context of a their social identity in a marginalized group within a dominant culture.

- **Racial and Ethnic Identity Development.** Four identity statuses may occur at any time during adolescence and into adulthood. These are statuses, not steps. Pre-encounter—may not be consciously aware of their race and how it may affect their life. Encounter—has a negative or positive encounter that initiates them into thinking about the role of racial identification. Immersion—searches for information about racial identity and are learning to cope as a member of a racial minority within a dominant culture. Internalization and Commitment—has developed a secure sense of racial identity and is comfortable socializing both within and outside their racial group.

  › **Identity Achievement and Identity Affirmation.** Minority individuals who identify more strongly with their minority group report greater psychological well-being.

  › **Cultural Identity.** Having a strong tie to one's cultural identity can strengthen social support networks within families or communities of shared cultural background.

  › **Oppositional Social Identity.** Those with an oppositional social identity resist certain forms of behavior as characteristic of Whites, and therefore to be avoided.

  › **Sexual or Gender Minority and Autistic Youth.** Sexual or gender minority and autistic youth are very often born into families that might not share their identities. The ability to connect with peers or mentors who share their identity is exceptionally important.

  › **Minority Stress.** The cumulative effect of many types of social stressors relating to the social marginalization experienced by minority group. The cumulative and constant stress contributes to significant mental and physical health concerns.

‣ **Affinity Groups.** Affinity groups allow students who share a marginalized identity to gather, talk in a safe space about issues related to that identity, and transfer that discussion into action that makes for a more equitable experience at school. Establish groups where students within the marginalized group and their allies are invited to participate to avoid legal concerns.

- **Self-Efficacy and Self-Regulation.** Self-efficacy is beliefs about what you can do with your abilities—the self-confidence to perform well and to achieve in specific areas of life including school, work, and relationships. The positive effects of feelings of self-efficacy are many and are long-lasting. Self-regulation is the process through which one controls thoughts, emotions, and actions. Self-regulation is crucial to success and well-being in almost every area of life.

• **Moral Development.** Moral development goes through a series of stages, similar to stages of cognitive development.

- **Preconventional Level.** Lasts until approximately age 9. Children do not have a personal code of morality. Moral decisions are made based on the standards of adults, the consequences of breaking rules, and physical consequences.

- **Conventional Level.** In middle childhood into early adolescence, the child begins to care about how outcomes of behaviors impact others. People value the good that can be derived from social norms, laws, or rules.

- **Postconventional Level.** From adolescence and beyond, people use abstract reasoning and self-chosen ethical principle sto justify behaviors and guide their moral judgement. Only a minority become capable of the abstract thinking necessary.

‣ **Rules and Social Norms.** Teens realize that rules are created by other people and may question their absolute authority. The "rule-based" approach to bullying prevention falls apart. They are attentive to culture and to the social norms they see at home, in school and in the mass media.

• **Traumatic Events.** A traumatic event is an event that threatens a person's life, safety, or well-being or the lives, safety or well-being of people around them. An ongoing traumatic situation is more chronic —ongoing distressing challenges. Both a traumatic event and ongoing distressing challenges are considered a form of trauma.

- **Focus on the Negative.** The human brain developed with a natural tendency to focus on potential danger and risk. Our brains naturally look for bad news, overreact to bad things, and store memories in the Hippocampus so that we can avoid risk in the future. Threat-focused memories and neural pathways can cause students to be overreactive when new challenging situations arise.

- **Threat Response.** If a student's brain detects that a threat may be present, their limbic system takes over. Many students encounter ongoing stressful situations. Their Amygdala is always on alert and their body always has higher levels of the stress hormones, adrenalin and cortisol. They will have a harder time feeling safe, calming down, sleeping, and learning.

  ‣ **Hippocampus Memories.** Increased stress hormones make it more challenging for the Hippocampus to function well. This results in challenges in telling the difference between past and present experiences. Situations that might resemble prior hurtful incidents can cause more intense panic—even though the current situation does not present a significant threat.

  ‣ **Triggering.** When students perceive they might be in danger, they are more likely to trigger. Because their prefrontal cortex has good "off-line" they are not able to think clearly. Because their emotional regulation center has also been affected, they have challenges self-regulating.

- **Neuroplasticity.** Neuroplasticity is a term that describes the brain's ability to change. If a student has feelings of self-confidence and positive connections with supportive others, it is less likely that the traumatic event or other distressing challenge will cause long term damage. It is possible to rewire the brain to achieve greater resilience and empowerment and to overcome the damage past challenging experiences have caused. Neuroplasticity is possible because of the capacity of their brain's neural pathways to change their synaptic connections in response to new information and experiences.

  - **Social Emotional Growth Mindset.** Neuroplasticity is the essence of having a Social Emotional Growth Mindset. Focusing on positive things that are happening can change the brain's neural pathways.

  - **Post Traumatic Growth.** Post Traumatic Growth is positive change that results from having experienced more significant challenges. People who endure psychological struggle following adversity can often see positive growth afterward. They can develop new understandings of themselves and the world they live in, how to relate to other people, the kind of future they might have and a better understanding of how to live life. Sometimes, our greatest enlightenment comes through the pain of our negative experiences.

DEVELOPMENT FACTORS AND HURTFUL BEHAVIOR

The reason for a more specific focus on teens is that as they enter puberty is when some of them become more hurtful. As was discussed in Chapter 2, there is an ethological basis for the hurtful behavior of Dominance Motivated Hurtful Students. As students enter puberty, these factors strongly emerge.

It is helpful that educators recognize the impact of brain development related to hurtful behavior. Note as discussed earlier, a meta-analysis of bullying prevention programs at the secondary level demonstrated zero effectiveness.[408] As Yeager and colleagues stated:

> *Strong developmental theory supports the prediction that anti-bullying programs might be less effective in older age groups compared to younger children. This involves the developmental changes in the content of bullying, the characteristics of those who bully, the underlying psychological causes of bullying, and finally an overall increase in reactance against controlling adults among older adolescents.[409]*

The developmental changes identified by Yeager and colleagues include the following:

- **Personal Identity** Adolescence is a time for developing personal identity and a sense of morality, as well as establishing independence and personal control. Telling teens simply to "Tell an adult" will often fall on deaf ears because this is translated as "admit personal failure."

- **Change in the Nature of Bullying Behavior.** Direct and observable forms of hurtful behavior, such as hitting and insults, decline as students go from elementary level to secondary level. More indirect forms of bullying, such as rumors and exclusion, increase. It is less likely that school staff will notice these more indirect forms of hurtful behavior.

- **Significantly Less Adult Supervision.** Teens are not as closely supervised in secondary school environment. They spend additional time with each other in environments without adult supervision. They are constant users of digital technologies and social media. Reliance on adult supervision is not a viable prevention approach.

- **Changes in Bullying Motivation.** Among younger children, bullying behavior is more often associated with their personal challenges. Students who most frequently bully others at the secondary level are more frequently focused on achieving dominance and social status.

- **Sexual Maturity.** Sexual harassment, disagreements between prospective, current, and former romantic partners, competition over romantic partners, disparagement based on perceived value as a romantic partner, and bullying of gender non-conforming students is frequent at the secondary level. Sexual digital images can be a significant concern.

- **Social Group Formation and Exclusion.** Teens form social groups with others who share their interests that, by their very nature, engage in exclusion. Teens deserve the right to decide who they will hang out with, who they like, and who they do not like. However, this should not lead to hurtful acts of exclusion.

- **Increased Autonomy.** Ample evidence from prevention programs that address smoking and drug abuse demonstrate that adults telling teens to "Just say 'No'" can have an opposite effect of increasing risk behavior.

TEEN BRAIN DEVELOPMENT

The teenage years are the time when young people start to explore and learn about the world.[410] Their brain is still "under development." Because of this, some challenges can arise in their decision-making—even when they are intent on making good decisions. The teen years are a time when they develop their own personal identity and move towards independence. Their brain is developing in the way it should to prepare them for adulthood.

Teens have an overwhelming desire to explore the world. They are also exploring essential questions about themselves—who they are, what skills they have, what directions they want to go in their life, and who they want close relationships with. As a result of how their brain is developing, they may be more likely to engage in behaviors that adults might consider to be "risky." Taking risks is actually a normal part of teen development. Another term for taking risks is "exploration."

Teens have a biologically driven need to explore. Through their explorations, they will acquire experience and become prepared to make the complex decisions they will need to make as an adult. What is important, obviously, is that they do not take risks that could potentially cause harm to their safety and well-being or the safety and well-being of others.

Parts of the Brain

To understand these behaviors, it is helpful to understand what is going on in the brain of the developing teen.[411] It is also very helpful for students to understand the parts of their brain and how they function.

The Prefrontal Cortex or "thinking center" of the brain is located near the top of the head, behind the forehead. The Prefrontal Cortex supports complex decision-making, planning skills, impulse control, and focused attention. When this area of the brain is fully functioning, they are able to think clearly, be aware of themselves and others, evaluate situations, engage in effective problem solving, and make good decisions. They think things through before they act. However, this area of the brain is not fully functional until they are around age 25.

The Anterior Cingulate Cortex or "emotional regulation center" of the brain is located next to the Prefrontal Cortex, but is deeper inside the brain. This area is responsible for regulating emotions. Their emotional regulation center helps them to remain calm. Ideally, their emotional regulation center is working closely with their thinking center. When this connection is working well, they are able to manage difficult thoughts and emotions without being totally overwhelmed. This fully supports their ability to evaluate situations and make effective decisions on how they will respond.

The Hippocampus or "memory center" is part of the limbic system. The limbic system is located deep inside of the brain. This is in an older part of the brain. The limbic system is focused on what is necessary for physical survival. The Hippocampus helps short term memories become long term memories. Remembering helps to learn from experiences to make better decisions the next time a similar situation arises. However, the Hippocampus can also store sad or distressful memories and this can cause them to overreact when a similar situation arises.

The Amygdala or "threat response center" is the other important part of the limbic system. The job of the Amygdala is to receive all incoming information—that is everything they see, hear, touch, smell, and taste— and answer one question: "Is this a threat?"

If the Amygdala detects that a threat may be present, sometimes informed by the Hippocampus because of past threats, the whole body goes into a "fight, flight, or freeze" mode. When this happens, stress hormones of adrenalin and cortisol rush through the body. Heart rate, blood flow, and breathing all increase to increase the ability to run or fight. When the Amygdala is fully in charge, the thinking center can shut down and become disconnected from the emotional regulation center.

This response to a threatening situation is just what we want brains and bodies to do when a physical threat like a dangerous wild animal is present. This response allows people to respond effectively to threats. These days, the threats young people face do not generally involve escaping wild animals. Many of the concerns they face require the ability to manage their emotions and engage in effective problem solving. A problem is that it is not possible to manage their emotions and engage in effective problem solving if they are feeling threatened.

In addition, many of the concerns teens face are more constant—constant pressure for grades or persistent bullying. Their threat response center can get stuck on "threat mode" more consistently. If this is happening to them, this means that stress hormones are always present. As a result, they are hyper vigilant and have difficulties thinking clearly. If they continue in this state, they will experience significant physical and mental health concerns.

Neurons—the Connections

The working parts of their brain are the neurons. Neurons are cells in the brain and nervous system that communicate with each other. Neurons form connections with other neurons that are called "synapses," "synaptic connections," or "neural pathways" to send messages throughout their body. It is said that these neurons are "wired together."

Neural pathways guide what they think about and how they respond. Experiences guide how their neural pathways are established. If they generally experience happiness and success, their neural pathways will be established in a way that will keep them on a happy and successful path. Unfortunately, if they are having more consistent negative experiences, their neural pathways will tend to keep their thinking focused on the negative experiences. This will undermine their happiness and success.

As the brain is developing during the teen years, it is engaged in synaptic pruning and the strengthening of their neural pathways. When someone prunes an apple tree, the weak branches are removed. This results in a healthier tree, with strong branches to bear fruit.

Synaptic pruning is basically the same thing. Pruning reduces weak and unnecessary synaptic connections. This allows more frequently used neural pathways to become stronger. This synaptic pruning occurs in childhood, throughout their teen years, and into early adulthood. The pruning is being facilitated by what they are experiencing.

It is possible to empower students to intentionally create neural pathways that can increase their resilience, empowerment, and happiness, as well as to enable them to more effectively engage in problem solving and action planning.

Challenges in Thinking and Problem Solving

The ability of young people to think and solve problems improves with age because the neural pathways that support this are being strengthened. During the teen years, their brain develops in a manner that emulates the the way in which our brains evolved over centuries. The neural pathways in the older portion of our brain, including the limbic system and the Amygdala, developed earlier. The neural pathways on their Prefrontal Cortex are the last part of their brain to mature. In fact, the synaptic pruning and strengthening in their their Prefrontal Cortex continues until they are around age 25. Even after this age, their brain is continuing to change and develop new and stronger neural pathways.

As their brain matures, the Prefrontal Cortex takes over greater control. They will have much greater ability to think things through before they act. Before the Prefrontal Cortex fully matures, the limbic system and the Amygdala are often more in charge. This means they may be more likely to act in a way that is a reaction, rather than thinking things through.

As their brain continues to develop and they have more experience, they will gain greater awareness, insight, and judgment. Every time they are involved in a new situation, they will learn from that experience and new neural pathways will be established. Their brain will store these memories in their hippocampus. The memory of each experience they have is stored. This helps to guide how they will respond to new similar situations.

As they get older, they will also become better at reasoning. They will be better able to predict the future consequences of their actions. This will support their ability to think and plan ahead. In addition to being better able to reflect on their own thinking, they will get better at detecting how others are motivated, thinking, and feeling.

During the teen years, however, their developing brain can lead to some actions that could raise concerns. These include the following:

- **Act Without Thinking**. One of the greatest challenge students face is acting without thinking. They are at much greater risk of engaging in impulsive actions if they are upset. If they act without thinking, they could cause harm to themselves or others—even if they do not want to cause such harm.

  - It is important that students learn to recognize when they are about to act without thinking and wait until they have calmed down and thought things through before they respond in any situation. This will help them to protect their reputation and relationships. What kinds of situations tend to make them upset? What steps can they take to avoid those situations? How can they recognize when they are in such situation? What plans can they make in advance for how they intend to remain in control of their actions?

- **Fail to Predict Consequences of Their Actions**. Teen may fail to predict or recognize the consequences of their actions on others. Their brain is learning to better understand how others think and feel. They may truly believe that they know what someone else is thinking or or how they are feeling—only to find out later that they were wrong. Knowing how someone else is thinking and feeling can be an especially challenging task when they are using social media. When they use social media, they cannot see how others are reacting. This can make it much more difficult to accurately recognize how others think and feel. They also may not recognize the consequences of their actions on others.

    - A critical component of effective problem solving is predicting the consequences of their actions. What might happen if they choose to act in this way or do this thing? When they pay close attention to the reactions of others, they will be better able to predict and recognize what others are thinking and how they are feeling. This will also help them to recognize the consequences of their actions on others.

- **Susceptible to Peer Influence.** When they were younger, they were more focused on how they were perceived by important adults. During the teen years, their focus is much more on how they are perceived by their peers. Because of this, they can very susceptible to peer influence. The last thing they want is to be excluded by their friends or "put down" by a peer. They may be more likely to engage in risky or inappropriate actions if their friends are also engaging in those actions. If they go to a party where everyone is drinking, they will likely feel compelled to drink also—even if this is not what they think they should do. Teens also may judge their value based on attention from others. Some teens appear to think that their value as a person is determined by how many friends they have. This is especially evident online. Some teens post outrageous material just to get attention. Some may be obsessed with how many "friends" they have or how many "likes" every one of their posts receive.

    - The strength of their focus on peer relationships is one reason why it is very important to encourage them to be careful when choosing which peers they want to have as close friends. Are their friends making the kinds of choices that are in accord with their personal values? Are their friends effectively thinking things through before acting? Are their friends making safe choices and being respectful to others? What is more important to them, the number of friends or the quality of their friendships?

- **Follow the Leader.** Teens often play "follow the leader." They are highly motivated to gain peer acceptance and not be excluded. This may lead they to think that it is necessary to go along with what someone who appears to be a "leader" does—even if this is against their personal values. They may feel even more pressure to do this if other teens follow this person's lead. If a popular student just posted something that is exceptionally hurtful about another student on social media, they may play "follow the leader" and "like" this post or add a hurtful comment. They may feel compelled to do this because if they do not support the popular leader, or if they object, they could be the next target.

  - This is why it is so important to seek to change student's perspectives on leadership—emphasizing the admiration of those who are Prestige Leaders. Schools should also encourage students who are friends of those who are hurtful to seek to influence their friend to stop being hurtful—and to assess their interest in continuing their friendship if they continue to be hurtful. They must understand that their reputation may be negatively impacted if they are viewed as someone who supports one who is being hurtful. This is also why it is so important to hold Hurtful Supporters accountable for the harm they have caused.

IDENTITY DEVELOPMENT

The major task in the teen years is identity development—the development of a strong and stable sense of self.[412] Answering the question "Who am I?" is the major task. Adolescence is the first time that people begin to think about how their identity may affect their lives. However, identity development occurs throughout one's lifetime.[413]

Developmental psychologists have researched multiple different aspects of identity development. This brief section will not come anywhere close to a comprehensive presentation of insight from this field. The focus of this research inquiry has been on identifying research insight that provides guidance on the processes by which teens can become more empowered and resilient. The focus is on identifying protective factors that support healthy identity development, especially for students who are within marginalized groups.

Early in adolescence, cognitive developments result in greater self-awareness and greater awareness of others and their thoughts and judgments.[414] Adolescents also gain the ability to think in abstract, entertain future possibilities, and consider multiple possibilities at once. As a result, they experience a significant shift from the simple and concrete thinking of younger children.

Identity is dynamic and complex, and changes over time. A person's self and social identities grow in response to both internal and external factors.[415] One's identity includes two components:

- **Self-identity.** This is how we define ourselves. During adolescence, the way a teen sees themselves will change in response to influences from their family, peers, school, and other social environments.

- **Social identity.** Social identity is how we view ourselves in reference to others. People can identify with different groups, such as their gender, race, nationality, or political party, and more. Intersectionality refers to identification in more than one identity group.

Erikson is credited for establishing the original framework for understanding identity development in adolescence.[416] His perspective was that adolescents are confronted by a crisis known as identity versus confusion. Marcia developed an expanded theoretical model of identity status.[417] This model proposes adolescents progress through a two-part developmental process that includes both identity exploration and commitment. This developmental process consists of four statuses. This is not a linear process.

- **Identity Diffusion.** The status of teens or adults who have not made a commitment to a particular identity.

- **Identity Foreclosure.** Committing to an identity prematurely, without time taken for exploration or choice.

- **Identity Moratorium.** A stage of active exploration coupled with low commitment to any particular identity.

- **Identity Achievement.** When the teen, having had the opportunity to closely explore an identity, chooses that identity with a high degree of commitment.

During the developmental phase of ages 12 to 25, teens and young adults move from identity diffusion and foreclosure toward moratorium and achievement. A great deal of the identity work is about values and goals —to articulate a personal vision for future objectives.[418] Identity development can be considered an ongoing process. Throughout adulthood, people can move back and forth between Moratorium and Achievement.[419] Among the key identities teens address include gender, sexual, vocational, religious, and political.

Students Within Marginalized Groups

Students who are from marginalized groups will have greater challenges in the identity development process.[420] Not only do they have to figure out who they are, they have to figure out who they are in the context of a their social identity in a marginalized group within a dominant culture.

These students may also be experiencing Identity-Based Bullying , from other students or from staff, as was discussed in Chapters 1 and 2. Unfortunately, in schools in the US, there is ample evidence of discriminatory prejudices that communicate to students from groups that are marginalized in our culture that they are less worthy. Therefore, as these students are asking the question "Who am I? they are also, unfortunately, also asking the question, "Am I worthy?"

It is also important to consider the impact of intersectionality within this discussion. Intersectionality takes into account the multifaceted nature of identities, which could include disabilities, race, ethnicity, gender, sexuality, and class. This intersectionality impacts experiences and development across the a person's lifespan.

As Tatum has pointed out in her seminal book, *Why Are All The Black Kids Sitting Together in the Cafeteria*, in mixed race elementary schools there is generally racial mixing.[421] But once students enter middle school racial clustering begins and continues through high school. Walk into the cafeteria and this racial clustering will be evident.

Most of the research in this area has focused on racial and ethnic identity development. An early model was developed by Cross.[422] Cross identified four identity statuses may occur at any time during adolescence and into adulthood when one's identity is associated with a marginalized group. These are statuses, not steps.

- **Pre-encounter.** The teen may not be consciously aware of their race and how it may affect their life.

- **Encounter.** The teen has a negative or positive encounter that initiates them into thinking about the role of racial identification. For minority youth, this experience is often a negative experience of an act of racism.

- **Immersion.** The teen searches for information about racial identity. They learn about racial identity through interaction with same race peers. At this time, they are learning to cope as a member of a racial minority within a dominant culture.

- **Internalization and Commitment.** At this point, the teen has developed a secure sense of racial identity and is comfortable socializing both within and outside the racial group they identify with.

Ghavami and colleagues proposed that there is an association between identity achievement, that is exploring and understanding the meaning of one's identity, and psychological well-being, that is mediated by identity affirmation.[423] The basis of this research is this understanding:

> *Minority individuals who identify more strongly with their minority group report greater psychological well-being. This association has been shown both for ethnic minority individuals and for lesbians and gay men.[424]*

Two key aspects of identity are considered important.[425] The cognitive aspect of social identity involves exploring and understanding the meaning of one's identity. The affective aspect includes the value and emotional significance one places on group membership and developing positive feelings and a strong sense of belonging to one's social group.

Having a strong tie to one's cultural identity can strengthen social support networks within families or communities of shared background.[426] The social identity theory developed by Tajfel recognizes the idea that feeling connected with a broader social group can enhance sense of self and self-esteem.[427] Emphasizing cultural pride and heritage have been identified as important approaches to support racial minority youth.[428]

Ghavami and colleagues assessed this the achievement-affirmation model with two groups of ethnic minority students and one group of sexual and gender minority students.[429] Their findings were:

> *By distinguishing between identity achievement and identity affirmation, we were able to investigate both their independent and joint contributions to psychological well-being. Our findings are consistent with developmental models of identity formation in showing that the process of identity achievement can serve as an important basis for developing positive feelings about and a sense of belonging to one's minority identity, which in turn contributes to psychological well-being. Moreover, this research confirms the social identity theory view that a sense of affirmation or group pride serves as an important basis for an individual's well-being.[430]*

Conversely, Fordham and Ogbu identified a psychological pattern they identified as oppositional social identity.[431] This is essentially an identity pattern that resists certain forms of behaviors as characteristic of Whites, and therefore to be avoided. A great insult of peers may be that they are "acting white."

More recently, Bothaa and Gillespie-Lynch addressed autistic identity development, using an intersectionality frame.[432] Many people who are autistic are also sexual or gender minorities and may also be racial minorities. Students born into racial and ethnic minorities families are born into a community of those like them. The closeness of the family support may help to protect these students. By comparison, sexual or gender minority and autistic students are very often born into families that might not share their identities. For these students, the ability to connect with peers or mentors who share their identity is exceptionally important. Many are connecting with others using the Internet.

"Minority stress" refers to the cumulative effect of many types of social stressors relating to the social marginalization experienced by minority groups, in addition to the everyday stress of life experienced by the general population.[433] People with marginalized identities often experience disadvantages within society that both shape and are shaped by their identities. The cumulative and constant stress contributes to significant mental and physical health concerns.

In our current society in the US, sexual and gender minorities are under significant attack, especially in more conservative states. The stress if they are also in families where their status would not be welcome is even greater. If students in non-accepting families are also being treated badly at school because of their known or perceived status, the risks of reaching out for help from the school are extremely profound.

Identity Politics

Unfortunately, in today's society, especially in the US but also evidenced elsewhere, identity development of young people is occurring within the context of identity politics. As demographics have changed and minority groups are more aggressively seeking remedies from the discriminatory practices they continue to experience, White people are becoming more anxious. As explained by Chua in her book *Political Tribes:*

> *When groups feel threatened, they retreat into tribalism. When groups feel mistreated and disrespected, they close ranks and become more insular, more defensive, more punitive, more us-versus-them.[434]*

For those on the Left, identity politics is seen as a means to confront and address discriminatory aspects of history and current society. White identity politics that has become mobilized around the idea that Whites are an endangered, discriminated-against group.

Unfortunately, almost no one is standing up for the idea of human identity—where both diversity and unity are welcomed. Engage Students to Embrace Civility has sought to avoid identity politics by focusing on the importance of all students feeling safe, welcomed, and respected.

Affinity Groups

The increased challenges experienced by students who are within marginalized groups has led schools to establish affinity groups for these students. An example of the reason for the establishment of affinity groups was explained in an article from Learning for Justice:

> *They allow students who share an identity—usually a marginalized identity—to gather, talk in a safe space about issues related to that identity, and transfer that discussion into action that makes for a more equitable experience at school. Guidance on the establishment of these groups includes ensuring the staff facilitator allows students to take the lead and focus on how this affinity group can translate the conversations around identity-related issues into action that helps address these issues at your school.[435]*

There is currently a critically important issue related to the establishment of these affinity groups in the US. Actions of some schools in establishing affinity groups are now being regularly challenged by an advocacy group called Parents Defending Freedom.[436] Sometimes, these groups are established in an exclusive manner—only allowing students who are within the marginalized group to participate.

As will be discussed in Chapter 10, this practice is being challenged based on the assertion that this is a violation of civil rights laws. Every school that has been challenged has backed off. In my opinion, rightly so. Schools could not set up a "Whites Only Club." They also cannot set up a "Blacks Only Club." The Gay Straight Alliance Network has established the appropriate path. Students within the marginalized group and their allies are invited to participate.

Self-Efficacy and Self-Regulation

One key aspect of identity is teens' self-concept—their image of who they are. Two components of self-concept appear most relevant: self-efficacy and self-regulation.[437] Self-efficacy refers to a person's belief that they are able to effectively engage in the actions necessary to attain a valued goal. The concept of self-efficacy has become one of the most thoroughly researched concepts in psychology.

Self-efficacy is your beliefs about what you can do with your abilities—your self-confidence to perform well and to achieve in specific areas of life that includes school, work, and relationships. As adolescence is the time when an individual is basically in the process of becoming who they are going to be. The effects of self-efficacy that develop in adolescence are long-lasting. One study found that greater social and academic self-efficacy measured in people ages 14 to 18 predicted greater life satisfaction five years later.[438]

Self-efficacy beliefs are influenced in five different ways:

- **Performance Experiences.** When you do well at a personal and achieve a desired goal, you feel that you will be able to do so in the future.

- **Vicarious Performances.** If someone similar to you succeeds, you think that you will be able to do so also.

- **Verbal Persuasion.** If someone you trust tells you they think you are capable of doing something, you are more likely to think you can.

- **Imaginal Performances.** You might imagine that you are able to do something.

- **Affective States and Physical Sensations.** When you associate positive moods and positive physical sensations with success.[439]

The benefits of a perspective that you have self-efficacy includes academic performance and willingness to strive to achieve moire challenging academic goals; healthy behaviors such as proper diet, exercising, sleep, and safer sex; and athletic performance. A person with strong perspective of personal self-efficacy has greater motivation to perform in areas where they have self-efficacy, are more likely to persevere through challenges in attaining goals, believe that they have more control over a situation and so are more likely to engage in the behaviors that will allow them to achieve their desired goal, and have more confidence in their problem-solving abilities and are able make better decisions, especially in the face of challenges and setbacks.[440]

As will be discussed in Chapter 8, a student's perspective of their self-efficacy is one of critical personal factors in whether they step in to help if they witness a hurtful situation. As discussed in Chapter 6, a research study that investigated the traits of students who experienced bullying at a younger age who were achieving success in high school identified three critical factors, one of which was a "sense of future possibility to persuade them that staying in school, despite the bullying, promised better things to come."[441] This factor is grounded in a perspective of self-efficacy.

Self-efficacy is an important component of self-regulation.[442] Self-regulation is the process through which one controls thoughts, emotions, and actions. Self-regulation is crucial to success and well-being in almost every area of life. Self-regulation is the capacity to change one's responses to bring your responses into line with some ideas about how they should be. People engage in self-regulation in four ways. They control their thinking, their emotions, their impulses, and their task performances. Students who are able to successfully self-regulate will have far greater success in their lives.[443]

MORAL DEVELOPMENT

The teen years is also the time when students are exploring questions about themselves and their values. There is an entire field of research called "moral development."[444] This work was stimulated in the 1980's by Kohlberg's studies on moral judgment.[445] Kohlberg's major premise was that moral development goes through a series of stages, similar to stages of cognitive development. As children develop cognitively, they also go through stages of moral thinking:

- **Preconventional Level.** This is the first stage of moral development, and lasts until approximately age 9. At this level, children do not have a personal code of morality. Moral decisions are made based on the standards of adults and the consequences of following or breaking their rules. Children often make decisions based on the physical consequences of actions.

- **Conventional Level.** In middle childhood into early adolescence, the child begins to care about how outcomes of behaviors impact others. They want to please and be accepted. At this level, people value the good that can be derived from holding to social norms. Generally, social norms are in the form of laws or rules. However, their perceptions about the accepted social norms can also be more informal. Hence, it is at this stage of moral development, that the Positive Social Norms approach can be most effective.

- **Postconventional Level.** From adolescence and beyond, people can use more abstract reasoning to justify behaviors and guide their moral judgement. Moral behavior is based on self-chosen ethical principles that are generally comprehensive and universal, such as justice, dignity, and equality. However, the research indicates that only about 10-15% of people become capable of the kind of abstract thinking necessary. Most people make decisions at the Conventional Level and adopt their moral views based on the views of those around them. Only a minority of people think through ethical principles for themselves.

Most teens are functioning at a Conventional Level of moral development. They are attentive to culture and to the social norms they see at home, in school and in the mass media. When they were younger they were more attentive to the values of their family environment. As noted, during teen years, the social norms of peers have a much greater influence. This includes what are acceptable qualities, values, and actions of those who they associate with.

They should be encouraged that when they see that someone has done something hurtful or is engaging in some other behaviors that are inappropriate, they ask themselves: "Is this in accord with my personal values?" "Do I want to be a follower of someone who is hurtful or does things I think are wrong?" They can be encouraged to decide what qualities in others they think are important at times that they are considering following their leadership.

In addition, because of their emerging cognitive development, they are able to realize that rules are created by other people. As a result, teens begin to question the absolute authority of parents, schools, government, and other traditional institutions.[446]

This is the time that the "rule-based" approach to bullying prevention falls apart. Students are told by their schools that there is a rule that they not engage in bullying. What is "bullying?" Try reading your school policy to see if this yields a firm understanding. On top of this lack of clarity, if someone is hurtful to them and they report to the school, the standard response in many schools is, "That is not bullying, so there is nothing I can do."

TRAUMATIC EVENTS

A traumatic event is an event that threatens a person's life, safety, or well-being or the lives, safety or well-being of people around them. A traumatic event is very stressful incident that has a significant, immediate impact on their emotional state. An ongoing traumatic situation is more chronic—ongoing distressing challenges. Both a traumatic event and ongoing distressing challenges are considered a form of trauma. NCTSN has excellent resources for educators on youth trauma.[447]

The human brain developed with a natural tendency to focus on the negative—to focus on potential danger and risk. This was necessary for survival. If they were a cave man, failure to note that a dangerous animal was close by could result in their death. Our brains naturally look for bad news, overreact to bad things, and do a really good job of storing memories of those bad things in their Hippocampus so that we can avoid risk in the future. Our brains will naturally pay more attention to the bad than to the good.

What is also happening is that those neurons that keep "firing together," to deal with the ongoing stressful situation, end up getting "wired together." This results in their brain creating neural pathways that cause them to be even more focused on potential threats and bad things. Instead of developing neural pathways that will support their success and happiness, their neural pathways are being formed in a way that seeks to ensure their survival in a dangerous world. These threat-focused neural pathways will cause them to be even more overreactive every time any new challenging situation arises.

As was discussed earlier, if their brain detects that a threat may be present, their limbic system and Amygdala take over. Their whole body goes into a fight, flight, or freeze mode. This response to a threatening situation is just what we want our brains to do when a threat is present, because this allows our physical bodies to respond effectively to that threat.

Unfortunately, many students encounter ongoing stressful situations. If they are experiencing distressing challenges, their Amygdala is always on alert and their body always has higher levels of the stress hormones, adrenalin and cortisol.

When their Amygdala is over-activated, they can experience chronic stress, fear, and anxiety. They will also have a harder time feeling safe, calming down, sleeping, or learning. Recall that their Hippocampus is in charge of the storage and retrieval of memories, as well as telling the difference between past and present experiences. The increased stress hormones make it more challenging for their Hippocampus to function well.

This can cause them to have more challenges in telling the difference between past and present experiences. Situations that might resemble prior hurtful incidents can cause more intense panic and fear—even though the current situation does not present a threat or that much of a threat.

Their brain has become filled with neural pathways that are trying to help protect them from danger. Painful memories can become reactivated by different "cues" from the outside world. This might be how someone looks at them or even being in a place where someone was hurtful to them in the past. They are always alert to when someone might be hurtful to them. They pay closer attention to who is around them and where they are so that they are prepared to respond. They are hyper vigilant.

Their brain has less of an ability to figure out whether a current situation is actually threatening or to determine how threatening the situation actually is. Their brain may translate a minor hurtful incident as being a more significant incident. They can be more easily triggered by a situation that they perceive to present a threat, even when no threat is present.

When they perceive that they might be in danger, they are more likely to trigger. They may respond in a way that is an overreaction—an outburst. At these times, they are reacting, not thinking. This is because the chemicals in their brain are preparing them to fight or run from that dangerous animal.

Their prefrontal lobe is not engaged. They are not able to think clearly. Because their emotional regulation center has also been affected, even when they want to calm down and feel better, they just can not do so. They are likely to have greater difficulties with concentration and attention. They are less able to think clearly. Because of this, they likely will have a harder time learning and remembering what they have learned. Because their brain is primed to look for the bad and potential threats, they may also not see the good things that are happening to them. If they are always worried about someone saying something hurtful to them, they may very well miss the fact that someone just smiled at them.

Teens respond to trauma and distressing challenges in different ways. This depends on the individual, as well as their past experiences, their levels of support, and what is happening. Experiencing a traumatic event or ongoing distressing challenges might leave a student with many legitimate questions about safety and control over their life. If they have been experiencing this and they have become emotionally distressed, it is important they talk with a trusted adult. Sometimes, it is hard to for them to recognize or acknowledge the symptoms of traumatic distress in themselves and to take actions to get help.

Neuroplasticity

The level of challenges teens face in their life varies from teen to teen. The degree to which a teen is impacted by trauma or other distressing challenges can also vary. If a teen has feelings of self-confidence and positive connections with supportive others, it is less likely that the traumatic event or other distressing challenge will cause long term damage. Even if they have experienced a traumatic event or another distressing challenges, is possible to change their brain so that the harm can be overcome. They can rewire their brain to achieve greater resilience and empowerment and to overcome the damage past challenging experiences have caused their brain to function.

Neuroplasticity is a term that describes the brain's ability to change. Neuroplasticity is possible because of the capacity of their brain's neural pathways to change their synaptic connections in response to new information and experiences. Even if neural pathways have formed in a way that keep their brain functioning in a hyper vigilant manner, with a focus on possible threats and a tendency to trigger, their brain does not have to remain in this way. Their brain can create new neural pathways that support greater calmness and happiness.

Neuroplasticity is the essence of being able to have a Social Emotional Growth Mindset. This is a very important concept to impart to students. By focusing on positive things that are happening in their life, they can change their brain's neural pathways. The key important insight into changing their brain relates to how their brain focuses more attention on negative, rather than positive experiences but that if they intentionally focus more on the positive, they can actually rewire their brain.

To rewire their brain to achieve greater resilience and empowerment, it is necessary to maintain significant focused attention on the positive things that are happening in their life. This rewiring is not going to happen rapidly. This will require intentional focused effort on their part. But this is possible. They can rewire their brain to be happier. They can rewire their brain so that they do not trigger and become dysregulated.

Post Traumatic Growth

Post Traumatic Growth is positive change that results from having experienced more significant challenges. Post-traumatic growth is a theory that explains how people can experience a transformation following trauma. Note that this also is a Social Emotional Growth Mindset.

This theory was developed by Tedeschi and Calhoun, PhD, in the mid-1990s.[448] The theory holds that people who endure psychological struggle following adversity can often see positive growth afterward. They can develop new understandings of themselves and the world they live in, how to relate to other people, the kind of future they might have and a better understanding of how to live life. There are seven areas of growth have been reported to arise from responding to adversity:

- *Greater appreciation of life*
- *Greater appreciation and strengthening of close relationships*
- *Increased compassion and altruism*
- *The identification of new possibilities or a purpose in life*
- *Greater awareness and utilization of personal strengths*
- *Enhanced spiritual development*
- *Creative growth.*[449]

When students are experiencing challenges, help them to look for the gems of insight they can gain that can help they to become an empowered person. Sometimes, our greatest enlightenment comes through the pain of our negative experiences.

Chapter 6.
Positively Powerful— Empowerment of Students

HIGHLIGHTS

- **Overall Empowerment Approach.** The objective of the positively powerful approach is to help young people gain dandelion-like qualities--the ability to grow and bloom anywhere. Students who are treated badly are often considered "misfits" who may always face the possibility of being treated badly. We must support them to reduce hurtful actions directed to them, respond effectively when this does occur, and not be unduly emotionally harmed as a result.

- **Positively Powerful Strategies.** There are a common set of factors that predispose children to positive outcomes in the face of significant adversity. These factors include the following: The availability of at least one stable, caring, and supportive relationship between a child and the important adults. A sense of mastery over their life circumstances. Strong executive function and self-regulation skills. Affirming faith or cultural traditions.

  - **Objective.** The objective of Positively Powerful strategies is to support students' resilience when things get tough and to increase their positive and happy feelings of empowerment. Each Positively Powerful Strategy will help students to form neural pathways that will help them to become more resilient and empowered. It is important for them to strive to focus on the positive things happening in their life, their strengths, and their successes. The Positively Powerful Strategies are:

- **Make Positive Connections**. I maintain positive connections with good friends and trusted adults.

- **Reach Out To Be Kind.** I reach out to be kind to others. Being kind to others will help to build a kind community around me.

- **Build and Use My Strengths.** I have many positive strengths. I use my strengths every day and when things get tough. I build new strengths and a positive future for myself.

- **Be Thankful.** I am thankful for the good things that are happening to me every day. I express my gratitude.

- **Be Mindful and Remain Calm.** I take time each day to achieve calmness and focus. If things get tough, I remain calm.

- **Keep My Personal Power.** I hold myself tall and strong. I do not allow what happens to me control how I think about myself or respond.

- **Think Things Through.** In any challenging situation, I think things through to decide what is best to do.

- **The Magic 5:1 Ratio**. For these strategies to work will require constant intentional repetition for a period of time. It is said that it takes five "positives" to undo one "negative."

- **Positively Powerful Happiness Thinking Questions.** The Questions are: Who did you have a positive connection with? Who were you kind to? What did you do that you are proud of? What happened to make you happy?

- **Positively Powerful Check In-Check Out.** A Positively Powerful CI-CO approach can be established for any student experiencing significant challenges—with a focus on these positive strategies.

- **Make Positive Connections.**

  - **Research Insight.** Positive connections with both good friends and trusted adults support student's emotional well-being and happiness. Students who have good friends appear to experience less distress if treated badly. Having a close connection with a trusted adult is the foundation for youth resilience.

  - **Core Insight for Students.** Good friends and trusted adults are people I can have fun with and who will provide me with support if things get tough. To have good friends, it is important that I am a good friend. To find new friends, I can be active doing the things I enjoy doing. I can find good friends and trusted adults who I feel comfortable talking with when things get tough and who will help me think things through to decide what I should do.

- **School-Based Activities.**

  ‣ **Relationship Mapping.** Ensure every student has one or more staff members who maintain a close connection with them.

  ‣ **Community Circle Time.** Will both increase positive staff-student connections and positive student-student connections.

  ‣ **Positive Acknowledgement.** The ideal is that students regularly receive 5 positive comments to every 1 negative comment or correction.

- **Positively Powerful CI-CO Strategy.** Evening: What friends or trusted adults did you have a positive connection with today?

• **Reach Out to Be Kind.**

  - **Research Insight.** Being kind to others results in a significant increase in feelings of happiness. Kindness is contagious. Being kind helps people feel stronger, more energetic, calmer, less depressed, and leads to increased feelings of self-worth.

    ‣ **Peer Acceptance.** Prosocial behavior is associated with academic achievement and social acceptance. Students who are consistently kind have higher levels of peer acceptance.

  - **Core Insight for Students.** Every day, I will reach out to be kind to others and spread kindness online by posting or sending positive comments to others. I know that that when I reach out to be kind, this increases happiness of the other person and my own happiness. Being kind to others will build a kind community around me. Being kind to others sets me on a path to a positive future of being of service and contributing to good in the world.

  - **School-Based Activities.**

    ‣ **School-Wide Kindness Activities.** The Student Leadership Team should focus on school-wide kindness activities.

    ‣ **Students with Challenges Positive Action Plan.** Strongly encourage challenged students to reach out to be kind to others at least 3 to 5 times a day, in person and online.

    ‣ **Accountability Process.** Require hurtful students to remedy the harm to the school by reaching out to be kind 3 to 5 times times a day.

  - **Positively Powerful CI-CO Strategy.** Morning: remind the student to reach out to be kind. Evening: ask the student to describe the times they were kind.

- **Build and Use My Strengths**.

  - **Research Insight.** Students who focus on their strengths and future directions are more resilient in response to challenges.

  - **Core Insight for Students.** I use my strengths every day and when things get tough. I know that situations and people can change and that every day in every way I can become better and better. I build new strengths and focus on my positive future. I use my strengths to create personal goals, take steps to achieve those goals, and effectively respond to challenges along the way. I make a positive difference in the world.

  - **School-Based Activities.**

    - **Character Strengths.** Have secondary students complete the VIA Institute on Character Character Strengths survey. Use Community Circles to discuss strengths. Ask students how they could use different strengths in challenging situations. Focus on one character strength a week.

    - **Social Emotional Growth Mindset.** Ensure Growth Mindset activities and messages incorporate social emotional growth.

  - **Positively Powerful CI-CO.** Morning: remind the student to use one of their strengths that day. Evening: ask the student to how they used one of their strengths or what they did that they were proud of. Encourage growth mindset language.

- **Be Thankful.**

  - **Research Insight.** Students who have positive feelings about themselves are less likely to demonstrate perceived weakness that could lead to being targeted and can better avoid thinking badly of themselves if this occurs. A consistent focus on the good things happening in their lives can help to support these positive feelings.

    - *Hardwiring Happiness* **Strategy**. To rewire the brain to be more happy. **Step 1. Have a Good Experience.** Either notice that something good has happened or create a positive experience. **Step 2. Enrich It.** Keep thinking about this experience for at least 10 seconds or longer. Feel the positive experience in your body. **Step 3. Absorb It.** Think about this positive experience as being absorbed deeply into your being.

  - **Core Insight for Students.** I am thankful for the good things that are happening to me every day. I take the time to notice people who make me feel happy, great things that happen, and what I do that I am proud of. I bring the happiness from those good things that happen into my heart. I keep a gratitude journal to maintain a focus on the positive things happening in my life.

- **School Based Activities.**

  ‣ **Gratitude Activities.** Another activity of a Student Leadership Team should be on school-wide gratitude activities.

- **Positively Powerful CI-CO.** Morning: remind the student to pay attention to the good things that happen. Evening: ask to describe a good thing that happened and to take a moment to feel the good feelings again. Encourage writing of thank you notes.

• **Be Mindful and Remain Calm.**

- **Research Insight.** Self-regulation is an essential skills when one is treated badly and to reduce the potential for impulsive retaliation. The practice of mindfulness creates the neural pathways to improve students' ability to self-regulate.

  ‣ **Mindfulness.** Research in mindfulness has identified a wide wide range of benefits in different areas of psychological health.

  ‣ **Self-Regulation.** Schools must have a comprehensive approach to support student self-regulation.

    - **Trauma Informed.** It is necessary to have a trauma informed understanding of what is happening when a student becomes dysregulated, as was discussed in Chapter 5.

    - **Social Emotional Growth Mindset.** Assure students they can change how they react when something has triggered them. The goal is to "flatten the curve"—to go from trigger, to slight escalation, back to calm—without an outburst.

    - **Approach.** Assist students to gain understanding about what triggers them. Then, identify the specific steps they can take to avoid going from a trigger to an outburst.

- **Core Insight for Students.** When I stay calm, I can handle the rough spots in life. I take time every day to become calm and mindful. I know what triggers me to get upset and know what I can do when this happens so I can stay calm and in control. If things get tough, I take a deep breath to stay calm and walk away to a place that is safe. If I get angry online, I do not respond until I have calmed.

- **School Based Activities.**

  ‣ **Mindfulness Practices in Schools.** Many sites provide excellent guidance on mindfulness practices in schools.

- ‣ **Happiness Thinking Mindfulness.** Have students practice mindfulness for a minute upon coming into class. Use a short guided meditation with the Happiness Thinking Questions.

- ‣ **De-escalation Strategies.** All school staff and students should be trained to understand the process by which anyone might become dysregulated and in effective de-escalation strategies. The strategies that must be avoided can be remembers by this term: TACOS: Threats. Arguments. Commands or criticism. Orders. Shaming.

- **Positively Powerful CI-CO.** Morning: Happiness Thinking Questions mindfulness activity. Remind them to calm when entering each new situation. Mention self-regulation strategies and their plan. Evening: ask if they had any challenges and how they responded. Rethink strategies if necessary. Celebrate success.

- **Keep My Personal Power.**

  - **Research Insight.** It is necessary to increase students' level of personal power. There are three strategies students can use.

    - ‣ **Hold Myself Tall.** Adopting a physical position that indicates power can result in increased feelings of confidence.

    - ‣ **Control My Thinking.** Students will never be able to control when or if someone might treat them badly, but they do have the ability to control their thinking about how they feel about themselves and how they respond in these challenging situations. This is how they can keep their personal power.

    - ‣ **Maintain a Positive Presence.** They can maintain a positively powerful presence by being known to be kind, respectful, and inclusive. When they use social media, they need to be careful about what they post or send because this can be forwarded to anyone and become permanent.

  - **Core Insight for Students.** I hold myself tall and am proud of who I am. I know that while I can't control what might happen to me, I can control what I think about myself and how I respond. I maintain a positive presence by being known as kind, respectful, and inclusive. I take care about what I post or send using social media, because this can be forwarded and become permanent. I maintain my positively powerful personal presence.

  - **Personal Power Activities in School.** Have students practice "feeling small" and "holding themself tall and proud. The Control My Thinking approach should be transmitted more informally.

- **Positively Powerful CI-CO.** Morning: practice "holding themselves tall." Remind them of the transitions strategy. Remind to keep their personal power—never give any other person the power to control what they think about themselves and respond.

- **Think Things Through.**

  - **Research Insight.** When students gain effective problem solving skills they are more resilient in figuring out how to respond if they are faced with any kind of a challenge. When they think things through, this is the opposite of acting without thinking.

    ‣ **Effective Problem Solving.** Four key interpersonal cognitive problem solving skills are: Means-ends thinking to reach a stated interpersonal goal by planning a step-by-step, sequenced means to reach that goal. Alternative solution thinking to identify alternative solutions to a stated problem. Consequential thinking to consider what might happen in certain situations. Weighing pros and cons to decide whether to carry out an act.

    ‣ These are the steps that are necessary to engage in effective problem solving: What is the situation? What do I want to accomplish? What strategies could I use? Is each in accord with my values and does each use my strengths? For each, what might happen? What is my best choice? How should I proceed? Did this work? What else could or should I do? Many times it is helpful to make a positive connection with a friend or trusted adult to think things through. They can also use this think things through strategy as part of a team.

  - **Core Insight for Students.** I can think things through to decide what to do. I ask these questions: What happened? What is my goal? What could I do? What might happen if I do this? I pick the best strategy, realizing that this might not work. I keep thinking things through until I succeed. I ask a good friend or trusted adult to help me think things through.

  - **Personal Power Activities in School.** Effective problem solving using the above strategy should be integrated into all aspects of instructional activities. The problem solving approach set forth above can be a valuable guide.

  - **Positively Powerful CI-CO.** Morning: ask if there are any challenges or problems they anticipate having to deal with during the day. Then, think things through to develop a strategy they can implement. At the end of the day, ask what challenges arose and how they thought things through to figure out what to do.

OVERALL EMPOWERMENT APPROACH

Essentially, the objective of the positively powerful approach is to help young people gain greater dandelion-like qualities--the ability to grow and bloom anywhere. Dandelion-like qualities are the essence of resilience.

This Chapter provides guidance on how to increase the resilience and empowerment of all students, especially those who are being more routinely treated badly. As was discussed in Chapter 1, students who are treated badly are often considered "misfits." They have aspects of their identity that, because of hurtful society norms, result in being looked upon as "less desirable." This includes both Targeted Students and Marginalized Hurtful Students.

Many of these students are within an identity group that is marginalized in our society. Most of these identity aspects are simply not going to change. With the recent rise in white nationalism, it appears that society has a long way to go in changing its norms of inclusion.

Nevertheless, as it is not possible for most students to change their identities and we remain a long way from social acceptance. This creates a reality that some students will always face the possibility that they will be treated badly—if not in school, elsewhere in society.

These students also face the toxic stress of knowing what is happening elsewhere that is harmfully impacting those who are within their identity group. Every shooting of a black person by a police officer, every statute that places restrictions on transgender youth, every political leader who argues against "woke" curriculum creates a moment of toxic stress for these students.

Thus, our challenge as educators is to empower students who are more likely to be targeted with a sufficient level of resilience and empowerment so that these anticipated negative incidents do not cause undue harm to their well-being. A primary focus in the effort is to support these students to reduce the level of hurtful actions directed to them, respond effectively when this does occur, and not be unduly emotionally harmed as a result.

However, a focus on student empowerment must go beyond just the students who are more often targets of hurtful behavior, including both Targeted Students and Marginalized Hurtful Students. All students will be benefitted by an increase in their personal power. This includes Dominance Motivated Hurtful Students who can hopefully see a more positive path to achieve the leadership goals they have, as well as Witnesses who are more likely to step in to help when they see a hurtful incident unfolding.

This Chapter sets forth the core insight into these issues and strategies to increase students' resilience, empowerment, and happiness. This insight can support all students.

Positively Powerful Strategies

The National Scientific Council on the Developing Child, associated with the Center on the Developing Child at Harvard University is a multidisciplinary, multi-university collaboration designed to bring the science of early childhood and early brain development to bear on public decision-making.[450] This statement on the foundations of resilience is from their excellent Working Paper 13.[451]

> *Multiple lines of research have identified a common set of factors that predispose children to positive outcomes in the face of significant adversity. These factors encompass strengths that derive from the child, the family, peer and adult relationships, and the broader social environments that build and support sturdy brain architecture. When these positive influences are operating effectively, they "stack the scale" with positive weight and optimize resilience. When these positive factors are absent, disrupted, or undermined, there is little to counterbalance the negative effects of significant adversity, thus creating the conditions for poor outcomes and diminished life prospects. These counter-balancing factors include the following:*
>
> - *The availability of at least one stable, caring, and supportive relationship between a child and the important adults in his or her life. These relationships begin in the family, but they can also include neighbors, providers of early care and education, teachers, social workers, or coaches, among many others.*
>
> - *Helping children build a sense of mastery over their life circumstances. Those who believe in their own capacity to overcome hardships and guide their own destiny are far more likely to adapt positively to adversity.*
>
> - *Children who develop strong executive function and self-regulation skills. These skills enable individuals to manage their own skills and emotions and develop and execute adaptive strategies to cope effectively with difficult circumstances.*
>
> - *The supportive context of affirming faith or cultural traditions. Children who are solidly grounded within such traditions are more likely to respond effectively when challenged by a major stressor or severely disruptive experience.*

The objective of these Positively Powerful strategies is to support students' resilience when things get tough and to increase their positive and happy feelings of empowerment. Resilience means "bouncing back" from difficult experiences and the ability to feel happy and be successful, even after something difficult or bad has happened.[452] Becoming empowered is a process of becoming strong and confident—allowing them to control their life and make their own decisions.

Each of these Positively Powerful Strategies will help students to form neural pathways that will help them to become more resilient and empowered. If they take the time to intentionally develop these inner strengths this can help them recover from pain they have experienced, cope with new challenges, maintain their emotional well-being, and move forward to a happy and successful life.

To build these strengths it is important for them to strive to focus on the positive. The goal is to increase the amount of time that they are focused on the positive things happening in their life, the strengths they are building, and the successes they are having. When they intentionally focus on these positive experiences, their brain will develop neural pathways that will make lasting positive changes in how their brain functions. These positive focused neural pathways will support their ongoing success and happiness. By intentionally focusing on the positive, they are building the neural pathways in their brain that will support their positive future.

The Positively Powerful Strategies presented in this Chapter are:

- **Make Positive Connections**. I maintain positive connections with good friends and trusted adults.

- **Reach Out To Be Kind.** I reach out to be kind to others. I know this makes us both feel happier.

- **Build and Use My Strengths.** I have many positive strengths. I use my strengths every day and when things get tough. I build new strengths and a positive future for myself.

- **Be Thankful.** I focus on the good things happening in my life. I am thankful and express my gratitude.

- **Remain Calm.** I take time each day to achieve calmness and focus. If things get tough, I remain calm.

- **Keep My Personal Power.** I hold myself tall and strong. I do not allow what happens to me control how I think about myself or respond.

- **Think Things Through.** In any challenging situation, I think things through to decide what is best to do.

The Magic 5:1 Ratio

These Positively Powerful Strategies have been demonstrated by the research outlined in the following sections to be effective. However, they will not work immediately. For these strategies to work will require constant intentional repetition for a period of time. Only then will they start to see positive results.

There appears to be a "magic formula." It is said that it takes five "positives" to undo one "negative." Every time they have a negative experience or thought, they should strive to counter the negative neural pathways this may have established by focusing on five positive things.

I have heard about this "magic 5:1 ratio" often—never with citations. The original research apparently arose in the arena of marital relationships.[453] As explained:

> To understand the difference between happy and unhappy couples, Dr. Gottman and Robert Levenson began doing longitudinal studies of couples in the 1970s. They asked couples to solve a conflict in their relationship in 15 minutes, then sat back and watched. After carefully reviewing the tapes and following up with them nine years later, they were able to predict which couples would stay together and which would divorce with over 90% accuracy.
>
> Their discovery was simple. The difference between happy and unhappy couples is the balance between positive and negative interactions during conflict. There is a very specific ratio that makes love last.
>
> That "magic ratio" is 5 to 1. This means that for every negative interaction during conflict, a stable and happy marriage has five (or more) positive interactions.[454]

There are several strategies students could be coached to use to increase their positive focus. These include:

- **Keep a Daily Journal.** It is recommended that students obtain a notebook to keep as their Journal. For many of these strategies, it will be suggested that they either take specific actions during the day, accomplish certain tasks, or reflect on what happened. It is helpful to write this on paper, rather than in digital format. This appears to help rewire their neural pathways when they write on paper. Alternatively, this journalling can take place in a Positively Powerful CI-CO interaction at school.

- **Use Transitions Strategies.** Students can use transition times to remind them to focus on certain positive actions. Transition times are the times when them are changing activities—like going from one class to another or leaving home to go to school. Some examples:

  - **Keep Their Personal Power.** They do this by holding themselves tall—paying attention to their physical posture. Just before they walk into school or get out of their seat to go to a new class, remind themselves to hold themselves tall.

  - **Be Mindful.** They do this by maintaining calmness. Remind them that when they sit down in class to take just a minute to breathe deeply to achieve mindfulness.

- **Reach Out to be Kind**. Encourage them to reach out to be kind to someone every day. They can also do this online. Every time they look on social media site, they can take the time to positively comment on someone's post or to send a message of thanks to someone.

What is happening in their brain every time they think to themselves, "hold myself tall," take a minute to achieve mindfulness, or Reach Out to Be Kind, is that a new positive neural pathway has been formed.

Positively Powerful Happiness Thinking Questions

The Positively Powerful Happiness Thinking Questions are the first four Positively Powerful strategies.

- Who did you have a positive connection with?

- Who were you kind to?

- What did you do that you are proud of?

- What happened to make you happy?

Several classroom strategies could be used in classrooms, homerooms, or advisories to focus on the Positively Powerful Happiness Thinking Question.

- Have the students engage in the Positively Powerful Thinking Questions as a class mindfulness activity, that is presented in the section Be Mindful and Calm below. Alternatively, this guided mindfulness session could be used with the entire school at the beginning of the day—asking to reflect on the previous day.

- Have a number of craft sticks and on each write the Positively Powerful Thinking Questions. Pass the sticks around during a Community Circle. Each student can pick one stick provide a response to the Question on that stick. If they do not have a response to this Question, they should be allowed to select another stick. Or if they have a burning desire to provide a response to a specific Question, allow them to do so.

- Have Positive Thinking Journal for every student. At the end of the day in elementary school ask them to write in this journal. "Today I: Made a positive connection with … Reached out to be kind to … Am proud that I … Was happy because …" Younger students could draw a picture.

Positively Powerful Check In-Check—Check-Out

Concerns about the use of CI-CO behavior cards were addressed in Chapter 3. It is recommended that schools consider the establishment of a Positively Powerful CI-CO approach for any student experiencing significant challenges. This includes Targeted Students and Marginalized Hurtful Students. The Positive Action Plan set forth in Chapter 11 is version of this practice.

As with a traditional CI-CO, students have some time they can check in with a Positively Powerful CI-CO mentor in the morning. Then, they also check out at the end of the day.

Keep in mind the "Magic 5:1 Ratio." The Positively Powerful CI-CO should be seen as a way to significantly enhance the student's experiences with positive. Reflect on how many negatives each of these students have experienced in their lives. For every negative, they need to experience 5 positives.

RESILIENCE STRATEGIES

The following are the seven Positively Powerful strategies.

Make Positive Connections

I will maintain positive connections with good friends and trusted adults.

Positive connections with both good friends and trusted adults are important for student's emotional well-being and happiness. Students who have good friends appear to experience less distress if treated badly. Having a close connection with a trusted adult is the foundation for youth resilience.

Friendships Insight

Research has clearly documented that students who are bullied, but who have supportive friends, experience less distress.[455]

There have been relatively few studies that have examined the link between friendship and important outcomes. A recent study by Lu and colleagues studied the importance of adult friendships through around the world.[456] This introduction to the importance of friendships also clearly holds true for young people:

Friendships enrich our lives in many ways. Friends give us both practical and emotional support when we need it. As a result, there are many emotional and physical health benefits of friendships—the more people prioritize friendships, the happier and healthier they are. ...

There is a reliable link between social support and mental and physical health across the lifespan, and one important source of support is our friends. Friends provide us with a strong sense of companionship, mitigate feelings of loneliness, and contribute to our self-esteem and life satisfaction. Perceiving greater support from friends is associated with a greater sense of purpose and control over one's life. In terms of predicting health, friendship occasionally predicts health to an equivalent and, in some cases, larger degree compared to spousal and parent–child relationships. Friends also help individuals institute healthy behaviors in their own lives. ...

However, friendship is not universally good for individuals—depression and negative health behaviors can also spread through friend networks. ... In sum, friends play a significant role in people's mental and physical well-being, for better and for worse.

Insight on Friendships to Impart to Students

To discuss friendships with students.

Having good friends can help you feel great about yourself and have more fun in your life. Having good friends also is very helpful if you are facing any challenges. Being able to get support from friends and talking through what has happened to decide what you might need to do can be exceptionally helpful.

To have good friends, you have to put forth the effort. No one is going to come knocking on your door to ask you to be your friend. When interacting with people, remember to smile and Reach Out to Be Kind. Smiling is an invitation to others that you want to interact with them.

Strive not to keep yourself in a "bubble." Present yourself as someone who wants to get to know other people. When you are around people, avoid focusing on your smart phone.

Be the friend that you want to have. Treat people the way you want to be treated. Be available to your friends when they need you. Make sure you are giving as much to your friend as you are getting from them. Let your friends know that you believe in them and support them.

The biggest barrier to finding new friends is fear of rejection. The best way to deal with that fear is to not place a high priority on achieving closer relations with everyone you interact with. Just focus on getting to know others better and reaching out to be kind to them. If a friendship happens, this is great. If it turns out that this person is not interested in a closer relationship, that is also fine. You can both get to know each other —without any more extensive expectations.

The best way to find new friends is by engaging in activities that you are interested in. Get involved in these activities with the idea of enjoying the activity—and possibly making a new friend. Do not create pressure for yourself that you intend to make a new friend. Just enjoy being with people who have fun doing the same things you like to do.

Give your friends space. Everybody needs time by themselves. Don't expect too much of your friend's time and attention. Don't be offended if they turn you down because they are busy or need some alone time. If you keep up with your own interests and have a wider circle of friends, you can share time with one or more friends depending on the circumstances.

Realize that friendship break-ups happen. This is a normal part of life. This does not mean that anything is wrong with either of you. If you have a friendship break-up, do not allow your pain to turn to anger and attack. Let go of your feelings of hurt by forgiving the other person. Forgiveness is something you do for yourself, to allow you to release and let go.

As hard as it may be, accept that the friendship is over, acknowledge it was meaningful, and take time to feel sad. Practice something kind to say about what happened if someone asks. Keep yourself busy doing things that you enjoy. Be open to meet new people.

- **Think About What Friendship Means to You.** What qualities would you like to have in a friend? Do you consistently act in this way with your friends and others?

- **Conduct a Friendship Audit and Create an Action Plan.** Who are your current friends? What interests do you share? What are the strengths of these friendships? What are any weaknesses? How can you build on these strengths? How can you make new friends? Create an action plan to increase your positive friendships.

- **Enjoy Your Interests to Find New Friends.** What are you interested in and what do you like to do? Is there a club at school you might want to join or a class you might want to take? Is there an after-school center, program, or class you could go to?

Trusted Adults Insight

The importance of positive connections with trusted adults cannot be overemphasized.[457] This statement is from the Harvard Center on the Developing Child's Working Paper 13. It is my strong recommendation that this paper be distributed to school staff.

Decades of research in the behavioral and social sciences have produced a rich knowledge base that explains why some people develop the adaptive capacities to overcome significant adversity and others do not. Whether the burdens come from the hardships of poverty, the challenges of parental substance abuse or serious mental illness, the stresses of war, the threats of recurrent violence or chronic neglect, or a combination of factors, the single most common finding is that children who end up doing well have had at least one stable and committed relationship with a supportive parent, caregiver, or other adult. These relationships provide the personalized responsiveness, scaffolding, and protection that buffer children from developmental disruption. They also build key capacities—such as the ability to plan, monitor and regulate behavior, and adapt to changing circumstances— that enable children to respond to adversity and to thrive. This combination of supportive relationships, adaptive skill-building, and positive experiences constitutes the foundations of what is commonly called resilience.[458]

The CDC has also identified "connectedness" as key to addressing the concerns of youth suicide, which is an identified risk for students being and engaging in bullying.

(R)eview of studies to date suggests that connectedness affects STB (suicide thoughts and behavior) through one or more of the following routes: (1) expanding intergenerational social networks; (2) heightening opportunities for soliciting and activating assistance from others or systems (e.g., schools, families, or other social systems); (3) enhancing the likelihood that worrisome affect and behavior, including early signs of distress or more direct warning signs for suicidal behavior, will be noticed and proactively addressed by proximal systems (parents, peers, schools); (4) increasing exposure to positive coping and help-seeking norms; (5) increasing positive emotion and, as a consequence, cognitive flexibility and emotion regulation capacity; and (6) enhancing opportunities for experiencing belonging and utility in a community of others.[459]

Insight on Connecting with Trusted Adults to Impart to Students

To discuss the importance of trusted adults with students.

Trusted adults are people you can turn to when you have a problem, when something bad is happening to you, or when you have embarrassing or difficult questions you need to ask someone you can trust. Trusted adults are also important for the positive times. They are someone you can learn from. You can share news of your successes with them and talk about your future plans.

It is generally best if you are able to identify a number of trusted adults who you could talk to in different situations. Trusted adults may include your parents or caregivers, grandparents, or other family members. They can also include a teacher, school counselor, coach, organization leader, faith leader, neighbor, and others.

To find trusted adults, it is necessary that you take the steps to reach out. Consider this a form of a quest—a quest to find some adults you can trust to support you. Some helpful standards are:

- A trusted adult is someone who you can talk to about anything and who you feel happy to be around

- A trusted adult is someone you feel comfortable talking with about something that makes you feel uncomfortable or confused—or a problem you might be having.

- A trusted adult should be a good listener—someone who will listen to your opinions and ideas, seek to understand your perspective by asking questions. They will honor your feelings, rather than tell you to stop feeling the way you do.

- A trusted adult should help you think things through and not immediately tell you their conclusion and directions about what they think you should do.

Before you decide to share information that is more sensitive with an adult you are not yet sure you can trust, try having a conversation with them about something that is not really important or personal, but about which they may have a difference of opinion. After this conversation, ask yourself: Did this adult truly listen to me? Did this adult accept my opinions?

Then, imagine yourself revealing something difficult or embarrassing to this adult. How would you feel sharing this information? Do you think this adult will listen to you? Would this adult support you to think things through—or would this adult try to take over and tell you what to do?

If you start to share more sensitive information with an adult you are not yet sure you can trust, do so slowly. Be very watchful for warning signs. Is this person listening to you with an open mind? Or are there signs that they might be wrongly judging you—a questioning look, a defensive body posture, statements that include "should," or a disapproving tone?

If any of these warning signs appear, stop explaining the situation, wait for this person to make one statement of "what you should do," thank this person for their guidance, change the subject, and find a reason to leave.

Then, find a trusted adult you can trust. When you do find a trusted adult, reach out when things get tough. Also, share your good news. If a trusted adult has been helpful to you, be sure to thank this person. A thank you note would be gratefully received.

- **Envision What You Want in a Trusted Adult.** Think of a conversation you had in the past with an adult where you walked away feeling that you were thoroughly heard and respected and the guidance and support you received made you feel empowered. What were the characteristics and qualities of the adult you spoke with that led you to feel heard and empowered? What did this adult do that made you feel heard and respected? What did this adult do that made you feel empowered?

- **Conduct a Trusted Adult Audit and Create an Action Plan.** Do you have a sufficient number of adults in your life you trust you can talk to about serious concerns? If not, go on a quest to find one or several trusted adults, using the guidance provided above. Create an action plan to make a good connection with several trusted adults.

Positive Connections Activities in Schools

Relationship Mapping

It is essential to ensure that every student has one or more staff members who are committed to maintaining a close connection with them—being the person who really cares about them at school. For students who are identified as being at a higher risk, several staff members should be specifically assigned to be mentors for these students.

The Harvard Graduate School Of Education's Making Caring Common's Relationship Mapping Strategy is an excellent approach.[460] Make sure newly entering students are added to this relationship map. Staff members should be required to check in regularly with their assigned students—taking the time to form a solid relationship.

Community Circle Time

A regular Community Circle time in classrooms, advisories, or homerooms will both increase positive staff-student connections and positive student-student connections. Community Circles are strongly recommended as a Restorative Practice. Community Circles are an important means by which a positive community can be established.

Positive Acknowledgement

The ideal is that students regularly receive 5 positive comments to every 1 negative comment or correction. This is especially important for students who are at higher risk. This requires constant focus on positive acknowledgement.

School staff must know that this formula is "magic." Focused staff attention on increasing positive acknowledgement and connections, especially of those students with greater challenges, will have magical results in improving emotional well-being and resilience of these students. It is important that positive acknowledgements be phrased in a Social Emotional Growth Mindset manner. Have some poster paper in the teacher's lounge that has suggestions of positive acknowledgements that are set forth in a Social Emotional Growth Mindset manner—not just related to intelligence, also positive attitudes, behaviors, and relationship activities. These are some strategies:

- Be specific. Positively acknowledge using Social Emotional Growth Mindset language. Acknowledge effort, strategy, and persistence even if this did not result in a positive outcome.

- Audio record a class session and then go over the recording to note how many comments are positive, negative or correction, or instruction. Periodically do this to improve on performance.

- Greet students as they enter the room, as this provides one positive connection to each entering student.

- Whenever a student responds to a question, positively acknowledge their response.

- Have in mind the students in each class who have greater challenges and be sure to note when they are engaged in positive behavior. Strive for a 5:1 ratio every class session with these higher risk students. Be sure to note the higher risk students who are more quiet.

- If a student is perceived to be getting off task, positively acknowledge the behavior of a student who is close to this student. Then, if this student shifts to on-task behavior, positively acknowledge this.

- Be at the door as students leave and positively acknowledge their accomplishments. Focus specifically on any students with greater challenges. This can be in the form of a question and positive response: "What did you do today you are proud of? Yeah, I noticed this. Nice job."

- If a redirection is necessary, following this with a positive acknowledgement and appreciation of the student's compliance.

- If a student starts to get agitated and then is able to self-calm, specifically note this accomplishment. If a student struggled during the day and overcame this, positively acknowledge this both at the time and at the end of the day.

Student Friendship Focus

It is very important that staff recognize the importance of peer friendships, identify students who appear to be having difficulties forming friendships, and a strategy be implemented to support all students in having good friends.

Be on the lookout for students who do not have friends:

- At the elementary school level, note which students are playing alone at recess.

- At the secondary level, note which students are sitting alone at lunch.

One strategy that has been mentioned, and I do not know the original source, is a teacher who asks students at the end of each week to provide a list of names of the students they would like to be partnered with on projects. What the teacher focuses on is those students who are not selected by any other student. These are the students who are at higher risk because other students do not seek connections.

Strategies to seek to increase students' friendships include encouraging students to consistently reach out to be kind, the next strategy. In addition, encouraging student participation in activities of interest to them can increase the potential of their forming friendships with others who share their interests.

Positively Powerful CI-CO Strategy

At the after school connection, ask the student: What friends did you have a positive connection with today? What trusted adult at school did you have a positive connection with today?

Reach Out to Be Kind

I will daily reach out to be kind to others. Being kind to others will help to build a kind community around me.

There are many positive benefits to engaging in acts of kindness, including better health, self-esteem, and optimism. Being kind also increases peer acceptance.

Kindness Insight

Research has identified that being kind to others results in a significant increase in feelings of happiness—creating greater feelings of happiness than spending on themselves.[461]

The Random Acts of Kindness Foundation provides great insight on kindness on their website.[462] The research they follow has documented this insight and these positive benefits of kindness. They have documented these outcomes from engaging in kindness:

- *Kindness is contagious--witnessing kindness leads other people to be kind.*

- *Witnessing acts of kindness increases hormones that lead to better health, self-esteem, and optimism.*

- *Being kind helps people feel stronger, more energetic, calmer, less depressed, and leads to increased feelings of self-worth.*

- *When you are kind to another person, your brain's pleasure and reward centers light up, as if you were the recipient of the good deed.*

- *Being kind stimulates the production of feel-good and pain killer hormones and lower stress hormones.*

- *Being kind can significant increase positive moods, relationship satisfaction and decrease social avoidance in socially anxious individuals.[463]*

It has been found that prosocial behavior is associated with academic achievement and social acceptance in adolescents.[464] One study assessed the impact on peer acceptance when students were encouraged to engage in acts of kindness. This study demonstrated that students who were instructed to perform kind acts for others every day experienced significant increases in peer acceptance.[465] As the researchers explained:

> *Research suggests that goals for happiness, prosociality, and popularity may not only be compatible but also reciprocal. Happy people are more likely to engage in prosocial behavior and have satisfying friendships. Similarly, students who are well-liked by peers (i.e., sociometrically popular) are also helpful, cooperative, and emotionally well-adjusted. Past studies indicate that the link between happiness and prosociality is bidirectional—not only do happy people have the personal resources to do good for others, but prompting people to engage in prosocial behavior also increases well-being*

The hypothesis of the researchers was that because prosocial behavior has a strong positive association with peer acceptance, and this relationship is likely bidirectional. Children who feel accepted are more likely to do kind things for others, and, in turn, children who do kind things for others might gain increased acceptance by their peers. So they assessed this.

The study focused on 9 to 11 year old students. They measured students' life satisfaction and peer acceptance. Then they instructed one group of students to perform acts of kindness to others, whereas the other group kept track of the places they visited. Students in both groups showed increases in life satisfaction. Of greatest importance, the level of peer acceptance of the students who engaged in acts of kindness increased significantly. As the researchers noted:

Our study demonstrates that doing good for others benefits the givers, earning them not only improved well-being but also popularity. Considering the importance of happiness and peer acceptance in youth, it is noteworthy that we succeeded in increasing both among preadolescents through a simple prosocial activity. Similar to being happy, being well-liked by classmates has ramifications not only for the individual, but also for the community at large. For example, well-liked preadolescents exhibit more inclusive behaviors and less externalizing behaviors (i.e., less bullying) as teens. Thus, encouraging prosocial activities may have ripple effects beyond increasing the happiness and popularity of the doers. Furthermore, classrooms with an even distribution of popularity (i.e., no favorite children and no marginalized children) show better average mental health than stratified classrooms, suggesting that entire classrooms practicing prosocial behavior may reap benefits, as the liking of all classmates soars. Teachers and interventionists can build on our work by introducing intentional prosocial activities into classrooms and recommending that such activities be performed regularly and purposefully.[466]

Clearly, encouraging all students to increase engaging in kind act can significantly improve school climate. However, increasing the acts of kindness those students who have greater challenges in how they are treated by others appears to be a positive path to increase their level of peer acceptance.

Insight on Kindness to Impart to Students

To discuss kindness with students.

One of the best ways you can improve your relationships with other students, reduce the potential of being treated badly, and improve your own happiness is to intentionally reach out to be kind to other students frequently during the day.

Research has documented many positive benefits of being kind to others. Being kind to others:

- Can significant increase your happiness.

- Can help you feel stronger and less depressed.

- Can increase your feelings of self-worth.

- Makes you feel as good the person you were kind to.

- Encourages other people to be kind and, in this way, contributes to establishing a community based on kindness.

You can use this insight to improve your relationships in school—simply by consistently making a practice of being kind to others.

A really helpful thing that researchers have found about kindness is that the more you reach out to be kind to others, the more others will like and accept you. If you occasionally experience other students being hurtful to you or you are sometimes excluded by others, one of the best things you can do is to make a commitment to consistently being kind to others.

Of course it is important you are kind to your friends and those within your social group. What about other students? You can reach out to be kind to someone you would like to become friends with, students in other social groups, and students who are more often excluded or treated badly.

If a student who sometimes treats you badly is not being hurtful right now, being kind to this person can reduce the potential that they will be hurtful in the future. Being kind to the friends of a student who has been hurtful, at a time that hurtful student is not present, can increase the potential this student's friends will tell them to stop being hurtful.

- **Think About Kindness.** Think of a recent time when you reached out to be kind. How did the person you were kind to respond? How did this make you feel?

- **Use the Copper Penny Strategy.** Get five bright copper pennies and begin the day with those pennies in your left pocket. When you intentionally reach out to be kind to someone, transfer one of those pennies over to your right pocket. This will help you keep track.

- **Reach Out to be Kind Using Social Media.** Every day, make an intentional point of posting a positive or supportive comment on the social media posts of others— especially if any person posts about some challenge they are having. Don't just "like" the post. Take the time to write something warm and supportive. Make this a daily practice.

- **Reach Out to be Kind During Transitions.** As you walk to a new class, reach out to be kind to a number of people. When you sit down in your new class, reflect on how you feel.

- **Try This Experiment.** On a scale of 1 to 5, rate the current quality of your relationships with other students: 1. Not at all good. 2. Not that good. 3. Middling. 4. Sort of good. 5. Really good. Implement the reach out to be kind strategy at least five or more times a day both in person and using social media. Do this for 30 days. Now rate the quality of your relationships with other students.

- **Write in Your Journal.** At the end of the day write in your Journal. What did you do to be kind? How did this person respond? How did this make you feel?

Kindness Activities in Schools

The Random Acts of Kindness Foundation has kindness lesson plans for K-12 educators.[467] They also have recommendations for school kindness activities that a Student Leadership Team could implement. Chapter 10 discusses the establishment of a Student Leadership Team. The principle activities of this Team should be on implementing school-wide kindness campaigns. There are plenty of ideas online. Search "kindness, schools."

For every student who is having challenges with being treated badly—both being treated badly and being hurtful, or is having other challenges with disruptive behavior—strongly encourage them to reach out to be kind to others at least 3 to 5 times a day. If they are secondary students and use social media, encourage them to intentionally post a kind comment on 3 to 5 other students' profile every day.

The Accountability Process described in Chapter 11 is for both Hurtful Students and Supporters. In addition to developing a remedy of harm for the student who they were hurtful to, they should be required to remedy the harm to the school community. A recommended strategy to do this is to require that for a period of time that they must reach out to be kind to others 3 to 5 times times a day. They should be required to keep a log of these kindness acts and report on a daily or weekly basis—for how long the school leader deems might be necessary to influence them to change their hurtful behavior.

Positively Powerful CI-CO Strategy

In the morning, remind the student to reach out to be kind at least 3 to 5 times that day. At the end of the day, ask the student to describe the times they were kind: Who they were kind to? What they did to be kind? How this made them feel?

Build and Use My Strengths

I have many positive strengths. I use my strengths every day and when things get tough. I build new strengths and a positive future for myself.

Students who focus on their strengths and future directions are more resilient in response to challenges. The Build and Use My Strengths strategy draws on the research insight into Character Strengths and Social Emotional Growth Mindset, set forth in Chapter 4. In addition, students who focus on their future possibilities are more resilient in the face of experiencing being treated badly.

Future Directed Insight

One additional research-based approach is also relevant. As noted earlier, in a research study, those students who were bullied, but who had positive outcomes, were found to have maintained a sense of future possibility that supported them in staying in school, despite the bullying. They maintained a focus on the promise of better things to come.[468]

A new effective, intervention approach has been developed for adults suffering from depression that does incorporates this future thinking approach, Future Directed Therapy (FDT).[469] As explained by the researcher who developed this approach.

> *The theoretical model of human behavior behind FDT is based on three primary concepts: (1) The desire to thrive is the primary drive of all human beings because it promotes the evolutionary process. (2) Thought and behavior are limited resources that humans utilize to promote their thriving. (3) Preparing for the future is essential to thriving and much of human functioning has evolved for the purpose of creating the future.*[470]

Essentially, the FDT process involves helping people understand how their thinking actually produces the future and how they can develop more positive thinking patterns. Additionally, participants are guided in developing practical skills for creating and achieving goals, planning, problem solving, learning to take action, and effectively dealing with obstacles or disappointments.

The Build My Strengths strategy should be implemented with the think things through strategy, discussed below. Students should be guided to think things through to develop goals and strategies to build their strengths with a focus on their positive future.

Insight on Character Strengths to Impart to Students

To discuss character strengths with students.

A team of social scientists from around the world engaged in a collaborative project to identify and classify the important human strengths they thought led to goodness in human beings—across cultures, nations, and beliefs. The strengths they identified are called Character Strengths.

The VIA Institute on Character has a free Character Strengths Inventory for teens on its website that you can complete (Search: VIA Character.) This survey will help you to identify your top Character Strengths. (Provide a list of the strengths to the students, or the more brief survey that is included as an Appendix on the Embrace Civility website.

Everyone has different strengths. You can also develop new strengths. Whenever you intentionally use one of your strengths this will most likely increase your happiness.

- **Each Day Use One of Your Strengths.** Every day, pick a one of your Character Strengths to use in a new way.

- **Build a New Strength.** Look over the list of strengths and those you already have. Pick a new strength do you want to build. Create an action plan to build this strength.

- **Use Your Strengths When Things Get Tough.** Think of the ways that you could respond in situations where things have gotten tough or you are becoming distressed. If you use one of your strengths at this time, this will help you be more effective in responding. Think about and practice ways you can use each of your top strengths in situations where you are facing a challenge or are about to get upset.

- **Write in Your Journal.** At the end of the day, write in your Journal about the Character Strengths you used and what you did. Also note how this makes you feel.

Insight on Social Emotional Growth Mindset to Impart to Students

To discuss Social Emotional Growth Mindset with students.

Our "mindset" is our way of perceiving things. Everyone has a mindset that shapes how they perceive the world and others around them. We may look at the world in a way that makes us feel strong and happy or in a way that makes us feel frustrated and weak.

People with what is called a Growth Mindset know the things that are happening to them can get better. They also know that they can change and get better. They keep trying, even when things are tough. People with a Fixed Mindset feel as if they are stuck with the way things or they are. So if things are not working the way they want, they are more likely to give up.

The kind of mindset you may have is not always the same. You could have a Growth Mindset in one area of your life and then more of a Fixed Mindset in another area. There may also be times in your life when things are going really well and you more consistently have a Growth Mindset. It is harder to keep a Growth Mindset when things are not working well.

When you try to do something that is new, this is when your brain has the opportunity to grow. Learning something new is hardest the first time you try something. Your brain is like a muscle that gets stronger every time things you repeat a new skill.

When something is difficult, you may get into Fixed Mindset thinking. You may feel frustrated and think about quitting. This is when you can change your thinking to a Growth Mindset.

There is a magical word that you can use to help maintain a Growth Mindset. That word is "yet." You can add the word "yet" onto the end of almost any sentence when feel like you are failing. If you think "I can't do this," change your statement to, "I haven't be able to do this yet."

Having either a Growth or Fixed Mindset profoundly affects the way that people respond to failure. People with a Fixed Mindset view failure as a result of their lack of ability. They feel like giving up. People with a Growth Mindset see failure as the opportunity to have figured out what was not going to work. People with a Growth Mindset use failure to expand their abilities. "Well, that clearly did not work. What else could I try?"

- **Pay Attention to Your Thinking.** Does your thinking focus on growing into the future or are you more focused on your what is now?

- **Have Fun with Challenges.** Challenges are fun and exciting. Easy tasks are boring. When you struggle to learn or do something, this is when you can have great accomplishments.

- **Use the Word "Yet" When You Have Not Yet Succeeded.** Shift from, "I can't do this," to, "I can't do this yet."

- **Embrace Your Mistakes and Failure.** Making mistakes and failing is part of learning. This is how you can learn and grow.

Strengths and Growth Mindset Activities in Schools

Character Strengths

Have secondary students complete either the VIA Institute on Character Character Strengths survey or the shorter survey provided in an Appendix that is on the Embrace Civility website. This provides an indication of what each student's strengths are. There are no "right answers" on this survey. Everyone has different strengths. Even the brief survey may be too complex for elementary students.

Teachers can use Community Circles in classrooms, homerooms, or advisories to discuss each these strengths. Students can do a collage art project that illustrates their personal strengths. They can go on a scavenger hunt to find the names of students who they share personal strengths with.

Whenever there is a class discussion on challenges or to address a general concern, students could be asked how they could use different strengths in this situation. For example, "If one or your strengths was humor, how could you use this strength in a hurtful situation?" Alternatively, in a discussion about challenges, the teacher could have a set of cards with each strength. In discussing a common concern in circle, the teacher could ask students to pull out 4 or so cards. Then the entire class could think things through to identify how that strength could be used to resolve the specific situation.

A class or the entire school could focus on one character strength a week. The Student Leadership Team could read a quotation each morning in morning announcements that relates to the Strength of the Week. Every student could be encouraged to find a way to use this strength. This can be discussed in circle. Younger students could do an art project illustrating this strength. Students could be encouraged to find examples of someone using this strength in their studies, especially in humanities classes.

In any intervention with a student who has an issue of concern, the teacher or school leader can ask that student what their strengths are and how they might use a personal strength to find a resolution for this problem situation.

Social Emotional Growth Mindset

There are a significant number of resources for schools and teachers on fostering a Growth Mindset.[471] However, many of these resources focus solely on academic performance or intelligence. It is exceptionally important to expand this concept to clearly incorporate social emotional growth. Strategies for school staff include:

- **Have a Social Emotional Growth Mindset Yourself.** To encourage a Social Emotional Growth Mindset in students, it is important for educators to have a Social Emotional Growth Mindset themselves. To have a Social Emotional Growth Mindset means having a strong conviction that all students can improve in their abilities to maintain positive relationships.

- **Focus on Effort, not Success in Relationships.** Positively acknowledge students for their effort in seeking to maintain positive relationships, as well as their effort in seeking to self-regulate, rather than their success. Focus on the process they take and the effort they make, not the end result.

- **Pay Attention to Words.** Frame language for students that fosters a Social Emotional Growth Mindset. There are many posters and worksheets that focuses on encouraging Growth Mindset language—

unfortunately, the vast amount of this is focused on academic performance, not relationships.

- **Focus on "Teachable Moments."** Struggles and failure in maintaining personal relationships and self-regulation provide the best opportunity to foster a Social Emotional Growth Mindset. Use these as "teachable moments" to reflect and encourage different or expanded skills.

Positively Powerful CI-CO

In the morning, remind the student to use one of their strengths that day. Perhaps discuss which strength they will try to use. At the end of the day, ask the student to how they used one of their strengths. Alternatively, ask them what they did that they were proud of.

In all conversations with students focus on their language. Identify when they are using Fixed Mindset language in relation to relationship activities. Encourage a change in their language to reflect an opportunity for growth on both their ability to maintain positive relationships, become happier, and self-regulate when things get tough.

Be Thankful

I am thankful for the good things that are happening to me every day. I express my gratitude.

Students who have positive feelings about themselves are less likely to demonstrate perceived weakness that could lead to their being targeted and better situated to avoid thinking badly of themselves if this occurs. A consistent focus on the good things happening in their lives can help to support these positive feelings.

Gratitude Insight

The Greater Good Science Center, that was introduced in Chapter 4, provides an excellent white paper on gratitude. This white paper noted:

> *Research suggests that gratitude may be associated with many benefits for individuals, including better physical and psychological health, increased happiness and life satisfaction, decreased materialism, and more.*

> *A handful of studies suggest that more grateful people may be healthier, and others suggest that scientifically designed practices to increase gratitude can also improve people's health and encourage them to adopt healthier habits.*

> *Many more studies have examined possible connections between gratitude and various elements of psychological well-being. In general, more grateful people are happier, more satisfied with their lives, less materialistic, and less likely to suffer*

from burnout. Additionally, some studies have found that gratitude practices, like keeping a "gratitude journal" or writing a letter of gratitude, can increase people's happiness and overall positive mood.

In recent years, studies have examined gratitude's potential benefits for children and adolescents. For example, studies have found that more grateful adolescents are more interested and satisfied with their school lives, are more kind and helpful, and are more socially integrated. A few studies have found that gratitude journaling in the classroom can improve students' mood and that a curriculum designed to help students appreciate the benefits they have gained from others can successfully teach children to think more gratefully and to exhibit more grateful behavior (such as writing more thank you notes to their school's PTA).[472]

Hanson, author of *Hardwiring Happiness*, has outlined the research that demonstrates that it is possible for people to rewire their brain to be more happy.[473] The approach Hanson recommends involves an intentional focus on positive experiences to change our brain. Hanson calls this approach the HEAL method—Have, Enrich, Absorb, Link. A version of this approach is included in the guidance for students below. However, I have omitted the Link portion of the strategy because this requires mental gymnastics of linking positive feelings to past sadness.

In pre-post intervention study that involved adult participants who took an online class to learn the HEAL method, the participants reported significant increases in composite measures of cognitive resources, positive emotions, and total happiness, and decreases in a composite measure of negative emotions. These results persisted two months after the course ended.[474]

Insight on Gratitude to Impart to Students

The following is language to discuss gratitude with students.

Our brain naturally wires itself to focus more on negative experiences than positive ones. If you have faced a lot of challenges, you may have created many negative neural pathways. These negative neural pathways will cause you to more frequently focus on negative things. A problem is that when people often focus on the negative, more negative things are more likely to happen to them.

Even if you have not experienced a lot of challenges, you can become happier when you focus on the good. The best way to maintain positive feelings is to focus on positive experiences and be grateful for those experiences.

You can rewire you brain to be more happy. When you intentionally focus on the good, this will help you brain build neural pathways to support greater happiness. As a result, more positive things are more likely to happen.

This is a strategy you can use to focus on the good.

- **Step 1. Have a Good Experience.** Either notice that something good has happened or create a positive experience for yourself.

- **Step 2. Enrich It.** Keep thinking about this experience for at least 10 seconds or longer. Feel the positive experience in your body. Enjoy it. Think about how wonderful this is. Really take the time to feel good.

- **Step 3. Absorb It.** Think about this positive experience as being absorbed by you— traveling deep into your mind and warming your heart. Bring the experience deeply into your being.[475]

Strive to focus on five positive experiences for every negative experience or negative thought. This means that every time you experience a negative incident or think a negative thought, strive to shift your focus to five positive things. This can help to prevent the negative experience from becoming wired as a negative neural pathway.

The more you can maintain positive feelings about yourself, the less likely you will act in ways that demonstrates a perceived weakness that could lead to your being treated badly. Also, the less likely you will be to think badly about yourself if someone is hurtful. -

- **Send a Note of Gratitude.** Send a private message or write a thank you note and sent this to a person who did something for you.

- **Focus on the Good as You are Transitioning.** As you are getting ready to leave one class for another, stop and think about one thing that happened in this class that made you feel good. Enrich this feeling and absorb it.

- **Focus on the Good in Response to a Distressing Experience.** If you experience something distressing, pull out a notebook and a pen and write down five recent positive experiences or things for which you are grateful. For each of these positive experiences, take a brief moment to enrich your positive feelings and absorb them. Then, if you find yourself thinking about the negative incident again, look at what you wrote and intentionally shift back to positive thinking.

- **Write in Your Journal.** In the evening, when you are writing in your Journal, be sure to write down five positive things that happened to you during the day. The act of writing itself provides another way to enrich and absorb the positive experiences.

- **Try This Experiment.** Rate how happy you are feeling on a scale from 1 to 5. 1: Not at all happy. 2. Not that happy. 3. Middling. 4. Sort of happy. 5. Really happy. Take the time to write in your Journal five thoughts that focus on the good. For each of these thoughts go through the two steps of enriching and absorbing. Now, rate how happy you feel.

Gratitude Activities in Schools

A search on the terms "gratitude, schools" will yield many sites with creative suggestions. A concern is that a primary focus of many sites relates to the Thanksgiving holiday in the US, a time for which the indigenous students are likely not feeling grateful. The Greater Good Science Center is an excellent source of insight into gratitude and gratitude activities in schools.[476]

The Greater Good Science Center recently collaborated with Emmons, a highly regarded researcher in gratitude in the creation of a new book, *The Gratitude Project: How the Science of Thankfulness Can Rewire Our Brains for Resilience, Optimism, and the Greater Good.*[477] This book is a collection of essays written by written by positive psychologists and public figures. It delves deeply into the neuroscience and psychology of gratitude, and explores how gratitude can be developed and applied for the positive benefit of all.

Positively Powerful CI-CO

In the morning, remind the student to pay attention to the things that happen that make them feel good. At the end of the day, ask the student to describe a positive thing that happened and to take a moment to feel the positive feelings again. If someone has done something that made this student feel good, encourage the student to write a note of thanks to provide to the person the following day.

Remain Calm

I take time each day to achieve calmness and focus. If things get tough, I remain calm.

The ability to self-regulate is an essential skills when one is treated badly. This can help the Targeted Student remain calm so as not to reward the student being hurtful. Self-regulation is also important to reduce the potential for impulsive retaliation. The practice of mindfulness creates the neural pathways to improve students' ability to self-regulate when things get tough.

Mindfulness Insight

Often students who are treated badly overreact in response, which appears to lead to additional hurtful experiences. Sometimes, they retaliate. Self-regulation is an important component of resilience. The practice of mindfulness helps people achieve calmness and focus—which builds the capacity of their brain to better self-regulate.[478]

The University of California—Los Angeles Mindful Awareness Research center is conducting a wide range of research studies on the benefits of mindfulness practice, including with young people. As stated on the page that has links to numerous published studies:

> *Research in mindfulness has identified a wide range of benefits in different areas of psychological health, such as helping to decrease anxiety, depression, rumination, and emotional reactivity. Research has also shown mindfulness helps to increase well-being, positive affect, and concentration.*
>
> *Practicing mindfulness can also be helpful to foster physical health by improving immune system function, quality of sleep, as well as decreasing blood pressure. Structural and functional brain changes have also been documented in areas associated with attention, emotional regulation, empathy, and bodily awareness.*
>
> *In addition to health, research has been made on the benefits of mindfulness in business and educational settings. In companies, results showed improved communication and work performance. In educational settings, mindfulness practices improved social-emotional skills, executive functions, and decreased test stress in students, as well as reduced stress and burnout in teachers.[479]*

Research has documented effectiveness of mindfulness training and practice in addressing stress-related concerns of children and adolescents, with documented positive results in their physical health, psychological well-being, social skills including emotional regulation, and academic performance.[480]

Insight on Mindfulness to Impart to Students

To discuss the importance of mindfulness.

The practice of mindfulness helps people achieve calmness and focus— to self-regulate. Being mindful is the basic human ability to be fully present, aware of where we are and what we're doing, and not overly reactive or overwhelmed by what's going on around us.

You can achieve greater mindfulness by routinely engaging in the practice of meditation. The following are the simple steps to meditate:

- **Be in a Safe Place.** Sit or lie in a safe place.

- **Ground Yourself.** If you are sitting, make sure your feet are on the floor. Whether sitting or lying, feel your energy go deep into the earth —grounding you there.

- **Reduce Input from Anything Outside of You.** Close your eyes or gaze downward. This will help you focus on you—and not what is going on around you.

- **Breathe.** Pay attention to your breathing. Take a slow breath in. Hold your breath for a short time. Release your breath out slowly. Keep repeating this.

- **Be There.** If your attention begins to wander, which it often will, gently return your thoughts to a focus on your breathing.

That's it. Consider how long this activity might take—not long at all. In fact, you can achieve a mindfulness state in a very short period of time—less than a minute.

The more you intentionally practice being mindful, the more effectively you will prepare your brain so that it does not trigger when someone is hurtful or a challenging situation emerges. Practicing mindfulness helps to build neural pathways so that you can remain calm even when challenging things happen.

You will also find that if you routinely practice meditation, you will increase your success in your learning. When you achieve mindfulness, this shifts your focus to your Prefrontal Cortex which is the thinking part of your brain. This allows you to think more clearly and concentrate.

Now, let's try something even more fun. When you feel calm while practicing mindfulness and your attention starts to wander, there is something else you can do. This is a guided mindfulness practice that uses the Positively Powerful Thinking Questions.

- **Positive Connections.** Take a breath and as you breath out think, "Who did I have a positive connection with?" Now, in the next several breaths think about several recent positive connections you had. Smile as you remember how happy you felt.

- **Kindness.** Take a breath and as you breath out think, "Who was I kind to?" Now, in the next several breaths think about several recent times you were kind to someone. Remember the smile on their face and how this made you feel.

- **Strengths.** Take a breath and as you breath out think, "What did I do today that used one of my strengths?" Or "What did I do today that I am proud of?" Now, in the next several breaths think about what you did that used a strength or did something that you are proud of. Smile as you remember how proud you are.

- **Thankfulness.** Take a breath and as you breath out think, "What happened today that made me feel really happy?" Now, in the next several breaths think about what happened that made you happy. Take the time to really feel happy and to bring that feeling of happiness into your whole body.

These are some other ways that you can achieve mindfulness:

- **Practice Mindfulness Every Day.** Take just a bit of time to practice mindfulness every day. You could do this both in the morning and at night before you go to sleep. Try to extend the time you can stay mindful.

- **Use the Positively Powerful Thinking Questions When You Meditate.** This will both help to build the neural pathways for you to be calmer and increase your happiness.

- **Engage in Movement Mindfulness.** You may take a yoga or a tai chi class, which is considered "movement mindfulness." There are also yoga and tai chi videos online.

- **Try Other Ways to Become Mindful.** This includes walking in nature, listening to music, watching a video, playing with a fidget tool, or reading a book.

- **Use a Transitions Strategy.** Every time you enter a classroom and take your seat, spend the next minute in a brief meditation to become mindful. Lower your eyes. Breathe slowly in and then release. Just a minute. Do this for a while and you will see that you are much better able to focus in class.

Self-Regulation Insight

Concerns of students who are not able to self-regulate and become disruptive are frequent in schools, especially as students have come back to the school environment after the pandemic.[481]

Schools across the country say they're seeing an uptick in disruptive behaviors. Some are obvious and visible, like students trashing bathrooms, fighting over social media posts, or running out of classrooms. Others are quieter calls for help, like students putting their head down and refusing to talk.

"This is a prolonged adjustment period," said Dr. Tali Raviv, the associate director of the Center for Childhood Resilience at Lurie Children's Hospital in Chicago. As children return to school, "There's much more interaction, there's much less downtime to recharge, there's much less flexibility."

The behavior issues are a reflection of the stress the pandemic placed on children, experts say, upending their education, schedules, and social lives. For students dealing with grief, mental health issues, or the layered effects of poverty and racism, big transitions can be even more challenging.

Anxiety and chronic stress also trigger a child's "survival brain," as Raviv put it. While some students retreat, others feel like they're on high alert — turning a nudge in the hallway into cause for an outburst, for example. "You can get these really big reactions over really small things," she said.

Coupled with staff exhaustion, the behavior challenges are making school environments more tense than educators and students had anticipated — and underscoring how much support students need right now.

In 2004, Colvin enunciated a framework called the *Stages of Behavior Escalation.*[482] This thinking and approach is connected with PBIS, thus is an approach that is grounded in behaviorism. This guidance has been presented to support the presentation of a framework that is informed by an understanding of trauma and a desire for student empowerment. Insight into trauma and the impact on dysregulated behavior has significantly increased since the time of the creation of this guidance. More insight into the process by which students become dysregulated is included in Chapter 5. According to Colvin, there are seven stages of behavioral escalation.

- *Phase 1: Calm. Supervise, reduce distractions, and provide quiet space. Establish and teach CLEAR expectations and acknowledge and praise compliance. Establish routines to decrease downtime and disruptions. Plan ahead for starter activities, transitions, and entry and exit routines.*

- *Phase 2: Triggers. Identify the situation where the behavior is likely to occur. Use pre-correction to teach appropriate response. Rehearse the expectations, prompt or remind students as needed, provide specific praise and reinforcement. Work with all staff and faculty to teach and reinforce social skills. School and non-school triggers. Group social skills, anger management, community services.*

- *Phase 3: Agitation. Show empathy: recognize the student's problem and communicate concern. Redirect and help the student become engaged in activity, lesson or task (passive or movement). Provide choices. Provide space in a quiet area or allow students to disengage briefly or put their heads down. Use proximity or brief interactions; show acceptance.*

- *Phase 4: Acceleration. Pause and Assess- "Is this an emergency situation?" Avoid escalating the student's behavior. Pausing rather than responding immediately shows students that while they may be out of control, staff are calm and controlled. Use a calm but serious tone. If the situation escalates, withdraw and follow school procedures for emergency situations.*

- *Phase 5: Peak. Focus on student and staff safety. Notify necessary staff of situations and provide directions for response. If needed, evacuate others. Contact appropriate assistance. If an Emergency Safety Intervention was used —Notify parents, document, debrief and learn from it.*

- *Phase 6: De-escalation. Monitory for health and safety. Once escalation is over, allow student space to calm down, under supervision. Avoid blaming—provide opportunity for non-judgmental discussion. Provide independent work that is fairly easy to complete to help regain focus. Debrief and document the incident to provide data for ongoing planning for safety.*

- *Phase 7: Recovery. Help student return to normal activities and engage in learning. Continue with planned consequence and do not discuss or negotiate.*

Acknowledge cooperative and appropriate behavior. Encourage and support student in changing problem behavior. Help student return to normal activities and engage in learning.

This insight must be updated to allow for a better understanding of what is happening within the brains of students when they are becoming dysregulated. Most importantly, the response approach must incorporate Social Emotional Growth Mindset strategies to empower students to be able to independently self-regulate.

When a student triggers and starts to become dysregulated, their Anterior Cingulate Cortex and Prefrontal Cortex is in the process of, or has become, disconnected. They are functioning in "fight, flight, or flee" mode. When students are in this state, the message their brain is telling them is, "You are not safe." When they reach this state, their ability to regulate their emotions and problem solve has been undermined. This interferes with their ability to process what a staff member is trying to tell them. There is one thing—and only one thing—that can help them at this point. That is to regain the feeling of being safe.

The other understanding that needs to be incorporated is an understanding of Social Emotional Growth Mindset. Students must be assured that they can change how they react when something has triggered them. The goal is to "flatten the curve"—to go from trigger, to slight escalation, back to calm—without ever climbing up to the peak. Students absolutely require the assurance that they can do this. The key to to assist students to gain more effective self-regulation is to help them to understand triggers them. Then, when something they know is likely to trigger them starts to happen, they can take steps to avoid going from a trigger to an outburst—to flatten the curve.

- **Phase 1. Calm.** All of the outlined tasks are necessary. Some additions are helpful. Implement a mindfulness program with mindfulness practice and mindful breaks after every transition. This can help students build the neural pathways that will better allow them to self-regulate. Teach all students how their brain functions, so that they understand how they or other classmates might become dysregulated. Also discuss with them the actions they can take if they start to to feel triggered. For students known to have challenges in self-regulation, when they are calm is the time to engage in participatory problem solving to identify several self-regulation strategies they can use. These should be for any location in the school where they may be. If they can walk away from the situation to get to a place where they can better self-regulate, this is best. They may choose to walk to a calm place in the classroom or they may need permission to leave wherever they are in the school and go to a calming room. Some manner of "code" to communicate to the teacher or an aide that they feel they are about to trigger will be helpful. For younger students, a laminated card of "My Calming Strategies" could be placed on their desk.

- **Phase 2. Triggers.** Notice how in this Colvin framework, insight into trauma was not integrated. Most of this research was not readily available. A key word to notice is the term "expectations." What this communicates is that the student is choosing to behave in a manner that is out of accord with "expectations" and that providing praise or reinforcement will help to control their choices. When a student is triggering, that student is in the process of flipping their lid. Something has happened that has caused them to not feel safe. They are losing the connection with their Prefrontal Cortex, which is reducing their ability to problem solve. They are not intentionally choosing to be noncompliant with "expectations." Note also that is some situations, the staff member may not yet be aware that the student has triggered.

- **Phases 3 and 4. Agitation and Acceleration.** It is unclear why these are two stages in the Colvin format. Every teacher has likely experienced a student who has gone to a hidden or not noticed trigger to a dysregulated peak in less than a minute. Many of these suggestions are helpful to assist a student become regulated. However, the most important issue of which to be cognizant is that the primary need of the student at this time is to feel safe. Students have not yet lost full capacity to problem solve. This is the stage that needs to be prepared for in advance, when the student is calm. Prepare for this stage helping the student identify strategies that are helpful for them to regain calm—to flatten the curve. Staff should use Reflective Listening at this stage. "It appears that you are becoming upset because ___. You have strategies you can use to regain calm. How can I help?" Note that this approach is student empowering, not focused on compliance with staff expectations.

- **Phase 5. Peak.** Obviously, this is the stage to avoid. If a student has become totally dysregulated, both their safety as well as that of the other students and staff are of concern. At this point, the student's Anterior Cingulate Cortex and Prefrontal Cortex are primarily off-line. All staff must be trained in effective de-escalation strategies. The key to effective deescalation is to recognize that what the student requires most of all is to regain the feeling that they are safe. Any reaction to them that continues their feelings of not being safe will not be effective in deescalation. The strategies that absolutely must be avoided can be remembers by this term: TACOS: Threats. Arguments. Commands or criticism. Orders. Shaming.

- **Phase 6. De-escalation.** This is also a stage to support student empowerment. Ask the student what they think they need to do to recover from the situation. After they have gotten themselves out of the immediate situation, they may also need to engage in some physical activity. When they trigger and start to get agitated, their Amygdala caused their body to release stress hormones of cortisol and adrenalin. It is important to get these hormones out of their system. Vigorous physical activity is the way to do this.

- **Phase 7 Recovery.** The biggest question of the Colvin guidance is the reasoning behind imposing a consequence. This suggests that the student intentionally chose to become dysregulated. Dysregulation is reactive behavior. Not proactive misbehavior. If while dysregulated a student has harmed another, the student should engage in an Accountability Process, such as is described in Chapter 11. It should be considered necessary for this student to develop a plan for how they will remedy the harm to anyone they harmed. However, a disciplinary consequence for a student's reaction to a situation that triggered and caused them to become dysregulated should not be considered appropriate.

Insight on Self-Regulation to Impart to Students

To discuss the importance of remaining calm.

If you are faced with a challenging situation, it is exceptionally important that you are able to self-regulate to remain calm. Failure to effectively self-regulate could lead you to engage in an outburst that could cause harm to you or others. When you frequently practice mindfulness this will help to create the neural pathways in your brain that will allow you to self-regulate more effectively. This is why daily mindfulness practice is so important.

If you have experienced bad things happening to you or ongoing distress, your brain is more likely to be hyper vigilant. You are concerned about and focusing on everything that is happening. You are more likely to have greater difficulties keeping yourself calm. Because of this, you are more likely to become disruptive something else happens that makes you upset.

When you know that this is the case, you have the ability to take the power into your own hands to better respond if this might occur. Because you know that there is a higher risk you will trigger and get upset, this knowledge gives you the power to change what could happen.

Alternatively, if you do not normally trigger but you know someone who does, you can use this insight to be on alert to the signs of emerging concern and reach out to help them.

There are several stages in going from calm to really upset and back to calm:

- **Calm.** You feel calm and relaxed.

- **Trigger.** Something happens that triggers you. You start to feel upset.

- **Agitation.** You become increasingly upset. You start having challenges in thinking clearly.

- **Outburst.** You become out of control and are disruptive.

- **De-escalation.** You now feel confused and embarrassed, but you are getting calm again.

- **Recovery.** The time it takes for you become calm.

The key to effective self-regulation is to have a good idea of what triggers you, so that when something like this starts to happen you know what might happen next. You can then take steps to avoid going from a trigger through agitation to an outburst. When you have triggered, this is the time to take a specific steps to stay calm.

Knowing when you might trigger is really helpful. At a time when you are calm, you can think things through to figure out what you can do to stop the trigger and get back to calm. It is important that you know that you absolutely have the ability to develop new strategies to keep yourself calm.

Take the time to think about what situations most often cause you to trigger. Then, think about your personal strengths. How can you use your top strengths to remain calm if or when something triggers you? Envision this kind of a situation occurring and practice using your strengths in such situations.

If you have a history of triggering and then becoming disruptive, talk with your teacher, a counselor, or a principal at your school to obtain special permission to leave any situation when you have triggered and start to feel agitated. There may be a calming corner in your room. They may agree to allow you to another place in the school to self-regulate. This might be the counselor's office or perhaps the school library. You should have some kind of a permanent pass, so that no other staff person stops you from going to a place to self-regulate.

The mindfulness meditation approach set forth above is a good approach for your initial response if something has triggered you. Make sure to ground yourself and hold yourself tall. Slowly and intentionally breathe in, hold your breath briefly, and then-breathe out. If your brain tries to shift your attention to the perceived threat, continue focus on your breathing.

After you have gotten yourself out of the immediate situation, you may also need to engage in some physical activity. When you trigger and start to get agitated, your Amygdala caused your body to release cortisol and adrenalin. It is important to get this out of your system. Vigorous physical activity is the way to do this.

- **Think Things Through.** If you have challenges with triggering, make a positive connection with a trusted adult to think things through to identify the common situations that you are more likely to trigger. Then, for each of these common situations, think things through to identify at least three things you can do if this common situation occurs.

- **Obtain Special Permission.** If you have a history of triggering, talk with your teacher, a counselor, or a principal at your school to obtain special permission to leave any situation when you have triggered and start to feel agitated.

- **Write in Your Journal.** Whenever you trigger, be sure to write about this in your Journal. Write out what happened and how you handled the situation. Did you become agitated and engage in an outburst or were you able to self-regulate? Note specifically what happened before you triggered so that you can be alert to when this might happen again. Do a self-evaluation of your effectiveness. It is perfectly okay if things did not work out right. You are rewiring your brain and learning this new self-regulation process. Decide whether there are strategies you might want to change in the future. It is most important not to focus on what you did that went wrong—but what you learned that can help you in the future. If you were able to self-regulate, congratulate yourself! Well done!

- **Connect with a Trusted Adult.** After you have gone through the journalling process, take the time to connect with a trusted adult. Share your thoughts and talk things through to get feedback on your thinking and plans for the future.

Mindfulness and Self-Regulation Activities in School

There are many sites that provide excellent guidance on establishing mindfulness practices in schools. These include: Mindfulness in Schools Project.[483] Mindful.[484] Mindful Schools.[485]

One very simple practice is to simply have students practice mindfulness for a minute upon coming into class after a transition. A minute of silence for self-calming. Then, at any time the students appear to be getting rambunctious, return to just a minute of silence until they have calmed.

A short guided meditation using the Positively Powerful Thinking Questions was set forth above. This guided mediation may be easier for students than the "clear your mind" kind of meditation practice. An alternative way to do this guided meditation could be asked is in a morning announcement for the entire school. Members of the Student Leadership Team could lead the guided mediation.

It is helpful for staff to have a trauma informed understanding of what is happening when a student becomes dysregulated. Seigel's approach to describing the process of becoming dysregulated is called "flipping your lid" is exceptionally helpful to use with students.[486]

Teachers can teach students about this by having them use their hand as a model of the brain to describe what happens when they trigger. The inner or downstairs brain is represented by their palm. The thumb represents the limbic system and can simulate its approximate position when they rest their thumb across their palm. This includes both the Hippocampus and the Amygdala. Curling their fingers over the top creates the Anterior Cingulate Cortex and the Prefrontal Cortex, the upstairs brain, in its proper place. If they become dysregulated, their fingers flip up—they have "flipped their lid"— and can no longer regulate their emotions or problem solve.

All school staff and students should be trained to understand the process by which anyone might become dysregulated. The key point that must be made is that the time that a student triggers is when they need to take action to self-regulate. This may be just at the start of when they are becoming agitated. The Prefrontal Cortex has not become entirely disconnected at this time, allowing for the opportunity to "flatten the curve."

All staff must be trained in effective de-escalation strategies. The key to effective deescalation is to recognize that what the student requires most of all is to regain the feeling that they are safe. Any reaction to them that continues their feelings of not being safe will not be effective in deescalation. Avoid TACOS: Threats. Arguments. Commands or criticism. Orders. Shaming.

Every student will have different ways that are best for them to self-regulate. Implement a Social Emotional Growth Mindset approach. When a student is calm, them them to think things through to determine what tends to trigger them and the best ways are for them to self-regulate when they have triggered. This is a participatory problem solving activity which can be done as a class or individually. Ask all students to respond with their best strategies and write this list on the board. Then, have all students select from this list their best self-regulation strategies. These should be written down. Be sure to include "get a snack" on this list. A drop in blood pressure often causes dysregulation. A term for this is "hangry."

Especially for students who are known to become dysregulated more easily, perhaps even laminate the list of self-regulation strategies they have chosen and have it on their desk. Also, develop a school-wide or class code for when a student feels they have triggered and need to take the time to calm. "I need to calm" may be sufficient. Or a teacher may note that a student looks anxious and ask, "Do you need to use a calming strategy?"

Positively Powerful CI-CO

In the morning, if there is time, it would be helpful to have a brief mindfulness activity with the student. Using the Positively Powerful Thinking Questions every day can accomplish this. Remind them of the transitions strategy that every time they enter a new situation they will take several deep breaths and remind themselves to calm. At the end of the day ask if they practiced this transitions mindfulness technique. Remind them also to practice meditation for a time at home.

The approach discussed above to positively address self-regulation, that includes identifying what situations tend to trigger them and their strategies to respond should be discussed with the student in the context of a longer Positively Powerful CI-CO discussion. Then, on a daily basis at the end of the day, discuss whether anything triggered the student and how they responded.

If they triggered and were not able to flatten the curve, engage in participatory problem solving to gain a better understanding of what happened to trigger the student and discuss how the strategy they tried to implement did not appear to work effectively. Approach this discussion with a Social Emotional Growth Mindset approach. "You learned what did not work. You can change your brain so that you do not become dysregulated. We just need to think things through to figure out something better you can do."

It will be especially important to positively acknowledge student's success in self-regulation. If escalation is a specific concern for any students, providing written positive acknowledgement to a parent or caregiver when the student successfully self-regulated would also likely be helpful. Self-regulating when you have triggered is really something to celebrate.

Keep My Personal Power

I hold myself tall and proud. I will not allow what happens to me control how I think about myself or respond.

To effectively address the concerns of hurtful behavior directed at, and sometimes by, students, it is necessary to increase students' level of personal power. This can be addressed both by a focus on how they are holding themselves physically and what they think when something challenging does happen to them.

Personal Power Insight

As was discussed in Chapter 1, students who have been treated badly in a serious or persistent manner have experienced trauma. Increasing their resilience and empowerment is necessary to address the harms caused by the adversities they have experienced. This will also support them in making behavior changes that reflect greater personal power, which should help to decrease the inclinations of those looking for disempowered targets to be hurtful to them.

The Keeping Their Personal Power strategies will also improve the ability of Targeted Students to respond more effectively when they are treated badly. Rather than trigger and have an outburst, which only encourages the Hurtful Students and Supporters, they will have a greater ability to remain calm, nonchalant, and simply walk away. Without the visible rewards of the results of their hurtful behavior, Hurtful Students will hopefully decrease their hurtful acts.

Hurtful behavior can essentially be considered a "power game," where a student is seeking to gain "power points." Students who seek greater personal power and dominance are seeking additional "power points" from their admirers. They are hurtful to students who have lower social power—have fewer "power points." When Targeted Students overreact to being treated badly, this proves to the Hurtful Student that they have been successful in taking the target's "power points."

When Targeted Students gain sufficient personal power, they will have a greater potential of reacting in a way that will not result in a loss of their "power points" when they are treated badly. Over time, with the other strategies that are advised, the Hurtful Student will hopefully come to realize that being hurtful is not working effectively to enable them to gain the "power points" they so desire.

Increased personal power of students can also increase the perspectives of Witnesses that they have sufficient personal power and self-efficacy to effectively step in to help. This is discussed more in Chapter 8. When witnesses, either individually or when working as a team with other students, have equivalent or greater "power points" as the Hurtful Student and Supporters, these Witnesses can gain additional "power points" by stepping in to help.

There are two strategies students can use that can help them to better keep their personal power, especially in situations where someone is trying to take their power from them: Hold Myself Tall and Control My Thinking.

Powerful Presence Insight

Research conducted by Cuddy, a professor at Harvard School of Business, has demonstrated that adopting a pose that indicates power—a "power pose"—can result in increased feelings of confidence.[487] An excellent TedTalk by Cuddy on Power Posing provides greater insight into this, as does her book, *Presence.*

Cuddy did an experiment where she had one group of college students in the business school stand using a power position for a period of time. Another group of students maintained a powerless position. These students were then interviewed as though they were applying for a job. Their interviews were video-taped.

People who knew nothing about what the students did before their interview judged the performance of the students on videos. These judges strongly favored the students who had stood in a powerful position before the job interviews.

What this study demonstrated is that holding a "power pose" before a challenging interpersonal relationship task allowed students to increase their effective performance. This showed that it is possible to "fake it" by assuming a power pose, which will then help a person "make it" by feeling more confident.

Insight on Powerful Presence to Impart to Students

To discuss the importance of holding oneself tall.

In both humans and other primates, standing tall with a very open posture indicates high power, whereas hunching over with your arms crossed over your chest reflects lower power. Many times, young people who are bullied maintain physical posture that demonstrate that they feel that they lack personal power.

Research by a professor at Harvard School of Business, demonstrated that if you hold a pose that indicates that you feel you have personal power—a "power pose"—this can increase your feelings of self-confidence. You can watch an TedTalk by Dr. Cuddy on Power Posing.

Dr. Cuddy did an experiment where she had one group of college students in the business school stand tall using a power position for a short period of time. Another group of students held themselves in a powerless position. These students were then interviewed as though they were applying for a job. Their interviews were video-taped.

People who knew nothing about what the students did before their interview judged the performance of the students on videos. These judges strongly favored the students who had stood in a powerful position before the job interview.

What this study demonstrated is that holding a "power pose" before a challenging interpersonal relationship task allowed students to increase their effective performance. This showed that it is possible to "fake it" by assuming a power pose, which will then help a person "make it" by feeling more confident. You can do this also. When you hold yourself tall and in a position of power you will then feel more powerful.

- **Try This Experiment.** Hold yourself in a position that indicates you have no power—shoulders hunched, arms crossed, head down. How does this make you feel? Now stand up tall or hold yourself tall. Shoulders back. Head held high. Arms out to you side or over your head in a celebration post, like you just won a race. How does this make you feel?

- **Practice Power Posing.** Every morning, stand or hold yourself for a few minutes in a position of personal physical power. Perhaps you can do this while looking at yourself in your mirror. Say an affirmation to yourself as you are holding yourself tall.

- **Use These Transitions Strategies.** Remind yourself to hold yourself tall whenever you come into school or go from one class to another. Also, whenever you in an area where you previously have experienced any challenges, remind yourself to hold yourself tall through this area.

- **If Something Bad Happens.** If something bad has happened, like a student says something hurtful, your first response should be to take a deep breath to remain calm and at the same time to shift your body posture to hold yourself tall.

Control My Thinking

Students will never be able to control when someone might treat them badly or if other bad things might happen to them. But they do have the ability to control their thinking about how they feel about themselves and how they respond in these challenging situations. This way they can keep their personal power.

This is an old theory. The underlying principles of the ancient Stoic philosophers, as set forth by Epictetus, who in the first century C.E. said: "Men are disturbed not by things, but by the views which they take of them."[488]

The key underlying premise of Rational Emotive Behavioral Therapy (REBT), created by Ellis, is that harmful consequences are not just caused by the bad adversities that happen to us, but also by our beliefs about those adversities.[489] While we can't control what might happen, we can control our beliefs. Ellis developed the A-B-C-model, which is described below.

Insight on Control Their Thinking to Impart to Students

To discuss the importance of controlling their thinking.

You will never be able to control when or if someone might treat you badly. You will never be able to control whether or if other bad things might happen to you. You do have the ability to control your thinking about how you feel about yourself and how you respond in these challenging situations.

The key understanding of the importance of controlling your thinking is to realize that harmful consequences are not just caused by the bad things that happen to us—but also by our beliefs about those bad things. While you can't control what might happen, you can control your beliefs and your thinking. This controls the outcome and how you feel.

This is an old theory. The underlying principles of this theory comes from the ancient Stoic philosophers, as set forth by Epictetus. In the first century C.E. he stated: "Men are disturbed not by things, but by the views which they take of them."

Think in terms of A-B-C-model.:

- A is the adversity or bad event.

- C is the consequence of how you feel or respond.

But A is not solely responsible for C.

- B is your belief—what you think or believe about A, not merely that A happened.

Thus, A + B = C. While it is not possible to change A, it is possible to be in control of B, and thus have greater control over the C.

Translation: We don't always have control over what happens to us. But we do have the ability to control what we think of ourselves and how we respond

- **Control Your Thinking.** If you are ever in a situation where someone has been hurtful or find yourself thinking about a past situation that occurred, think to yourself, "I will not give that person the power to control what I think about myself or how I respond."

- **Write in Your Journal.** If you experienced a situation where someone was hurtful or something else bad happened, write about this. Write out what happened and how you handled the situation. Do a self-evaluation of your effectiveness in controlling your thinking. Decide whether there are things you might want to change in the future. It is most important not blame yourself. Rather focus on what you have learned.

- **If Something Bad Happens.** Stand or hold yourself tall are you breathe slowly and deeply to remain calm. Then, think to yourself, "I can't control what happens. I can control how I feel about myself and respond."

Personal Power Activities in School

An excellent TedTalk by Cuddy on power posing provides greater insight into standing or holding oneself tall. This TedTalk is quite appropriate for secondary students to watch and discuss.[490]

For elementary students, talking about standing or holding themselves tall can be supported by watching the highly popular "Let It Go" music video from the movie *Frozen*.[491] Have them note how powerless Else appears in the first of the video. Then, note when she holds herself tall and proud. Have them practice "feeling small" and "holding themself tall and proud. Students love this video—likely because they yearn to be able to demonstrate their level of personal power.

The message that while it is not possible to control what happens, but it is possible to control how you respond and feel about yourself will need to be transmitted more informally in every situation where a student is feeling distressed about something that happened to them.

Positively Powerful CI-CO

In the morning as they are about to leave your meeting, have them practice "feeling small" and then "holding themselves tall." Remind them of the transitions strategy of remembering every time they are getting ready to move to a different place in the school they should remind themselves to hold themselves tall. Also, always remind them every day, both in the morning and before they leave, to keep their personal power —never give any other person the power to control what they think about themselves and respond.

Think Things Through

In any challenging situation, I will think things through to decide what is best to do.

When students gain effective problem solving skills they are more resilient in figuring out how to respond if they are faced with any kind of a challenge. When they think things through, this is the opposite of acting without thinking.

Problem Solving Insight

Some students who are most often bullied lack critically important relationship skills. When students gain greater interpersonal relationship problem solving skills—that is learn how to think of their own solutions to problems, consequences to their actions, and how they and others feel about things--they are less likely to engage in risk behavior and are more resilient in figuring out how to respond if someone is hurtful to them.

Shure has done significant work focused on supporting young people in effective problem solving.[492] Four key interpersonal cognitive problem solving skills are:

- Means-ends thinking to reach a stated interpersonal goal by planning a step-by-step, sequenced means to reach that goal.

- Alternative solution thinking to identify alternative solutions to a stated problem.

- Consequential thinking to consider what might happen in certain situations.

- Weighing pros and cons to decide whether to carry out an interpersonal act.

As was discussed in Chapter 4, an excellent intervention approach for students who have engaged in misbehavior is called Collaborative Problem Solving, also called Collaborative and Proactive Solutions.[493] This process engages school staff in problem solving with students. Parents and caregivers can also use this approach.

Knowing how to effectively solve problems provides the foundation for success in school, higher education, family life, and in their employment. It is also important to know how to think things through as part of a team. When they develop their skills in goal setting and action planning and use these skills consistently, this can support their positive future.

Think Things Through

To discuss how to engage in effective problem solving.

When you gain effective problem solving skills you can become more resilient in figuring out how to respond if you are facing any kind of a challenge. Thinking Things Through is the opposite of acting without thinking.

Knowing how to effectively solve problems provides the foundation for success in school, higher education, family life, and in your employment. It is also important to know how to think things through as part of a team. These are the steps that are necessary to engage in effective problem solving:

- **What is the Situation?** Step back from the situation and think about what has happened to make sure you have a clear understanding.

- **What Do I Want to Accomplish?** Determine what you would like to achieve or what outcome you desire.

- **What Strategies Could I Use?** Identify several different strategies or actions you could take to resolve the problem or respond.

- **Is Each in Accord With my Values and Does Each Build and Use My Strengths?** Evaluate these strategies based on your own personal values and whether each strategy or action Uses Your Strengths.

- **For Each, What Might Happen?** Think about and try to predict or envision what might happen if you followed each of those strategies or actions.

- **What is My Best Choice?** After thinking through what might happen as a consequence of each strategy you thought of, then weight the pros and cons to decide which strategy or action would be the best to take.

- **How Should I Proceed?** Determine what steps to take to accomplish this strategy or action.

- **Did This Work?** Evaluate your effectiveness. Realize that the first thing you try might not work. The fact that the first thing you tried did not work is totally okay. You learned what would not work.

- **What Else Could or Should I Do?** Repeat this process if the first strategy or action did not achieve your desired goal or if you learned something that leads you to decide that some other action is necessary.

Positively Powerful Strategies

- **If Something Bad Happens.** Think to yourself, "I got this. I can think things through to decide what is best to do."

- **Working With a Team.** Use the think things through steps when working with a team on a project.

- **Engage in Goal Setting and Action Plans.** You may want to set goals for a day, for a week, or for a month or for even longer.

- **Write in Your Journal.** At the end of the day, in your Journal, think about what happened during the day and whether you faced a situation where you needed to engage in effective problem solving. Write about what happened and how you used the think things through strategy. How did this work?

Problem Solving Activities in School

Effective problem solving should be integrated into all aspects of instructional activities, especially in history and cultural affairs as well as science. Problem solving is the basis for all scientific exploration. "What problem were these people trying to solve? What had happened? What was their goal? What strategy did they use? Did this work? Remember, the first thing people try to do to solve a problem often does not work? What else did they try?"

Problem solving should especially be incorporated into Community Circles whenever there is a discussion of a concern or relationships issue. "What has happened? What do we think should be the goal? What strategies could be used? Let's think about the Character Strengths. Can we think of some strategies that use some of these strengths? Are all of these strategies in accord with our school's values? What do you think might happen if this approach was tried? What about this other approach? Based on this analysis, what do you think would be the best strategy to try first? How will be determine if this was effective? What should we do if it is not effective? We have to remember that many times the first thing we try might not work and that is okay."

Positively Powerful CI-CO

In the morning, ask if there are any challenges or problems that the student anticipates having to deal with during the day. Then think things through to develop a strategy they can implement. At the end of the day, ask what challenges arose and how they thought things through to figure out what to do.

Chapter 7.

Accountability and Remedy

HIGHLIGHTS

- **Accountability is Critical.** Every student who has been hurtful to another student must be held accountable and required to remedy the harm both to this student and the school community. This includes both Hurtful Students and Supporters. The intervention approach presented in Chapter 11 integrates insight into how to hold students accountable that is set forth in this Chapter..

  - **Stop, Own It, and Fix It.** Students must be held accountable to accept personal responsibility for their wrongdoing, to stop engaging in this hurtful behavior, and to agree to take steps to remedy the harm to both the student they treated badly and to the community. Hurtful Supporters must also be held accountable.

  - **Distinguish between Reactive and Proactive Aggression.** Interventions must distinguish between those students who were proactively aggressive, acting with the intent of being hurtful, and those who were reactively aggression, being hurtful in response to harmful behavior being directed towards them. Interventions with Marginalized Hurtful Student must be grounded in an understanding of trauma.

- **Restorative Practices.** Restorative Practices is grounded in research regarding shame management. The response to shame can be adaptive or maladaptive. The adaptive response to shame is to acknowledge wrongdoing, accept responsibility, and engage in remediation. The maladaptive response leads to shame displacement —which can include withdrawal, attacking self, avoidance, and attacking others. Punitive approaches generally result in maladaptive shame displacement. Restorative approaches can foster accountability and reintegration for those who engaged in harmful acts.

- **Principles of Influence.** Discussed in Chapter 4.

  - **Implementation Strategy.** To increase accountability.

    ‣ **Reciprocity—the Golden Rule.** Ask: "How would you feel if someone treated a good friend like you treated this person?"

    ‣ **Commitment and Consistency.** Ask students to judge their actions by their commitments they made on the Personal Relationships Commitments Statement.

    ‣ **Social Proof.** Ask students to reflect on what school data demonstrates about how others think about those who act in hurtful ways or support those being hurtful.

    ‣ **Liking.** Hold Hurtful Supporters accountable and discuss strategies to encourage their friend to not be hurtful.

    ‣ **Authority.** Ask: "What would your mom or dad or other adult who you respect think about your actions?"

    ‣ **Scarcity or Possible Loss.** Reflect on the possible loss of reputation or friendships.

- **Mechanisms of Moral Disengagement.** To hold students who engaged in wrongdoing accountable requires they accept personal responsibility for the harm they have caused. They must "own it" before they can be expected to agree to "fix it."

  - **Four Key Strategies.** Mechanisms of Moral Disengagement describes the process by which people convince themselves that certain ethical standards do not apply to their behavior in particular situations.

    ‣ **Reconstruing Conduct (Justify and Spin).** Moral justification, use of euphemistic labeling, and comparing actions to worse behavior.

    ‣ **Displacing or Diffusing Responsibility (Deny Personal Responsibility).** Blame someone else for encouraging the action, or thinking someone else should to intervene.

- ▸ **Disregarding or Misrepresenting Injurious Consequences (Deny the Harm).** Minimize, ignore, or even dispute the harmful consequences of actions.

- ▸ **Blaming the Victim (Blame the Other).** Dehumanize and blaming the victim as deserving their suffering.

- **Moral Disengagement and Bullying.** The degree to which moral disengagement is shared by classmates has been linked to greater aggression, bullying perpetration and victimization, pro-bullying behavior of witnesses, passive witness behavior, and less defender behavior.

  - ▸ Moral justification and blame the victim are most associated with direct bullying. Blame the victim most associated with in-direct bullying. Diffusion of responsibility and blame the victim most associated with hurtful actions of supporters.

  - ▸ Use of mechanisms of moral disengagement can be decreased through education and this may result in a reduction of hurtful behavior and an increase in defending behavior.

  - ▸ School leaders or staff may also rationalize not responding to the hurtful incidents they witness or are reported to them.

- **Collaborative Problem Solving.** Kids with challenging behavior do not lack the will to behave well—they lack the skills. The CPS process: Identifying triggers to a student's challenging behavior and the specific skills they need help developing. Collaborate with the student to build skills and develop lasting solutions to problems that work for everyone. Implementation of CPS has been consistently associated with significant reductions in disciplinary outcomes such as restraints, seclusion, suspensions, and alternative placements.

  - **Implementation Strategies.** The Accountability Process set forth in Chapter 11 does not strictly follow this CPS process, and is referred to as "participatory problem solving." The CPS Thinking Skills Inventory is an excellent tool to use with any Marginalized Hurtful Student (and some Targeted Students). Additional questions are recommended.

- **Impulsive Retaliation.** It appears that retaliation, which could be impulsive/reactive or planned/proactive, is a source of significant student disruption. Battles between rivals that are frequently referred to students as "drama" tend to involve significant repeated rounds retaliation. Students appear to have mixed feelings about retaliation.

The following approach to reduce retaliation combines the research in Chapters 4, 5, 6 and this Chapter.

- **Self-Regulation**. Students with effective self-regulation skills will be less likely to engage in impulsive reactions.

- **Keeping Their Power**. When students keep their personal power, they realize that they can remain in control of how they feel about themselves and respond if someone is hurtful.

- **Knowing that People Can Change**. If students think that the person who was hurtful will always be hurtful, this justifies their hurtful response. But when they know that people can change holding out for a more positive resolution is a better path.

- **Problem Solving**. Having a problem solving process to use if someone has been hurtful helps them to identify a positive and powerful response.

- **Make a Positive Connection**. Connecting with a good friend or trusted adult should facilitate obtaining personal support, which will help with self-regulation and problem solving.

THE IMPORTANCE OF ACCOUNTABILITY

Every student who has been hurtful to another student must be held accountable and required to remedy the harm both to this student and to the school community. This includes in situations there they acted in retaliation against someone who was hurtful to them. In this situation, both students should be considered Targeted Students and Hurtful Students.

The interventions in situations where students were hurtful must distinguish between those students who were proactively aggressive, who were acting with the intent of being hurtful, and those who were reactively aggression, being hurtful in response to harmful behavior being directed towards them.

A discussion on motivations for being hurtful was set forth in Chapter 2.[494] The Proactive Aggression motivations identified in the research literature included dominance, status and popularity, resources, justice, belonging, romance, identity, entertainment. The motivation that would more often fall under the nature of Reactive Aggression is revenge or retaliation.

Chapter 1 addressed the concerns of students who have both been targeted by hurtful behavior and are also aggressive—the "bully/victim" student who in this book is referred to as the Marginalized Hurtful Student. The challenges faced by this student and the process to intervene with this student must be grounded in an understanding of trauma, thus the strategies set forth in Chapter 6 are highly relevant to the concerns of these students. Unless and until the harm they are experiencing is identified and effectively addressed, it is unlikely that much success will be achieved in influencing them to stop being hurtful.

However, Marginalized Hurtful Students must be also be held accountable. This means the research-based approaches set forth in this Chapter to influence students to accept personal responsibility and agree to take steps to remedy the harm apply fully to these students also.

Strategies to address the concerns of Dominance Motivated Hurtful Students will not likely focus on any personal challenges these students face. Thus, the intent in these situations is to hold these students accountable to accept personal responsibility for their wrongdoing, to stop engaging in this hurtful behavior, and to agree to take steps to remedy the harm to both the student they treated badly and to the community.

The other students who must be held accountable and agree to take steps to remedy the harm are the Hurtful Supporters. These students must accept personal responsibility for supporting or encouraging the Hurtful Student. The supportive role they play is significant. Their remedy of the harms should include a remedy of harm to the Targeted Student, a remedy of harm to the school community, an agreement to discontinue any support for the Hurtful Student, and an agreement to seek to encourage this Hurtful Student to not be hurtful in the future.

RESTORATIVE PRACTICES

The essence of Restorative Practices is that students who have been hurtful are supported to stop their hurtful acts, acknowledge personal responsibility, and take steps to remedy the harm to both the student or students who they have been hurtful to, as well as to the school community.

An extensive discussion of the current concerns associated with Restorative Practices was set forth in Chapter 2. Nevertheless, implementing activities that are grounded in Restorative Practices is considered essential. This section will delve more deeply into this approach.

The Restorative Practices approach to discipline is grounded in research regarding shame management. Shame is a central feature of social regulation.[495] The response to shame can be adaptive or maladaptive. The adaptive response to shame is to acknowledge wrongdoing, accept responsibility, and engage in remediation. The maladaptive response leads to shame displacement—which can include withdrawal, attacking self, avoidance, and attacking others.[496] The key factor determining whether shame becomes adaptive or maladaptive is whether wrongdoing is treated in a way that is stigmatizing or reintegrative.

Punitive approaches generally result in maladaptive shame displacement. This is why punitive disciplinary actions are so frequently ineffective in creating a positive change in behavior. This is also why the slight shift many schools have made to an approach of logical consequences, while an improvement, does not appear to be achieving desired results. This response still involves the person in authority imposing a consequence. This also includes the practice of imposing a logical consequence, which is better than punishment. However, this still involves an adult authority imposing a consequence.

As effectively set forth in Zehr's *The Little Book of Restorative Justice,* the punishment or logical consequences approach seeks to find who is to blame and asks these questions:

- *Who did it?*
- *What "rule" was broken?*
- *How should the offender be punished?*[497]

Restorative approaches can foster accountability and reintegration for those who engaged in harmful acts. Interventions pursuant to Restorative Practices interventions view transgressions as harm done to people and communities and encourage adaptive shame management. Restorative practices ask these questions:

- *What is the harm to all parties involved and to the community?*
- *What needs to be done to repair the harm?*
- *Who is responsible for this repair?*
- *What needs to occur to prevent similar harm in the future?* [498]

As noted earlier, the International Institute for Restorative Practices has contributed significantly to the promotion of restorative practices.[499] A very excellent set of resources are also available on the Minnesota Department of Education website, most notably a Restorative Intervention Implementation Tool Kit.[500]

Implementation Strategy

The *Engage Students to Embrace Civility* intervention approach presented in Chapter 11 is grounded in restorative practices thinking and integrates other insight into how to influence positive behavior that is set forth in this Chapter. This includes insight gained from research into Principles of Influence, Mechanisms of Moral Disengagement, and Collaborative Problem Solving.

The concerns associated with restorative conferences or circles and the shift from restorative to logical consequences were addressed in Chapter 3. To overcome those concerns, it is considered most important to engage with the Targeted Student privately, which then follows that the intervention with the Hurtful Student and Supporters would also be private.

The key reason for this is the imbalance of power between the Targeted Student and those who are hurtful. It is also important to engage with the Hurtful Supporter privately, not with the Hurtful Student. Hurtful Students often have significant power over their Supporters. If a Supporter is concerned that any evidence of less than total allegiance to the Hurtful Student may place them at risk, that student needs to be bale to address this concern privately.

The process that is outlined in Chapter 11 suggests engaging with the Hurtful Student and each Supporter being engaged in a series of questions called an Accountability Process. This Accountability Process is based on the research set forth in this Chapter.

Once the student has gotten to the point of truly accepting accountability for their wrongdoing, the conversation them shifts to problem solving. This is a participatory problem solving process that is similar to what is called Collaborative Problem Solving, which is discussed below.[501] "You have taken excellent steps in acknowledging that what you did was wrong. Now, how do you propose you might remedy the harm you caused to (name of targeted student) and to our school community?"

PRINCIPLES OF INFLUENCE

The research on Principles of Influence was set forth in Chapter 4.[502]

Implementation Strategy

These principles provide an effective discussion strategy to seek to influence acceptance of personal responsibility and an agreement to remedy the harm by both Hurtful Students and Supporters. The following is a description of how these principles can be utilized in the context of engaging in an Accountability Process with students who have been hurtful and their supporters.

- **Reciprocity—the Golden Rule.** When intervening with a student who has been hurtful or supporter, questions like this can be asked: "How would you feel if someone treated you or a good friend of yours like you treated this person?" "How would you feel if someone treated you like your friend treated ___?" This will generate thinking in accord with the influence of reciprocity. Note in the *Embrace Civility Student Survey* that when asked why they would not be hurtful: 78% of students responded that "How I would feel if someone did this to me" was an important consideration.

- **Commitment and Consistency.** The approach of having students create a statement of their Personal Relationships Commitments Statement, which was discussed in Chapter 4, is grounded in this strategy. These statements should be retained by the school in a digital format that is easily accessible by school leaders.

  - When intervening with Hurtful Students or Supporters, having these students' written Personal Relationships Commitments Statement and asking them to judge their actions by their commitments will be exceptionally more powerful in changing behavior than accusing them of breaking a school rule. "How did your recent behavior fit with the commitment you made?"

- **Social Proof.** In an intervention, asking students to reflect on what the school data demonstrates about how others in this school think about those who act in hurtful ways or support those being hurtful should have a helpful influence.

- **Liking.** The liking and friendship principle can be incorporated by ensuring that when a hurtful incident occurs, both the primary student who is being hurtful and this student's supporters, are engaged in a discussion about accountability and remedying the harm. Further discussions can be held with the Hurtful Supporters about strategies they can use to encourage their friend to not be hurtful.

- **Authority.** This principle can be incorporated into into a discussion with a Hurtful Student and Supporter by asking the student, "What would your mom or dad or other adult who you respect think about your actions?"

- **Scarcity or Possible Loss.** The *Embrace Civility Student Survey* will reveal the actual accurate thinking of students and the possible loss of reputation or friendships. Hurtful Students and Supporters can be asked what their thoughts about their actions are based on the school's survey that has demonstrated that a significant percentage of students do not admire those who are hurtful or support those being hurtful. This strategy combines the influences of Social Proof and Possible Loss.

MECHANISMS OF MORAL DISENGAGEMENT

To hold students who engaged in wrongdoing accountable requires they accept personal responsibility for the harm they have caused. They must "own it" before they can be expected to agree to "fix it."

Very often, people will rationalize their wrongdoing—which will interfere with ensuring that they stop, accept responsibility, and take steps to remedy the harm. To establish school environments where students treat each other with kindness, respect, and inclusion requires the staff in these schools maintain the same standards for their actions.

Research has consistently shown that students judge bullying as a severe moral transgression and consider it wrong—independently of school rules. They most often judge this behavior as wrong by referring to the harm that it causes to the victim.[503] However, those who engaging in bullying tend to judge bullying as less wrong. They also appear to consider the possible harmful effect of their behavior less frequently in their justifications of their bullying actions.

Bandura introduced the concept of Mechanisms of Moral Disengagement.[504] This relates to social and psychological thinking strategies can interfere with one's actions and acceptance of personal responsibility. Bandura's theory of the Mechanisms of Moral Disengagement describes the process by which people convince themselves that certain ethical standards do not apply to them in particular situations.

People establish personal moral standards they intent to follow. People like to think of themselves as one who engages in ethical and moral behavior. Through the use of these mechanisms, a person's moral self-sanctions can be disengaged. The self-regulation of their actions in accord with their values can be deactivated. In turn, this promotes or facilitates behaviors that harm others without feelings of remorse or guilt. When their behavior is in a violation of the moral standards they have established for themselves, they create rationalizations or excuses for why these standards should not apply to their actions in the current situation.

Bandura's insight provides an effective framework to understand how students who engage in hurtful behavior and others might seek to excuse their behavior. The four primary approaches that people, youth and adults, use to support moral disengagement and rationalize wrongdoing are these:

- **Reconstruing Conduct (Justify and Spin).** Reconstruing conduct is done in three ways: moral justification of using worthy ends or moral purposes to justify actions, euphemistic labeling, and advantageous comparison of making a negative behavior seem less negative by comparing it to a worse behavior. Actions are portrayed as serving some larger purpose or euphemistic terms are used to describe the action. "Someone needed to speak out." "I was just joking around." "It was a prank." "This was locker room talk." "This is just drama, not bullying."

- **Displacing or Diffusing Responsibility (Deny Personal Responsibility).** This can occur if many are engaging in certain behavior, if someone else can be blamed for encouraging the action, or someone else ought to intervene to stop the wrong. "Everybody does it." "Someone else started it." "It wasn't my fault." "Someone else should be responsible for stopping this."

- **Disregarding or Misrepresenting Injurious Consequences (Deny the Harm).** This allows people to minimize, ignore, or even dispute the harmful consequences of their actions. "What I did or what happened wasn't that bad." "They are overreacting."

- **Dehumanizing or Blaming the Victim (Blame the Other).** This involves dehumanization and blaming the victim by thinking that the victim deserves their suffering. Those who are targeted may have personal characteristics that make it easier to blame them as being "deviant" or "misfits." When someone is dehumanized, it is easier to rationalize that hurtful actions were justified. "They deserved it."

Moral Disengagement and Bullying

Many researchers are focusing on moral disengagement as the process by which some people rationalize their hurtful acts or their failure to step in to help when they witness wrongdoing. A recent meta-analysis by Killer and colleagues of 47 independent studies of the association of moral disengagement with both bullying and defending was conducted. A significant relationship between moral disengagement and bullying behavior was consistently found in these studies.[505]

Students who display higher rates of moral disengagement are more inclined to engage in bullying behaviors and other aggressive acts.[506] Moral disengagement is positively associated with aggression including both those who are bullying and marginalized students who are both being and engaging in bullying. Further, students who who display higher levels of moral disengagement are more prone to support those who are being hurtful.

One study of moral disengagement mechanisms among students identified moral justification and dehumanizing or blaming the victim as the rationalizations most associated with engaging in direct bullying.[507] Indirect bullying was only associated with dehumanizing or blaming the victim.[508] It appears that diffusion of responsibility and dehumanizing or blaming the victim are associated with greater pro-bullying behavior by supporters.

Researchers have started to explore whether moral disengagement as a group-level, such as in the classroom or school, is related to bullying. If the norms of the classroom appear to support individual moral disengagement, this has been shown to be associated with a higher prevalence of bullying in the classroom or school.[509]

In addition, an assessment of student perceptions of the degree to which moral disengagement is shared by classmates has been linked to greater aggression, bullying perpetration, bullying victimization, pro-bullying behavior of witnesses and passive witness behavior, and also to less defender behavior.[510] Students who scored higher on individual assessment of moral disengagement were even more likely to engage in bullying when they were in a classroom in which reinforcing bullying was the more prevalent reaction by witnesses.[511]

The question of whether inclination to morally disengage precedes bullying or is developed subsequently, to explain such behavior, is not clear. However, a recent study in Sweden, provided some insight.[512] This study assessed both inclination to morally disengage and bullying behavior in both 4th and 5th grade years. What was found was this:

> ...(C)hildren who are more prone to moral disengagement tend to be more inclined to bully others. Also, children who more often bully others are more prone to develop a higher tendency of moral disengagement over time, independent of their initial levels of moral disengagement. In other words, bullying perpetration precedes moral disengagement over time in middle childhood. ...(O)ur study suggests that bullying perpetration in middle childhood might initiate a more frequent and intense use of moral disengagement over time. Moral disengagement might then become stable as a trait-like characteristic that in turn predicts and increases the likelihood of engaging in bullying perpetration during adolescence... Bandura argues that individuals conduct milder forms of aggressions that they can tolerate with some discomfort, and by a gradual increase in moral disengagement through repeated aggressions, inhumane behaviors increase over time and become thoughtlessly routinized.[513]

Two studies have investigated strategies implemented in schools designed to undermine the use of moral disengagement to be hurtful.[514] One with elementary students used guided discussions of children's literature that focused on the use of moral disengagement. Students who underwent the program decreased their likelihood to justify hurtful behavior and reported decreased experience of others treating them badly. The other, with high school students related to cyberbullying that included awareness-raising and interactive discussions, demonstrated decrease in use of moral disengagement on questionnaires. Unfortunately. this study did not measure behavior.

As is clear from the research, students who engage in hurtful behavior are very likely to use these mechanisms of moral disengagement when faced with an accusation of such hurtful behavior. Their parents or caregivers may also do this. In addition, when students think they should intervene, but do not, they are also likely to create rationalizations for why they did not intervene. However, it appears that the use of mechanisms of moral disengagement can be decreased through education and this may result in a reduction of hurtful behavior and an increase in defending behavior.

Staff Use of Mechanisms of Moral Disengagement

School leaders or staff may also use Mechanisms of Moral Disengagement to rationalize not responding to the hurtful incidents they witness or are reported to them. Many students and parents have reported to this author of hearing principals say such things as: "It was just a joke." "This is not bullying, so there is nothing I can do." "This is off-campus, not my job." "You are overreacting, it wasn't that bad." "If you would only stop (fill in the blank), this would not happen to you."

The significant negative ramifications of filing bullying reports with USDOE's OCR, required under *ESSA*, has very likely contributed to a very significant increase in school leadership use of rationalizations to justify not considering a reported incidents to meet the standards requiring a report.

It is important to distinguish between rationalizations and reasons. The "blame the victim" rationalization is grounded in perception that the targeted student is "deviant." If a student states: "She has been spreading nasty rumors about me" this is a reason. This is a report of hurtful behavior directed at this student that must be addressed.

Implementation Strategy

As limited research has documented, it is possible to specifically teach students and staff about Mechanisms of Moral Disengagement and rationalizations and this may lead to a reduction in the use of rationalizations to support being hurtful or not stepping in to help.

Listening to politicians or other leaders when publicly accused of engaging in inappropriate behavior provides ample opportunity to witness these mechanisms in action in a manner that is apart from the school environment. It is suggested that teachers pay attention to situations in which these common rationalizations are set forth in news stories and discuss these mechanisms for what they are—excuses for not engaging in ethical behavior. All of society would be benefitted by a greater understanding of these mechanisms are used so often, frequently by people in power, to rationalize and justify their harmful actions.

The best way to challenge these rationalizations is using questions that are based on the Principles of Influence, especially Commitments and Social Proof, and to engage in a form of Reflective Listening. Reflective Thinking responses provide the opportunity for the student who is engaging in rationalizations to hear their words coming back to them. "If I am hearing you correctly, you feel that you were justified in (description) because (expressed rationalization). Can you help me understand how that fits with your Personal Commitment for how you will treat others? How do you think other students think about your actions?"

Note, that Mechanisms of Moral Disengagement are a strategy to rationalize behavior that varies from a person's individual values and social norms. The above statement challenges the Hurtful Student on both aspects.

COLLABORATIVE PROBLEM SOLVING

The Collaborative Problem Solving approach was originally developed by Greene when he was at Massachusetts General Hospital. This theory was described in books he authored including, *Lost at School*.[515] For a reason unknown to this author, Green and others at Massachusetts General had a falling out. The trademark Collaborative Problem Solving was retained by Massachusetts General. Green's approach is now called Collaborative & Proactive Solutions.[516] The Massachusetts General approach is called Collaborative Problem Solving and is presented on its website,

Think:Kids.[517] The Collaborative Problem Solving approach is described on the Think:Kids site in this manner:

> *Our Collaborative Problem Solving approach recognizes what research has pointed to for years – that kids with challenging behavior are already trying hard. They don't lack the will to behave well. They lack the skills to behave well.*
>
> *CPS helps adults shift to a more accurate and compassionate mindset and embrace the truth that kids do well if they can – rather than the more common belief that kids would do well if they simply wanted to.*
>
> *Flowing from this simple but powerful philosophy, CPS focuses on building skills like flexibility, frustration tolerance and problem solving, rather than simply motivating kids to behave better. The process begins with identifying triggers to a child's challenging behavior and the specific skills they need help developing. The next step involves partnering with the child to build those skills and develop lasting solutions to problems that work for everyone.[518]*

As should be apparent the Collaborative Problem Solving approach is in line with the Social Domain Theory:

- **Competencies.** Students who demonstrate behavior challenges have lagging skills and need assistance in developing new skills.

- **Control.** These students will be engaged in problem solving process, whereby they will be asked to develop strategies to address their concerns. Thus, they have control.

- **Connections.** The problem solving process is collaborative, a process that involves a supportive adult who remains engaged to support the student in implementing their developed strategy.

The effectiveness of Collaborative Problem Solving in school settings has been described as follows:

> *Findings from published research and unpublished reports indicate that the implementation of CPS in educational settings has been consistently associated with significant reductions in disciplinary outcomes such as restraints, seclusion, suspensions, and alternative placements. Teachers trained in CPS have reported reductions in student-related stress as well as improved confidence and relationships with students, and the initial evidence suggests that CPS may be positively associated with peripheral variables such as student attendance and family participation. Preliminary results also suggest that treatment with CPS may be associated with improved social skills and executive functioning; future research needs to explore whether improvements in these skills drive decreases in restrictive disciplinary practices such as suspensions, restraints, and seclusions. Rigorous and controlled research will be necessary in order to validate these preliminary, but promising, findings.[519]*

This is an additional helpful description of the underlying premise of Collaborative Problem Solving:

CPS is a conceptual and therapeutic model that posits that chronic and severe externalizing behavior is the product of lagging cognitive skills that interfere with a child's ability to comply with adult expectations. Consider this: in order to meet adult expectations, a child must have an adequately developed set of cognitive skills allowing him to accurately comprehend and interpret the expectations, to flexibly respond to different expectations in different situations, to consider a range of responses, to predict consequences of each of those responses, to express his or her needs or difficulties in meeting expectations, and to tolerate frustration in the face of unexpected results. CPS asserts that if a child is lacking one or more of these skills, he or she will be unable to adaptively respond to demands and that, as a result, maladaptive behavior (defiance, outbursts, and so on) will ensue.[520]

It must be noted and emphasized at this point, the use of Collaborative Problem Solving to support students who are having challenges in personal relationships should not be focused on an effort to address "children's ability to comply with adult expectations." This must be an effort to increase students' abilities to engage in positive relationships with peers and adults in all settings. It must be recognized that some students, both Targeted Students and Marginalized Hurtful Students engage in behaviors that are disapproved by their peers and this often results in their being treated badly.

This statement should not be interpreted as blaming the student for the fact that they are being treated badly. Reducing these disapproved behaviors should be considered component of a strategy to address the overall concern. Increasing student tolerance for a wider range of behaviors considered acceptable from their peers must be an equally importance component.

Implementation Strategies

Both of these Collaborative Problem Solving programs have a well-defined set of practices. The Accountability Process that is set forth in Chapter 11 does not strictly follow this Collaborative Problem Solving process. The approach I referred to as "participatory problem solving."

Thinking Skills Inventory

The Collaborative Problem Solving Thinking Skills Inventory is an excellent tool to use with any Marginalized Hurtful Student.[521] This also can be used in the context of a Targeted Student who appears to have some behavioral concerns that are contributing to their victimization. If either the Marginalized Hurtful Students or Targeted Students is receiving special education services, this assessment should be integrated into their Individualized Education Plan (IEP) or Section 504 Plan.

The shift in thinking issue that must be pointed out relates to the identification of specific cognitive skills deficits. This is a description of the Collaborative Problem Solving process:

> *In order to assess the specific cognitive-skills deficits for a particular child, it is first necessary to identify the demands or expectations that trigger their externalizing behaviors. Because the same challenging behavior (e.g., verbal outbursts) could be caused by a wide range of lagging skills, the specific type of challenging behavior is of little importance. The focus is on identifying the demands that trigger the behavior (e.g., transitions or spelling homework). Once a list of triggers is identified, the caregiver or clinician can use this list to inform hypotheses about lagging skills. For example, a child who frequently overturns his or her school desk (the challenging behavior) in response to the end of free time and the start of work (the trigger) may have difficulty with transitions/set-shifting (executive functioning) or with tolerating frustration (emotion regulation). ...[522]*

It is suggested that an expanded version of the Collaborative Problem Solving Thinking Skills Inventory be used with any student who has identified behavior challenges that appear to be implicated in their victimization. When this approach is implemented in the context of reducing hurtful incidents, the "triggers" that also must be assessed include the specific issues related to the hurtful incidents.

In addition, in a manner that is in accord with the regulations under federal civil rights laws, aspects of the school environment that may be contributing to such concerns must also be assessed and plan must also be developed and implemented to address these environmental aspects. This may include staff who are engaging in hurtful behavior.

It is recommended that these additional questions be added to an expanded Collaborative Problem Solving Thinking Skills assessment:

- What cognitive skills defects does this student appear to have?

- What relationship skills defects does this student appear to have?

- What situations appear to trigger this student to be hurtful?

- What traumatic or toxic stress situations has this student or is this student experiencing?

- What strengths does this student possess?

- What is happening in relation to the manner in which student is experiencing hurtful treatment or behaving in a hurtful manner and their relationships with the other players?

- What aspects of the school environment may be contributing to this student's behavior or the behavior of others in relation to this student?

- What are this student's relationships with school staff and how can these be strengthened?

Problem Solving Approach

The problem solving approach of Collaborative Problem Solving is described as follows:

> *Plan B—a seminal element of CPS—is used when the adult attempts to solve the problem collaboratively with the child. Implementation of Plan B consists of three components, performed sequentially. In the first component, the adult gathers information in order to gain a clear understanding of the child's concerns about a particular recurring problem or issue (e.g., "I don't like stopping free time when I'm in the middle of reading, because it's hard for me to find my place again later.") In the second, the adult states his or her concern or perspective ("My concern is that we need to move on to math at that time. I don't want you to miss out on the beginning of math, because it will be hard to catch up later.") When both the child's and adult's concerns are clear, the third component can be implemented: the adult and child brainstorm solutions that will address both their concerns. The child is given the first opportunity to generate a solution (e.g., "What if you warn me when we have a few minutes left, so I can find a good stopping point?"). No solutions are dismissed outright, and the adult helps the child to think through whether each solution addresses the concerns of both parties and whether it is realistic and feasible. Plan B is successfully completed when both adult and child have agreed on a mutually satisfactory and realistic solution. This process, however, is iterative; after a Plan B conversation, the child and adult implement the solution and return to discuss whether it was successful. If it was not, they discuss what other concerns arose, and they try again with another solution until they have found one that works.[523]*

As will be set forth in Chapter 11, the manner in which the Collaborative Problem Solving approach should be applied in situations of seeking to address hurtful incidents will follow a similar pattern: gathering information, identification of concern, discussion of solutions with the student fully engaged in the process, implementation of the agreed upon strategy, revisiting the discussion to assess effectiveness and determine whether any other strategies need to be implemented.

However, when implemented with students who have been hurtful, several additional research-based strategies have been incorporated to ensure that the Hurtful Student accepts personal responsibility for their hurtful actions. These include strategies to undermine their use of Mechanisms of Moral Disengagement to rationalize their hurtful behavior and Principles of Influence strategies that strive to influence acceptance of personal responsibility and more positive behavior.

In addition, this includes addressing an exceptionally important additional component must be implemented—Restorative Practices. The concept of

Restorative Practices has not been integrated into Collaborative Problem Solving. After the student has reached a personal acceptance that they engaged in behavior that has caused harm to another student and to the school climate, they must be engaged in a restorative Accountability Process to identify how they will remedy this harm.

IMPULSIVE RETALIATION

As noted earlier, one of the motivations for being hurtful involves retaliation, in response to situations that from the perspective of the Hurtful Student involved harm being directed at them. Many times Marginalized Hurtful Students will engage in Reactive Aggression—impulsive retaliation.

Dominance Motivated Hurtful Students or Targeted Students may also engage in retaliation. Battles between two rivals, especially related to interpersonal relationships, that are frequently referred to students as "drama" tend to involve significant repeated rounds of hurtful behavior that is retaliatory.

Note how on the *Embrace Civility Student Survey*, where a combination of the top two responses for why they were hurtful—"I acted too fast when I was angry and really did not 'think'" at 47% and "This student had been hurtful to me or a friend of mine" at 44% translates to "impulsive retaliation."

Note also in the discussion on Positive Social Norms in the Chapter 4, when asking about student norms, this response was highlighted: "Were treated badly and retaliated." Only 18% of students did not admire this action, a significant 52% had mixed feelings, and 30% approved of retaliation. Thus, it is challenging to rely on Positive Social Norms to reduce such retaliation. Several more questions have been added to the new *Embrace Civility Student Survey* that will seek to better demonstrate more positive responses to being treated badly.

Helpful research was presented in Chapter 4 in the section on Social Emotional Growth Mindset. Of key importance was Yeager and colleagues research study that involved teaching students about Social Emotional Growth Mindset. Providing instruction about Social Emotional Growth Mindset very effectively demonstrated a reduction in retaliation.[524]

It appears that there are a combination of Social Emotional Growth Mindset strategies that students can learn that would assist in avoiding impulsive retaliation.

- **Self-Regulation**. The positive benefits of self-regulation and strategies to increase self-regulation were addressed in Chapter 6. Students who gain in their self-regulation skills will be less likely to engage in impulsive action in response to being treated badly. "I can change how I respond when things get tough and stay calm."

- **Keeping Their Power**. Assisting students in keeping their personal power was also addressed in Chapter 6. When students increase their ability to keep their personal power, they realize that they can remain in control of how they feel about themselves and respond if someone is hurtful. By holding themselves tall and remaining calm, Targeted Students also can keep their personal power. "Even if I do not feel strong when someone is hurtful to me, I know that I can hold myself tall and control my thinking so that I keep my personal power."

- **Knowing that People Can Change**. This is the Social Emotional Growth Mindset insight, understanding that people can change, as discussed in Chapter 4. If students think that the person who was hurtful will always be hurtful, this justifies their hurtful response. But when they know that people can change they can understand that holding out for a more positive resolution is a better path. "I know that the other student has been hurtful to me. But I also know that this other student can change. If I respond in a positive manner, this can help the other student to change and not be hurtful to me in the future."

- **Problem Solving.** Also discussed in Chapter 6 is the think things through problem solving strategy. Having a problem solving process to use if someone has been hurtful helps them to identify a positive and powerful response. "I can think things through to figure out how to respond to this situation."

- **Make a Positive Connection**. The guidance to connect with a good friend or trusted adult should facilitate obtaining personal support, which will help with self-regulation and problem solving. "I can make a positive connection with a good friend or trusted adult who will provide me with support, as well as help me to think things through."

Chapter 8.
Positive Peer Intervention

HIGHLIGHTS

- **Importance Of Positive Peer Intervention.** Most often, bullying takes place in front of the peer group, who either supported or not. The objective of this analysis is to increase the likelihood that when students witnesses a hurtful incident they will step in to help.

  - **Effective, but Most Do Not.** Many students indicate that they would like to help when they see someone being hurtful or excluded. When students do intervene, they are often successful in getting the hurtful situations to stop. Bullied students who have supportive friends experience less distress. Students strongly admire those who step in to help. Unfortunately, when bullying situations do occur, most often witnesses do not step in to help.

  - **Social Norms Evidence.** On PISA 2018, students overwhelmingly reported negative attitudes towards bullying and very positive attitudes about defending targets of bullying.

- **Bystander Research.** Individuals are less likely to intervene on behalf of a distressed individual when there are other observers.

  - The five steps of the bystander model are: Notice the event. Interpret the event as an emergency that requires help. Accept responsibility for the intervention. Know how to intervene or provide help. Implement intervention decisions.

- **Bullying Research on Bystanders.**

  - **Participant Roles.** Different patterns of witness involvement are called "participant roles:" Assistants of the one being hurtful. Reinforcers of the one being hurtful. Outsiders who stay away from bullying situations and do not take sides with anyone. Defenders of the one being treated badly.

  - **What Research Has Not Considered.** Research has not considered the role of students who both engage in bullying and are treated badly or situations that involve retaliation.

  - **Social Preference and Perceived Popularity.** Researchers measure student status of "social preference" (how well liked) and "perceived popularity." But this research has not considered insight of Dominance or Prestige Leaders. My opinion is that this is significant. Most students do not have personal power to directly challenge the actions of a Dominance Motivated Hurtful Student.

  - **Programs.** The level of research effectiveness of programs has varied. Programs implemented at the secondary level have not generally achieved any success.

- **The *Engage Students to Embrace Civility* Framework.** The following is my research-based peer intervention framework.

  - **Witness Roles.** When students witness bullying or other hurtful behavior, they can be a: Hurtful Supporter—provide support for Hurtful Students. Passive Observer—do not become involved in the situation. Helpful Ally—step in to help.

    › **Helpful Allies.** Helpful Allies can: Step in to Help. Reach out to be kind to the person being hurt or left out, help this person walk away, support those who are having challenges, and help others resolve conflict. Say, "Stop." Publicly or privately tell the person being hurtful to stop. Report Concerns. Tell an adult who can help.

  - **Hurtful Supporter.** It is exceptionally important to focus on the role of these Hurtful Supporters and seek to shift their path by also holding them accountable.

  - **Passive Observer.** Our society and schools encourage students to be Passive Observers. Their perception of their own social status and the safety risks will often shape their decision-making. Passive

Observer students who do care and want to step in to help, can be encouraged to help in a private manner.

- **Helpful Ally.** The most active Helpful Allies tend to have higher social status and personal power. They also have a higher level of compassion and effective social relationship skills. Much research appears to lack an understanding of the ethological basis for hurtful behavior involving the drive for social dominance.

- **Research to Support Positive Peer Intervention.** Three key personal factors and three key environmental factors.

  - **Personal Factors.**

    ‣ **Motivation Grounded in Personal Values.** This includes compassion, a feeling of personal responsibility for well-being of others, acceptance of differences, affective empathy, and a feeling of personal connection.

    ‣ **Personal Power.** The comparative personal power between the one being aggressive and the Witness. Directly stepping in raises the risk of embarrassment, retaliation, physical harm, or damage to reputation.

    ‣ **Self-Efficacy.** Believing in one's capabilities to engage in actions that are required to achieve desired goals—includes both effective skills and confidence in those skills.

  - **Social and Environmental Factors.**

    ‣ **Friendships.** Friendship status is highly influential in decisions to intervene.

    ‣ **School Climate.** Defending is more likely in schools that have low levels of moral disengagement and higher levels of school connectedness. The school must maintain a culture of acceptance and celebrate differences. Staff must always treat all students with kindness and respect. Of significant importance is that staff intervene effectively in hurtful incidents they witness.

    ‣ **Perceived Expectations of Peers—Social Norms.** What students think other students think about those who are hurtful and those who step in to help appears to be highly influential in increasing the willingness of students to positively intervene.

- **Barriers to Intervention.**

  - **Bystander Perceived Barriers.** Diffusion of Responsibility —"Someone else should be responsible." Audience Inhibition—"I could fail or embarrass myself." Social Influence—"No one else is doing anything—nobody else thinks this is wrong."

  - **Mechanisms of Moral Disengagement.** Students who step in to help do not display high rates of moral disengagement.

  - **Fears and Fixed Mindset.** Legitimate fears, including differences in personal power and a perceived lack of skills to safety and effectively intervene are a barrier. Students who have a Social Emotional Fixed Mindset are also likely to think that this hurtful behavior cannot be stopped, and there is nothing they could do.

IMPORTANCE OF POSITIVE PEER INTERVENTION

Positive peer intervention refers to the actions of peers when they witness hurtful incidents. The objective of this analysis is to increase the likelihood that when students witnesses a hurtful incident they will step in to help. Most often, bullying takes place in front of the peer group.[525] Bullying behaviors are either supported or not supported by peers. Peers can inhibit and discourage bullying or they may reinforce, support, or otherwise encourage bullying.

Many students indicate that they would like to help when they see someone being hurtful or excluded.[526] When students do intervene, they are often successful in getting the hurtful situations to stop.[527] Bullied students who have supportive friends experience less distress.[528] Students strongly admire those who step in to help.[529]

Unfortunately, when bullying situations do occur, most often witnesses do not step in to help.[530] Simply telling students how horrible bullying is and not to be a "bystander" is an approach that does not appear to have demonstrated any effectiveness. It is necessary to better understand the dynamics of Witness decision-making to increase the number of Witnesses who are willing to step in to help.

The research in this area generally uses the term "bystanders." I dislike this term, because I think it conveys the underlying message of "standing by" or deciding not to become engaged. I also dislike the term "upstander" as a contrivance. I choose to use the term "Witness."

However, all of the research uses the term "bystander." So sometimes I will use the term "bystander" in the discussion of the research. I encourage schools to use the term "Witness."

Encouraging bystanders to step in to help, also called "defend" in the research literature, is an important strategy to reduce the level of bullying behavior in schools.[531] Students who might potentially defend are likely easier to influence than those being hurtful. These students often feel bad for the one being targeted by the bullying and indicate that they want to help. They also strongly support, in the abstract, the idea that supporting a student who being bullied is something they should do.

As was discussed in Chapter 1 and 4, the PISA 2018 contained questions on bullying, including some very helpful attitude questions.[532] When asked about their feelings towards bullying, students overwhelmingly reported negative attitudes towards bullying. They also reported very positive attitudes about defending targets of bullying:

- *It irritates me when nobody defends bullied students*—81% agreed or strongly agreed.
- *It is a good thing to help students who can't defend themselves*—88% agreed or strongly agreed.
- *I like it when someone stands up for other students who are being bullied*—90% agreed or strongly agreed.

These findings clearly suggest that if we can better support Witnesses to take action against bullying, prevalence rates could be reduced.[533]

Embrace Civility Student Survey

Interesting insight was obtained on the earlier version of the *Embrace Civility Student Survey*.

Question: In the last month, how frequently have you witnessed a student being hurtful to another student at school?

- Almost every day—12%.
- Once or twice a week—22%.
- Once or twice a month—33%.
- Never—32%.

Question: What did you do when you saw this hurtful incident?

- Tried to help resolve the situation—63%.
- Immediately reached out to the student who was treated badly—56%.
- At a later time reached out to the student who was treated badly—54%.

- Publicly told those being hurtful to stop—51%.
- Told a school staff member—47%.
- Privately told those being hurtful to stop—46%.
- Ignored the situation—38%.
- Filed an abuse report online—29%.
- Watched with interest—24%.
- Encouraged the student being hurtful—23%.

In general, students reported very positive responses. However, the actual level of positive responses must be assessed in accord with the perspectives of those who were treated badly, this question:

Question: Did any other student do the following?
- Reached out to be helpful to me—47%.
- Publicly told the person being hurtful to stop—37%.
- Helped both of us resolve the situation—29%.
- Reported the incident to a school staff member—26%.

The responses on the question of whether they stepped in to help are very likely biased in accord with a socially desirable response, as they are not in accord with the reports of those who are targeted. (These questions have been revised on the new survey.)

However, a positive interpretation is that the responses to "what did you do" are the actions that students want to take. The fact that students who were treated badly did not validate this level of positive peer intervention likely reflects the concerns of the barriers that likely got in the way between positive intent and actual action.

Bystander Research

The behavior of bystanders has been the focus of research outside the bullying arena for decades. This research is generally referred to as the "bystander effect."[534] This research has found that individuals are less likely to intervene on behalf of a distressed individual when there are other people observing the situations. Latane and Darley developed a five-step model that leads to intervention in an emergency, however, this research has not been applied in the context of bullying.[535] The five steps of the Latane and Darley bystander intervention model. However the text integrates relevant research regarding bullying.

- **Notice the event.** Noticing that an emergency situation exists is necessary.

- Bullying incidents that involve physical aggression or loud verbal aggression against specific identifiable victims are likely to draw attention.[536] More subtle acts of relational aggression may not be as noticeable.

- **Interpret the event as an emergency that requires help.** After noticing an event, it needs to be interpreted as an emergency worthy of help or intervention. The decision-making process at this stage can be impeded when others are present who do not appear to consider this a serious event.[537]

  - Many bullying situations are the more minor kinds of incidents. The damage comes from the persistent nature of of the harm. The more minor incidents may not be translated as "serious" or an "emergency" by student who witness them.

- **Accept responsibility for the intervention.** When there are many people present, it is easier to rationalize that you do not personally have an obligation to intervene because someone else ought to do this.

  - Having moral values of compassion for others and an empathic response to the student's distress, may increase the likelihood of feeling responsibility for intervening.[538] However, when in school, students may not think that they are responsible. They are very likely to think that the staff should have done something. They may also have been told some variation of "mind you own business." School messaging to students may discourage positive peer intervention.

- **Know how to intervene or provide help.** Having the necessary skills to effectively intervene, without placing themselves at risk is a necessary consideration.

  - Student's perception of their own self-efficacy, the belief that they can act in a way that will be helpful, will contribute to a decision to intervene.[539] Many students may fear their potential actions to intervene will be ineffective or that they will become the victim.[540] Before a student will take the chance to intervene, they will consider the potential costs to them for doing so. Here, another consideration likely comes into play. This is an assessment of respective levels of social status and personal power. This goes to the question, "Is it safe for me to intervene?"

- **Implement intervention decisions.** The final step in the model is taking the steps to intervene.

Bullying Research on Bystanders and Defenders

In 1997, Craig and Pepler published findings from observational study of bullying on the school playground.[541] They determined that in about 85% of incidents, other children were present. Several studies found that only about 17–19 percent of bystanders intervene in bullying.[542] A helpful observational study by O'Connell and colleagues found that peers spent 54% of their time passively observing, 21% of their time actively supporting those who were bullying, and 25% of their time intervening on behalf of those being victimized.[543] A greater number of peers present results in a longer duration of bullying behavior.

When peers do defend those who are targeted, they are very often effective in stopping the bullying.[544] In addition, having someone step in to defend them is important to the well-being of the students treated badly.[545] Students who are treated badly in front of peers and who are not defended by peers have worse emotional outcomes than those who are defended. Students who are defended in these situations experience fewer emotional problems, have higher self-esteem, and are less likely to be rejected by peers.[546]

Stepping in to help may also be helpful for bystanders. Witnessing bullying incidents negatively impacts the stress levels, emotions, school satisfaction, and mental health of bystanders.[547] If, as the research clearly documents, students do not like to see bullying and think they should step in to help—but they do not—this likely creates dissonance between what they think they should do, but did not do. They are likely to feel guilt or shame knowing that what happened was wrong, they wanted to help, but they did not help.[548] However, if they think they should have stepped in to help, but did not, they likely rationalize their failure to do so using the Deny Personal Responsibility Mechanism of Moral Disengagement rationalization discussed in Chapter 7.

When students defend those who are bullied, this influences the norms of the school. The level of bullying in a school is positively linked to the presence of bystanders who provide reinforcement and social rewards for bullying behaviors.[549] Schools where students defend those who are bullied have lower rates of bullying than schools where bullying behavior is reinforced by peers.[550] Students who engage in moral disengagement to support their hurtful behavior are even more likely to bully others if they belonged to a school where the bystanders reinforce such behavior.[551] When Hurtful Students see that others defend those they have targeted, they may reconsider their actions and have a harder time rationalizing that what they are doing is appropriate.

Participant Roles

Salmivalli and colleagues identified different patterns of involvement in bullying, which they called "participant roles."[552] These are roles that students may play in a specific situation, not what they do at all times. In addition to the student being hurtful and the one targeted, there are peers in the group may play different participant roles. These research findings have been validated in many countries.[553] The four witness participant roles include:

- **Assistants of the one being hurtful.** These students do not start the bullying, but join in after it has been started.

- **Reinforcers of the one being hurtful.** These students encourage bullying by cheering, laughing, coming to see what is happening, encouraging the one being hurtful. Subsequent research has suggested merging the categories of assistants and reinforcers into one category as "followers."[554]

- **Outsiders who stay away from bullying situations and do not take sides with anyone.** These students are passive and remain uninvolved.

- **Defenders of the one being treated badly.** These are prosocial students who comfort and support the victim, try to intervene to make others stop bullying, or tell an adult to intervene.

It should be noted, however, that most research on participant roles has not considered the role of students who both engage in bullying and are treated badly. These students are generally disliked, as well as feared. They are far less likely to have peer supporters, unless they are active in a group of other marginalized students. These incidents are more likely to involve some form of physical violence, which can make intervening at the time more dangerous.

Another factor that may be present is that the student who at this time appears to be the target, may have actually triggered the aggressive response by being hurtful to the student who is now being aggressive. This may be a retaliation situation. If this is the case, making a decision to intervene is even more complicated.

As was discussed in Chapter 5 under brain development, teens will often follow the lead of a stronger teen. The way in which they express actions in front of the peer group, is influenced by their development in the context of peer group dynamics. To them, there is significant importance of determining who is in their group and how members of their group want them to behave.[555]

As was discussed in Chapter 2, most students use bullying behavior as a means to acquire dominance and social status. The role of followers is of exceptional importance to this end objective. These followers could be the students who passively observe, who are providing the attention the Hurtful Student desires. Followers could also be Hurtful Supporters who are more actively supporting. The supportive acts of both Passive Observers, who pay attention, and Hurtful Supporters validate the dominance of the one being hurtful. In addition, being associated with the Dominance Motivated Hurtful Student can increase the status of the Hurtful Supporters.[556]

Social Preference and Perceived Popularity

Researchers in this field have measured student status among peers by using measurements of "social preference" and "perceived popularity."[557] Social preference is how well liked and appreciated the student is. This is often measured by asking students which other students they like. Perceived popularity essentially measures how popular students are among peers. Perceived popularity is considered to be an assessment of the reputation, social dominance, and power of the student, regardless of how well they are liked. However, on the instruments to assess popularity, students are not given a definition of the term "popular."

When children are younger, social preference and perceived popularity are strongly correlated—that is, some students are both liked and perceived to be popular. As student become teens, this starts to change. Teens attach a greater importance to perceived popularity. Some become more effective in using relational aggression to obtain it. A quest for popularity is becomes associated with aggressive behaviors. Thus, these hurtful students are perceived to be "popular," but they are not well liked.[558] Unfortunately, it does not appear that having peers dislike them dissuades them from engaging in such behavior. By contrast, most of those victimized are considered unpopular and disliked.

My thinking on the issue of popularity is slightly different due to my discovery of the research that distinguishes between Dominance Leaders and Prestige Leaders, as was introduced in Chapter 2 and further discussed in Chapter 4. Recall that this research literature has not yet been integrated into bullying research literature.

Effectiveness of Programs focused on Bystanders

The *KiVa Antibullying* program, which has been implemented in Finnish schools and in other parts of the world, is strongly focused on influencing participants to stop reinforcing the bullying behavior and instead step in to help.[559] Salmivalli and colleagues, who have conducted significant research into bystanders and defending behavior are the developers of this program.[560] An intervention of KiVa that specifically target bystander behaviors was found that decreases in reinforcing the one engaged in bullying resulted in decreases in both self and peer reported bullying.[561] Research on the KiVa program has indicated a lack of effectiveness at older grade levels.[562] Of concern when considering the potential effectiveness of this program in other countries, such as the US, is the radical differences in the management of schools between the two countries.

A recent published evaluation of a program developed by the University of New Hampshire's Prevention Innovations Research Center, *Bringing in the Bystander* (BIBT) shed light into the difficulties of increasing positive peer interventions.[563] BIBT is a program developed during the early 2000s to address interpersonal violence among college students.

BIBT was implemented in an evaluation study in high schools. This program is a seven lesson curriculum that teaches students how to safely and effectively intervene before, during, and after situations of relationship abuse and sexual assault to both prevent and stop these forms of abuse from happening, as well as supporting victims in the aftermath of these experiences. Thus, BIBT is focusing on one aspect of hurtful behavior that *Engage Students to Embrace Civility* seeks to address.

The results of this evaluation study were mixed. There was an indication of a reduction in some forms of sexual aggression. However, this program appeared to have no impact on influencing bystander behaviors. The researchers thought that it was possible that classroom-delivered bystander-focused violence prevention curricula is not particularly effective in increasing bystander interventions, as there appear to be more issues involved in influencing positive peer intervention. The additional components that were suggested by the researchers when assessing the ineffectiveness of their program included focusing on peer norms, a focus on friendships, the involvement of popular opinion leaders, and the need to focus more on teaching effective bystander intervention skills. These components that have been included in the *Empowered to Embrace Civility* student program, described in Chapter 10.

THE *ENGAGE STUDENTS TO EMBRACE CIVILITY* FRAMEWORK

The following research-based peer intervention framework is helpful in developing strategies to engage and empower more students to step in to help when they witness bullying situations.

When students witness bullying or hurtful behavior, they can be a:

- **Hurtful Supporter.** Provide support for Hurtful Students.

- **Passive Observer.** Do not become involved in the situation.

- **Helpful Ally.** Students who do step in to help.

Helpful Allies can help in a variety of ways. The three ways they can step in to help addressed in the *Embrace Civility* student instruction program are these:

- **Step in to Help**. Reach out to be kind to the person being hurt or left out, help this person walk away, support those who are having challenges, and help others resolve conflict.

- **Say, "Stop."** Publicly or privately tell the person being hurtful to stop.

- **Report Concerns.** Tell an adult who can help.

Hurtful Supporter

In line with research on the ethological basis of dominance theory, alpha chimpanzees have Hurtful Supporters.[564] Dominance motivated bosses in corporate environments or dominance motivated politicians, always have a band of supporters who cheer their dominance activities. A Dominance Motivated Hurtful Student will most definitely have a band of followers who step in to support them. Those who participate with Dominance Motivated Hurtful Students may perceive their social status to be linked to their "leader."

Hurtful Supporters who support Socially Marginalized Hurtful Students are frequently at a similar low social status level and also at higher risk. Hurtful Supporters of Dominance Motivated Hurtful Students, also tend to be both popular and disliked. However, they are less popular or dominant than the student they are supporting.[565] These students tend to engage in increasingly more hurtful behavior over time, especially targeting those students who the "ringleader" has targeted.[566]

Note from Chapter 2, one of the motivations for engaging in hurtful behavior is Belonging. A Dominance Motivated Hurtful Student will insist that their Hurtful Supporters are also hurtful to be allowed to stay or belong in the Dominance Motivated Hurtful Student's graces and group of followers. They must continue to be Hurtful Supporters to belong to the group.

It is exceptionally important to focus on the role of these Hurtful Supporters and seek to shift their path. Their involvement in hurtful situations is very frequently ignored. School leaders generally identify and focus primarily on the student who was most hurtful. These are students who face the "consequences." Both the Hurtful Student and all identified

Hurtful Supporters must be held accountable. This is discussed in Chapter 11.

Further, it may be possible to shift some of these followers from their Hurtful Supporter roles. These students may be more reachable than the students who are most hurtful. If the support of these students can be redirected away from the Hurtful Student or if these Hurtful Supporters can be provided with motivation and skills into how they might shift the thinking of the student they have been supporting, this could lead to a reduction in hurtful behavior. All of the strategies discussed in Chapter 7 relate to strategies to seek to influence the behavior of Hurtful Supporters.

Passive Observer

A Passive Observer ignores what is happening or walks away.[567] There may be three variations of Passive Observers:

- Curious and paying attention, which rewards the Hurtful Student.

- Truly not interested and not inclined to become involved in the personal relationship "drama" that they witness and so they walk away.

- Inclined to want to step in to help—but perceive they lack the personal power and skills to do so safely and effectively. This last group of students should have a primary focus. The more of these students a school can switch over to Helpful Ally status, the better the efforts to reduce hurtful behavior will be.

In many ways, our society and schools encourage students to be Passive Observers. Have your students heard these messages: "Mind your own business." "Don't get involved." "Stay out of what does not pertain to you." Encouraging them to "Be an Upstander!" is not likely to be effective when these messages have been predominant.

Passive Observers frequently do not have a high level of social status or personal power. This is a significant factor. Students do evaluate the their positions on the school's social leader" in relation to the student being hurtful when trying to decide how to respond during a hurtful incident.[568] Their perception of their own social status, compared to others in the peer group and those being hurtful will often shape their decision-making.

A lower social status Passive Observer would face a clear risk if they were to try to step in to tell a powerful, Dominant Motivated Hurtful Student and their Hurtful Supporters to stop. Physical safety risks would also be present in situations of Reactive Aggression of a Marginalized Hurtful Student. Students who are at a lower social status may choose not to defend for fear becoming targets themselves or damaging their reputation and status by being associated with a low social status Targeted Student.[569]

However, the research has demonstrated that those who have been treated badly are known to defend others. Ma and colleague's recent meta analysis demonstrated that students who identified as those who had been victimized were more likely to defend.[570] This is why it will be really important to include students who have been targets of bullying on the school Student Leadership Team. This is a strategy to help shift these students from "victim" to Helpful Ally and more powerful leaders for social justice.

In addition to an assessment of their social status, students who are more likely to be Passive Observers also assess their level of self-efficacy. If they feel that they do not have adequate skills to intervene, they will be less likely to step in.

The Passive Observer students who do care and want to step in to help, but do not, must be a strong focus of school efforts. These are the students who can more easily become Helpful Allies. This will require addressing both their fears of personal risks, risks to their reputation, and their perception that they lack effective skills.

Helping students who are generally Passive Observers learn effective ways they can safely and privately step in to help the one who was treated badly after the incident will hopefully increase their efforts in doing so and reshape them into Helpful Allies. To intervene privately does not require the same level of personal power as directly telling someone to stop. Reaching out privately to support the one who was targeted can be very supportive of that student. It should be emphasized to all students that those who support Targeted Students privately are every bit as helpful as those who have more personal power to more safely intervene directly and publicly.

Helpful Ally

The most active Helpful Allies tend to have higher social status and personal power. They also have a higher level of compassion and effective social relationship skills. They are generally well-liked by peers.[571] Both being popular and being liked or accepted by peers are important factors.[572] Having a higher social status among the peer group enables them to defend others will less fear of negative repercussions.[573]

Some research has documented that girls typically engage in higher levels of defending.[574] However, a recent meta analysis indicated this effect appears to disappear in adolescence.[575] It has been suggested that girls may defend more because they are fulfilling stereotypical gender roles.

A significant amount of research has demonstrated that younger children are more apt to defend than those in adolescence. However, a more recent meta-analysis suggests this may not be accurate.[576] Research has documented a general increase in prosocial behavior from childhood to adolescence.[577] Further, as young people develop, they become more effective in perspective taking, which can assist in effective defending. This may enable students to become more effective in defending in ways that do not place their social status at risk.

Some Helpful Allies step in to help by directly confronting the one being hurtful. Others are more indirectly helpful by privately comforting the target or reporting the concern to the school.[578]

Publicly telling the person being hurtful to stop requires that the Helpful Ally have sufficient personal power and social status. Interestingly, there is some evidence that students who engage in direct defending may be more likely to also engage in hurtful behavior—unlike those who engage in victim-oriented defending.[579] It has been suggested that some students may defend those who are bullied in order to achieve their own goals of social status.[580] Direct or visible defending may be an effective strategy for them reach their social status goals, as students do admire those who step in to help.[581]

Privately reaching out to support the Targeted Student and reporting concerns are indirect ways to intervene. Targeted Students who receive such support have a much better sense of well-being. As the Targeted Students are also at a lower social status level, they also can very well understand why many students would not be able to directly and publicly challenge those being hurtful. Students engage in more indirect defending appear to do so more out of an altruistic motive.[582] Although they are well-liked by peers, they do not appear to be more driven by social status goals. They also do not have a sufficient level of personal power to effectively directly tell the one who is being hurtful to stop.

The emerging research in this area has become quite extensive. The research findings on defending are sometimes mixed and confusing. Researchers are continuing their research and do not feel they have everything precisely sorted out.

Of concern is that much of this research appears to perceive those who engage in bullying as the "at risk" marginalized students who are being hurtful—the inaccurate "public stereotype" that was discussed in Chapter 2. Much of this research appears to lack a critical understanding of the ethological basis for hurtful behavior in relation to the manner in which those who engage in bullying are motivated by their drive for social dominance, the Dominance Motivated Hurtful Students. This is clearly of significant importance because any student who might directly intervene by telling this person to stop must have an equivalent level of personal power, otherwise they will place themselves at risk.

This bullying bystander research has also not integrated the important insight discussed in Chapters 2 and 4 on the differences between Dominance Leaders and Prestige Leaders. As was discussed, students who have leadership inclinations can demonstrate behavior patterns of dominance or prestige approaches. The students who are most likely to be active in directly intervening in these situations are the Prestige Leaders. Increasing the engagement of the Prestige Leaders in your school as Helpful Allies is critical to increasing positive peer intervention.

Research to Support Positive Peer Intervention

Taking a deep dive into the research literature and looking for the factors that might increase positive peer intervention revealed that there appear to be three key personal factors, as well as three key environmental factors. In addition, consideration must be made of the barriers and how Mechanisms of Moral Disengagement may play a role.

Personal Factors

Motivation Grounded in Personal Values

Motivation is grounded in personal values. This includes compassion, a feeling of personal responsibility for well-being of others, acceptance of differences, affective empathy, and a feeling of personal connection.[583] Several meta analyses have documented that defenders score higher in both affective empathy—sharing another person's emotional state—and cognitive empathy—taking the perspective of others.[584] Several other factors are associated with defending behavior, including anti-bullying attitudes, a sense of social justice, high sense of responsibility for the well-being of others.[585]

Mechanisms of Moral Disengagement are used by people who act against their personal values. Students who do not tend to morally disengage are more likely to feel that they have some obligation to intervene, hence they are acting in accord with their personal values. One study showed that if early adolescents anticipated that they would feel guilt or shame from not defending, they were more likely to defend.[586] This demonstrated that they were not as inclined to rationalize to avoid acting in accord with their values.

However, as is evidence in the PISA 2018 data as well as the *Embrace Civility Student Survey* data, the overwhelming majority of students do not approve of bullying behavior, admire those who step in to help, and think they should do so. This indicates that while motivation is a factor, lack of motivation may not be the most significant determining factor in whether students actually do step in to help.

This also means that instructional programs that simply seek to increase students' compassion and empathy for those who are bullied are likely to be not significantly effective. A significant majority of students truly understand that those who are treated badly are being harmed and they do not like to see this happening. Lack of motivation and lack of empathy are likely not the significant barriers.

As was outlined in Chapter 6, it is recommended that schools have all students draft a document where they set forth their Personal Relationships Commitments Statement to positive relationships. This strategy is grounded in the Principle of Influence of Commitment and Consistency. If students state and make a commitment to what their values are, they are more likely to act in accord with those values. One of the statements of commitment asks what students will do if they see someone being hurtful to another student.

Personal Power

The personal power factor is related to comparative personal power between the one being aggressive and the Witness.[587] As already discussed, if a Witness does not feel as powerful as the student being hurtful, directly stepping in by telling this person to stop raises the risk of embarrassment or retaliation. If a Witness is not as physically strong as one being hurtful in a physical harm situation, directly stepping in raises the risk of physical harm. Also, if a Witness directly steps in to support the Targeted Student, they may be perceived as being associated with lower social status student. This can raise a risk of embarrassment, teasing, or damage to their own reputation.

It is not likely possible to dramatically change the personal power or social status of most Witnesses. However, the strategies discussed in Chapter 6 can assist in this process. Because of this, the strategies to address the personal power factor must be creative:

- Seek to influence and increase the positive actions of those Witnesses who do have higher personal power to be Helpful Allies who can directly step into help by helping them gain insight into effective strategies that will increase their feelings of self-efficacy.

- Lower the perceived personal power barrier using a Positive Social Norms approach, described in Chapter 4. This will help to reduce the perception that those who engage in hurtful behavior are admired and increase the perceived status and power of those who step in to help.

- Recognize that many students are likely to not ever think that they have sufficient personal power to directly stand up to someone being hurtful. Provide guidance on more private strategies Helpful Allies can use that will avoid direct, public confrontation with the one being hurtful. Ensure that students realize that these private strategies are exceptionally valuable in supporting the Targeted Students.

Self-Efficacy

A factor that is significantly associated with the inclination of Witnesses to be Helpful Allies appears to be self-efficacy—believing in one's capabilities to engage in actions that are required to achieve desired goals.[588] Students' perspectives of their own self-efficacy has been positively associated with actual defending behavior.[589] Self-efficacy includes both effective skills and confidence in those skills. The confidence factor is likely related to the students' perception of their own level of personal power and social status.

Self-efficacy can be gained from past accomplishments, modeling others, and encouragement by others including parent, caregivers, family members, peers, or teachers. The companion student program, *Empowered to Embrace Civility*, teaches these skills.

Students who demonstrate high self-efficacy generally seek out challenges and quickly recovers from failures or defeat. Student who have low self-efficacy have a tendency to avoid challenges. They tend to focus more on risks than opportunities. In addition, feelings of general social self-efficacy, such as the ability to make new friends or express themselves in a group, is associated with greater defending. In other words, students with a Social Emotional Growth Mindset perceive they have the self-efficacy to step in to help—and are willing to take the risks associated with failure.

Strategies to assist students in gaining self-efficacy to positively intervene that reduce the risks of embarrassment or retaliation include:

- Teach students to problem solve—to think things through from the perspective of being a Helpful Ally: What do they want to accomplish in their efforts to help? What actions could they take? Is each action in accord with their personal values? What might happen for each action and would this be safe for them? What is their best first option? What could they do next if this was not effective?

- Teach students the importance of using private strategies, such as privately reaching out to be kind, privately telling a friend to stop being hurtful, or reporting to an adult who can help. As self-efficacy is connected to personal power, more students are likely to gain feelings of self-efficacy in the use of private strategies than they would if there is a strong focus is made on direct interventions approaches.

- Teach safer strategies to publicly tell the Hurtful Student to stop. These safer strategies include working in a team with other students and making sure not to turn the situation into a confrontation or argument. Knowing that they tried, but their efforts to intervene did not achieve success and shifting to a strategy of enlisting an adult to help is a strategy that demonstrates self-efficacy.

- Encourage a Social Emotional Growth Mindset. Especially make it clear that students who do step in to help may actually fail. Failure is an important way to gain even better insight and skills. Stepping in to help someone who is being treated badly means you cared and you tried. This is to be celebrated.

Social and Environmental Factors

Friendships

Students who witness hurtful behavior may have friendships with either those being hurtful or those targeted.[590] These friendships are highly influential in decisions to intervene. Students are more likely to step in to support a student involved in a hurtful incident if that student is a friend, rather than a "neutral" peer.[591] Peer pressure to intervene promotes defending behavior.[592]

Students are members of distinct social groups within the school community. When students share the same group membership as the student who has been targeted or is being hurtful, they are more likely to step in to support that student.[593] This means the friendship factor can cut different ways.

- Those who are friends of the Targeted Student are likely to privately reach out to help their friends or, if they have sufficient personal power and self-efficacy, tell the one being hurtful to stop.

- The friends of Hurtful Students are more likely to join in, encourage, or support their friend who is being hurtful.

- If Witness are friends with both, they may help to resolve or mediate the incident, or they may just do nothing.

- Those Witnesses who are friends with neither could step in to help, do nothing, or join in the harm, all depending on the other personal factors.

The following are recommendations to best use friendships to foster positive behavior:

- Seek to increase positive intervention by those who are friends of Targeted Students by increasing their self-efficacy in doing so, especially by providing instructional insight into how they can best help their friend simply walk away if they are being treated badly and help their friend to stay calm, hold themselves tall tall, and problem solve so they do not become dysregulated, as well as how they can support their friend.

- Encourage those who are friends with those who are hurtful to help their friends stop and remedy the harm by increasing their self-efficacy to do so. This particular group of Hurtful Supporters could potentially play a very valuable role if they can be convinced to privately encourage their friend to stop being hurtful and to make things right. Seek to increase their motivation by pointing out that, based on the school's Positive Social Norms, as a perceived supporter of someone who is hurtful, their reputation will also be damaged. In addition, ensure that they know that is is possible to help their friend change by speaking in terms that are in accord with a Social Emotional Growth Mindset—their friend does have the capacity to change and make better choices. The Personal Relationships Commitments Statement also includes a statement of what they will do if a friend is hurtful. Suggest they consider their friendship if their friend continues to be hurtful.

  - In resolving hurtful situations, as discussed in Chapter 11, also address the hurtful behavior of Hurtful Supporters. Require that Hurtful Supporters are also held accountable. One of the specific agreements to obtain with the Hurtful Supporters is their commitment of what they will do in the future if their friend is hurtful.

- Ensure students have effective conflict resolution skills to enable them to help their friends or others resolve conflicts or stop cycles of hurtful acts between friends.

- Address the other personal factors, school climate, and perceived peer norms to increase the willingness of students who are not close friends with the participants to increase their willingness to intervene.

School Climate

School and class climate is clearly a factor that influences students' willingness to help a bullied peer.[594] Defending is more likely in schools that have low levels of moral disengagement and higher levels of school connectedness.[595] An Authoritative School Management approach that focuses on fostering community where all voice are heard and considered is foundational. The school must maintain a culture of acceptance. All staff members must demonstrate a celebration of differences. School staff must reinforce the importance of shared responsibility and intervening. Staff must always treat all students with kindness and respect.

The quality of staff–student relationships and the willingness of students to intervene is of significant importance.[596] Positive staff–student relationships can enhance students' feelings of self-efficacy by providing support and encouragement in strategies to manage social relationships. When staff pay attention and note with positive comment when they witness students who do top in to help, this will increase the likelihood this student will continue to do so.

Of significant importance is that staff intervene effectively in the hurtful incidents they witness. Recall the data from Chapter 3.

- While only 7% of school staff thought they made things worse when they intervened in bullying situations, 61% of middle school students and 59% of high school students reported that staff who tried to stop bullying only made things worse.

- While 97% of school staff said they would intervene if they saw bullying, 43% of middle school students and 54% of high school students reported they had seen adults at school watching bullying and doing nothing.[597]

If it is your desire to see bullying and hurtful behaviors reduced, this cannot be the situation in your school. Staff likely require professional development in strategies they can use in these situations.

Schools should regularly assess climate issues related to conditions to reduce hurtful behavior and support positive peer intervention through surveys and focus groups. The *Embrace Civility Student Survey* contains questions that assess school climate and staff-student relationships, as well as student perspectives of the frequency and effectiveness of staff interventions in hurtful incidents.

Perceived Expectations of Peers—Social Norms

The perceived expectations of peers, or social norms, has already been identified as a critically important factor.[598] What students think other students think about those who are hurtful and those who step in to help appears to be highly influential in increasing the willingness of students to positively intervene.[599] Norms around the appropriateness of moral disengagement to rationalize behavior that is not in accord with school values are also highly influential.[600]

Instructional activities should allow students to realize the actual Positive Social Norms held by their peers—disapproval of hurtful behavior and admiration of Helpful Allies who step in to help. These strategies are included in the *Empowered to Embrace Civility* student program.

Barriers to Intervention

Perceived Barriers

Latane and Darley identified the key perceived factors that appeared to discourage intervention by witnesses.[601] These include:

- **Diffusion of Responsibility**. "Someone else should be responsible."

- **Audience Inhibition**. "I could fail or embarrass myself."

- **Social Influence.** "No one else is doing anything—nobody else thinks this is wrong."

Mechanisms of Moral Disengagement

Note that these barriers appear to be a combination of Mechanisms of Moral Disengagement and the Principles of Influence, with the addition of perceived lack of skills.

There appear to be additional factors related to the perceived barriers to intervene in bullying situations. Many are grounded in legitimate fears. These fears are generally related to the very real differences in in levels of personal power and a perceived lack of skills to safety and effectively intervene. Students who have a Social Emotional Fixed Mindset are also likely to think that this hurtful behavior cannot be stopped, and there is nothing they could do.

The impact of Mechanisms of Moral Disengagement must be considered. A significant relationship has been found a significant negative relationship between moral disengagement and defending. Students who step in to defend do not display high rates of moral disengagement.[602]

Moral identity, which is a personal perspective of how important moral qualities are to one's own self-concept, has also been positively associated with stepping in to help.[603] Feeling moral distress, distress that occurs when a person is recognizes the morally appropriate action, but cannot carry out that action because of an obstacle appears to predict students' willingness to intervene in bullying incidents instead of remaining passive.[604] When students were more inclined to morally disengage they were less likely to report moral distress when they did not intervene as witnesses of a bullying incident.[605]

Studies of the relationship between moral disengagement and being a passive witness have yielded inconsistent findings.[606] A probable explanation for the mixed findings may be the failure to make a distinction between two types of passive witnesses—those who are unconcerned and those who feel guilty for not feeling that it was safe to step in to help. The factor of feelings of self-efficacy are implicated. One study showed that students who scored low in moral disengagement were inclined to defend victims if they were high in defender self-efficacy, but inclined to remain passive as bystanders if they scored low in defender self-efficacy.[607]

Those who see a hurtful situation and fail to step in to help often rationalize why they did not help. This can allow them to reduce or eliminate the feelings of guilt for not acting in a way that, based on their moral values, they think they should have acted.[608] The most frequent mechanism for disengagement is to deny personal responsibility.

Fears and Fixed Mindset

Legitimate fears are also a barrier. These fears are generally related to the very real differences in in levels of personal power between the Witness and the Hurtful Student. A Witness with lower personal power is at clear risk if they try to publicly tell a Dominance Motivated Hurtful Student to stop. A Witness also faces risks if they intervene in a physically violent situation. Witnesses may also perceive that they lack the skills to safety and effectively intervene.

Students who have a Social Emotional Fixed Mindset are also likely to think that this hurtful behavior cannot be stopped, and there is nothing they could do.

Embrace Civility Student Survey

On the earlier *Embrace Civility Student Survey* the key barriers students identified to stepping in to help. It is clear that the barriers to intervene that have been identified in the bystander intervention research literature were also identified by students as barriers in this survey

- I didn't know what I could do—59%. (Self-efficacy.)
- It was none of my business—34%. (Deny personal responsibility.)
- I could have failed and embarrassed myself—32%. (Personal power, self-efficacy, and social environment.)
- Other students might have teased me if I tried to help—28%. (Personal power and social environment.)

- School staff is supposed to handle this—28%. (Deny personal responsibility.)
- The student being hurtful could have retaliated—27%. (Personal power.)
- It wasn't that bad—18%. (Deny the harm.)
- Others thought it was funny—14%. (Social environment.)
- The student being treated badly deserved it—11%. (Blame the target.)
- Other reason—10%.

A version of this question has been included on the new *Embrace Civility Student Survey*. Guidance is provided on instructional strategies the Student Leadership Team can use to help all students learn to distinguish between fears, perceived lack of skills, or Social Emotional Fixed Mindset and excuses or rationalizations. To address the perceived barriers, it is necessary to ensure students have effective intervention skills, that will reduce the potential of failure or embarrassment and a school climate that fully supports positive peer intervention.

Holocaust Rescuers

Fascinating insight in positive peer intervention can be derived from studies of people who acted to rescue the Jews during the Holocaust.[609] Fogelman, daughter of a survivor, conducted interviews with such rescuers and found four very common attributes:

- They had well-developed inner values, acceptance of differences, and a strong belief that individual action mattered.

- They came from loving homes, where parents used reasoned discipline rather than punishment. They had an altruistic caregiver who modeled compassionate values and had suffered a loss in their own family that had given rise to increased sympathy for others.

- They had a strong sense of self-competency and in their ability to find creative solutions to the very difficult situations.

- There were enabling situations that occurred that helped to support their efforts. This included a support network of like-minded rescuers.

Essentially, what Fogelman discovered in her research is fully in line with the insight that this author identified through extensive academic research.

PART III
Legal Issues

Chapter 9.

Legal Issues—Civil Rights and Free Speech

HIGHLIGHTS

This Chapter presents insight into the requirements under the US civil rights regulations.

- **Federal Civil Rights Laws.**

  - **Federal Laws.** Several federal laws govern discriminatory harassment. These laws are enforced through agency actions by the USDOE's OCR or litigation.

  - **Civil Rights Laws.** The four federal civil rights laws are: *Title IX of the Education Amendments of 1972* prohibits discrimination on the basis of sex, including orientation and gender. *Title VI of the Civil Rights Act of 1964* prohibits discrimination on the basis of race, color, or national origin in any educational program or activity receiving federal funds. *Section 504 of the Rehabilitation Act of 1973* prohibits discrimination on the basis of disability in programs or activities receiving federal financial assistance. *Americans with Disabilities Act of 1990* prohibits discrimination on the basis of disability.

- Public school districts violate federal civil rights laws when discriminatory harassment based on race, color, national origin, sex, or disability is sufficiently serious or persistent to create a Hostile Environment, and school staff encourage, tolerate, do not adequately address, or ignore such harassment. These statutes also provide the basis for litigation against public schools

- **2010 OCR Dear Colleague Letter.** "Harassment creates a Hostile Environment when the conduct is sufficiently severe, pervasive, **or** persistent so as to interfere with or limit a student's ability to participate in or benefit from the services, activities, or opportunities offered by a school. When such harassment is based on race, color, national origin, sex, or disability, it violates the civil rights laws that OCR enforces."

  - **"Or."** It is exceptionally important that educators note the term "or." Minor incidents that are persistent or pervasive can create a Hostile Environment.

  - **Civil Rights Requirements.** If a school has identified a Hostile Environment is present, the school must: End the harassment. Remedy the harmful effects on the target. Correct the hostile environment. Monitor to ensure effectiveness. My perspective is these comprehensive requirements should guide all instances of serious, pervasive, **or** persistent hurtful situations targeting any student—whether or not a member of a Protected Class.

- **Civil Rights Litigation.** Schools can be financially liable if they are "deliberately indifferent to known acts of student-on-student sexual harassment and the harasser is under the school's authority," so long as the harassment is "so severe, pervasive, and objectionably offensive that it can be said to deprive the victims of access to the educational opportunities or benefits provided by the school."

  - **Elements.** The five elements of a case include: Student is a member of, or perceived to be a member of, a Protected Class under federal statutes and the hurtful behavior is associated with the student's Protected Class status, or perception thereof. The school had actual knowledge of the harassment. The student or students engaging in the harassment were under the school's authority. The harassment was so severe, pervasive, and objectionably offensive that it deprived the student of access to the educational opportunities or benefits provided by the school. The school was deliberately indifferent to this harassment.

- **Deliberate Indifference.** "Where a school district has actual knowledge that its efforts to remediate are ineffective, and it continues to use those same methods to no avail, such district has failed to act reasonably in light of the known circumstances."

• *Individuals with Disabilities Education Act* **and** *Section 504.* Schools are required to take steps to reduce the bullying of and by students with disabilities and remedy the harmful effects. Students with disabilities who are being harassed are often being denied their right to a Free and Appropriate Public Education (FAPE).

  - **Students with Disabilities.** Three federal laws govern situations related to bullying of or by students with disabilities: *Section 504 of the Rehabilitation Act of 1973 (Section 504). The Americans with Disabilities Act of 1990 (ADA). Individuals with Disabilities Education Act (IDEA).*

  - **Bullying of or by Students with Disabilities.** Failure to effectively address the harassment or bullying of students with disabilities is governed under both *Individuals with Disabilities Education Act (IDEA)* and *Section 504.*

    ‣ **FAPE.** When the hurtful conduct a student is receiving is interfering with or limiting that student's ability to participate in or benefit offered by a school, this is a Hostile Environment and is also interfering with FAPE.

    ‣ **IEP and 504 Plan.** If a student on an Individual Education Plan (IEP) or 504 Plan is being bullied, the school must convene the IEP or 504 Team to address the situation and modify the Plan as necessary.

    ‣ **Functional Skills and Supplementary Aids and Services.** A revised IEP or 504 Plan should address both Functional Behavior Objectives to support the student in improving their personal relationship skills and Supplemental Aides and Services that address the actions the school will commit to take to stop the harassment and correct the apparently Hostile Environment.

  - **Child Find — Bullied Students with Mental Health Concerns.** If any student, whether or not originally considered to have a disability, is experiencing mental health concerns associated with being bullied, this student should be considered for placement on a *Section 504* Plan. This Targeted Student may or may not need any other special education or related aids and services.

- **Affinity Groups.** Some schools have recently been challenged when they established Affinity Groups to focus on equity concerns that have been limited to one group of students or parents. This approach is clearly a violation of civil rights laws. Include allies.

- **Free Speech Issues.**

  - **Supreme Court Cases.** There have been five Supreme Court cases addressing student free speech rights. Four of these relate to situations when considering student speech that disparages other students.

    - *Tinker v. Des Moines.* Schools may only restrict student speech if there are reasons to believe it could cause a substantial disruption or a significant interference with other students.

    - *Bethel v Fraser.* School administrators could respond to student speech that was lewd, vulgar, plainly offensive, and contrary to the school's educational mission, not off-campus speech.

    - *Morse v. Frederick.* The manner in which the Supreme Court approached its analysis in *Morse* focused on student safety—in this case, drug abuse. This decision is directly applicable to the situation involving speech that could harm other students, including situations involving bullying.

    - *Mahanoy Area School District v. B.L.* A student's vulgar off-campus online postings is protected speech. Schools can only intervene in situations of student off-campus speech if such speech has or reasonably could create a substantial disruption at school or interference with the rights of other students.

    - **Applied to Bullying and Cyberbullying Situations.**

      - The problems associated with bullying have been well-documented through research.

      - Schools are encouraged to reduce bullying in schools. Schools are required by state statutes to have bullying prevention policies in place and to respond to reports of bullying.

      - Schools must teach students socially appropriate behavior, including the need to treat others with respect.

      - If schools tolerate student speech that disparages their peers, this will pose a major challenge in the ability of schools to protect students who have been entrusted to their care.

Failure to restrict such speech could also lead to liability for discriminatory harassment.

- Schools can intervene in student off-campus that has or reasonably could create interference with the rights of a student who is being bullied or harassed.

- **Two Important Lower Court Cases.**

  › *Saxe v. State College.* It is appropriate for schools to prohibit speech that would substantially interfere with a student's educational performance.

  › *Kowalski v. Berkeley County.* The student's off-campus actions had interfered with bullied student's learning while at school..

- **Disparaging Speech on Campus.**

  › **Restricting Disparaging Speech.** Schools must be able to restrict speech that includes derogatory terms, symbols that have historically been associated with the oppression of a group of people, or statements that communicate an opinion of the inherent inferiority of a student, group of students, or group of people which may include students.

  › **Evidence of Substantial Disruption.** To restrict such speech requires that schools are able to reasonably forecast of disruption at the school or interference with the rights of other students. The cases where the courts did not support the school's restriction, were based on the lack of sufficiency of the evidence to determine whether the school's restriction of student speech was supported.

  › **Sufficiency of Local Evidence is KEY!** Schools must have local data and evidence, backed up by research and/or expert analysis, to justify their conclusion, that similar speech has created, and therefore can be reasonably expected to create conditions at school that significantly interfere with the rights of other students to receive an education and participate in school activities or a substantial disruption, that could include violence.

FEDERAL CIVIL RIGHTS LAWS

Several federal laws govern discriminatory harassment. These laws are enforced through agency actions by the USDOE's OCR.[610] These statutes also provide the basis for litigation against public schools. The four civil rights statutes are:

- *Title IX of the Education Amendments of 1972* prohibits discrimination on the basis of sex by an educational program or activity receiving federal funds.[611] This includes students who are lesbian, gay, bisexual, transgender, queer, questioning, asexual, intersex, nonbinary, and individuals who identify their sexual orientation or gender identity in other ways.[612]

- *Title VI of the Civil Rights Act of 1964* prohibits discrimination on the basis of race, color, or national origin in any educational program or activity receiving federal funds.[613] OCR has taken the position this includes discrimination based on religion, if grounded in national origin.[614]

- *Section 504 of the Rehabilitation Act of 1973* prohibits discrimination on the basis of disability in programs or activities receiving federal financial assistance.[615]

- The *Americans with Disabilities Act of 1990* prohibits discrimination on the basis of disability.[616]

States also have constitutional provisions and statutes that protect against discrimination, most generally including sex, race, color, religion, and national origin. Some state statutes have been expanded to include other protected classes, including sexual or gender minority protections.

Public school districts violate federal civil rights laws when discriminatory harassment based on race, color, national origin, sex, or disability is sufficiently serious or persistent to create a Hostile Environment, and school staff encourage, tolerate, do not adequately address, or ignore such harassment.[617] These students are considered within a Protected Class.

2010 OCR Dear Colleague Letter

One notable guidance document is the *Dear Colleague Letter (DCL)* issued by the OCR in October 2010.[618] This *DCL* addressed the intersection between bullying and discriminatory harassment as follows:

> *Harassment creates a Hostile Environment when the conduct is sufficiently severe, pervasive, **or** persistent so as to interfere with or limit a student's ability to participate in or benefit from the services, activities, or opportunities offered by a*

school. When such harassment is based on race, color, national origin, sex, or disability, it violates the civil rights laws that OCR enforces.[619]

It is exceptionally important that educators note the term "or." One of the likely reasons it appears that the disciplinary code approach is ineffective is that the result of an investigation into a reported situation is a determination of whether the accused student engaged in behavior that was significantly serious to warrant a disciplinary response—actions that created a "substantial disruption."

Principals are likely to not consider these more minor hurtful incidents to meet this standard. Students who are hurtful to achieve dominance rarely will engage in hurtful actions that could be considered to constitute a "substantial disruption." Their hurtful acts are most often persistent. If many students within a Protected Class are experiencing hurtful conduct, this is a pervasive Hostile Environment.

The critical factor is whether such serious **or** pervasive **or** persistent conduct has had the result of interfering with or limiting a student's ability to participate in or benefit from the services, activities, or opportunities offered by a school.

Based on the 2010 *DCL*, schools must respond to situations of discriminatory harassment that they know or reasonably should know about. The examples included make clear that to avoid an adverse agency action, schools must not only intervene in reported incidents, they must engage in comprehensive efforts to change the school culture that underlies such incidents. The requirements set forth in the *DCL* included:

(S)chools should have well-publicized policies prohibiting harassment and procedures for reporting and resolving complaints that will alert the school to incidents of harassment.

When responding to harassment, a school must take immediate and appropriate action to investigate or otherwise determine what occurred. The specific steps in a school's investigation will vary depending upon the nature of the allegations, the source of the complaint, the age of the student or students involved, the size and administrative structure of the school, and other factors. In all cases, however, the inquiry should be prompt, thorough, and impartial.

If an investigation reveals that discriminatory harassment has occurred, a school must take prompt and effective steps reasonably calculated to end the harassment, eliminate any Hostile Environment and its effects, and prevent the harassment from recurring. These duties are a school's responsibility even if the misconduct also is covered by an anti-bullying policy, and regardless of whether a student has complained, asked the school to take action, or identified the harassment as a form of discrimination.

...

When the behavior implicates the civil rights laws, school administrators should look beyond simply disciplining the perpetrators. While disciplining the perpetrators is likely a necessary step, it often is insufficient. A school's responsibility is to eliminate the Hostile Environment created by the harassment, address its effects, and take steps to ensure that harassment does not recur. Put differently, the unique effects of discriminatory harassment may demand a different response than would other types of bullying.[620]

Complying with Federal Civil Rights Regulations

The standards under civil rights regulations apply to all situations where a student is experiencing serious or persistent bullying, or when many students in a Protected Class are experiencing pervasive hurtful conduct. Schools must be mindful that failure to take these steps could provide the basis for an agency action or litigation.

To reiterate, under civil rights guidance, if a Hostile Environment is suspected or alleged to exist, schools are required conduct a prompt, thorough and impartial investigation. If this investigation revels that a Hostile Environment exists, the school must intervene by taking prompt and effective steps that are reasonably calculated to:

- **End the Harassment.** Engage the Hurtful Student and Supporters through an Accountability Process, where they are required to accept responsibility, take steps to remedy the harm to the target and school community, and agree to discontinue all further acts of harm. Disciplinary consequences should be implemented upon failure to agree to or comply with this Accountability Agreement. Create a Protections Plan to ensure any necessary protections for the Targeted Student.

- **Remedy the Harmful Effects.** Identify and address the challenges any involved students. Put a Positive Action Plan into place to address these challenges. This includes both Targeted Students and Marginalized Hurtful Students. This plan should also address harms that the Targeted Student has experienced, including both academic harms and emotional harms.

- **Correct the Hostile Environment.** Make any necessary corrections to school environment to address concerns identified in the prompt, thorough, and impartial investigation. This includes corrections of staff hurtful behavior or failure to intervene, as deemed necessary. This also includes other aspects of the environment. The investigation should have determined whether the serious or persistent conduct directed at one student is actually evidence of a pervasive hurtful situation impacting many students within this Protected Class.

- **Monitor to Ensure Effectiveness.** Engage in ongoing monitoring takes place to ensure that things are better for all involved students. Conduct an evaluation involving all parties to the hurtful incident or situation to determine effectiveness of the school's investigation and intervention and identify any ongoing concerns.

When students within a Protected Class are treated badly in a pervasive manner, a very comprehensive analysis of the environment and school climate must be taken to identify and determine how to correct harmful aspects to better eliminate the overall Hostile Environment—not only for this student, but all students within this Protected Class. This aspect of the required civil rights intervention response is most important from the perspective of the overall objective of ensuring all schools maintain a safe and respectful environment for all students in this Protected Class and that aspects of the school environment that are supporting ongoing harmful acts against many students in this class are addressed.

Why Just Protected Class Students?

The perspective taken by *Engage Students to Embrace Civility* is that these comprehensive requirements should guide all instances of serious **or** persistent **or** pervasive hurtful situations targeting any student—whether or not this student is a member of a Protected Class. There is no justifiable reason why a student who might not fall into a class that receives protections under federal civil rights laws do not deserve this kind of comprehensive investigation and intervention.

This recommendation is certainly not for the purposes of downplaying in any way the significant importance of schools addressing the increased concerns that students who are in Protected Classes face. For students in Protected Classes, being treated badly based on their minority status will have a profound harmful impact. These are the situations that are also likely to be pervasive. Therefore, schools must be highly attentive to the importance of ongoing actions that seek to remedy this harm.

The intent of suggesting that the actions required under the civil rights laws should also guide the kinds of actions taken for students who are not within a Protected Class is to ensure consistency and a sufficiently comprehensive approach to also stop the harms all students are experiencing—stopping the hurtful behavior, remedying the harm to the target, identifying any environmental aspects that may be contributing to the hurtful situation, and ongoing monitoring to ensure the hurtful behavior has stopped.

Civil Rights Litigation

In 1999, in the case of *Davis v. Monroe County Board of Education*, the Supreme Court held that schools can be financially liable under *Title IX* if they are "deliberately indifferent to known acts of student-on-student sexual harassment and the harasser is under the school's authority," so long as the harassment is "so severe, pervasive, and objectionably offensive that it can be said to deprive the victims of access to the educational opportunities or benefits provided by the school."[621]

Breaking the above statement down, the five elements of a case include:

- Student is a member of, or perceived to be a member of, a Protected Class under federal statutes and the hurtful behavior is associated with the student's Protected Class status, or perception thereof.

- The school had actual knowledge of the harassment. ("Should have known" is the standard for agency enforcement.)

- The student or students engaging in the harassment were under the school's authority.

- The harassment was so severe, pervasive, and objectionably offensive that it deprived the student of access to the educational opportunities or benefits provided by the school.

- The school was deliberately indifferent to this harassment.

This liability standard is based on the principle that recipients of federal funds should be held liable only for their own misconduct and not the misconduct of others. Thus, *Title IX* does not make a school district liable for the conduct of students who are engaged in aggression. Rather, a district is liable only for its own misconduct in failing to respond to known harassment in a diligent manner.

The key element that is frequently in most contention in these cases is whether the school was deliberately indifferent. The most frequently quoted standard on this is from *Vance v. Spencer Cnty. Pub. Sch. Dist.*, a Sixth Circuit case.[622] In interpreting the *Davis* standard, the Court stated:

> *Where a school district has actual knowledge that its efforts to remediate are ineffective, and it continues to use those same methods to no avail, such district has failed to act reasonably in light of the known circumstances.*[623]

A very excellent jury instruction in the case of *Zeno v. Pine Plains* sets forth an excellent description of this standard:

> *Deliberate indifference means that the defendant's response or lack of response to the alleged harassment was clearly unreasonable in light of the known circumstances. Deliberate indifference may be found where a defendant takes*

remedial action only after a lengthy and unjustifiable delay or where defendant's response was so inadequate or ineffective that discriminatory intent may be inferred. In other words, deliberate indifference requires a finding that the District's actions or inactions in response to known harassment effectively caused further harassment to occur.[624]

Unfortunately, two more recent cases in other circuits have taken the position that if the district is following the guidelines of the state bullying statute, that is, the district has a policy and a reporting approach, and upon report the principal investigated and responded in some way, this does not constitute "deliberate indifference."[625] If this guidance is upheld in other circuits this does not bode well for the protection of students. It clearly should be understood that simply following state bullying prevention is not equivalent to the enhanced and more comprehensive intervention requirements under federal civil rights laws.

BULLYING OF OR BY STUDENTS WITH DISABILITIES

Schools are required to take steps to reduce the bullying of and by students with disabilities and remedy the harmful effects. Students with disabilities who are being harassed based on their disability or bullied on any basis are also most often being denied their right to a Free and Appropriate Public Education (FAPE). Three federal laws govern situations related to bullying of or by students with disabilities:

- *Section 504 of the Rehabilitation Act of 1973 (Section 504).*[626]

- *The Americans with Disabilities Act of 1990 (ADA).*[627]

- *Individuals with Disabilities Education Act (IDEA).*[628]

The importance of addressing the risks associated with bullying and students with disabilities was recently reinforced by the USDOE. In 2013, USDOE's Office for Special Education and Rehabilitation Services (OSERS) issued a *DCL* that called upon schools to better address bullying of or by students with disabilities who are receiving services under the *IDEA.*[629]

In 2014, OCR issued a *DCL* that made it clear that failure to effectively address the harassment or bullying of students with disabilities is also governed under Section 504, both for students receiving services under *IDEA* and those receiving services under Section 504.[630]

A major concern noted in all of these documents is the interference with a student's FAPE. Note the similarity in the concept of FAPE and the standards by which a Hostile Environment is considered to be present:

> *Harassment creates a Hostile Environment when the conduct is sufficiently severe, pervasive, or persistent so as to interfere with or limit a student's ability to participate in or benefit from the services, activities, or opportunities offered by a school.[631]*

Essentially, when the hurtful conduct a student is receiving is interfering with or limiting that student's ability to participate in or benefit from the services, activities, or opportunities offered by a school, this is also interfering with FAPE. The 2013 OSERS *DCL* stated:

> *Whether or not the bullying is related to the student's disability, any bullying of a student with a disability that results in the student not receiving meaningful educational benefit constitutes a denial of FAPE under the IDEA that must be remedied.[632]*

The OSERS *DCL* placed an express requirement on schools related to any target of bullying who is also on an Individual Education Plan (IEP):

> *Schools have an obligation to ensure that a student with a disability who is the target of bullying behavior continues to receive FAPE in accordance with his or her IEP. The school should, as part of its appropriate response to the bullying, convene the IEP Team to determine whether, as a result of the effects of the bullying, the student's needs have changed such that the IEP is no longer designed to provide meaningful educational benefit.[633]*

While schools may seek to protect students with disabilities who are being bullied or engaging in bullying by placing them in a more restrictive environment away from the mainstream school community, the *DCL* specifically warns:

> *(S)chools may not attempt to resolve the bullying situation by unilaterally changing the frequency, duration, intensity, placement, or location of the student's special education and related services.[634]*

Further requirements set forth in the OSERS *DCL* related to situations when a student with disabilities is engaging in bullying behavior:

> *If the student who engaged in the bullying behavior is a student with a disability, the IEP Team should review the student's IEP to determine if additional supports and services are needed to address the inappropriate behavior. In addition, the IEP Team and other school personnel should consider examining the environment in which the bullying occurred to determine if changes to the environment are warranted.[635]*

The 2014 OCR *DCL* directed that if a student is on a Section 504 Plan, these concerns must be addressed in a 504 Team meeting. Note, this provision must be considered in relationship to the use of exclusionary practices.[636] A student with disabilities who is both bullied and engaging in hurtful behavior, who is suspended, expelled, or arrested for engaging in such hurtful behavior raises the potential of a challenge based both on FAPE and civil rights discrimination.

In 2016, USDOE OCR issued an excellent guide, *Parent and Educator Resource Guide to Section 504 in Public Elementary and Secondary Schools.*[637] This guide also provides a section on bullying and harassment:

> *Section 504 prohibits disability-based harassment by peers that is sufficiently serious to deny or limit a student's ability to participate in or benefit from the school's education programs and activities (in other words, creates a Hostile Environment). When a school district knows or reasonably should know of possible disability-based harassment, it must take immediate and appropriate steps to investigate or otherwise determine what occurred. If an investigation reveals that the harassment created a Hostile Environment, the recipient must take prompt and effective steps reasonably calculated to end the harassment, eliminate the Hostile Environment, prevent the harassment from recurring, and, as appropriate, remedy its effects. …*

> *Schools also have responsibilities under Section 504's FAPE requirements when a student with a disability is harassed or bullied on any basis (for example, bullied based on disability, or national origin, or homelessness, or appearance). This is because the bullying or harassment can result in a denial of FAPE under Section 504 and, if that occurs, it must be remedied. FAPE may be denied to a student when, for example, the effects of the bullying include adverse changes in the student's academic performance or behavior.*

> *If the school has reason to suspect the student's needs have changed, the Section 504 team must determine the extent to which additional or different services are needed, ensure that any needed changes are made promptly, and safeguard against putting the onus on the student with the disability to avoid or handle the bullying.*[638]

Both *IDEA* and *Section 504* address concerns associated with the suspension or exclusion of students with disabilities, either a 10 day suspension or a series of suspensions.[639] As OCR stated in the *DCL*:

> *OCR also considers a series of short-term exclusions (each 10 school days or fewer) from the educational program to be a significant change in placement, if the short-term exclusions total more than 10 school days and create a pattern of removal.*[640]

While this language relates to suspensions, this provides the basis to argue that if the harassment a student is receiving has interfered with that student's ability to participate in learning and any school activity and this has happened more than ten days, this is a significant change in placement and denial of FAPE. This has created a pattern of exclusion that is a violation of *Section 504* and must be addressed in a *Section 504* or IEP meeting.

Functional Skills Objectives

Under *IDEA*, within a student's IEP, schools must assess and develop objectives for both academic skills and functional skills. Functional skills include social emotional competencies and personal relationship skills. Any involvement in bullying raises a "red flag" that the student has challenges in maintaining personal relationships that must be better addressed.

To incorporate a strategy into an IEP or *Section 504* Plan to address bullying, it may be necessary to conduct a Functional Behavioral Analysis to identify whether this student has challenges in personal relationships related to their being treated badly. This analysis will lead to the development of Functional Behavior Objectives the student improve their personal relationship skills.

The development of Functional Behavior Objectives must be done in a way that does not blame the student for the fact that they are being treated badly. The goal of any Functional Behavior Objectives should be to assist the student in gaining personal relationship skills that honor who they are. This is especially important in situations where a student is neurodiverse and is behaving in ways that other students may consider to be inappropriate or "weird." There has been an unfortunate effort in the special education of neurodiverse students to try to teach them to "act normal."[641] Functional Behavior Objectives should also include increasing skills in personal advocacy and strategies for how to effectively respond if someone is hurtful to them on the basis of the fact that they are "different."

Supplementary Aids and Services

The additional, and much more critical, focus in the *Section 504* Plan or IEP meeting must be on the actions the school will commit to take to stop the harassment and correct the apparently Hostile Environment. The school's plans to stop the harassment and correct the environment should be addressed within in a discussion about what Supplementary Aids and Services the student requires. The requirements under Supplementary Aids and Services are described as follows:

> *(d) A statement of the specific special education and related services and supplementary aids and services, based on peer-reviewed research to the extent practicable, to be provided to the child, or on behalf of the child, and a statement of the program modifications or supports for school personnel that will be provided for the child:*
>
> *(A) To advance appropriately toward attaining the annual goals;*

(B) To be involved and progress in the general education curriculum and to participate in extracurricular and other nonacademic activities; and

(C) To be educated and participate with other children with disabilities and children without disabilities.[642]

If this student is being bullied or engaging in hurtful behavior, achieving objectives (A), (B), and (C) are all of concern and should be fully addressed. This student will have greater difficulties focusing on studies, being involved in educational activities and extracurricular activities, and participating with other students. Therefore, the school must create a plan of action that will be incorporated into Supplementary Aids and Services section of the 504 Plan or IEP to allow this student to effectively learn and fully participate—without other students or staff members being hurtful to them or them responding in a hurtful way.

While not naming or addressing any specific Hurtful Student or staff member specifically, it will be necessary to generally talk about what the school intends to do in regards to any situations where any student or staff member is hurtful to this student, even if in a minor way, as part of a general plan to stop the harassment.

Child Find — Bullied Students with Mental Health Concerns

If any student, whether or not originally considered to have a disability, is experiencing mental health concerns associated with being bullied, this student should be considered for placement on a *Section 504* Plan.

Under *Section 504*, schools must identify and locate all children in the district's jurisdiction who are disabled under *Section 504* and are not receiving FAPE.[643] Schools must also notify students with disabilities and their parents or caregivers of the district's responsibility under *Section 504*.[644] Section 504 also provides system of procedural safeguards that are designed to inform parents or caregivers of a school district's actions or decisions and to provide parents or caregivers with a process for challenging those actions or decisions.

The *Section 504* definition of physical and mental impairment also includes any mental or psychological disorder that substantially limits a major life activity.[645] Major life activities include learning, concentrating, and thinking. This list, however, does not provide every possible major life activity. If an activity is not listed, it might still be considered a major life activity under Section 504.[646] Most specifically, the ability to fully participate in learning and other activities at school should be considered a major life activity for any student. If the bullying this student is receiving is substantially limiting such learning or participation, then this should be considered interference with an important life activity.

Thus, any student who has developed a mental health disability, as documented by a doctor or counselor, as a result of being bullied in a serious or persistent manner, which has created a substantial limitation on their ability to learn, concentrate, think and fully participate in classroom and school activities, the situation of this student must be evaluated by a *Section 504* Team to make a determination regarding placement on a *Section 504* Plan.

The result of the bullying this student is receiving is interfering with their FAPE. Thus, this student, whether or not they were originally perceived to be within a Protected Class under civil rights laws, should now be considered to receive protections under *Section 504*—as they now have a mental health condition caused by the bullying.

This Targeted Student may or may not need any other special education or related aids and services. *Section 504* does not obligate a school district to provide aids or services that a student does not need. But, even if a student with a diagnosed mental health condition that is interfering with their life activities does not need other kinds of more typically provided services, this student is protected from disability-based discrimination under *Section 504's* general non-discrimination requirements.[647]

School leaders and counselors must recognize that if a student is reporting being bullied by peers or staff, and this student has now received a mental health condition diagnosis, and the bullying has created a substantial limitation on the ability of this student to learn, concentrate, or think and is interfering with the ability of this student to fully participate in learning and school activities, thus denying FAPE, under *Section 504*, this student must be evaluated for a *Section 504* Plan.

Even if this student does not require any additional support services, the bullying this student is receiving must be addressed in a *Section 504* Plan, developed by a *Section 504* Team—that includes the parent or caregiver and should include the student. This *Section 504* Plan will be legally enforceable.

Guidance on the issues to be addressed in a *Section 504* Plan or IEP to address concerns of bullying of a student with disabilities, including a student recently diagnosed at having a mental health condition associated with being bullied, is set forth in Chapter 11.

Affinity Groups

A recent issue associated with civil rights laws has emerged related to school-based Affinity Groups. An advocacy group called Parents Defending Freedom has called upon their followers to report concerns they deem involve schools integrating Critical Race Theory, to which they object. This is resulting in complaints or litigation.

One issue they are concerned about, and have filed complaints on, are schools that implement Affinity Group activities in a way that directly excludes some students or parents or caregivers—specifically White students or parents or caregivers. Parents Defending Freedom are asserting that this is a violation of civil rights laws.[648]

In every situation Parents Defending Freedom have raised this complaint, the school district has backed down. And rightly so. To exclude any student or parent or caregiver from any school group or activity based on race, national origin, sexual or gender status, is a clear violation of civil rights laws. US civil rights laws were enacted to address the concerns of "Whites Only" restrictions. For schools to say "No Whites Allowed" is clearly also unacceptable.

The Gay Straight Alliance Network, very effectively has avoided any potential challenges in this manner.[649] This Affinity Group approach is opening and welcoming of allies. As schools want to better focus on increasing inclusion, all students must be welcome in all student groups. All parents or caregivers must be welcome in all parent or caregiver activities. The National Association of GSA Networks has a dynamite advisory guide, *GSA Advisor Handbook*, that provides insight that is valuable for any advisory group.[650]

A challenge may emerge in some schools. This is the potential that students or parents or caregivers who do not support activities or initiatives that provide expanded support for students and families in marginalized groups may seek to join or participate in these Affinity Groups. A situation was reported to me of a school that had established a support group for sexual and gender minority students that attracted a student who was curious about those who might be questioning their sexuality, then used this information to denigrate and be hurtful to these students. There are two strategies that can address this concern:

- **Have Group Agreements**. As the *GSA Advisor Handbook* described:

  Many groups have group agreements in order to ensure that group discussions are safe, confidential, and respectful. Many groups have a group agreement that no assumptions or labels are used about a group member's sexual orientation or gender identity. This can help make straight allies and transgender students feel comfortable about attending the club.[651]

- **Hold Restorative Circles.** This is the one situation where my guidance on holding Restorative Circles, set forth in Chapter 3, should not hold. IIRP has an excellent guide on *Restorative Circles, Restorative Circles in Schools: A Practical Guide for Educators*.[652] The mentor for any Affinity Group should have training in managing Restorative Circles. If any member of an Affinity Group violates the Group Agreements of that group, a Restorative Circle should be held so that this student can hear the opinions of all of the other group members about this person's hurtful conduct. Restorative Practices work best in communities that have established community agreements about behavior. Remember, that the goal of a Restorative Circle is acceptance of personal responsibility, agreement to remedy the harm, and reconciliation.

FREE SPEECH ISSUES

It is helpful to frame this discussion with an analysis of the historical underpinnings of the free speech provision in the First Amendment. There is considerable disagreement about exactly what the framers of the Bill of Rights were thinking.[653] However, the natural rights philosophy advocated by John Locke, who was revered by many early leaders, was likely influential. The natural law perspective was expressed as follows:

> *Without Freedom of Thought, there can be no such Thing as Wisdom; and no such Thing as Publick Liberty, without Freedom of Speech: Which is the Right of every Man, as **far as by it he does not hurt and control the Right of another**; and this is the only Check which it ought to suffer, the only Bounds which it ought to know.*[654]

An excellent contemporary discussion of these issues from the perspective of schools was recently set forth in a document entitled, *Harassment, Bullying and Free Expression: Guidelines for Free and Safe Public Schools:*

> *It is important to distinguish between speech that expresses an idea, including religious or political viewpoints—even ideas some find offensive—and speech that is intended to cause, or school administrators demonstrate is likely to cause, emotional or psychological harm to the listener. **Words that convey ideas are one thing; words that are used as assault weapons quite another**.*[655]

Note the great similarity between this statement and the prior statement by Locke. Essentially, the line at which students' free speech rights crosses over to speech that can be restricted in school is when such speech intrudes with other important student rights that schools must also protect, specifically the right to receive an education.

Supreme Court Cases

There have been five Supreme Court cases addressing student free speech rights. Four of these relate to situations that could be involved when considering student speech that disparages other students. These are: *Tinker v. Des Moines Ind. Comm. Sch. Dist., Bethel School District v. Fraser,* and *Morse v. Frederick.*[656]

Tinker v. Des Moines.[657] The *Tinker* case involved the right of students to wear black arm bands to protest the war in Vietnam. The Court made strong statements related to the protection of students' free speech rights, but also indicated schools may restrict student speech if there are reasons to believe it could cause a substantial disruption or a significant interference with other students. A key comment from the case:

> *In order for the State in the person of school officials to justify prohibition of a particular expression of opinion, it must be able to show that its action was caused by something more than a mere desire to avoid the discomfort and unpleasantness that always accompany an unpopular viewpoint. Certainly where there is no finding and no showing that engaging in the forbidden conduct would "materially and substantially interfere with the requirements of appropriate discipline in the operation of the school," the prohibition cannot be sustained.*

Bethel v Fraser.[658] The next Supreme Court case addressing student free speech was *Fraser*, which involved student speech presented during an assembly that included an explicit sexual metaphor. While the Court again reinforced the importance of respecting students' free speech rights, it also noted that the "constitutional rights of students in public school are not automatically coextensive with the rights of adults in other settings." The Court determined that school administrators could respond to student speech that was "lewd, vulgar, plainly offensive, and contrary to the school's educational mission."

An important statement also appeared in the *Fraser* case, in the concurring opinion of Justice Brennan. This statement relates directly to the issue of off-campus speech. Justice Brennan stated:

> *If respondent had given the same speech outside of the school environment, he could not have been penalized simply because government officials considered his language to be inappropriate.*

Thus, the *Fraser* standard provides support for school administrators in inculcating habits and manners of civility, but this only applies to on-campus student speech.

Morse v. Frederick.[659] The case of *Morse* involved student display of a sign that read "Bong Hits 4 Jesus" at what the Court considered to be a school event, where students were watching the Olympic torch passing the school. The manner in which the Supreme Court approached its analysis in *Morse* focused on student safety—in this case, drug abuse. As such, this decision is directly applicable to the situation involving speech that could harm other students, including situations involving bullying.

Laying the groundwork for the concern of drug use, the Court quoted from the *Vernonia* case, where it had upheld school-based drug searches and spoke extensively on the dangers of youth drug abuse. Then, the Court engaged in an extensive discussion of the need and demand for school-based efforts to address drug abuse. The Court's process of analysis was:

> *The problem (of drug abuse) remains serious today. (Citing several sources of supporting data.) ...*
>
> *Congress has declared that part of a school's job is educating students about the dangers of illegal drug use. ... (Referencing such statutory efforts.)*
>
> *Thousands of school boards throughout the country ... have adopted policies aimed at effectuating this message. Those school boards know that peer pressure is perhaps "the single most important factor leading schoolchildren to take drugs," and that students are more likely to use drugs when the norms in school appear to tolerate such behavior. Student speech celebrating illegal drug use at a school event, in the presence of school administrators and teachers, thus poses a particular challenge for school administrators working to protect those entrusted to their care from the dangers of drug abuse.*

The concurring opinion in *Morse*, Justice Alito, along with Justice Kennedy, should also be viewed as influential. In this opinion, Justice Alito focused on the issue of student safety:

> *[A]ny argument for altering the usual free speech rules in the public schools cannot rest on a theory of delegation but must instead be based on some special characteristic of the school setting. The special characteristic that is relevant in this case is the threat to the physical safety of students. School attendance can expose students to threats to their physical safety that they would not otherwise face. Outside of school, parents can attempt to protect their children in many ways and may take steps to monitor and exercise control over the persons with whom their children associate. Similarly, students, when not in school, may be able to avoid threatening individuals and situations. During school hours, however, parents are not present to provide protection and guidance, and students' movements and their ability to choose the persons with whom they spend time are severely restricted. Students may be compelled on a daily basis to spend time at close quarters with other students who may do them harm. Experience shows that schools can be places of special danger.*
>
> *... [D]ue to the special features of the school environment, school administrators must have greater authority to intervene before speech leads to violence.*

Mahanoy Area School District v. B.L.[660] ***141 S. Ct. 2038 (2021)*** The Supreme Court ruled on June 23, 2021 that a public high school student's off-campus social media postings in which she used vulgar language and disparaged school programs constituted protected speech. The Court declined to provide a bright-line rule stating what counts as "off-campus speech" and when such speech is protected. Instead the Court focused on three "features" of off-campus speech that often diminish a school's ability to regulate it.

First, off-campus speech normally falls in the zone of parental, rather than school-related, authority. Second, if off-campus speech and on-campus speech can both be regulated by schools, this would leave students with little to no opportunity to speak freely. Third, public schools, play a role in supporting democracies, and thus should have an interest in protecting unpopular student expression, especially off campus. The Court rejected the arguments that the school had an interest in teaching good manners off-campus or that the posts significantly disrupted school. The Court said it would "leave for future cases to decide where, when, and how these features mean the speaker's off-campus location will make the critical difference."

Schools can only intervene in situations of student off-campus speech if such speech has or reasonably could create a substantial disruption at school or interference with the rights of other students. The Court provided a few examples where off-campus behaviors may call for school regulation. These include: serious or severe bullying or harassment targeting particular individuals; threats aimed at teachers or other students; the failure to follow rules concerning lessons, the writing of papers, the use of computers, or participation in other online school activities; and breaches of school security devices, including material maintained within school computers.

I wrote an extensive law review article on off-campus student speech that was published in 2012.[661] The Supreme Court's decision in this case was in full accord with what I set forth in 2012.

Two Important Lower Court Cases

Two important lower court cases illustrate how the standards of *Tinker* and *Morse,* and sometimes *Fraser,* have been applied in situations of bullying and speech that disparages others and thus contributes to a "culture of bias."

A key federal court case that applied the *Tinker* standard in the context of a bullying policy is **Saxe v. State College.**[662] In *Saxe,* the school district's anti-harassment policy had been challenged on the basis that it was over broad and could impact speech that someone might find merely offensive. The objections to the school's bullying policy had been raised by the legal guardian for two students who believed that this policy would restrict the ability of students to speak out about their religious beliefs, including their belief that homosexuality is a sin.

The Third Circuit Court, in an opinion by then-Judge Alito, initiated the discussion with the following statement:

> *There is of course no question that non-expressive, physically harassing conduct is entirely outside the ambit of the free speech clause. But there is also no question*

that the free speech clause protects a wide variety of speech that listeners may consider deeply offensive, including statements that impugn another's race or national origin or that denigrate religious beliefs.

In other words, there are no concerns with respect to statutory bullying prevention restrictions against hurtful physical conduct. The free speech concerns are associated with provisions that impact student speech. In discussing the school district's policy, the court stated as follows:

We agree that the Policy's first prong, which prohibits speech that would "substantially interfere with a student's educational performance," may satisfy the Tinker standard. The primary function of a public school is to educate its students; conduct that substantially interferes with the mission is, almost by definition, disruptive to the school environment.

Note also that the court essentially equated the *Tinker* concept of "substantial disruption" with "interference with a student's educational performance." Note also the use of the terms "a" student, meaning the disruption does not have to be school-wide. The interference may be of only one other student.

In another location in the decision, the court also stated that it was appropriate to assess the distress of a student based both on the subjective perspective of the student bullied, as well as an objective perspective looking at all of the circumstances, including frequency, severity, and degree of interference.

However, the court did find the second prong to be unconstitutional because it included the term "offensive." The court stated:

In any case, it is certainly not enough that the speech is merely offensive to some listener. ... Because the Policy's "Hostile Environment" prong does not, on its face, require any threshold showing of severity or pervasiveness, it could conceivably be applied to cover any speech about some enumerated personal characteristics the content of which offends someone. This could include much "core" political and religious speech: the Policy's "Definitions" section lists as examples of covered "negative" or "derogatory" speech about such contentious issues as "racial customs," "religious tradition," "language," "sexual orientation," and "values." Such speech, when it does not pose a realistic threat of substantial disruption, is within a student's First Amendment rights.

Kowalski v. Berkeley County.[663] This Fourth Circuit case, addressed a situation involving off-campus cyberbullying involving hurtful speech directed at one student by another student. Because this speech was off-campus, the court declined to rely on the *Fraser* standard. The court made its determination supporting the disciplinary actions of the school based on the *Tinker* substantial disruption standard, noting the evidence of how the student's off-campus actions had interfered with the bullied student's learning while at school.

However, in discussion the court also set forth an analysis approach that was very similar to the manner in which the Supreme Court approached its decision in *Morse*:

> *According to a federal government initiative, student-on-student bullying is a major concern in schools across the country and can cause victims to become depressed and anxious, to be afraid to go to school, and to have thoughts of suicide. ... [Schools have a duty to protect their students from harassment and bullying in the school environment ... Far from being a situation where school authorities suppress speech on political and social issues based on disagreement with the viewpoint expressed, ... school administrators must be able to prevent and punish harassment and bullying in order to provide a safe school environment conducive to learning.*

Thus, in this case, we can see the reliance on *Tinker*, but strong support from a *Morse*-based analysis related to student safety.

Applied to Bullying and Cyberbullying Situations

The manner in which the Supreme Court and two Circuit Courts analyzed the situation in these three cases can be readily followed when supporting the important role of schools in effectively addressing the concerns of bullying or disparaging student speech:

- The problems associated with bullying have been well-documented through research. These concerns include long-term emotional harm, school avoidance and failure, and suicide ideation.[664]

- In its interpretation of numerous civil rights statutes, the USDOE's OCR has declared that part of a school's job is preventing discriminatory harassment of students.[665]

- The Federal Government has launched a broad-based initiative to reduce bullying in schools.[666]

- Throughout this country, schools are required by state statutes to have bullying prevention policies in place and to respond to reports of bullying.[667]

- The freedom to advocate unpopular or controversial views in schools must be balanced against the school's role in teaching students the boundaries of socially appropriate behavior and the "habits and manners of civility," including the need to treat others with respect.[668] (However, do not attempt to use this argument to justify restriction of student off-campus speech.)

- If school administrators and teachers tolerate student speech that disparages peers, this will pose a major challenge in the ability of schools to protect students who have been entrusted to their care.

- Failure to restrict such speech could also lead to liability for discriminatory harassment because such speech could contribute to a Hostile Environment or "culture of bias" against certain students.[669]

- Schools can intervene in student off-campus that has or reasonably could create interference with the rights of a student who is being bullied or harassed.

Disparaging or Hate Speech on Campus

Restricting Disparaging or Hate Speech

It is necessary for schools to be able to restrict and respond to disparaging speech to ensure that the school does not allow an underlying "culture of bias" against typically targeted students that may reenforce more egregious, continuing bullying or harassment. Clearly, to ensure a school climate that supports all students, schools must restrict instances of disparagement that may not reach the level of bullying or harassment, but could, in a cumulative manner, support and sustain a Hostile Environment. Interventions in this regard should, as best as possible, be instructional in nature.

To do so, schools must be able to restrict speech that includes derogatory terms, symbols that have historically been associated with the oppression of a group of people, or statements that communicate an opinion of the inherent inferiority of a student, group of students, or group of people which may include students. This kind of speech will be referred to as disparaging speech.

Most of the cases addressing the authority of schools to restrict disparaging speech have been in situations involving student dress codes. These cases have not specifically focused on situations involving bullying or harassment. Some of these kinds of cases have involved what could be viewed as lewd or vulgar speech.[670] The courts have generally upheld the authority of schools to restrict such speech relying on the standards expressed in *Fraser*. In most, but not all, cases the courts have upheld schools' decisions to prohibit the Confederate flag at school, under *Tinker*, because past racially charged incidents allowed the officials to predict that the display of the Confederate flag foreseeably could substantially disrupt the schools. These cases present examples:

- *Melton v. Young*.[671] In the four years since the high school was racially integrated, the school had experienced significant racial tension.

- *West v. Derby Unified Sch. Dist.*[672] There had been actual fights at school involving racial symbols, particularly the Confederate flag.

- *Scott v. Sch. Bd. of Alachua County.*[673] The school had a history of racial tensions including racially based altercations.

However, a different decision was made in *Castorina ex rel. Rewt v. Madison County School Board.*[674] In this case, the Sixth Circuit reversed the District Court's grant of summary judgment to the school. The court noted the lack of evidence suggesting that a ban on the Confederate flag was needed to prevent disruptions and emphasized that the Confederate flag appeared to have been specifically targeted by school administrators, who let other potentially divisive racial symbols go unpunished. The reasons for this will be discussed further below.

In cases where the issue has been anti-homosexual speech based on religious objections or anti-Islamic speech, the decisions have been more varied. By way of example are these cases:

- *Nixon v. Northern Local School District Board of Education.*[675] A Federal District Court upheld the right of a student to wear a T-Shirt that stated: Homosexuality is a sin! Islam is a lie! Abortion is murder! Some issues are just black and white!

- *Zamecnik v. Indian Prairie School Dist. #204.*[676] The Seventh Circuit upheld the right of students to wear a T-shirt stating: "Be Happy, Not Gay."

- *Harper v Poway.*[677] In 2006, the Ninth Circuit upheld the school's right to restrict Harper's anti-homosexuality speech, but this decision was vacated on appeal by the Supreme Court.

- *Sapp v Alachua.*[678] A Federal District Court supported the decision of a school in a suit brought by students who were prohibited from wearing t-shirts stating: "Islam is of the Devil."

Evidence of Substantial Disruption

Determining why these decisions were different requires a focus on the quality of the evidence presented by the school to justify its decision to restrict such speech. To restrict such speech requires that schools are able to reasonably forecast of disruption at the school or interference with the rights of other students.

By way of background on the issue of local evidence forecasting substantial disruption, consider the statements made in several key cases. In *Tinker*, the Supreme Court stated:

> *[T]he record does not demonstrate any facts which might reasonably have led school authorities to forecast substantial disruption of or material interference with school activities, and no disturbances or disorders on the school premises in fact occurred.*[679]

In *Saxe*, the Third Circuit noted:

> However, if a school can point to a well-founded expectation of disruption--especially one based on past incidents arising out of similar speech--the restriction may pass constitutional muster.[680]

Justice Alito's concurring opinion in *Morse*, stated:

> [I]n most cases, Tinker's "substantial disruption" standard permits school administrators to step in before actual violence erupts.[681]

Failed to Meet Evidentiary Requirement

The following are statements from court decisions regarding the sufficiency of the evidence in cases where the school's restriction of student speech was not supported. In *Castorina*. In the above-mentioned Confederate flag case, the Sixth Circuit stated the following in regards to the sufficiency of the evidence:

> If the students' claims regarding the Malcolm X-inspired clothing (i.e. that other students wore this type of clothing and were not disciplined) and their claims that there were no prior disruptive altercations as a result of Confederate flags are found credible, the court below would be required to strike down the students' suspension as a violation of their rights of free speech as set forth in Tinker. In addition, even if there has been racial violence that necessitates a ban on racially divisive symbols, the school does not have the authority to enforce a viewpoint-specific ban on racially sensitive symbols and not others. Conversely, if the students cannot establish their factual claims, then the principal and school board may have acted within their constitutional authority to control student activity and behavior. In either circumstance, the facts are essential to the application of the legal framework discussed herein. Accordingly, the summary judgment is reversed and the case remanded to the district court for trial.[682]

In similar manner in *Nixon*, the anti-homosexual, anti-abortion, anti-Islam T-shirt case, the court expressing its opinion of the sufficiency of the evidence as follows:

> Defendants concede that James' shirt did not cause any disruptions at school. ...
> They do assert, however, that the shirt had the potential to cause a disruption.
> This is presumably based on the fact that the school includes students and/or staff members who are Muslims, homosexuals, and those who have had abortions. The mere fact that these groups exist at Sheridan Middle School, and the fact that they could find the shirt's message offensive, falls well short of the Tinker standard for reasonably anticipating a disruption of school activities.[683]

In *Zamecnik*, an anti-homosexual T-shirt case, the court explained that the three forms of evidence the school submitted were entirely deficient, noting:

> *To justify prohibiting their display the school would have to present "facts which might reasonably lead school administrators to forecast substantial disruption."* ... *Such facts might include a decline in students' test scores, an upsurge in truancy, or other symptoms of a sick school*—**but the school had presented no such facts in response to the motion for a preliminary injunction.**[684]

The court rejected the school's evidence of prior incidents of harassment as negligible because the single school administrator who presented testimony about these incidents was unable to confirm any details about any incidents. He reportedly was relying on comments made by other unidentified school administrators, based on unconfirmed statements, made by unidentified students.

The school had also submitted evidence of incidents of harassment by students against Zamecnik, the student who wore the T-shirt. The court determined that the school could not rely on retaliatory conduct by persons who are offended by speech to prohibit such speech. Finally, the school had offered expert testimony, which the court described:

> *There is nothing in the report to indicate that Russell knows anything about Neuqua Valley High School, for there is no reference to the school in the report. No example is given of "particularly insidious" statements about homosexuals. No example is given of a "homophobic slur" or "derogatory remark" about them that has ever been uttered in any school, or elsewhere for that matter. Though the report calls "be happy, not gay" particularly insidious, it does not indicate what effects it would be likely to have on homosexual students. It gives no indication of what kind of data or study or model Russell uses or other researchers use to base a prediction of harm to homosexual students on particular "negative comments." No methodology is described. No similar research is described.*
>
> *... Dr. Russell is an expert, but fails to indicate, however sketchily, how he used his expertise to generate his conclusion. Mere conclusions, without a "hint of an inferential process," are useless to the court. ... Russell's is as thin an expert-witness report as we've seen.*[685]

The focus on local evidence in these three cases makes it clear that what courts will pay attention to the most is not the substance of the speech itself, but the quality of the local evidence presented to justify restricting such speech based on the foreseeability of interference with rights of other students at that particular school.

Met the Evidentiary Requirement

Compare the lack of evidence in the above cases to that which was submitted in *Harper* and *Sapp*, where the authority of the school to restrict disparaging speech in a specific incident and in a policy, was upheld.

In *Harper*, the school provided information about a series of incidents and altercations occurred on the school campus as a result of anti-homosexual comments that were made by students, including a confrontation that required the principal to separate students physically.[686]

The school also provided extensive research insight that demonstrated the academic underachievement, truancy, and dropout of homosexual youth that were the probable consequences of violence and verbal and physical abuse at school. Further, it was known that this case was occurring in the context of litigation that had been brought against the district for failure to prevent the harassment of students based on sexual orientation.

In *Sapp*, the school district also provided extensive local evidence of disruption.[687] This included a number of student altercations related to the disparaging speech, and significant disruption of student events. Additional evidence was that parents had contacted the school expressing concerns about the safety of their children. Four administrators testified about how, in their professional experience, such speech was offensive and demeaning and could lead to a Hostile Environment that was interfering with the delivery of instruction.

Sufficiency of Local Evidence is KEY!

Thus, the decisions in support of the students' disparaging speech in *Castorina, Nixon,* and *Zamecnik* were quite clearly based on lack of sufficient local evidence to demonstrate that the school had a well-founded expectation that the speech could foreseeably cause a significant interference in the rights of other students to receive an education. The decisions were not based on the character of the speech itself.

In fact, in the decision in *Zamecnik,* the court went to such great lengths outlining the insufficiency of the evidence, one could reasonably "read between the lines" in this decision that the court wanted to rule in the opposite manner and was frustrated by the lack of evidence that would support its doing so. Essentially, this decision provided extensive instruction by the court to schools on the evidence necessary to support a conclusion upholding a school restriction of student speech that disparages others.

Recommendations

To restrict student speech that disparages other students without facing the threat of litigation for free speech, school district must ensure that they have local data and evidence, backed up by research and/or expert analysis, to justify their conclusion, that similar speech has created, and therefore can be reasonably expected to create conditions at school that significantly interfere with the rights of other students to receive an education and participate in school activities or a substantial disruption, that could include violence.

Schools are advised to obtain such local evidence on a regular basis, just in case an objection to an action to restrict disparaging speech occurs. An annual survey and focus groups are the perfect vehicle to obtain sufficient evidence of the negative impact of cumulative disparaging statements on students' well-being, learning, and participation.

If any increased efforts are planned to better address disparaging speech or bias incidents, the following strategy is recommended:

- Gather all following evidence that addresses the findings of the negative impact of disparaging speech or bias incidents on students' ability to learn and participate in school activities that includes.

  - Data from an annual survey of students.

  - Focus group data from students that are likely targeted that focuses on specific incidents involving disparaging speech, as well as the cumulative negative effect of such speech on their emotional well-being and the resulting impact on their ability to learn and participate in school activities.

  - Stories that document occasions when such students have avoided school, classes, or school activities due to the expressions of disparaging speech by other students. Focus on the cumulative effect of such disparaging speech.

  - Data from actual incidents to back up the presence and negative impact of such speech.

- Back up the validity of these findings with academic published studies.

  - If there is an expectation of a contentious response to any restrictions or a threat of litigation, arrange for an external expert to review this report to provide additional credibility to the findings.

- Emphasize that any school response to these situations will focus on instruction, accountability, and remedying the harm—and not punishment.

  - Focus attention on the important role of schools to impart the habits and manners of civility that are essential to a democratic society which includes tolerance of divergent political and religious views, but also must take into account the sensibilities of other students. Incorporate language from *Brown, Tinker,* and *Fraser.*

- Have students who are typically targeted present this report to any policy body, such as the school board or a site council.

- This report can justify any necessary changes in policy related to disparaging speech or information for students or parents or caregivers about school standards.

- If the above has not been done and contention arises in the context of litigation or threatened litigation, quickly prepare the above documentation.

The Bottom Line

If a school district is in any situation where restrictions are being imposed on a student's exercise of speech or a disciplinary consequence is being imposed, be sure to thoroughly document, at the time, why such restriction or action is warranted in terms of how this speech has, or foreseeably could (based on very solid part experience or known experience in other schools) cause a significant interference in the ability of any other student to receive an education or could create a substantial disruption of a number of students at school.

PART IV
Instruction and Intervention

Chapter 10.
Empowered to Embrace Civility

Chapter provides recommendations on strategies to more fully engage students in maintaining positive relationships and civility. This Chapter provides insight on the establishment of a Student Leadership Team and insight into the implementation of an indirect instruction strategy to transmit information about the Positive Social Norms of a school, as well as personal relationship skills. The approach and objectives of the companion student program, *Empowered to Embrace Civility* are addressed in this Chapter.

As this Chapter presents an implementation approach, there is no Highlights section.

STUDENT LEADERSHIP TEAM

Establishing a Student Leadership is a critically important component of *Engage Students to Embrace Civility* approach. The leaders who should serve on the Student Leadership Team are the Prestige Leaders among different groups of students in the school. These are the students who have a long standing reputation of being kind, respectful, and inclusive. They also consistently reach out to help others, especially those students who are perceived to be "different."

In this book, the name Student Leadership Team has been used. Please encourage your students to select a name for themselves. For example, the (Name of School) Kindness Team. Or (Name of School) Unite Together.

Identifying the Student Leaders

The student leaders you will want to have involved are the students who provide leadership within the social groups of students who they affiliate with. It is especially important to identify students who have influence with the school's different social groups. Ensure the Team includes students from all school grades, all racial and ethnic groups of the school, students with minority gender identities and sexual orientation, and students from groups that are less connected to school or active in school activities, and student with disabilities. However, at the elementary school level, it may be best to have a Team oof only the top two grade levels.

These students may not be considered "high-achievers." They also may not currently be highly engaged in current overall school activities. Sometimes, school leadership groups have become more populated by the Dominance Leaders. The students you are looking for may be involved in more quiet leadership activities. For example, these students may be the leaders in a sexual minority support group or students who are working as mentors with students with disabilities.

Be careful that you do not include those students who are merely thought to be "popular" and "cool." It may be that these students have been the ones who have achieved high social status by being hurtful to others. Make sure the students selected have a long history of being kind and compassionate. Failure to do this could undermine the acceptance of the guidance of the Team by other students.

A experience I had might help to understand how careful it is to select the right students for this team. Some news articles appeared in my local community in reference to an incident where someone had taken images of texts that a principal and assistant principal were sending to each other while watching a game.[688] The texts denigrated a student who had been going to their school, who had recently transferred to this new school. She had joined the cheer team. After these texts came to light, these two administrators resigned.

I met in person with one of the young ladies who was the target. She did have weight problems—for which she had been bullied throughout school. She almost died as a young child because she has Type I diabetes. She told me that while in high school, she had applied several times to be in the student leadership class. Every time, she was turned down. The school's popular athletes were always the ones chosen for this leadership class—by the assistant principal—who was also the athletic director. The students who were included in the leadership class were also the ones who had bullied her since elementary school.

BE EXCEPTIONALLY CAREFUL IN YOUR DETERMINATION OF WHO YOU CONSIDER TO BE LEADERSHIP STUDENTS!

Specifically identify and invite students who appear to have latent leadership capacity, who have also experienced being treated badly. Being asked to serve on this Team will be empowering for them. They also have the ability to speak with knowledge about the concerns of students being hurtful.

Application or Nomination

It is recommended that all members of the Student Leadership Team be required to submit an application or be nominated by other students or by staff. The recommended approach to identify students should be nominated or encouraged to apply is:

- Ask school staff to identify students using the above criteria, paying particular attention to selection of students from all social groups.

- Ask students who are in minority population groups within your school to identify which students they think would be strong representatives to express the concerns that members of their community face. Ask these students to nominate those they think should especially be part of the Team.

  - Alternatively, hold focus group discussions with these students to ask them about their concerns. In the process of these discussions, identify the students who appear most articulate and dedicated and appear to be viewed as leaders by their peers.

It is suggested that the Student Leadership Team nomination form provide and solicit this information:

This Student Leadership Team is being established to promote civility, kindness, respect, and inclusion for all students at (name of school). Using this form, you can nominate a student who you think should be invited to serve on this Leadership Team.

- What is the name and grade of the student you think should be a member of the Student Leadership Team?

- Please explain why you think this student should be a member of this Team.

- Please explain a time when you saw that another student was being treated badly and the student you are nominating stepped in to help the student being treated badly.

- Please explain a time when you saw the student you are nominating step in to help resolve a conflict between students.

- Please explain a time when you saw that another student was being hurtful and the student you are nominating told the student being hurtful to stop.

It is suggested that the Student Leadership Team application form provide and solicit this information:

This Student Leadership Team is being established to promote civility, kindness, respect, and inclusion for all students at (name of school). Using this form, you can apply to serve on this Leadership Team.

- Please explain why you want to be a member of this Team.

- Please explain a time when you saw another student was being excluded or treated badly and you stepped in to help the student. How did you step in to help? What did you learn from this?

- Please explain a time when you stepped in to help resolve a conflict between students. What did you learn from this?

- Please explain a time when you stepped in to tell a student who was being hurtful to stop. What did you learn from this?

- Please explain a time when you made a mistake and were hurtful. How did you handle the situation afterwards? What did you learn from this?

Using a combination of this input, identify students to ask to serve on the initial Student Leadership Team. It is likely that all students who are nominated and those who apply are exactly the students you will want to serve on the Team.

After the initial Team has been established and has established protocols, schools are advised to consider allowing any other interested student to join this Team. The bigger the Team, the greater the potential impact. It should also be possible for students who have had difficulties in being hurtful, but are now demonstrating signs of a desire to maintain more positive relationships, be added to the Team.

Ideally, the school will establish an initial Student Leadership Team that can either take full or partial responsibility for *Empowered to Embrace Civility*. At younger grades, the students may require greater assistance from their mentor(s).

Sources of Strength

Empowered to Embrace Civility can also be integrated into other student leadership programs your school has established. The lessons of *Empowered to Embrace Civility* are highly compatible with an excellent suicide prevention program called Sources of Strength.[689] More on Sources of Strength later in this Chapter.

COORDINATION

Relationship Building

Especially at the start, the staff mentors and student leaders should take time within the activities of the Student Leadership Team, especially at the start, for activities that are specifically designed to build relationships and break down barriers. Conduct a search for "ice breaker activities for students" will yield many positive suggestions.

Students Leaders Think Things Through

The most important job of the mentors for the Student Leadership Team is to take the role of a "Guide by the Side." One of the best things the staff mentor can do is help the students learn and practice a strategy that engages the members of the Student Leadership Team in Thinking Things Through to decide what to do.

The think things through strategy was set forth in Chapter 6. A slight shift is necessary for use of this approach with the Student Leadership Team in deciding on strategies. The recommended approach:

- What is the situation or issue that we would like to address?

- What strategies could we use?

- How is each strategy in accord with our school's values?

- For each strategy, what might happen as a result of implementing this strategy? Especially identify any challenges that may emerge and develop plans for how to address such challenges.

- What is our best choice or choices?

- What is our plan for implementation? Who will take what responsibilities? What resources or permissions will we need?

- How will we evaluate success?

Key *Empowered to Embrace Civility* Activities

The key activities of the Student Leadership Team were already introduced in Chapter 4.

- Engage the Team in the development of objectives for student improvement in maintaining positive relationships.

- Engage the Team in the presentation of *Empowered to Embrace Civility*, which includes the Positive Social Norms data, as well as the incident and insight data, and recommendations on skills to better manage personal relationships to students.

- Engage the Team in the creation of additional images that illustrate the data and skills as posters, bookmarks, and log on screens, or create short videos that illustrate the skills and Positive Social Norms data.

Additional Activities for the Team

The Student Leadership Team can expanding on these messages of increasing civility, kindness, respect, and inclusion throughout the school year. These are activities that should be under the direct leadership of the Student Leadership Team. The students should be encouraged to think of their own ideas. These are some idea that could be considered by the Student Leadership Team:

- **Welcome to School Display.** Create a display at the entrance of the school incorporates a word cloud incorporating the most frequently selected words to illustrate the concept of civility or a statement created that incorporates these words.

- **Kindness Campaign.** Implement a Kindness Campaign in the school. Random Acts of Kindness Foundation site has lots of activities to promote kindness.[690] Conducting a search on "kindness, schools" will yield additional ideas.

- **Posters, Screen Savers, Bookmarks, and Short Videos.** Create posters, screen displays, book-marks, or short videos that illustrate the schools's Positive Social Norms data and positive relationship skills. Or hold a contest for the entire student body.

- **T-shirt.** Host a competition for a t-shirt design for students to promote their commitment to civility, kindness, respect, and inclusion.

- **Daily or Weekly Announcements.** Make a daily or weekly public school announcements related to Embrace Civility.

  - Here is an example of what a member of the Civility Student Leadership Team could say: "Hi. I am ____ a member of the Student

Leadership Team. Here is your quote of the day: 'If I can help somebody as I pass along, if I can cheer somebody with a word or song, if I can show somebody he's traveling wrong, then my living will not be in vain.' Dr. Martin Luther King, Jr. Please take a moment today to Reach Out to Be Kind or help someone decide on a positive path. Remember also to say thank you to someone who reaches out to be kind to you. We are having a meeting of the Student Leadership Team ___. Remember, membership on this Team is open to anyone who makes a commitment to be kind, respectful, and inclusive and who wants to help our school community live by these values."

- **Special Days in Association with Organizations.** Promote special days activities. Participate in events promoted by other organizations to allow students to know that their local school activities are connected at a larger level. These are some examples:

  - **Beyond Differences—special days to promote social inclusion.** Beyond Differences, promotes a number of wonderful activities to help students promote social inclusion.[691] These are events that take place on one day and include No One Eats Alone, Know Your Classmates, and Call It Out.

  - **GLSEN No Name Calling Week.** GLSEN hosts a No Name Calling Week generally mid-school year.[692] Their website has excellent resources to support this effort. Like a participation in the Beyond Differences days, the Student Leadership Teams participation in the GLSEN activities allow the school effort to merge with national initiatives.

- **Mindfulness and Mindful Movement.** Coordinate the school's mindfulness activities, including setting up a student-led "mindful movement" program at lunch time or before school.

- **Quote Competition.** Encourage students to find and submit a quote by a famous person that relates to the objectives of Embrace Civility. The quotes could be posted in categories. Students could vote on their favorite quotes. These quotes could be turned into posters, bookmarks, or screen displays.

- **Video.** Create a video to share what the school is doing to support students in maintaining positive relationships.

- **Frowny Faces Paper Plates Display.** The school's data will likely reveal that around 90% of the students express that they really do not like to see students being hurtful. When this data is shared in an assembly, it is recommended that ten Student Leadership Team members have creatively decorated paper plates as faces—nine with frowny faces and one laughing. The students can show these paper plate faces demonstrating how many students really do not like to see someone being hurtful. Then, the paper plates can be put on display at the entrance of the school, with a sign stating: "If you are hurtful to someone at (name of school), this is how many students watching you do not like to see this happen."

- **Wall of Thanks.** Create a bulletin board area in the school as a Wall of Thanks. Provide ample "sticky notes" nearby and pens. Encourage everyone in the school community—students, staff, parents, and caregivers —to regularly write personal messages of gratitude to others or for anything they are personally thankful for.

  - To expand on this activity, members of the Student Leadership Team could pick out a few messages each day to read over the intercom in the morning. Instruct them to specifically pick out messages of gratitude sent to students who are known to have greater challenges.

- **Celebrating and Building Strengths.** Implement activities celebrating Character Strengths. As noted in Chapter 4, schools are encouraged to have secondary students complete the VIA Institute's Character Strengths survey.[693] The VIA site contains many activities and approaches that can be used to promote the different strengths. The Student Leadership Team could lead a campaign to focus on one character strength a week.

- **School Board and Other Presentations.** Make a presentation on their findings and efforts to the School Board and to other community organizations. (Hint: community organizations may be a source of funding for some projects that require funding.)

- **Community Service Day.** Set up one day a month where students go into the community to provide service.

- **Flash Dance.** Create a flash dance to perform at a local mall. If you have not seen this video, watching it is a must: https:// www.youtube.com/watch? v=MhYyAa0VnyY. Search: Anti-Bullying Flashmob January 2011." Or this one: https://www.youtube.com/ watch?v=vmDId5UPhIMAnti Bullying Flash Mob February 2017.

Additional Resources

There are a number of additional excellent sites online that have wonderful ideas, programs, or resources that could be integrated into school activities, especially students in older grades. Among the best are:

- **Greater Good Science Center.** The Greater Good Science Center has excellent resources on supporting a meaningful happy life.[694]

Student Leaders could sign up to receive their news letter and create Expansion Activities related to the insight that is provided.

- **Learning for Justice Resources.** Southern Poverty Law Clinic's excellent Learning for Justice program has a wealth insight and resources for activities that can easily be student led.[695] The resources on this site can be used to expand on the Embrace Civility lessons in older grades.

- **No Place for Hate.** The Anti Defamation League's (ADL) No Place for Hate website has a significant number of effective resources to provide anti-bias instruction.[696] I have some overall concerns about how this program is implemented. I prefer to use language that is positive in nature—working for something positive, rather than against something negative. I have significant concerns about the high pressure to sign a statement written by ADL. My approach is to have students answer their own questions about their commitments. I think this is more powerful. I do not think schools should be required to notify ADL of incidents. However, notwithstanding these concerns, some of the informational materials on the site appear to be helpful.

- **One and All.** One and All is a site established by Harvard Graduate School of Education that focuses on Strategies to Protect Students, Reject Bullying, and Build Communities Where Everyone Thrives.[697]

EMPOWERED TO EMBRACE CIVILITY

As has been noted, the *Empowered to Embrace Civility* student program is a separate program that is available from Embrace Civility. The cost is based on the average student population of the school. More information is at http://embracecivility.org.

Empowered to Embrace Civility focuses on strengthening positive student relationships and supporting students in responding effectively when someone is hurtful—as a Witness, the Hurtful Student, or the Targeted Student. This program can be used in middle and high school. It is also advised that districts have their middle school Student Leadership Team make a presentation, using middle school data, to the students in the intermediate grades at their companion elementary schools.

The objectives for this program are included in an early question on the *Embrace Civility Student Survey*. The students at your school will:

- Treat other students with civility, kindness, and respect while at school.

- Treat other students with civility, kindness, and respect while using social media.

- Step in to help if they see someone being treated badly.

- Tell students who are hurtful to stop.

- Report serious or unresolved situations to an adult who can help.

- Stop themselves and say they are sorry if they were hurtful.

- Respond in an effective way if someone treats them badly.

Empowered to Embrace Civility Positive Relationship Skills

Empowered to Embrace Civility teaches insight and skills in five core areas:

Step in to Help

- Reach out to be kind to those who are being treated badly, have been left out, or are going through a challenging time

- Help others to think things through or resolve conflict.

Say "Stop"

- Publicly tell someone being hurtful to stop.

- Help someone who was hurtful decide to stop, own it, and fix it.

- Encourage friends to make the right choices.

Report Concerns

- Tell an adult who can help if I know of a situation that is a serious and has or could cause harm..

Stop, Own It, and Fix It

- Always remember that my choices show who I truly am.

- Stop myself and make things right if I have been hurtful.

Be Positively Powerful

- Make positive connections, reach out to be kind, build my strengths, be thankful, remain calm, keep my personal power, and think things through.

- Respond in a positively powerful way if someone is hurtful to me.

Components of the Program

In the development of this program every effort has been made to create the resources in a way that will allow for creative modified use by schools. *Empowered to Embrace Civility* contains the following components:

- **An Implementation Guide**. This Guide includes Instructional Objectives and Activities.

- *Embrace Civility Student Survey*.

- **Template Slideshow for the *Empowered to Embrace Civility* Assembly.** This is a slideshow that will need to be revised to set forth the data that is obtained through the local *Embrace Civility Student Survey*.

- **Instruction Posters.** These slides from the slideshow can also be turned into posters , bookmarks or screen displays. Alternatively, the text on these slides can be set forth on posters, bookmarks, or screen displays created by students that could use the school colors.

- **Personal Commitment Statement.** This document provides questions students can respond to that will help them to think more deeply about what has been discussed and how they might apply this insight to their own values and actions. The use of a Personal Commitment Statement was introduced in Chapter 4 in the discussion of Principles of Influence.

- **Character Strengths Short Survey.** It is recommended that schools encourage secondary students to complete a free teen survey on the VIA Institute of Character website.[698] However, a shorter survey has been developed with approval from the VIA Institute on Character that could be used as an alternative.

Indirect Instruction

As was discussed in Chapter 4, *ESSA* set forth four evidence levels to guide schools in selecting evidence-based programs and approaches that have a Likelihood of Success. *Empowered to Embrace Civility* should be considered to meet the standards for the category of "Demonstrates a

Rationale." The student program fully embraces all of the research set forth in Chapters 4 through 7. Thus, clearly, this program has a rationale that it fully supported by research.

This category also requires evaluation, preferably local evaluation. *Empowered to Embrace Civility* incorporates a Continuous Improvement Approach that incorporates ongoing evaluation. The *Embrace Civility Student Survey* will both support Positive Social Norms-based messaging and will provide data necessary both for needs assessment and ongoing evaluation of effectiveness. As noted in Chapter 4, the Student Leadership Team should be fully engaged in the establishment of objectives for improvement based on data from the survey.

The practical reality is that many schools, especially in the US, have such a strong focus on having students achieve academic outcomes, finding time in the school schedule to directly teach about how to maintain positive relationships is a challenge. Another challenge is that, based on the data set forth in Chapter 3 related to student perspectives of school staff insight into bullying, students may simply not think that school staff really understands their relationship concerns.

Positive Social Norms

The section on Positive Social Norms in Chapter 4 set forth research that supports the implementation of an indirect instruction approach through the use of posters that set forth the data obtained through a local survey. In a research study, simply displaying posters that had graphics demonstrating the school's norms resulted in a decrease in bullying.

In the digital age, these posters can be provided online as screen displays on the school's instructional website. In addition to posters, bookmarks, and screen displays, the Student Leadership Team members can create short videos illustrating effective personal relationship skills.

Relationship Skills Instruction

The effective indirect instruction approach using posters is also grounded in the insight from a University of New Hampshire campaign to reduce sexual assault at the college level called, *Know Your Power*.[699] This program was developed by University of New Hampshire's Prevention Innovations Research Center. Note, in a discussion earlier, another program developed by this Center that sought to achieve the same aims—but through adult delivery of direct instruction—was deemed to be ineffective. This was discussed in Chapter 8.

The *Bringing in the Bystander* (BITB) direct instruction by teacher program appeared to have no positive impact on influencing bystander behaviors. The researchers thought that it was possible that classroom-delivered bystander-focused violence prevention curricula is not particularly effective in increasing bystander interventions.

The UNH *Know Your Power* implemented an informal messaging campaign using graphic images that illustrated effective bystander strategies. The images used were photographs of college students in situations of sexual assault, this included pre-, during, and post- situations. The posters included communication "bubbles" illustrating what was being said. These images were produced as posters, bookmarks, bus signs, screen displays, and the like. The images also include the program's name and a tagline such as: "Friends watch out for one another... Especially when there is alcohol involved."

An early evaluation of the campaign found that an increase target audience members' awareness regarding sexual and relationship violence, increased willingness to get involved in reducing violence, and increased reported likelihood to act as an active bystander.[700] It appeared that the more greater the frequency of seeing these posters and like, the increase in positive impact. Further, when students considered that they saw themselves in the images, there was a greater influence.

A study implemented the use of these posters and like over a four week period of time. This study assessed before, during, and one month after the implementation found that the campaign appeared to change undergraduate students' attitudes. For example, there was a reduction of their acceptance of common rape myths. In addition, the students exposed to the campaign reported an increase in the actions they had taken to reduce sexual and relationship violence on their campus.[701]

Student Leadership

Sources of Strength is one of the first suicide prevention programs that implemented the use of peer leaders to enhance protective factors associated with reducing suicide at the school population level. From it's website:

> *A best practice youth suicide prevention project designed to harness the power of peer social networks to change unhealthy norms and culture, ultimately preventing suicide, bullying, and substance abuse. The mission of Sources of Strength is to prevent suicide by increasing help seeking behaviors and promoting connections between peers and caring adults. Sources of Strength moves beyond a singular focus on risk factors by utilizing an upstream approach for youth suicide prevention. This upstream model strengthens multiple sources of support (protective factors) around young individuals so that when times get hard they have strengths to rely on.*

The resilience factors that Sources of Strengths focuses on are highly compatible with the resilience factors discussed in Chapter 6. As excellent as Sources of Strength is, it currently lacks a strong focus on bullying and other hurtful behavior. However, the manner in which the program is implemented in schools allows for the flexibility of the student leaders to implement initiatives they perceive would be helpful for the student body. *Empowered to Embrace Civility* would clearly fit in with both the peer leadership approach and the strong focus on resilience.

Positive Social Norms and Relationship Skills Indirect Instruction

The indirect instruction approach of *Empowered to Embrace Civility* student program is fully grounded in the research on the effectiveness of the Positive Social Norms posters in a middle school and the *Know Your Power* posters and other media at the college level. This program incorporates aspects that were recommended by the researchers in their evaluation of the ineffectiveness of the adult-delivered BITB program. The additional components that were suggested included focusing on peer norms, a focus on friendships, the involvement of popular opinion leaders, and the need to focus more on teaching effective bystander intervention skills.

This program can be implemented in an indirect manner using the following approach:

- Establish a Student Leadership Team, identify one or more staff mentors, and initiate relationship building activities within the Team.

- Conduct the *Embrace Civility Student Survey*.

- Modify the *Empowered to Embrace Civility* slideshow to demonstrate the data from the local school survey. This slideshow contains slides that set forth the data, as well as the recommended strategies to increase students' skills in maintaining positive relationships.

- Have the Student Leadership Team present the slideshow to groups of students. At the upper elementary school level, it likely will be necessary for the staff mentor to take the leadership in presenting the slideshow, with participation of the Student Leadership Team. Especially the first year, when the Student Leadership Team is just getting started in its instructional role, it is likely that presentations to smaller groups of students would be preferable.

- Turn the slideshow slides into posters, bookmarks, and screen displays. Alternatively, create posters, bookmarks, or screen display using the text of the slides, but with local student-created graphics. Encourage the Student Leadership Team to create short videos that set forth the data and strategies.

If desired, it also is possible to implement Embrace Civility through direct instruction by teachers. The instructional objectives and possible instructional activities are provided in the Guide. The instructional objectives are also presented in this Chapter. There are seven groups of lessons contained in *Empowered to Embrace Civility*. However, within each group lesson, there are multiple mini lessons, each one of which could be a short lesson and discussion in and of itself.

Curriculum Standards

The Health Education Curriculum Analysis Tool (HECAT) is an assessment tool developed by the CDC in partnership with health education experts representing state education agencies, school districts, schools, colleges, and national organizations.[702] Most state standards have been developed in reference to these. The 2012 HECAT for Violence Prevention Curriculum provides this definition:

Violence is defined as any threat or actual use of force or power against oneself (self-inflicted injury or suicide), against another person, or against a group that results in or has a high likelihood of resulting in injury, psychological harm, abnormal growth or development, deprivation, or death.[703]

While *Empowered to Embrace Civility* does not choose to use the term "violence" in the description or objectives, these are the curriculum objectives that are most relevant. The Health Behavior Outcomes (HBO) should enable students to:

- *HBO 1. Manage interpersonal conflict in nonviolent ways.*

- *HBO 2. Manage emotional distress in nonviolent ways.*

- *HBO 3. Avoid bullying, being a bystander to bullying, or being a victim of bullying.*

- *HBO 4. Avoid engaging in violence, including sexual harassment, coercion, exploitation, physical fighting, and rape.*

- *HBO 5. Avoid situations where violence is likely to occur.*

- *HBO 6. Avoid associating with others who are involved in or who encourage violence or criminal activity.*

- *HBO 7. Get help to prevent or stop violence including harassment, abuse, bullying, hazing, fighting, and hate crimes.*

- *HBO 8. Get help to prevent or stop inappropriate touching.*

- *HBO 9. Get help to stop being subjected to violence or physical abuse.*

- *HBO 10. Get help for oneself or others who are in danger of hurting themselves.[704]*

The *Empowered to Embrace Civility* lessons directly address the knowledge and student skills expectations in the HECAT violence prevention objectives.

Embrace Civility Student Survey

The *Embrace Civility Student Survey* is a powerful tool in this program. The questions support both indirect instruction and assessment. What will be discovered is that students are exceptionally interested in what their data says about how they treat others or which their peers would treat others. This survey is available for preview on the Embrace Civility website at http://embracecivility.org..

As is evident in the survey language itself, students should be given the option of deciding whether or not they will complete the survey. Notice should be sent home to parents or caregivers informing them of the survey and giving them the opportunity to opt their child out. Some states in the US and some other countries may require signed parent or caregiver consent.

It is not necessary at the elementary school level to use all of the survey questions that have been provided. These are provided as options. An alternative strategy for the elementary level would be to use the middle school data from the school which these students will attend. A key effort is to reduce the increase in hurtful behavior that occurs when students enter the middle school environment and puberty kicks in more strongly. Showing these upper elementary students the data that demonstrates the Positive Social Norms of middle school students may actually be helpful.

The *Embrace Civility Student Survey* asks these kinds of Questions:

- Questions about overall school climate from the perspective of how students treat each other and relationships with staff.

- Positive Social Norms questions about students' perspectives about hurtful and helpful student behavior.

- Questions about incident rates of hurtful behavior. This includes questions about how frequently in the last month students witnessed someone being hurtful, were hurtful, had someone be hurtful to them, and witnessed staff being hurtful to a student.

  - There are follow-up questions to these incident questions that focus on behaviors that are desired to be increased, which includes stepping in to help, telling students who are hurtful to stop, telling a friend who was hurtful to stop, stopping and saying they were sorry if they were hurtful, and responding to someone treating them badly in an effective way. The survey questions will allow for important comparisons to be made. For example, students who witness hurtful incidents are asked if they stepped in to help. Students who reported someone was hurtful to them are asked if anyone stepped in to help. The resulting data will try likely demonstrate differences—which can lead to valuable discussions.

- An extended question that asks about the frequency of hurtful behavior associated with identity groups or school activities.

The *Embrace Civility Student Survey* addresses staff issues. This portion of the survey results should be analyzed by staff and staff should identify objectives for improvement.

Empowered to Embrace Civility Presentation and Media

The *Empowered to Embrace Civility* presentation is contains both Positive Social Norms data and relationship skills guidance:

- **Positive Social Norms.** Data from the survey is presented to the students by the Student Leadership Team. As is evident from both use of an earlier version of the *Embrace Civility Student Survey* and the PISA 2018 attitude data, this presentation will demonstrate that the majority of students hold positive values related to how they think they and their peers should treat others. This approach emulates the prior Positive Social Norms approach that achieved success in middle schools.

- **Relationship Skills.** The slides also demonstrate effective skills incorporating strategies identified as Core Personal Relationship Skills earlier in this Chapter. This is similar to the *Know Your Power* approach. However, the skills presented are more extensive. Further, these slides also incorporate the related Positive Social Norms data.

Empowered to Embrace Civility includes both a presentation and follow-up media:

- **Presentation.** The presentation of both the Positive Social Norms data and relationship skills guidance is initially made to students in groups by the Student Leadership Team.

- **Media.** The slides from the presentation and other graphics created locally are then displayed in posters and computer screens.

It would be best if key members of the Student Leadership Team present this data. The staff mentors may also assist, especially for younger grades. An approach of using high school students to make a presentation at the middle school and middle school students present at the elementary school could also be considered. As noted, it also would be acceptable to have the middle school students use middle school data in presentations to older grade students at the elementary school level. These students are often very focused on what life will be like for them as they move to the middle school.

INSTRUCTIONAL OBJECTIVES

Civility and Positive Norms

- Understand that civility means being kind and respectful even if you disagree.

- Recognize the key values of students related to maintaining positive personal relationships.

- Understand that the majority of students do not like to see students be hurtful to others.

- Understand that the majority of students admire those who: are respectful; reach out to help others; help a friend stop being hurtful; report serious concerns; stop, own it, and fit it if they are hurtful; and respond in a positive manner if treated badly.

- Understand that the majority of students do not like and admire those who are disrespectful, create hurtful "drama" to get attention, support those being hurtful, and ignore hurtful situations.

Be a Helpful Ally

- Recognize that when they see someone being hurtful or disrespectful, they have three choices. They can be a Hurtful Supporter, Passive Observer, or Helpful Ally.

- Identify the reasons why they would want to step in to help.

- Understand that there are three basic ways they can be a Helpful Ally include reaching out to be kind, saying "stop," and reporting concerns.

- Understand that Helpful Allies can be very effective in stopping hurtful incidents and are admired by their peers when they do step in to help.

- Recognize the common barriers to being a Helpful Ally are legitimate fears related to their own abilities and fears related to the possible reactions of others, including possible safety and reputation concerns —however, these concerns can be addressed.

- Recognize that they might rationalize or make excuses for not stepping in to help because they want to continue to consider themselves to have good character.

- Understand that there are safe and effective ways they can be a Helpful Ally.

Step In to Help

- Learn how they can help someone who is being treated badly think things through to identify desired goals, think of possible strategies they could use and the potential consequences, decide on a strategy and determine how to proceed, and realize that what they initially try may not work, so they may need to use another strategy.

- Learn how to help others who are engaged in a conflict think things through to resolve that conflict. Identify the steps of conflict resolution, which include helping those who are in conflict express their feelings about what has happened in a manner that can lead to resolution, generate possible strategies to resolve the situation, come to an agreement on the best strategy, and the steps they will take if that does not work.

- Learn safe strategies to help someone who is being treated badly leave the situation without getting into an argument with the one who is being hurtful. Recognize that if they are not able to help, they should report their concerns to someone who can help.

- Learn how they can support a friend who is going through a challenging time.

Say "Stop"

- Recognize the common rationalizations or excuses people use when they are hurtful to try to deny that they have done anything wrong. Learn how to use a form of Reflective Listening to challenge these common rationalizations.

- Learn the important safety guidelines for telling someone who is being hurtful to stop, including the importance of assessing the situation to keep themselves safe, not retaliating, not increasing attention to someone who wants attention, and working with others.

- Encourage their friends to make good choices by assessing their friends values and actions, not joining in when their friend is hurtful, and encouraging their friend to stop, own it, and fix it.

- Understand the importance of thinking things through if their friend refuses to stop, own it, and fix it related to their own personal values and the possible damage to their own reputation if they continue this relationship.

Report Concerns

- Recognize the warning signs that a peer or they are at higher risk.

- Identify situations that are serious or have been unresolved, especially if there is risk of harm. Recognize that in these situations should be reported to an adult

- Understand what information should be reported to an adult.

- Understand who these situations should be reported to and what to do if the first adult they report to fails to respond.

Stop, Own It and Fix It

- Identify the reasons why they would not want to be hurtful to another. Recognize that they may rationalize being hurtful and understand that such rationalizations are excuses for behaving in ways that are not in accord with their own values.

- Understand the differences between students who are striving for social status by being kind and compassionate, as compared to those who are hurtful to others to achieve social dominance. Privately reflect on their motivations.

- Understand that in situations where they have been treated badly, there is a possibility they may engage in impulsive retaliation. Recognize that people can change and hurtful situations can be stopped. Understand that engaging in retaliation will undermine to potential for maintaining positive relationships.

- Learn how to think things through if they were hurtful, decide to stop, own it, or fix it.

Be Positively Powerful

- Learn strategies to become more positively powerful, which can help to reduce the potential other students are hurtful to them and will reduce the potential of their experiencing emotional harm, including:

  - Make positive connections with good friends and trusted adults.

  - Reach out to be kind to others.

- Build their personal strengths and focus on their future goals.

- Be thankful for good things that are happening in their lives.

- Practice mindfulness every day so that they build the neural pathways to remain calm.

- Maintain a positive presence, both in person and when using social media.

- Know how to think things through to decide what to do.

• Learn how to effectively respond to being treated badly in a manner that enables them to keep their own power if someone is hurtful to them and reduce the harmful impact on them.

- Recognize the importance of remaining calm when someone is hurtful to them and not overreacting in response.

- Recognize that while they can't control what happens to them, they do have the ability to control what they think about this, and therefore how this makes them feel.

- Learn how to think things through to determine a powerful positive response of someone treats them badly.

- Understand the importance of connecting with a good friend or trusted adult after this occurs to gain support and to help them to think things through to determine whether there is something further they should do.

Personal Relationships Commitments Statement

The following are my Personal Relationships Commitments regarding how I intend to maintain positive relationships.

- I commit to treat other students in the following way:

- If I witness someone being hurtful to another student, I will:

- If I make a mistake and am hurtful to someone, I will:

- If a friend of mine is hurtful to another student, I will:

- If someone is hurtful to me, I will:

Chapter 11.

Intervention and Empowerment

This Chapter provides guidance on how school leaders and staff can positively intervene in hurtful incidents. There are two objectives of this intervention approach. One is to stop the hurtful behavior, remedy the harm to the target, and correct the Hostile Environment. The second underlying objective is, through this process, to impart insight and skills to students to more effectively resolve hurtful incidents in the future.

As this Chapter presents an implementation approach, there is no Highlights section.

HURTFUL INCIDENTS OR SITUATIONS

In this Chapter, the term "Incident" refers to a more minor incidents that students should be able to resolve on their own or with a limited staff intervention. "Situations" are those that are more serious or persistent and are having a harmful impact on the ability of the Targeted Student to participate in instruction or other school activities. The term "Situation" can also be applied to pervasive situations where many students who are within an identity group are all experiencing hurtful treatment.

Hurtful behavior between students obviously occurs along a continuum. Therefore, these definitions must be viewed with some flexibility.

It should be recognized by all staff that what at first appears to be an Incident may be one of a series of more persistent or pervasive incidents —which would constitute a Situation.

In US civil rights legal terminology, a Situation is also a Hostile Environment, as was discussed in Chapter 9. The foundation of the intervention guidance set forth in this Chapter, for Situations is fully based on the guidance provided in Chapter 9 on the requirements to respond to Hostile Environments.

- **End the Harassment.** Engage the Hurtful Student and Supporters through an Accountability Process, where they are required to accept responsibility, take steps to remedy the harm to the target and school community, and agree to discontinue all further acts of harm. Disciplinary consequences should be implemented upon failure to agree to or comply with this Accountability Agreement. Create a Protections Plan to ensure any necessary protections for the Targeted Student.

- **Remedy the Harmful Effects.** Identify and address the challenges any involved students. Put a Positive Action Plan into place to address these challenges. This includes both Targeted Students and Marginalized Hurtful Students. This plan should also address harms that the Targeted Student has experienced, including both academic harms and emotional harms.

- **Correct the Hostile Environment.** Make any necessary corrections to school environment to address concerns identified. This includes corrections of staff hurtful behavior or failure to intervene, as deemed necessary. This also includes other aspects of the environment. The investigation should have determined whether the serious or persistent conduct directed at one student is actually evidence of a pervasive hurtful situation impacting many students within this Protected Class.

- **Monitor to Ensure Effectiveness.** Engage in ongoing monitoring takes place to ensure that things are better for all involved students. Conduct an evaluation involving all parties to the hurtful incident or situation to determine effectiveness of the school's investigation and intervention and identify any ongoing concerns.

OVERVIEW OF RESPONSE AND INTERVENTION STRATEGIES

The positive strategies for investigation and intervention include:

- Engage all students who have been involved in an Incident or Situation in the efforts to resolve this Incident or Situation in a manner that empowers them to independently maintain positive relationships in the future and respond effectively when hurtful conduct does occur.

- Respond to Situations as a "potential allegation" of a violation of the district policy against bullying or civil rights laws that initially will be responded to as a "Restorative Diversionary Intervention."

- Implement a modified MTSS framework that in addition to an assessment of the challenges of the involved students, also focuses on three tiers of hurtful conduct that need to be addressed within the school.

- Increase the effectiveness of staff in responding to Incidents in a positive, restorative, and instructive manner. Ensure that staff follow up after intervening in this Incidents to ensure the matter has been resolved.

- Ensure that staff identify and report evidence that suggests a more serious, persistent, or pervasive Situations that require a more intensive investigation and intervention by a Designated Staff Person.

- Conduct a prompt, comprehensive, and unbiased investigation of any potentially serious, persistent, or pervasive Situation.

- Distinguish between Reactive or Proactive Aggression, as this will provide insight into the underlying motivations of the Hurtful Students.

- Implement a Positive Action Plan to increase resilience of any student who has been involved in a Hurtful Situation who has any identified personal relationship or self-regulation challenges. This may include either Targeted or Marginalized Hurtful Students.

- Ensure a Protections Plan is put into place, if necessary, to provide any protections for any Targeted Student or Marginalized Hurtful Student.

- Hold both Hurtful Students and Supporters accountable through an Accountability Process that results in an Accountability Agreement.

- Address concerns of students with disabilities who are currently on an IEP our 504 Plan who are either being bullied or engaging in bullying in an IEP or 504 team meeting. Address both Functional Skills and necessary Supplemental Aids and Supports.

- Identify any Targeted Student who is now experiencing emotional distress, that has been determined to be a mental health concern which has created a substantial limitation of their ability to learn, concentrate, or think. Make a determination regarding placement of this student on a 504 Plan and a resolution of this Situation within the context of a 504 Plan.

- Investigate and correct aspects of the school environment that may be contributing to a Hostile Environment.

- Conduct an evaluation of the effectiveness of school's interventions in Hurtful Situations by asking all involved students and their parents or caregivers if the situation has gotten better.

- Consider the establishment of a Peer Assistance and Accountability Team.

Restorative Diversionary Intervention

School leaders in the US are presented with a multiple directions Catch-22 situation when it comes to responding to reported or witnessed Hurtful Incidents or Situations.

- As was explained in Chapter 3, at the federal level under *ESSA* and in many states, there are statutes that report any bullying incidents. This appears to have led to a disinclination of principals to consider Hurtful Situations to meet the standards of "bullying" or "harassment" under their district's policy.

- As was discussed in Chapter 9, schools must respond to Hurtful Situations that involve a student who receives protection under civil rights laws in a manner that is in accord with the requirements of comprehensive civil rights regulations. Failure to do so could lead to an adverse agency action or litigation.

It is not my anticipation that *ESSA* or state statutes will be amended any time soon. Assuming your district's legal council agrees this is is permissible, it is suggested principals view serious, persistent, or pervasive Hurtful Situations as "potential allegations" of a violation of the district policy against bullying and harassment or civil rights laws. However, choose to proceed with a Restorative Diversionary Intervention.

Note that under *ESSA*, Restorative Practices are encouraged. When a school engages in a Restorative Practice, this is not viewed as a "disciplinary consequence" that must be reported. The recommended Restorative Diversionary Intervention is in line with this reasoning.

The Restorative Disciplinary Intervention approach does not anticipate a disciplinary consequence unless the student who was hurtful fails to abide by the Accountability Agreement they will enter into. Only if such hurtful behavior continues will the Situation be upgraded to an "actual allegation" of a violation of the policy, thus requiring reporting under *ESSA* or possibly under state statute.

It should be noted that the Restorative Diversionary Intervention approach presented in this Chapter does incorporate the more extensive requirements considered necessary to respond to a Hostile Environment under the federal civil rights laws, as discussed in Chapter 9.

It is recommended that this more comprehensive intervention approach be provided for all students, not just those protected under civil rights laws, as this is a more effective way to address the concerns.

This information should not be interpreted as legal guidance. Please consult with your district's local counsel on what has been set forth in this subsection and Chapter.

Engagement and Empowerment

The underlying perspective of the Restorative Diversionary Intervention approach to intervene can be summed in two words: Engage. Empower. It is necessary that all students who have been involved in Incidents or Situations be fully engaged in the resolution of the concerns.

The process of resolution should seek to achieve empowerment of all involved students. These Incidents or Situations should be viewed as "teachable moments" to allow all involved parties to gain greater insight into skills they can use in the future to maintain more positive relationships and respond effectively to hurtful conduct in the future. The objective is that all students will gain the expertise to respond to Incidents or Situations in an effective manner independently—whether the one being treated badly, the one who was hurtful, or a witness. The intervention approach must also be instructional and empowering.

Student Voice in Interventions

It is recommended that educators not assume the perspective that they "the adult" needs to step in and decide what should be done. These Incidents and Situations involve challenges in interpersonal relationships. Student voice and participation, especially of the Targeted Student, is essential.

The people who know best what is happening are the students involved. All of the students involved in a problem situation should have both the right and the responsibility to be proactively engaged in determining the resolution. The intervention approach must focus on empowering these students by ensuring Authentic Student Voice.

A Targeted Student is generally in a position of lower personal power than the one who was hurtful. Educators can help this student regain personal power by being treated as a full partner in the decision-making regarding what needs to be done. Recall the concerns of these students as outlined by extensive research in Chapter 3.

Recall that most of these students are extremely concerned by the fact that information about the hurtful behavior has become known to school leadership because of the very real potential that what leadership does will make matters worse for them. From the outset, they must know that leadership will be attentive and respond appropriately to their concerns. To accomplish this:

- Recognize that a Targeted Student may not want the Hurtful Student to be held accountable through the school's Accountability Process. This student may simply desire the opportunity to discuss what is happening, receive emotional support, and brainstorm possible strategies this student can use independently to respond. Discuss response options this student might be able to independently use.

- This student may not want the school to respond to this present report, as this would result in them being accused of "tattling." They may want to ensure staff are present where these incidents are occurring, so that a staff member can detect the next incident. This will greatly reduce the potential that reporting to the school could damage the Targeted Student's reputation or lead to retaliation. If this is the incidents are persistently occurring in a specific location, setting up this kind of a scenario is strongly advised. Suggest this possibility to the Targeted Student and follow their desires.

- Indicate to the Targeted Student that the school will seek to enter into an Accountability Agreement with the Hurtful Student. Indicate the purpose of this Accountability Agreement approach is to ensure the Hurtful Student will accept personal responsibility, agree to a Protection Plan if necessary, develop a plan to remedy the harm, and commit to discontinue any further harm.

  - Ask the Targeted Student if there is a desire to prepare or approve a statement that describes what happened and the harmful impact of what happened that will be provided to the Hurtful Student.

  - Ask what the student desires or requires in terms of a Protection Plan, including a "no contact" order or any necessary changes in classroom seating or attendance.

  - Ask the Targeted Student's opinion on the approach to intervene with the student who was hurtful. This student may wish that the school to coordinate a Restorative Practice intervention discussion and resolution that includes both of the students together.

Sometimes a student or the student's parent or caregiver, will want the school to "punish" the student who was hurtful. This is a natural response. In some situations a disciplinary consequence may be called for.

Explain to the student and parent or caregiver how the school will seek hold this student Accountable in a way that has been developed to achieve greater effectiveness and that the school will remain fully engaged to ensure the hurtful behavior is stopped.

Explain to the Targeted Student that as this is a Restorative Diversionary Intervention that requires acceptance of personal responsibility; agreement to a Protection Plan, if necessary; actions that will be taken to remedy the harm; and an agreement to discontinue such harm, this is not a "disciplinary consequence." It would presumably not be considered a violation of FERPA to provide part of the Accountability Agreement entered into by the Hurtful Student and Supporters to the Targeted Student.

However, this information should not be interpreted as legal guidance. Please consult with your district's local counsel on what has been set forth in this section.

It is also important to engage in collaboration with both the Hurtful Student and Supporters, allowing them also to have Authentic Student Voice. The Accountability Process engages the authentic voice of both the Hurtful Student and their Supporters in extensive discussions about their actions and supportive development of plans to remedy the harm.

The essence of Restorative Practices is that the one who engaged in wrongdoing is engaged in problem solving to identify a strategy to remedy the harm both to the individual harmed and to the community. The essence of Collaborative Problem Solving is that the student who is misbehaving is fully involved in the development of strategies to stop these actions. Principles from both Restorative Practices and Collaborative Problem Solving have been integrated into the Accountability Process and Agreement.

Self-Regulation

All staff must understand how to effectively respond to a dysregulated student to support that student in achieving regulation, so that they can be appropriately engaged in achieving a resolution of the Hurtful Incident of Situation. Attempting to reason with or resolve a Hurtful Incident or Situation at a point in time when any involved student is dysregulated, will not be effective.

The difference between Proactive or Reactive Aggression has been addressed throughout this book. School leaders and all staff will need to be alerted to this distinction so that intervention responses can be informed.

Any student who has engaged in Reactive Aggression has been, by definition, dysregulated. Reactive Aggression is characterized by high emotionality which makes the person prone to impulsive reactions after provocation. If this student is still diysregulated, their ability to explain their actions and to engage in problem solving has been undermined—their current actions are largely being directed by their Amygdala. Students who have engaged in Proactive Aggression are likely not to be dysregulated. The Targeted Student may also have become dysregulated, thus complicating and immediate intervention.

Strategies to assist students in becoming regulated were addressed in Chapter 6. Remember, the most important assurance that a dysregulated student needs is the assurance that they are safe and supported. Therefore, even if a dysregulated student has been hurtful to another, the first step in an immediate intervention are the actions necessary to support them in feeling safe and becoming regulated.

All staff should receive professional development in strategies to help dysregulated students become regulated. After all students who have been involved in a Hurtful Incident or Situation have become regulated, this is when an appropriate investigation and intervention can occur.

For staff dealing with a dysregulated Hurtful Student, this may feel as though they are being "kind" to a student who has been hurtful. A statement such the following is advised: "Right now what do you need to help you feel safe and get under control? We can address the situation after you have calmed down."

Modified Multiple Tier Approach

Implementing a modified Multiple Tier System and Supports (MTSS) approach will provide a foundation for effectiveness. However, the MTSS approach must be modified to effectively address hurtful behavior. One reason for this is that those competent students who are hurtful to achieve dominance and social status are not functioning in a manner that would be considered "at risk."

MTSS is an excellent three tiered, prevention approach that originated in the public health field.[705] The focus of MTSS has always been on those students who are at a greater risk. There are three Tiers:

- **Tier I.** Universal prevention efforts directed at all students.

- **Tier II.** Targeted supplemental interventions required by students who need additional support.

- **Tier III.** Intensive interventions required by students who face significant challenges.

Sometimes students who have been involved in a Hurtful Incident or Situation will require intervention at a Tier II or III level. This is especially true or Marginalized Hurtful Students.

Essentially, with a modified change in perspective, MTSS can also function effectively as a framework to address prevention efforts, as well as interventions in hurtful situations. This must include addressing the concerns of students who are not considered "at risk, as well as the concerns related to staff who witness Hurtful Incidents or Situations and do not respond appropriately. This will also include situations of staff who engage in behavior that is considered hurtful to a student.

The following are portions from a description of MTSS by PBIS.[706] This insight helps to explain the modification of MTSS in the effort to both prevent and intervene effectively in Hurtful Incidents or Situations. These statements from PBIS are provided because they provide an excellent opportunity to gain insight into the traditional understanding of the application of MTSS to risk prevention and how this understanding must be modified to more effectively address the concerns of hurtful behavior.

Tier I

From the PBIS document:

> *At Tier I, all students and staff are taught directly and formally about how to behave in safe, respectful, and responsible ways across all school settings. The emphasis is on teaching and encouraging positive social skills and character traits. If implemented well, most students will benefit and be successful.[707]*

This statement and approach requires some additions to more effectively support maintaining positive relationships. Recommended thinking: "All students and staff will gain the insight and skills to maintain positive relationships across all school settings, as well as when communicating online. This includes knowing how to prevent and effectively respond to and seek to resolve all Hurtful Incidents, if they are treated badly, are hurtful, or are a witness. At the Tier I level, all staff know how to effectively assist students in resolving Tier I level Incidents and identify possible Situations."

Tier II

From the PBIS document:

> *At Tier II, students whose behaviors do not respond to Tier I supports are provided additional preventive strategies that involve (a) more targeted social skills instruction, (b) increased adult monitoring and positive attention, (c) specific and regular daily feedback on their behavioral progress, and (d) additional academic supports, if necessary.[708]*

The Tier II level requires a change in perspective to support positive relationships and address the concerns of Situations. Note that under traditional MTSS analysis, Tier II students require more targeted personal relationship skills instruction and feedback on their behavioral process—hence, this applies to students who have been identified as being "at risk." This student-focused perspective is entirely appropriate for three kinds of students:

- Students who are being hurtful who have personal relationship skills challenges—the Marginalized Hurtful Students.

- Some Targeted Students who have personal relationship skills challenges that appear to be contributing to their vulnerability and/or inability to effectively respond.

- Any Targeted Student in a Situation who is experiencing emotional distress, who should be considered for designation under *Section 504*.

All three of these kinds of students should receive a Positive Action Plan, which is considered a Tier II intervention. Components of a Positive Action Plan are discussed later in this Chapter.

However, Dominance Motivated Hurtful Students are not otherwise going to be considered "at risk" or to have "behavioral concerns" warranting a Tier II intervention. They generally have excellent personal relationship skills, when they choose to exercise such skills, are competent, and are compliant to adult staff. These students would likely not ever be perceived as requiring Tier II personal interventions—and yet they are the source of most hurtful behavior in schools.

The modified MTSS guidance is to consider all Situations—the serious, persistent, or pervasive situations—to require a Tier II level intervention. Tier II level interventions require a more comprehensive investigation and a more extensive intervention approach, the effectiveness of which is monitored until such time as all students will indicate that things have gotten better. In other words, Tier II intervention is situational based. Not, "this student requires Tier II intervention." Rather, "this Situation requires a Tier II intervention."

An important aspect of Tier II level is expressed as "(b) increased adult monitoring and adult attention." Given the concerns of students about reporting and the evidence of the low level of effectiveness of staff interventions, clearly it is imperative that Situations be monitored in an ongoing manner.

A Tier II level investigation and intervention can also be implemented in any situation where a staff member has been accused of engaging in more minor hurtful or disrespectful behavior or has been present when a Incident or Situation occurred and did not intervene appropriately. It would be desirable that this situation be perceived as requiring a corrective action through professional development and support, and not a disciplinary action. This approach will hopefully avoid challenges with the staff member's union representation.

Tier III

From the PBIS document:

At Tier III, students whose behaviors do not respond to Tier I and II supports are provided intensive preventive strategies that involve (a) highly individualized academic and/or behavior intervention planning; (b) more comprehensive, person-centered and function- based wraparound processes; and (c) school- family-community mental health supports.[709]

Some very serious Situations should be addressed at a Tier III level, especially when there is evidence that of students with serious behavioral challenges or have experienced trauma and, individually, they require a Tier III intervention. A Tier III level intervention may also be required when a Tier II level Situation intervention has not achieved effectiveness. If there is evidence of pervasive hurtful treatment of a group of Protected Class students, the intervention required, which will include comprehensive interventions to address a the school climate, should be considered to be a Tier III level intervention.

Tier III level intervention should also be considered necessary to respond to more egregious staff conduct or what are originally considered to be Tier II staff intervention, to which the staff member has not responded in an effective manner.

INVESTIGATION AND INTERVENTION PROCESS

It is presumed that districts have adopted a disciplinary code that includes provisions in accord with their respective governing statute. This almost always has established a reporting process, both at the school and district level, that can be used by students, parents, caregivers, or staff to report Incidents or Situations.

As noted, the recommended intervention approach should be considered Restorative Diversionary Intervention. It is possible that language could be added to the district policy. Alternatively, implementation practice guidelines could be developed. The following practices may already be established:

- Identify one or more staff members at the school as "Designated Staff Person," who are responsible for investigating and intervening in the serious, persistent, or pervasive Situations. The Designate Staff Person will generally be the principal or assistant principal, or could be a school mental health professional.

- Identify one or more district staff personnel who are available to provide assistance to school level Designated Staff Person and who are also responsible for investigating Situations that have not been resolved at the school level. The district staff person should also be called upon to support the Designated Staff person in investigating and intervening in any situation where a staff member has been witnessed or reported to have been hurtful to a student.

- Establish standards for staff regarding their intervention and reporting responsibilities. This should include guidelines for how they are expected to respond to the Incidents or serious Situations they witness or are reported to them by students, as appropriate based their staff position and job responsibilities.

  - All staff should immediately report any serious Situation to the Designated Staff Person. If in their response to what appeared at first to be a more minor Incident, becomes upon questioning evidence of a persistent or pervasive Situation, this should also be reported to the Designated Staff Person.

  - All staff members should be expected to seek to stop any Incident. If a classified stamp member intervenes in an Incident, this staff member should report to the certified staff member they work with. This certified staff member may engage in further investigation and intervention, if deemed necessary.

  - The Designated Staff Person should be responsible for investigating and intervening in Situations, including what originally were considered Incidents that have either not been effectively resolved by staff or that the staff member has received insight this may be a persistent or pervasive Situation.

  - If a staff member witnesses another staff member engaging in behavior that is disrespectful or abusive of a student, the staff member must report this to the Designated Staff Person. If there appears to have been no effective response to this report or alternatively for any reason, the staff person should or could report to the district level staff person. Confidentiality of the staff member reporting should be assured.

Intervention in Incidents by Staff

Objectives of this Approach

Schools must set forth steps to be taken by both certified and classified staff when they: witness Incidents; an Incident is reported to them; they witness a serious Hurtful Situation; upon their investigation what originally appeared to be an Incident, evidence of persistence or pervasiveness such hurtful conduct is revealed and, therefore, this should be reported as a possible persistent Hurtful Situation; or in their follow-up investigations into an Incident they thought had been resolved, concerns have remained. The objectives of this intervention approach:

- Take into account the reality of how staff can respond, given their other job responsibilities.

- Use this incident as a "teachable moment." Maintain a focus on helping students learn strategies to independently resolve all kinds of Incidents or Situations, not simply identify whether "bullying" has occurred and report this.

- Recognize that the hurtful behavior staff has witnessed may not be the whole story and inquire further.

- Empower Targeted Students in a way that will reduce the potential of lasting emotional harm and assist them in learning skills to more effectively respond to similar Incidents that may occur in the future.

- Ensure Hurtful Students and Supporters accept personal responsibility for their wrongdoing, take steps to remedy the harm, and agree to discontinue in any further hurtful acts.

- Follow-up to ensure that the resolution was effective.

Action Steps for Incidents

The key actions steps in an initial intervention by certified staff member should include:

- **Stop the Hurtful Conduct.** The staff member may directly intervene, if safe to do so. If it is not safe, this should be considered a serious Situation, which should be immediately reported to the Designated Staff Person.

  - Ensure safety of all students. Especially ensure the student who was the target is secure. Also, be attentive to safety needs of any other participants. This step should take place while waiting for assistance, if it has been called.

- Help all involved students self-regulate, if necessary. If any students are having difficulties with self-regulating, this step must take place prior to seeking to respond to what has happened.

- Support the Targeted Student. The Targeted Student may be striving to effectively respond to the situation in some manner. It is very important that stuff members not take power away from this student. Rather, staff should take actions to support this student in expressing to the Hurtful Student that they should stop. "It appears that you are being hurtful and (name of student) is doing an excellent job in expressing that you need to stop. Can you help me understand why you are having a hard time understanding that your actions are hurtful?"

- **Assess the Situation.** Assess whether this is a more minor Incident or a Situation that should be immediately referred to the Designated Staff Person. This initial assessment should determine the apparent degree of severity.

  - If identified as a Situation, immediately refer to the Designated Staff Person.

  - If any of the involved students have been unable to self-regulate, report to the Designated Staff Person or handle in the process that has been established by the school.

  - Identify whether the hurtful behavior appears to be Reactive or Proactive. Reactive hurtful behavior will be evidenced as involving emotionality and impulsive actions. Reactive Aggression is likely to be impulsive retaliation to a prior hurtful act that was not witnessed. The student who is initially perceived to be the Hurtful Student may have reactively responded to being treated badly by the student who is now perceived to be the Targeted Student. In any situation that appears to involve Reactive Aggression both students have been targeted and both have been hurtful. Both need to be held accountable for their hurtful actions and take steps to remedy the harm to the other. If these hurtful actions were minor, this is still a situation that the staff member can handle.

    - Ask the Targeted Student questions to establish whether any other Incidents are occurring that involve this Hurtful Student or Supporters. The targeted student should be asked about this privately. What appears to the staff member to be a single minor Incident may just one Incident in a more persistent Situation. If concerns of persistence arise from these questions, refer the possible Situation to the Designated Staff Person.

- If the Targeted Student is a member of an identity group that may be experiencing hurtful treatment, ask the Targeted Student whether hurtful conduct that was witnessed is occurring to other students within their identity group. This will allow the staff member to determine whether the Incident witnessed is evidence of a pervasive Hurtful Situation involving a group of students based on their identity

- If the staff member is classified, it is possible that the Incident should be referred to the certified staff person who the classified staff member works with or who is providing supervision in the school location. There may be exceptions to this for certain classified staff members who have expertise in behavior management.

- **Resolve the Hurtful Incident.** If the Incident appears to be minor and the students have self-regulated, seek to support the students in effectively resolving the Incident. Do so at this time, if possible—unless staff has other pressing responsibilities. If at a later time, making interim arrangements for "separate paths" and arrangements to meet. Or refer to the Designated Staff Person.

  - Consider using "shuttle diplomacy"—talking with each student independently to reach a resolution. If the students are self-regulated, they may be able to both be present to resolve the matter.

  - If using shutter diplomacy, talk with the Targeted Student to gain greater understanding into the dynamics. Find out how this student wants to proceed and what would be an effective resolution from this student's perspective. Follow this student's lead in achieving a resolution to support this student's empowerment.

  - Realize that if this is an impulsive retaliation situation, the identification of the involved students as "Target" or "Hurtful" may switch. The student first presenting as the Target may have been the one who initially engaged in hurtful behavior.

  - Ask **Accountability Questions for Hurtful Student** (below). Identify the Hurtful Student's motivations and to help this student agree to accept personal responsibility, remedy the harm, and agree to discontinue the hurtful behavior.

  - After the Hurtful Student proposes a remedy, check with the Targeted Student to determine whether this is acceptable or what modifications are desired.

  - If Hurtful Supporters were involved, ask **Accountability Questions for Hurtful Supporters** (below). Help them also agree to accept personal responsibility, remedy the harm, and agree to discontinue supporting the hurtful behavior.

- If a resolution cannot be achieved, refer to Designated Staff Person.

- If this Incident appears to be a minor bi-directional conflict between students of equivalent social power, privately ask each students if they would be willing to engage in **Conflict Resolution** (below). Make arrangements to accomplish this at this time or later, with another staff member, with a peer mediator, or by themselves with a report back to the staff member.

- **Report.** Report as required by the school. If the Incident appears to have been resolved and has not been identified as part of a persistent or persistent pattern that is possibly a Situation, a school could decide that these Incidents do not have to be reported. However, if any involved student is on an IEP, 504 Plan, or other Tier II intervention or is a member of a Protected Class, this Incident likely should be reported.

- **Follow-up.** For the next several weeks, follow-up daily with both the Targeted Student, Hurtful Student, and Supporters to ensure the resolution was effective.

Action Steps for Conflict

When staff intervene in a Hurtful Incident, it may quickly become apparent that this is more of a conflict situation, where both students have been hurtful. The following is a Conflict Resolution process.

- Make sure each is self-regulated and agrees to listen to the other.

- Engage in Reflective Listening. Ask each person to explain what happened and how this made them feel. Guide them to use an "I" statements: "I feel _____ when you _____."

- After each person explains, reflect this back by saying: You are feeling (describe feelings), because (description of what happened). Is this correct? Ask if the other person understood.

- When you are sure both understand how the other is feeling and why, then ask them to brainstorm strategies that would remedy the harm their behavior caused to the other and resolve the conflict.

- What are some strategies you could use to resolve this?

- For each of the identified strategies, ask them to think about what might happen if they used this strategy and whether this outcome would be acceptable.

- Help them come to an agreement on which strategy or strategies they will try first and if this does not work, what they will do as a back-up.

- Possibly put the solution in writing that they both sign.

- Follow-up with each privately to ensure the conflict was resolved and things got better.

Interventions in Serious, Persistent, or Pervasive Hurtful Situations

Comprehensive Investigation

In Situations, a prompt, comprehensive, unbiased investigation is required.[710] A comprehensive investigation is necessary first step to create an Intervention Plan. The Appendix on the Embrace Civility website sets forth an Investigation Protocol for a Designated Staff Person to effectively investigate the Situations. This includes identifying those that may constitute discriminatory harassment under federal or state civil rights laws. This also includes digital and social media situations, as well as Situations involving students who are receiving special education services.

This Investigation Protocol has been designed to raise attention to all issues that should be considered to fully understand the Situation, the challenges faced by any involved student, and what may be necessary to address a Hostile Environment. Such insight is deemed necessary to support an effective intervention.

This Investigation Protocol is quite extensive and should be considered, in part, for the purpose of professional development. Over time, it is assumed that a Designated Staff Person will be able to more effectively identify the key issues involved in a Situation without having to go through each item in the Investigation Protocol.

This Investigation Protocol has been designed to support the Designated Staff Person in their investigation and planning to correct Situations that could give rise to an agency action or liability for discriminatory harassment under federal or state civil rights laws and to avoid potential liability for violation of free speech for an intervention response to off-campus digital speech in a manner that will presumably not raise such concerns. These issues were discussed in Chapter 9.

However, this information should not be interpreted as legal guidance. Please consult with your district's local counsel on what has been set forth in this section.

Investigation Protocol

This Investigation Protocol is designed to identify:

- **Dynamics of the Situation.** There should be a comprehensive understanding of where, who, how, and when the hurtful behavior is occurring. The assessment will identify whether the situation is serious, persistent or pervasive or whether the situation involves bi-directional harm or impulsive retaliation. This assessment will also allow an appropriate Protection Plan to be set in place, if necessary.

- **Protected Class Status.** Whether the Targeted Student is within a class of students who receive protection under civil rights laws or if there is some other marginalized identity basis which appears to be implicated.

- **Disabilities.** Whether any involved student has disabilities and is receiving services on an IEP or 504 Plan, which will require a comprehensive intervention plan to be developed within the context of this student's 504 Plan or IEP.

- **Mental Health Diagnosis.** Whether a mental health diagnosis has been made of the Targeted Student and whether this student is experiencing challenges to their ability to receive FAPE, especially related to the hurtful treatment they are experiencing. If these concerns are present, this student should be evaluated for the receipt of *Section 504* services. This will include a comprehensive intervention plan to be developed within the context of this student's 504 Plan.

- **Relationship Skills Challenges.** Concerns that relate to relationship skills challenges of any involved students. These should be addressed by a Positive Action Plan to assist these students in gaining more effective personal relationship skills and greater resilience and empowerment. This may also include issues related to home situations that may require referral to community mental health.

- **Motivations.** The motivations of the Hurtful Student and any history of the relationship interactions. This will lay the groundwork for an approach that will assist the Hurtful Student to be held accountable. This analysis should include an assessment of whether the hurtful behavior appeared to be Reactive or Proactive, and the apparent social status of the Hurtful Student in relation to the Targeted Student. This assessment must allow for a determination of whether this appears to be a Marginalized Hurtful Student or a Dominance Motivated Hurtful Student and what actions will be required to support this student in stopping such hurtful behavior.

- **Hurtful Supporters.** The identification of Hurtful Supporters to ensure they are also held accountable.

- **Staff Behavior.** Any concerns related to staff behavior, including whether any staff member has been hurtful to any of the involved students at this time or in the past and whether any staff member was present during an Incident or Situation and how that staff member responded. This will allow for plans to correct staff behavior and improve the skills of staff in effectively responding to such hurtful behavior.

- **School Environment.** Aspects of the school environment that may need to be addressed to support greater inclusion and to address a Hostile Environment. If the Targeted Student is within a Protected Class or other marginalized identity group, as assessment must be made regarding this is an isolated situation or whether there is evidence of pervasive concerns that other students within this identity group are also being treated badly—which will require more expensive corrections to the school climate. This assessment should also consider the behavior management approach that has been implemented by the school to assess whether the Targeted Student or Marginalized Hurtful Student is experiencing management practices that appear to designate them in the eyes of other students as "less worthy." This includes the use of any extrinsic rewards or behavior charts or cards. These concerns were addressed in Chapter 3.

DIVERSIONARY RESTORATIVE INTERVENTION

This recommended Diversionary Restorative Intervention incorporates Restorative Practices and Collaborative Problem Solving principles, along with MTSS for individual students, where necessary and appropriate. This model includes:

- A **Positive Action Plan** for any student involved who is experiencing relationship and/or self-regulation challenges. This could include both the Targeted Student and a Marginalized Hurtful Student.

- A **Protections Plan**, if deemed necessary, for the Targeted Student or Marginalized Hurtful Student.

- An **Accountability Process and Agreement** for Hurtful Students and any Supporters. This includes both Marginalized Hurtful Students and Dominance Motivated Hurtful Students.

- A **Hostile Environment Corrections Plan** to accomplish necessary corrections to the school environment that appear to be supporting hurtful behavior, especially based on students' membership in an identity group or Protected Class.

- An **Evaluation Plan**.

If either the student who was targeted or the one who was hurtful is on an IEP or 504, the Intervention should be addressed at an IEP or 504 meeting and incorporated into the student's IEP or 504 Plan.

Bi-Directional Hurtful Situations

If the Situation involved bi-directional hurtful acts, then all participants who have been hurtful, or who have supported someone who was hurtful, should participate in the Accountability Process and enter into an Accountability Agreement. This would be all involved students.

The Accountability Agreement should include provisions that will resolve the Situation. A Protections Plan or Positive Action Plan may also be necessary for any of the participants. To resolve this Situation, use of Shuttle Diplomacy may be necessary. Alternatively, if there is not an imbalance of power between the parties, a Restorative Practice mediation may be possible.

Positive Action Plan

Interventions with Targeted Students should be shaped based on the concerns faced by these students, with the objective of improving their personal relationship skills and building their resilience and empowerment. Realize that if these students continue to be treated badly, this predicts ongoing victimization at school, challenges with dating or domestic violence, and workplace victimization. Use this insight to also encourage parent or caregiver support for intervention efforts.

The Positive Action Plan is also important for Marginalized Hurtful Students. Positively addressing the harms they have suffered is essential to helping them to improve their personal relationship skills and to increase build resilience and empowerment, especially increasing their ability to self-regulate so that they will stop their hurtful acts directed towards others.

The recommended Positive Action Plan has been developed to provide this level of support. This Positive Action Plan should be considered a Tier II or III level individual intervention. The foundational research that has been relied on in the creation of this recommended approach was outlined in Chapter 6. If any involved student is on an IEP or 504 Plan, the Positive Action Plan can be incorporated into this Plan, as discussed in Chapter 9.

In discussions with the student about the Positive Action Plan, which should be developed collaboratively, it will be important to initially engage in Reflective Listening. This will support the Targeted Student in knowing that they are being heard and their concerns are truly being addressed.

Simply jumping to adult generated "solutions" in the interaction process will seriously undermine effectiveness. Ensure that the process that is being followed is one that is involving the authentic voice of the Targeted Student and involves this student in Collaborative Problem Solving. Remember at all times that the fact that this student was treated badly has had the impact of this student's personal power being taken from them. The best way to empower this student is to ensure they are fully engaged and collaborating in creating this Positive Action Plan.

A focus on Social Emotional Growth Mindset is imperative. The Targeted Student must be assured that they, the students who are hurtful, and the situation can change.

The Positive Action Plan might address:

- **Happiness Thinking Journal and Acts of Kindness.** Provide the student with a small blank journal. Encourage the student to write in this journal every evening, who they had a positive connection with, how they reached out to be kind, something this student did they are proud of, what happened that made them happy. Encourage the student to set a goal of intentionally reaching out to be kind to another student at least 3-5 times a day. This is exceptionally important to improve this student's level of peer acceptance.

  - Advise the student that if, at any time, things feel bad, to think of some of the positive things that were recently written. If anyone has said or done something negative, think about what has been written in this journal. Advise the student that the entries in this journal can and should also be shared with their Staff Allies and their parent or caregiver.

- **Remedy of Harm to Academic Success.** This student may have suffered harm to their academic progress. The Positive Action Plan should incorporate the steps the school will take to assist this student in getting onto a path to academic success. This may require tutoring or other forms of academic support, preferred enrollment in any important classes, the ability to improve grades by doing an extra credit assignment, and the like.

- **Identify and Address Challenges the Student Has Related to Personal Relationship Skills.** Determine whether this student's lack of personal relationship skills may be contributing to the challenges the student is facing. This may include how the student is presenting, effectiveness in reading social clues, and how the student responds when treated badly.

- The best tool to use will be the Collaborative Problem Solving Thinking Skills Inventory, with a specific focus on Emotional and Self-Regulation Skills and Social Thinking Skills within this inventory.[711] Place a strong focus on also identifying this student's strengths and effective strategies.

- Collaboratively develop strategies to assist the student in moderating the behaviors to lessen the potential for being targeted. This MUST be done in a way that does not in any way appear to be blaming this student for how they are being treated. There also must be a focus on how the school environment can assist all students in accepting that some students simply behave differently and should not be treated badly because of this.

• **Self-Regulation.** A specific focus should be made on strategies to increase this student's ability to self-regulate, hold themselves tall, and think things through when they are hearted badly so that they do not lose their personal power. Provide the student's parent or caregiver with insight into how to assist their child in self-regulation, personal power, and problem solving. As was discussed in Chapter 6, the regular practice of meditation can assist in building neural pathways in the brain that can assist a student in being better able to self-regulate when under stress. Finding a way to support the student in meditation while at school and at home.

• **Identify and Address Any Traumatic Distress or Other Mental Health Concerns.** Determine whether this student is demonstrating symptoms that indicate traumatic distress or other mental health concerns that may be contributing to or the result of the Situations. This may also include identified challenges related to the family situation. If this is a concern, a Tier II or III level assessment and team-developed intervention plan within an IEP or 504 Team meeting will be necessary. Referral of the student and family to community mental health services may also be advisable.

• **Designate Staff Allies.** Ask the student to identify several staff members, at a minimum two, who the student feels very comfortable with. Contact these staff members and enlist their ongoing participation in checking in with the student on a regular basis and report any concerns. Advise this student to regularly check in with their Staff Allies, especially if distressed, but also to report successes and good things.

• **Determine Need for a Daily Positive Action CI-CO.** A daily Positive Action CI-CO, may be required if there are significant concerns. The daily check-in may be with the principal, a counselor, or a Staff Ally. During the daily Positive Action CI-CO:

- Ask questions about any ongoing or new Incidents and the effectiveness of the current Safe Passages Plan (below).

- Focus on positive developments in this student's life and relationships. Ask the four Positively Powerful Happiness Thinking Questions: Who did you have a positive connection with today? How were you kind to someone else? What did you do that you are proud of? What happened today that made you happy and you are thankful for? Also discuss any times when the student felt distressed or had to handle a challenging situation and how this worked. Discuss strategies that could improve their effectiveness.

• **Develop and Practice an Incident Response Plan of Action.** Collaboratively help the student develop effective incident responses in situations where someone is hurtful. Discuss and practice specific strategies this student can use, in the moment, if someone says or does something hurtful to ensure that they do not demonstrate distress.

- Discuss with the student that the probable goal of the one being hurtful is to cause them to become distressed. Showing any degree of distress can reinforce this hurtful behavior, because the Hurtful Student accomplished a goal. By remaining calm and not showing any degree of distress can help to end the hurtful behavior.

- It may be helpful to discuss this in reference to "power points" like are gained in a computer game. "When a student is being hurtful, it is their intent to obtain your power points. If you appear to be upset or angry, this is a power point reward for the Hurtful Student. If you can keep your cool and not respond with distress or anger, you are able to keep your power points. In many situations, this will also enable you to gain power points from the Hurtful Student."

- Engage this student in an analysis of the data on the *Embrace Civility Student Survey*, so they can recognize that in situations where other students are afraid to step in, the vast majority to not like what they are seeing. Responding in a positive manner will increase the admiration of other students.

- Recommended immediate responses if someone is hurtful:

  ‣ Immediately focus on their body language, shifting into a more powerful pose—holding themselves tall, shoulders square, head up. Take a deep breath and remain calm. Think, "I choose not to let this person control how I feel about myself or respond."

- Either ignore the person totally or send a brief glance that communicates, "Your efforts are not going to get to me." Generally, do not say anything to the Hurtful Student.

- Walk away from the situation to a place where there are more people, especially including school staff. But do not talk to a school staff member in the presence of the Hurtful Student. Immediately running to a staff person and appearing to report, could be translated as "tattling" and could lower the Targeted Student's social status. An exception to this is if physical violence is threatened.

- If online or receive a hurtful text or message, do not immediately respond directly to this person. Do save what was posted and immediately report this person to the site. Possibly block this person.

- After getting away from the situation, talk with a friend, parent or caregiver, Staff Ally, the Designated Staff Member, or a counselor to gain emotional support and to discuss how to respond further, if deemed necessary.

- If this hurtful act was done by a student who is currently under an Accountability Agreement, this should be reported because this will be a violation of that Agreement.

- **Address Digital and Social Media Activities.** Review the student's digital and social media activities with the student and the student's parent or caregiver. Discuss ways to protect the student from digital aggression and lessen the possibility that digital and social media activities may be contributing to concerns.

  - Encourage this student to post positive comments every time they are using social media. Encourage them to frequently make positive comments on other student's posts. This is beyond just clicking on a "like" button. If the Targeted Student will take the small amount of time necessary to add ten positive comments to other student's posts, this will very likely yield significant benefits in an increase in their peer acceptance. If a student has specifically reached out to be kind to them that day, they should be sure to create a post acknowledging and thanking this person.

- **Help the Student Identify and Build Upon Character Strengths.** If this has not been done as a school-wide activity, encourage the student to complete Character Strengths Inventory at the VIA Character Institute or the brief version that is included as an Appendix on the Embrace Civility website. If this has been done, review the student's results to identify this student's strengths.

- In situations with students who have any significant challenges both complete the online survey and obtain a report on the survey findings from the Institute, along with a guidebook. There is a modest cost for this. This would likely be a very good investment to more effectively assist this student in gaining positive insight and guidance focused on their personal strengths.

- Encourage the student to find ways to use their personal strengths every day. Also identify strategies the student could use to respond in tense situations that use their personal strengths.

• **Identify Strategies to Strengthen Student's Friendships.** Explore the current status of the student's peer relationships. Develop strategies to improve and increase positive peer relationships. This may require parent or caregiver involvement to support additional out-of-school peer activities. Determine if there are any school activities or organizations the student could participate in that would increase positive peer relationships. Within the school environment, identify ways the student could associate with students who have similar interests, through school organizations or activities.

• **Identify Strategies to Increase Advancement and Provide Service.** Explore with the student their current interests and activities, as well as continuing education or career interests. Work with parent or caregiver to identify expanded ways that the student could be more actively involved in pursuing these interests and activities. Develop strategies where the student can better pursue these interests at school. Identify possible adult mentors, community volunteer activities, or other ways in which this student can shift focus to future opportunities and exploring interests. Encourage volunteer activities that are in service to others.

Protection Plan for Targeted Students

A Protection Plan may be necessary in situations of serious or persistent harmful conduct when the level of commitment of the Hurtful Student to stop being hurtful may be necessary. As with the Positive Action Plan, this is a plan that should be developed collaboratively with the Targeted Student. The plan should address the following:

• **Staff Ally for Check-in/Check-Out.** This was advised for the Positive Action Plan. This should be considered necessary for a Protection Plan.

• **Place of Refuge and Calming.** Identify several places in the school where the student feels most safe. The school library, counseling office or calming room might be the places where the student may feel safest. Arrangements should be made for the student to have the ability to go to one of these places if there is a potential someone may be hurtful. A "travel pass" will likely be necessary.

- **Safe Passages.** Identify any physical areas of the school, to or from school, or any involvement with activities that present greater concerns. Make arrangements to increase safety in these areas. This may include increased supervision or a requirement that the person who was hurtful avoid this location.

- **No Contact Order or Other Requests.** If the Targeted Student has specific reasonable requests of the student who was hurtful for "no contact," this should be honored. It will be necessary to incorporate a No Contact Order into the Accountability Agreement for Hurtful Student and possibly the Accountability Agreements of Hurtful Supporters.

- **Not Change in Target's Schedule or Activities.** What the Protection Plan should NOT contain is any requirement that the Targeted Student change classes or disengage in school activities, unless truly desired by the student. If any change is necessary to ensure the protection of the Targeted Student, the Hurtful Student and Supporters must make those changes.

Accountability Process and Agreement

Intervention with Hurtful Students and Supporters

The Accountability Process could be considered a Restorative Diversionary Intervention—with any disciplinary consequence held in abeyance. This Process incorporates principles of Restorative Practices and Collaborative Problem Solving. Additional insight related to Self Determination Theory, Positive Social Norms, Principles of Influence, Mechanisms of Moral Disengagement, and Social Emotional Growth Mindset have also been incorporated. The research behind this approach is addressed in both Chapters 4 and 7.

The results of the *Embrace Civility Student Survey* and the student's Personal Relationships Commitments Statements will be instrumental in supporting both Hurtful Students and Supporters to accept personal responsibility and agree to take actions to remedy the harm.

Use of Reflective Listening throughout the discussions is also exceptionally important. The Hurtful Student or Supporter will have some level of fear because they are in a discussion with a staff member or Designated Staff member about their behavior. People do not make good decisions if they are coming from a place of fear. Especially at the start of the conversation, the use of Reflective Listening, will help to dissipate the fear and help the Hurtful Student or Supporter understand that they are being listened to and their perspective is being heard.

The other beneficial aspect of Reflective Listening is that when these students hear a reflection of their values and attitudes spoken back to them, they will hopefully hopefully engage in reflection themselves about the values and attitudes they are espousing. Upon such reflection, they may, themselves, start to take issue with their more concerning values.

In addition to the identified Hurtful Student, any students who were clearly identified as being Hurtful Supporters—who took actions that were clearly indicated as being supportive of the hurtful behavior of the Hurtful Student—should also be held accountable.

The Accountability Process is designed to lead a Hurtful Student and Supporters to acknowledge their wrongdoing, understand the negative impact on the other Targeted Student, accept personal responsibility, create a plan to remedy the harm, and commit to avoiding any further harm. If necessary, this will also include agreement to abide by the Targeted Student's Protection Plan. This agreement also requires actions to remedy the harm to the school community.

If a student successfully abides by the terms of the Accountability Agreement, they will avoid a disciplinary record and should learn a very valuable lesson that will support success in the future. This approach should alleviate the concerns about a permanent disciplinary record, which will likely generate greater parent or caregiver support for responsible behavior and compliance.

The process is initiated by offering the Hurtful Student or Supporter the option of participating in an Accountability Process to develop an Accountability Agreement. The student and parent or caregiver should be required to agree to allow a portion of the Accountability Agreement to be shared with the student who was harmed and their parent or caregiver. While under federal privacy law FERPA, this should be considered permissible, a signed waiver of the student's possible privacy rights under FERPA has been included in the Accountability Agreement.

However, this information should not be interpreted as legal guidance. Please consult with your district's local counsel on what has been set forth in this section.

Disclosing the designated portion of the Accountability Agreement is important because this will help the Targeted Student and their parent or caregiver gain closure and assurance. In terms of "power points" this is a way to provide "power points" back to the Targeted Student—the Hurtful Student acknowledged their wrongdoing.

Accountability Questions for Hurtful Students

These Accountability Questions, in a brief manner, can be used by a staff member intervening in an Incident. The more complete manner can be used by the Designated Staff Member. For the Designated Staff Member, prior to the meeting, obtain a digital version of that student's statement or ask student what commitments they made related to treatment of others and how they would respond if they were ever hurtful. Have the Positive Social Norms data from the *Embrace Civility Student Survey*. These are extensive questions. At any point in time, the Hurtful Student may be willing to indicate they are willing to accept personal responsibility and remedy the harm.

- Set forth the expectations. Tell the Hurtful Student, "We can resolve this matter without a disciplinary consequence (or without sending you to the office) if you accept personal responsibility for the fact that you were hurtful, agree to remedy the harm, and make a commitment that you will not continue to be hurtful."

- Assuming your school had students complete the *Embrace Civility Student Survey*, ask: "Do you recall our data about how (name of school) students think about those who are hurtful? Do you recall what they think about someone who was hurtful who refused to accept responsibility and say they were sorry? "Do you recall what students think about someone who acknowledges that they treated someone badly and takes steps to make things right? (Self Determination Theory—Connections and Principles of Influence—Positive Social Norms and Threat of Loss.)

- Ask: "Can you help me understand what happened and what were you trying to accomplish?" Seek to solicit and affirm the Hurtful Student's motivation using Reflective Listening after each statement made by the student. As discussed in Chapter 2, this motivation could be dominance, resources, revenge, justice, belonging, romance issues, identity, well-being, or entertainment. Listen carefully to determine whether the hurtful acts were Reactive or Proactive Aggression. This may require asking about what was happening in the relationships prior to these hurtful acts. Realize that the identity of who is the original Hurtful Student may change. This may shift to the need to hold both involved students accountable.

- Ask: "Can you help me understand why you thought what you did was okay?" Listen for and challenge Rationalizations—justify or spin, deny responsibility, deny harm, blame target. (Mechanisms of Moral Disengagement.) Continue a form of Reflective Listening: "So what I think I hear you saying is that you think that because this student (describe what was explained) that then means it should be considered okay for you to (describe what this student did)? Can you help me understand if I am hearing what you are saying properly?" Keep track of the Rationalizations the student makes. Do not challenge at this time.

- Share Personal Relationships Commitment Statement with student. If a staff member does not have access to this document, just ask in general. "Do you recall what commitments you made about how you were going to treat others? Can you help me understand how and why your actions do not appear to be consistent with the commitments you made?" "Do you recall what commitments you made about what you are going to do if you made a mistake and were hurtful? (Principles of Influence—Commitment and Consistency.)

- Now go back to the Rationalizations. You told me that what you did should be considered okay because (identify the stated Rationalization), but this appears to be contrary to your Personal Commitment Statement where you said (what student had written). Can you help me understand how your actions and your excuses appear to be inconsistent?" (Principles of Influence—Commitment and Consistency.) You could also add "How would you feel if someone treated your best friend the way you treated (name of student)?" (Principles of Influence—Reciprocity.) Or, "How would your parent or caregiver or other adult whose opinion you value think about your actions?" (Principles of Influence—Authority.)

- Ask: "Are you willing to accept personal responsibility for your actions, agree to remedy the harm, and make a commitment that you will not continue to be hurtful?"

- If, by this point in the discussion with a staff member, the student has been unwilling to accept personal responsibility, it is time to consider this a Hurtful Situation and refer to the Designated Staff Person. If this discussion is with the Designated Staff Person, this process should shift to a disciplinary intervention.

- If the student has accepted personal responsibility, the discussion should shift.

    - Ask: "What do you think you can to do to make things right to (name of student)? What commitments will you make to not be hurtful to (name of student)?"

    - If this is a discussion with the Designated Staff Person, it would also be appropriate to bring into the conversation any requirements being placed on this student's actions pursuant to the Targeted Student's Protection Plan.

- Also, if this is a discussion with the Designated Staff Person, a remedy to the school community is also necessary. Ask: "What do you think you can to do to make things right to our school community?"

- It is also recommended that the school place a requirement of harm to the school community on this Hurtful Student. This is a requirement that they reach out to be kind to (number of) students who are not in their social group, every day for a period of time determined by the Designated Staff Person. They should keep a log of this and provide that log in a manner decided.

- If these Accountability Questions have been asked by a staff member, a verbal expression to the Targeted Student of acceptance of personal responsibility, indicating they are sorry for their actions, and a commitment not to be hurtful in the future should suffice. If this is a Situation being resolved by the Designated Staff Person, a shift should be made to complete the **Hurtful Student Accountability Agreement.**

Accountability Questions for Hurtful Supporters

- Tell the Hurtful Supporters: "It appeared that you were supporting _____ (name of Hurtful Student). We can resolve this right now if you accept personal responsibility for supporting someone who was being hurtful, agree to remedy the harm, and agree to not continue to support this person in being hurtful or be hurtful yourself."

- Ask: "Is there anything you know about this Incident that you think might be helpful in making sure that it does not continue? Why do you think Hurtful Student was being hurtful?" Explore their perspective of the motivations of their friend.

- Assuming your school had students complete the _Embrace Civility Student Survey_, ask: "Do you recall our data about how (name of school) students think about those who support those who are hurtful? Do you recall what they think about those students who encourage a hurtful friend to stop and say they are sorry? (Self Determination Theory—Connections and Principles of Influence—Positive Social Norms and Threat of Loss.)

- Ask: "Can you help me understand why you thought it was okay for you to be supporting (name of student) in being hurtful?" In like manner to the Hurtful Student, after asking this question, the process should shift to Reflective Listening.

  - Listen for and challenge Rationalizations, as was discussed above.

- Listen for any possible challenges that this student may face if they indicate that the Hurtful Student's behavior was not acceptable. They may face the potential of retaliation from the Hurtful Student. If there is any possibility that this may occur, this is an issue that should be added to the Accountability Agreement of the Hurtful Student.

- Share Personal Relationships Commitment Statement with student. If a staff member does not have access to this document, just ask in general. "Do you recall what commitments you made about how you were respond if a friend of yours was hurtful. (Principles of Influence—Commitment and Consistency.)

- Ask: "What are your thoughts now about how you were supporting someone who was being hurtful? Do you accept personal responsibility for your supportive actions?"

- If the student has not by this point acknowledged wrongdoing of the Hurtful Student and accepted personal responsibility for their actions in support of this, ask some of the questions set forth above for Hurtful Students. If there is still a refusal, this could be turned into a disciplinary action. However, the continuing refusal may be grounded in a profound, and quite possible, threat of retaliation by the Hurtful Student. This will obviously be a more challenging situation that will require an additional discussion with the Hurtful Student.

- Ask: "What do you think you can to do to make things right to the (name of Targeted Student)?" Ask also: "In the future, how do you think you could encourage (name of Hurtful Student) or any other student to stop being hurtful and make things right if they were?"

- If these Accountability Questions have been asked by a staff member, a verbal expression to the Targeted Student of acceptance of personal responsibility, indicating they are sorry for their actions, and a commitment not to be hurtful or support someone being hurtful in the future should suffice. If this is a Situation being resolved by the Designated Staff Person, a shift should be made to complete the **Hurtful Supporter Accountability Agreement**.

Accountability Agreement for Hurtful Students

The Accountability Agreement for a Hurtful Student should be completed on a form with the school filling in information designated as for the Designated Staff Person. If your school had students participate in creating a Personal Relationships Commitments Statement, integrate the commitments the student made related to treatment of others, actions if witnessing someone being hurtful, and how this student would remedy the harm if hurtful into this Accountability Agreement using their words.

This Accountability Agreement should be in two parts. The first part should be provided to the Targeted Student, as this is a remedy of harm to that student. The second part should not be shared.

Part I—To be disclosed to Targeted Student

- Please write a statement that describes what you did:

- Please write a statement that acknowledges that what you did was wrong and that you accept personal responsibility for this wrongdoing:

- Please write a statement where you commit that you will avoid engaging in any further harmful acts directed at this student or others:

- Please describe what you will do to make things right for this student:

- (If considered necessary.) The school is imposing a No Contact Order on you until further notice. This means you are not to have any close contact with (name of student) either in person or via digital technology or social media. Please write a statement where you commit you will agree to abide by this No Contact Order:

- (If considered necessary.) The person who you were hurtful to has asked that you do or avoid doing this: (Will need to be filed in with reasonable requests by the Targeted Student that are included in the Protection Plan.) Please write a statement where you commit you will agree to abide by these requests:

Part II—Not to be disclosed to Targeted Student

- My personal commitments related to how I will treat others, actions I will take if I witness someone being hurtful, actions I will take if a friend of mine is hurtful, and my commitment to remedy the harm if I am hurtful are: (Taken from their Personal Relationships Commitments Statement. Can be revised.)

- Please write a statement of what you will you say to your friends about this situation:

- If necessary, add a commitment that they will not be hurtful to any Hurtful Supporter who also met with you.

- Please describe what you will do to make things right to our school community:

- The school is imposing one additional obligation on you as way to remedy the harm to the school community. For the next ___ days (recommend 20-30 school days), you will reach out to be kind to at least ___ students (recommend 3-5). These need to be students who are outside of your social group. You will be provided with a form to complete that will describe what you did, what happened, how you felt. This form will be turned in to the office on a daily basis for the first 5 days, and a weekly basis thereafter—or daily basis continuing.

- Write a statement acknowledging that you recognize that any violation of this agreement will be considered a violation of the disciplinary code and will subject you to a disciplinary consequence:

- Your signature on this document indicates that it is acceptable to provide Part I of this Accountability Agreement to the student you treated badly.

Signatures of the Hurtful Student and Parent/Caregiver.

Accountability Agreement for Hurtful Supporters

The Accountability Agreement for a Hurtful Supporter should be completed on a form with the school filling in information designated as for the Designated Staff Person. If your school had students participate in creating Personal Relationships Commitments Statement, integrate the commitments the student made related to treatment of others, actions if witnessing someone being hurtful, what this student will do if a friend of theirs is hurtful, and how this student would remedy the harm if hurtful into this Accountability Agreement.

This would not likely need to be disclosed to the Targeted Student. If part is, permission from the parent or caregiver should be obtained.

- Write a statement that describes what you saw happen and how you responded:

- Write a statement that acknowledges and accepts personal responsibility the fact that you were supporting someone who was being hurtful:

- Write a statement that acknowledges why what the student being hurtful did was wrong:

- Write a statement that acknowledges why how your support of these hurtful acts was wrong:

- Please describe what you will do to make things right for the student who was harmed:

- (If considered necessary.) The school is imposing a No Contact Order on you until further notice. This means you are not to have any close contact with (name of student) either in person or via digital technology or social media. Please write a statement where you commit you will agree to abide by this No Contact Order:

- (If considered necessary.) The person who you were hurtful to has asked that you do or avoid doing this: (Will need to be filed in with reasonable requests by the Targeted Student that are included in the Protection Plan.) Please write a statement where you commit you will agree to abide by these requests:

- My personal Commitments related to how I will treat others, actions I will take if I witness someone being hurtful, actions I will take if a friend of mine is hurtful, and my commitment to remedy the harm if I am hurtful: (Taken from their Personal Relationships Commitments Statement. Can be revised.)

- The school is imposing an obligation on you as way to remedy the harm to the school community. For the next ___ days (recommend 5-10 school days), you will reach out to be kind to at least ___ students (recommend 3-5). These need to be students who are outside of your social group. You will be provided with a form to complete that will describe what you did, what happened, how you felt. This form will be turned in to the office on a weekly basis.

- Write a statement indicating your agreement to avoid engaging in any further harmful acts or supporting any further hurtful acts directed at this student:

- Please recognize that any violation of this agreement may be considered a violation of the disciplinary code and may subject you to a disciplinary consequence.

Signature of the Hurtful Supporter: (This can be sent to the parent or caregiver, but does not need to be signed.)

BULLYING INVOLVING STUDENTS WITH DISABILITIES

All aspects of the 504 Plan or IEP should be developed in coordination with the Targeted Student in a collaborative manner.[712] The concerns should be identified. The student, their parent or caregiver and other members of the Team should outline and discuss possible strategies to address these concerns. It is especially important to include the student in this collaborative discussion, as this helps to support their personal power.

Note that is is assumed in this section that if the bullying of any student on any basis has reached the point where this student has a diagnosed mental health condition, the fact that that student had developed a mental health condition as the result of persistent bullying, which has created a substantial limitation on their ability participate in learning or other school activities requires that this student be evaluated for a 504 Plan. Assuming these conditions exist, a 504 Plan should be established to address the bullying concerns and their resulting harms.

Investigation

A prompt, comprehensive, unbiased investigation is required. The outline for an Investigation has been set forth above, and an Investigation Protocol is set forth in the online Appendix. Two enhancements are noted.

- Sometimes within the environment of a student with disabilities, the Hurtful Student may also be a student with disabilities. Under *Section 504*, and the *DCLs* discussed , the concerns of this student's bullying of other students must be addressed in this Hurtful Student's *Section 504* Plan or IEP. This Hurtful Student may also be the target of hurtful behavior by others. There may be two kinds of situations:

  - The Hurtful Student may be engaging in Reactive Aggression to situations when they have difficulties—a Marginalized Hurtful Student.

  - The Hurtful Student may be being hurtful in a Proactive Aggression in an effort to achieve dominance within the community of students who have disabilities or challenges—basically a combination of both aspects of both Marginalized and Dominance Motivated Hurtful Students.

  - While a full discussion of any disabilities or challenges faced by a Hurtful Student within the context of the Targeted Student's *Section 504* Plan or IEP is inappropriate, it is necessary to understand the motivations behind those being hurtful to ensure that all appropriate protections are put into place for the Targeted Student, to support the actions necessary to ensure the hurtful behavior is stopped.

- A comprehensive assessment of the Targeted Student's personal relationship skills—especially the skills necessary to allow this student to form positive relations with others and to respond effectively in situations where someone is hurtful. A recommended tool to conduct this evaluation is the Collaborative Problem Solving Thinking Skills Inventory, with a specific focus on Emotional and Self-Regulation Skills and Social Thinking Skills.[713]

- Note: this comprehensive assessment should not be implemented in the manner that is currently recommended for a Functional Behavior Analysis, that looks at Antecedents, Behavior, and Consequences. This is an inadequate analysis, as it is grounded in a behaviorism perspective of behavior and is very frequently focused on compliance.

Stop the Hurtful Behavior and Prevent it From Recurring

Within the Targeted Student's 504 Plan or IEP, the school should outline the following strategies it will engage in to stop the hurtful behavior and prevent it from recurring—without individually identifying the student or students who are currently being hurtful.

- What strategies will be used to support unmet needs and challenges of any Hurtful Student?

- What strategies will be used to ensure the Hurtful Student and Supporters accept personal responsibility and will take steps to remedy the harm to this student?

- What steps, if necessary, will be taken to ensure that the Hurtful Student and Supporters will abide by the Protection Plan that may be developed for the Targeted Student?

All aspects of the general requirements placed on these Hurtful Students and Supporter should be disclosed within the *Section 504* or IEP meeting.

If any changes in schedules or activities need to be made, those changes should be made by the Hurtful Student or Supporters—not the Targeted Student. If the Targeted Student is enjoying a class they are in with a Hurtful Student or Supporters and the continuation of both in the same class is perceived to present challenges, the Hurtful Student or Supporters should be removed from the class.

Remedy Harm and Provide Support

The Supplemental Aids and Supports section of the Targeted Student's 504 Plan or IEP should be modified to incorporate the following:

- **Protection Plan.** As described above, the Protection Plan should be set forth to ensure the safety and emotional well-being of the Targeted Student within school building and grounds, going to and from school, and in classes and school activities. This Protection Plan should address risk in all of the locations that were identified in the investigation to present possible concerns. As noted, Hurtful Students and Supporters should be required to acknowledge agreement to any aspects of this Protection Plan that relate to their location or other requirements, such as a "no contact order." This Protection Plan should include specific instructions for the Targeted Student on how to respond and report any further hurtful incidents. This Protection Plan will need to be conveyed to all staff who might be responsible for ensuring its effectiveness.

- **Positive Action Plan**. A Positive Action Plan should be developed to provide support, remedy emotional harm, and address any personal relationship challenges the Targeted Student might have. This Positive Action Plan may also need to remedy any impact of hurtful conduct the Targeted Student's learning and achievement. This may include tutoring, extra credit opportunities, and priorities in scheduling for classes.

- **Functional Behavior Objectives**. If the Targeted Student has identified concerns in personal relationship skills, which is likely, this must be addressed in a positive manner in the Functional Objectives section of their 504 Plan or IEP. A solid plan should be included for how these objectives will be accomplished. The inclusion of Functional Objectives to support improved personal relationships should not make the Targeted Student feel blamed for why others are treating them badly.

  - Sometimes, in students' 504 Plan or IEP, Functional Behavior Objectives relate primarily to the students' compliance with adult authority. These kinds of objectives will be entirely ineffective in addressing the Targeted Student's personal relationship challenges.

  - Because the Targeted Student has been experiencing adversities, they may also be engaging in inappropriate behavior as a result. It is important to ensure the personal relationship skills Functional Behavior Objectives are developed with insight into trauma.

Correct the Hostile Environment

The Supplemental Aids and Supports section of a Targeted Student's 504 Plan or IEP should also set forth a brief discussion of the strategies the school intends to implement strategies to improve the school climate to address how the Targeted Student is being treated, as well as to increase inclusion of all students with disabilities.Correcting the environment will likely require more comprehensive, school-wide initiatives, which would not need to be included in an individual student's 504 Plan or IEP.

Four important components of this Hostile Environment correction plan are recommended:

- **Correct any Hurtful Staff Behavior.** The investigation may have identified concerns related to how the Targeted Student is being treated by all school staff. If any staff member is treating this student with disrespect, this is unacceptable modeling to other students. Such behavior must be changed. Some aspects of enforcing such a change will be considered confidential, as this relates to the staff member's employment. However, the student's 504 Plan or IEP should outline that this correction will occur and the precise steps the Targeted Student and their parent or caregiver should take if any such inappropriate staff behavior continues to occur.

- **Correct how Staff Respond.** The investigation may have identified concerns related to how staff are responding if the Targeted Student is treated badly in their presence or reports this to them. If there are any concerns associated with this, the student's 504 Plan or IEP should outline the school's commitment to agreed upon standards for how staff will respond, insight into how staff will receive training, and the precise steps the student or their parents or caregivers should take if there are any future hurtful incidents where staff responds ineffectively.

- **Assess Behavior Management Approaches.** Determine whether any behavior management approaches used by the school model the denigration and exclusion of students who have challenges. Too many schools are using behavior management approaches that are profoundly damaging from the perspective of children who have disabilities or other challenges. These approaches include behavior management charts, token rewards, and behavior cards that model the disparagement or exclusion of some students. Correcting the harmful use of these behavior management approaches requires a shift to approaches grounded in trauma and neurodiversioty informed practices. This is a more significant undertaking than should be set forth in an individual student's 504 Plan or IEP. However, reference to the concern, the harmful impact of this concern, and the school's intention to change these harmful practices should be incorporated.

- **Increase Inclusion Activities.** There are many innovative approaches schools are implementing to increase the positive inclusion of students with disabilities. These also are a more significant undertaking than should be set forth in an individual student's 504 Plan or IEP. However, reference to the intent to increase inclusion strategies is advised.

Monitoring and Compliance

The 504 Plan or IEP should set forth how this situation will be monitored and addressed if challenges continue. The Targeted Student and their parents or caregivers should know how to report concerns and have the expectation that a prompt response will occur. Information on how to report such concerns should be incorporated into the 504 Plan or IEP. Provisions that are incorporated into a 504 Plan or IEP are enforceable. A parent or caregiver can file a complaint if the school fails to abide by the commitments set forth in this Plan.

CORRECT HOSTILE ENVIRONMENT

It is necessary to investigate and take actions to correct aspect of the school environment that are contributing to hurtful behavior directed at any student.

In the US, if the Targeted Student in a Situation is within a class that receives protection under federal civil rights laws, based on race, national origin, color, religion grounded in national origin, gender identity or orientation, sex, or disability, and a Hostile Environment is deemed to be present, schools must take actions reasonably calculated to correct the Hostile Environment. In situations of pervasive hurtful conduct that has created a Hostile Environment for many students within one or even several protected classes, the primary activity of the school must be focused on correcting the Hostile Environment

Continuous Improvement Approach

This effort should follow a Continuous Improvement Approach, as discussed in Chapter 4. Some components of the assessment component of a Continuous Improvement Approach have been incorporated into the Investigation Protocol, that is part of the online Appendix. The key to effectiveness of this Continuous Improvement Approach is the effective analysis of evaluation data.

In Oregon, where I live, there has been a consistent question on the youth wellness surveys that solicits a 4-part agree-disagree response to a variety of statements. One statement reads: "At least one teacher/adult in my school really cares about me." Positive connections between students and at least one staff member in school is of exceptional high importance. For over a decade, the results on this question have not improved.

The use of evaluation data to assess progress to desired outcomes is totally ineffective if schools simply conduct surveys year after year and do nothing to address the environmental factors that are contributing to a failure of this data to document improvement.

These steps set forth a recommended process to be followed by schools that holds a likelihood for success in remedying a Hostile Environment.

- **Use a Team Approach.** Remedying a Hostile Environment will require involvement of a number of school staff, including the principal, counselors, school psychologist, and others who can bring different expertise to the situation, as well as potentially involving law enforcement and advocates from community-based identity group organizations. The Team should include representatives from the Student Leadership Team and the school's parent or caregiver organization who are reporting to and receiving feedback from their respective groups.

- **Engage in Effective Assessment.** Effectively remedying an Hostile Environment requires a comprehensive assessment of the nature of the environment. As noted in Chapter 4, it is recommended that schools regularly conduct surveys to assess school climate, bullying, and harassment. The Investigation Protocols from recent Hurtful Situations will also contain valuable insight. If a Hostile Environment is suspected, school officials should also conduct focus groups with the students who are within the identity group that is suspected of being harassed in a serious, persistent, or pervasive manner, as well as parents or caregivers and community-based identity group organizations. If there are pervasive problems, they may well have been reported to these community-based identity group organizations and not to the school.

  - The *Embrace Civility Student Survey* contains several school climate questions. These questions can provide some indications. If significant environment issues are documented, it is highly recommended that schools use additional school climate surveys.

- **Develop an Action Plan**. The school team should conduct an overall assessment of the school's approach to reducing hurtful student behavior and supporting students in maintaining positive relationships and develop an action plan to remedy any identified concerns.

- **Provide Professional Development.** The overall effectiveness of school staff in detecting, intervening, and reporting Incidents should be assessed and action plans should be put into effect to remedy any identified concerns. These plans should include directives to staff and professional development on strategies for staff to more effectively intervene. The professional development plans may also require a focus on assisting the staff in gaining greater cultural competence, specifically in relation to the identity groups students who are frequently treated badly belong to. Issues of implicit bias must be effectively addressed as the boas of staff many be implicated in their behaviors that are modeling disrespect to students in these identity groups.

- **Ensure Corrections of Staff Behavior** (if necessary). Questions have been included on the *Embrace Civility Student Survey* and in the Investigation Protocol that is in the online Appendix, to solicit information from all of the involved students related to instances where they have experienced a staff member be hurtful or disrespectful to them or when a student was hurtful to them a staff member was present and failed to intervene correctly.

  - As noted above, it is recommended that challenges with staff behavior be addressed within the context of Multiple Tier System thinking, generally with a Tier II professional development approach. However, the manner in which this must be handled will be dictated by employee relations requirements. If any concerns associated with disrespectful or abusive staff behavior are raised in the *Embrace Civility Student Survey* or are being consistently identified in investigations, it is recommended that serious discussions be held with the unions representing both certified and classified staff to develop an approach to address these concerns that does not result in protracted adverse conflict.

- **Develop an Evaluation Plan.** Ongoing evaluation is necessary using the same approach as outlined in **Assessments.**

MONITORING

Interventions in Situations must include ongoing monitoring and follow-up until all involved students report that things are better. It is exceptionally important also that the Designated Staff Person conduct a Post-Situation Evaluation of the effectiveness of the intervention in every serious or persistent Situations.

- Request of feedback from all parties involved, including the Targeted Student and parent or caregiver, the Hurtful Student and parent or caregiver.

- Continue periodically for several months. If after several months of consistent response that things have gotten and stayed better, this follow-up can be discontinued.

In situations where it has been discovered that a Hostile Environment has existed for groups of students, most likely identity groups, conduct routine focus groups with students, parents or caregivers, and community advocates to assess progress in correcting the Hostile Environment. Also assess progress by analyzing the annual data and incident reports/

PEER ACCOUNTABILITY AND ASSISTANCE TEAM

Schools are advised to consider the formation of a Peer Assistance & Accountability Team (PAAT). Establishing a PAAT is an idea that combines the concepts of peer mediation, teen court, and peer support. This approach will allow your Prestige Leaders to gain even greater expertise in leadership.

A PAAT can be established as a program within the Student Leadership Team. Students involved in the PAAT would require additional training in issues of peer support, trauma and resilience, Positive Psychology, self-regulation, conflict resolution, peer mediation, and the like.

The recommended activities of a PAAT could include the following:

- **Accountability Process.** Follow a scripted process to implement the Accountability Process and an Accountability Agreement with Hurtful Students and Hurtful Supporters.

- **Peer Mediation/Restorative Practices.** Engaging in peer mediation or a peer led restorative conference to assist students in resolving drama or conflict using a Conflict Resolution Protocol. It is important to note that peer mediation in situations of conflict is different from resolving situations of one directional serious, persistent, or pervasive hurtful behavior where there is an imbalance of power.

- **Peer Support Services.** Providing "open office" peer support services for students who are facing any personal challenge to come and talk with compassionate peers. This may also include providing support services to students who are being targeted or are involved in a conflict, where the students do not wish to pursue a more formal school intervention with an adult staff member.

Accountability Process

To implement the Accountability Process and an Accountability Agreement with Hurtful Students and Supporters the PAAT students will essentially follow a scripted Accountability Process set forth in this Chapter. Prior to allowing the PAAT engage in this process, information should be provided to the parent or caregiver and their signed permission should be received.

First, they would go through a process of asking the questions set forth above in Accountability Questions for Hurtful Students or Supporters.

They would then work with the Hurtful Student or Supporter to draft an Accountability Agreement. The Designated Staff Person would meet with the parent or caregiver of the Hurtful Student and present the Accountability Agreement to their parent or caregiver to obtain their agreement and signature.

Before turning this process over to a PAAT, the Designated Staff Person would need to conduct an investigation into the challenges that the Hurtful Student might face. The kinds of challenges this student might face might dictate whether the situation is handled by the PAAT or not. Hurtful Situations involving Marginalized Hurtful Students may be best handled by the Designated Staff Person.

Each Accountability Process intervention should involve at least three PAAT members. Ideally, the following kinds of students should be included on a PAAT for any involvement in the Accountability Process and development of an Accountability Agreement:

- One student from a more powerful social class of students within the school. This student will convey the influence of student leadership and convey the message that to be acknowledged a "true leader" requires the avoidance of hurtful behavior and support for those who are targeted.

- One student from an identity group in the school that is more frequently targeted. This student will convey a message that those students who are often thought to lack personal power and social status have, in this school, gained sufficient social status and power to be in a position of authority over those who engage in hurtful acts.

- One student who has also engaged in or supported hurtful behavior in the past, who is serving on the PAAT as part of required community service under the terms of an Accountability Agreement and who has demonstrated by their actions as being truly remorseful and desiring to maintain a change in their behavior. This student will likely be in recognizing and challenging the Hurtful Student or Hurtful Supporter on any rationalizations for their wrongdoing. This student will convey a message that redemption and a shift to positive action is possible.

The students who participate on a PAAT must be required to sign an agreement that they will respect confidentiality of all participating students. Training in the importance of privacy protections will also be necessary. Because of the potential of privacy concerns under FERPA, parental/caregiver permission should be required for any reliance on a PAAT with any Hurtful Student or Hurtful Supporter.

It is highly probable that peer involvement in interventions with those who are hurtful and their supporters will support greater accountability and effectiveness.

- Clear expression of disapproval by peers can communicate a strong positive norm of opposition to hurtful behavior and supporting hurtful behavior.

- Increased expectation that failure to comply with agreements under the Accountability Agreement will lead to detection.

- An important part of shame management is the expectation of continued acceptance within the community. The PAAT can communicate the essential message that forgiveness and reconciliation within the school community is possible through the Accountability Process.

Peer Mediation/Restorative Practices

There are helpful resources online for establishing a peer meditation program. A search on "peer mediation in schools" will lead to a wealth of helpful resources.

Williams has recently published an excellent book that outlines how to engage students in Restorative Practices activities in your school, *Peacekeepers: An Implementation Manual for Empowering Youth Using Restorative Practices.*[714]

Peer Support Services

Peer Support Services or Peer Support Workers is an approach that first emerged in addition recovery. As described by SAMHSA:

> *Peer support workers are people who have been successful in the recovery process who help others experiencing similar situations. Through shared understanding, respect, and mutual empowerment, peer support workers help people become and stay engaged in the recovery process and reduce the likelihood of relapse. Peer support services can effectively extend the reach of treatment beyond the clinical setting into the everyday environment of those seeking a successful, sustained recovery process.*[715]

Most of the states in the US have a process to license Peer Support Workers that requires they engage in a certified training program.

Peer Support Services are emerging in the college and university level. A recent evaluation indicated excellent effectiveness of this practice.[716] A conclusion from this study is:

Peer support and the establishment of on-campus peer support services can be very beneficial to university and college students in helping them better cope with the numerous stressors in their academic environment. The Peer Support Centre appears to fulfil its mandate of providing empathetic, confidential, non-judgemental and non-directional support to students at McGill University in an accessible manner. Taken together, the establishment of an on-campus peer support service is beneficial and relied upon by students at a university campus.[717]

Especially given the harmful impacts of the pandemic on student mental health and the abject lack of school counselors in many schools, establishing a Peer Support Service program should likely have a high priority of schools. The American School Counselor Association has taken a position in strong support of these program:

ASCA Position

Peer support programs help students develop an improved sense of well-being, social confidence and health behaviors. The informed implementation of peer support programs enhances the effectiveness of school counseling programs and provides increased outreach and expansion of services.

The Rationale

Development of relational peer networks in schools can improve students' academic achievement and social support. Specifically, peer support programs can be defined as peer-to-peer interaction in which individuals who are of approximately the same age take on a helping role, assisting students who may share related values, experiences and lifestyles. Peer support programs include activities such as assistance in one-to-one and group settings, academic/educational help, new student aid and other diverse activities of an interpersonal helping nature.[718]

The Adolescent Peer Support League is an organization that is dedicated to creating a system of peer support programs for mental health in high schools throughout the country.[719] They have excellent resources to support these programs.

Index

Footnotes

[1] On his website, Quote Investigator, O'Toole traced, the link between insanity and repetition back to at least the 19th century, but noted its use in a Narcotics Anonymous pamphlet as well as novels (including Brown's), TV shows and various other sources..https://quoteinvestigator.com/2017/03/23/same/.

[2] https://www.nationalacademies.org/news/2002/05/no-single-solution-for-protecting-kids-from-internet-pornography.

[3] https://web.archive.org/web/20071001215743/http://stopbullyingnow.hrsa.gov/index.asp?area=main.

[4] The Institute for Civility in Government. https://www.instituteforcivility.org/who-we-are/what-is-civility/.

[5] https://dpcpsi.nih.gov/sgmro.

[6] Thornberg, R. (2011). "She's weird" – The social construction of bullying in school: A review of qualitative research. *Children & Society*, 25, 258–267.

[7] I was unable to figure out where this quote came from. Further, this quote has also been attributed to Stephen Jobs, but I think he was quoting without citing.

[8] Olweus, D. (1993). *Bullying in school: What we know and what we can do.* Malden, MA: Blackwell Publishers.

[9] Hellström, L. Thornberg, R. & Espelage D.L. (2021) Definitions of Bullying. *Wiley Blackwell Handbook of Bullying: A Comprehensive and International Review of Research and Intervention.* Wiley Blackwell.

[10] Vivolo-Kantor , A & Gladden , R.M. (2014) What is Bullying? A New Uniform Definition for Research..gov. http://www.stopbullying.gov/blog/2014/02/10/what-bullying-new-uniform-definition-research.

[11] Id.

[12] Hamburger M.E., Basile K., & Vivolo A.M. (2011) *Measuring Bullying Victimization, Perpetration, and Bystander Experiences: A Compendium of Assessment Tools.* Atlanta, GA: Centers for Disease Control and Prevention, National Center for Injury Prevention and Control. https://www.cdc.gov/violenceprevention/pdf/bullycompendium-a.pdf.

[13] Ybarra M.L., Boyd D, Korchmaros JD. (2012) Defining and measuring cyberbullying within the larger context of bullying victimization. *Journal of Adolescent Health* 2012;51(1):53-58. DOI: 10.1016/j.jadohealth.2011.12.031.

[14] In the US, Title IX of the Education Amendments of 1972. 20 USC. §§ 1681-1688. Title VI of the Civil Rights Act of 1964. 42 USC. §§ 2000d-2000d-7. Section 504 of the Rehabilitation Act of 1973. 29 USC § 794. The Americans with Disabilities Act of 1990. 42 USC. §§ 12131-12134.

[15] USDOE-OCR, 2010 *Dear Colleague Letter.* https://www2.ed.gov/about/offices/list/ocr/letters/colleague-201010.html.

[16] https://www.stopbullying.gov/resources/laws.

[17] Stuart-Cassel, V, Bell, A. & Springer, J.F. (2011) *Analysis of State Bullying Laws and Policies.* US Department of Education. http://www.ed.gov/ news/press-releases/us-education-department-releases-analysis-state-bullying-laws-and-policies.

[18] Görzig, A., Wachs, S. & Wright, M. (2021) Cultural Factors and Bullying. *Wiley Blackwell Handbook of Bullying: A Comprehensive and International Review of Research and Intervention.* Wiley Blackwell.

[19] Smith, P. K., Kwak, K., & Toda, Y. (2016). School bullying in different cultures: Eastern and western perspectives. *Cambridge:* Cambridge University Press.

[20] Smith, P.K, Robinson, S. & Slonje, R. (2012) The School Bullying Research Program: Why and How It Has Developed. *Wiley Blackwell Handbook of Bullying: A Comprehensive and International Review of Research and Intervention.* Wiley Blackwell.

[21] United Nations (2019) *UN Strategy and Plan of Action on Hate Speech.* https://www.un.org/en/genocideprevention/documents/UN%20Strategy%20and%20Plan%20of%20Action%20on%20Hate%20Speech%2018%20June%20SYNOPSIS.pdf

[22] UCLA Diversity & Faculty Development (2014) *Diversity in the Classroom.* https://equity.ucla.edu/wp-content/uploads/2016/06/DiversityintheClassroom2014Web.pdf

[23] Title IX of the Education Amendments of 1972. 20 USC. §§ 1681-1688.

[24] Wolke, D. & Lereya, S.T. (2015) Long-term effects of bullying. *Arch Dis Child.* Sep; 100(9): 879–885. doi: 10.1136/archdischild-2014-306667.

[25] Cook C.R., Williams K.R., Guerra N.G., Kim T.E., & Sadek S. Predictors of bullying and victimization in childhood and adolescence: a meta-analytic investigation. *School Psychol Q* (2010) 25:65. doi: 10.1037/a0020149.

[26] Kochel K.P., Ladd G.W., Bagwell C.L., & Yabko B.A. 2015. Bully/Victim Profiles' Differential Risk for Worsening Peer Acceptance: The Role of Friendship. *J Appl Dev Psychol.* 41:38-45; Nansel, T. R., Overpeck, M. D., Pilla, R. S., Ruan, W. J., Simons-Morton, B., & Scheidt, P. C. (2001). Bullying behaviors among US youth: Prevalence and association with psychosocial adjustment. *Journal of the American Medical Association* (JAMA), 285(16), 2094–2100.; Juvonen, J., Graham, S., & Schuster, B. (2003) Bullying among young adolescents: the strong, the weak, and the troubled. *Pediatrics.* 112(6 Pt 1):1231-7.

[27] Juvonen, et. al. (2003), supra.

[28] Green V.A. (2021) The Role of Teachers. *Wiley Blackwell Handbook of Bullying: A Comprehensive and International Review of Research and Intervention.* Wiley-Blackwell.

[29] Dodge K.A. (1991) The structure and function of reactive and proactive aggression *Dev. Treat. Child. Aggress.*, 16 (5), pp. 201-218, 10.1111/j.1467-6494.2009.00610.x

[30] Gini G & Pozzoli T. (2009) Association between bullying and psychosomatic problems: a meta-analysis. *Pediatrics.* 2009 Mar; 123(3):1059-65; Copeland WE, Wolke D, Angold A, & Costello EJ (2013) Adult psychiatric outcomes of bullying and being bullied by peers in childhood and adolescence. *JAMA Psychiatry.* Apr; 70(4):419-26.

[31] Nansel, et. al. (2001), supra.

[32] Juvonen, et. al. (2003), supra; Kowalski R.M. & Limber S.P. (2013). Psychological, physical, and academic correlates of cyberbullying and traditional bullying. *J Adolesc Health.* 53(1 Suppl):S13-20.

[33] Nakamoto J. & Schwartz D. Is peer victimization associated with academic achievement? A meta-analytic review. *Soc Dev* 2010;19:221–42. 10.1111/j.1467-9507.2009.00539.

[34] Glew G.M., Fan M.Y., Katon W., Rivara F.P., & Kernic MA. (2005). Bullying, psychosocial adjustment, and academic performance in elementary school. *Arch Pediatr Adolesc Med.* 159(11):1026-31; Schwartz D. 2000 Subtypes of victims and aggressors in children's peer groups. *Journal of Abnormal Child Psychology* 28:181–192; Wolke, et. al (2013), supra.

[35] van Geel M., Vedder P., & Tanilon J. 2014. Bullying and weapon carrying: a meta-analysis. JAMA *Pediatric.* 168(8):714-20; Klomek A.B., Sourander A., & Elonheimo H. (2015). Bullying by peers in childhood and effects on psychopathology, suicidality, and criminality in adulthood. *Lancet Psychiatry.* 2(10):930-41.

[36] Wolke, D., Copeland, W. E., Angold, A., & Costello, E. J. (2013). Impact of bullying in childhood on adult health, wealth, crime, and social outcomes. *Psychological Science,* 24(10), 1958–1970. doi:10.1177/0956797613481608.

[37] Ford R., King T., Priest N., & Kavanagh A. (2017). Bullying and mental health and suicidal behaviour among 14- to 15-year-olds in a representative sample of Australian children. *Aust N Z J Psychiatry.* 51(9):897-908.

[38] Wolke, D., Copeland, W. E., Angold, A., & Costello, E. J. (2013). Impact of bullying in childhood on adult health, wealth, crime, and social outcomes. *Psychological Science,* 24(10), 1958–1970. doi:10.1177/0956797613481608.

[39] Woods S. and White E. (2005). The association between bullying behaviour, arousal levels and behaviour problems. *J Adolesc.* 28(3):381-95; Fanti K.A .& Kimonis E.R. (2013) Dimensions of juvenile psychopathy distinguish "bullies," "bully-victims," and "victims." *Psychology of Violence,* Vol 3(4): 396-409.

[40] Guy, A., Lee, K. & Wolke, D. (2019) Comparisons Between Adolescent Bullies, Victims, and Bully-Victims on Perceived Popularity, Social Impact, and Social Preference. *Psychiatry,* 22 https://doi.org/10.3389/fpsyt.2019.00868.

[41] Thornberg, R. (2003) She's Weird! - The Social Construction of Bullying in School: A Review of Qualitative Research, 2011, *Children & Society,* (25), 4, 258-267.

[42] Pouwels, J.L. & Garandeau, C.F. (2021) The Role of the Peer Group and Classroom Factors in Bullying Behavior. *Wiley Blackwell Handbook of Bullying: A Comprehensive and International Review of Research and Intervention.* Wiley-Blackwell.

[43] Cantin, S., Brendgen, M., Dussault, F., & Vitaro, F. (2019). Transactional links between adolescents' and friends' victimization during the first two years of secondary school: The mediating role of likeability and friendship involvement. *Social Development,* 28, 743–757.b doi:10.1111/sode.12355

[44] Pouwels & Garandeau, (2021), supra.

[45] Espelage, D.L. (2021) What Do We Know About Identity-Based Bullying? *Virtual Symposium: Understanding and Preventing Youth Hate Crimes and Identity-Based Bullying.* OJJDP. https://oijdp.ojp.gov/programs/preventing-youth-hate-crimes-bullying-initiative.

[46] https://ojjdp.ojp.gov/programs/preventing-youth-hate-crimes-bullying-initiative.

[47] United Nations Educational, Scientific and Cultural Organization (UNESCO) (2017) *School Violence and Bullying: Global Status Report.* https://unesdoc.unesco.org/ark:/48223/pf0000246970.

[48] Flentje A., Heck N.C., Brennan J.M. & Meyer I.H. (2020) The relationship between minority stress and biological outcomes: A systematic review. *J Behav Med.* 2020 doi: 10.1007/s10865-019-00120-6.

[49] Meyer, I. H. (2003). Prejudice, social stress, and mental health in lesbian, gay, and bisexual populations: Conceptual issues and research evidence. *Psychological Bulletin,* 129, 674–697. doi:10.1037/00332909.129.5.674

[50] Bhushan D., Kotz K., McCall J., Wirtz S., Gilgoff R., Dube S.R., Powers C., Olson-Morgan, J., Galeste M., Patterson K., Harris L., Mills A., Bethell C., & Burke Harris N. (2020) Office of the California Surgeon General. *Roadmap for Resilience: The California Surgeon General's Report on Adverse Childhood Experiences, Toxic Stress, and Health.* Office of the California Surgeon General DOI: 10.48019/PEAM8812.

[51] Garnett B.R., Masyn K.E., Austin S.B., Miller M., Williams D.R., & Viswanath K. (2014) The intersectionality of discrimination attributes and bullying among youth: an applied latent class analysis. *J Youth Adolesc.* (8):1225-39. doi: 10.1007/s10964-013-0073-8.

[52] Jones, L.M, Mitchell, M. & Turner, H. (2021) Characteristics of Hate Crimes Involving Juveniles: Findings From the National Hate Crime Investigations Study (NHCIS). *Virtual Symposium: Understanding and Preventing Youth Hate Crimes and Identity-Based Bullying.* OJJDP. https://ojjdp.ojp.gov/programs/preventing-youth-hate-crimes-bullying-initiative.

[53] Title 18, USC., Section 249 - *Matthew Shepard and James Byrd, Jr., Hate Crimes Prevention Act.*

[54] Jones, et. al., (2021) supra.

[55] Kuldas, S. Dupont. M. & Foody M. (2021) Ethnicity-Based Bullying: Suggestions for Future Research on Classroom Ethnic Composition, *Wiley Blackwell Handbook of Bullying: A Comprehensive and International Review of Research and Intervention.* Wiley Blackwell

[56] Fandrem, H., Strohmeier, D., Caravita, S.C.S. & Stefanek, E. (2021) Migration and Bullying, *Wiley Blackwell Handbook of Bullying: A Comprehensive and International Review of Research and Intervention.* Wiley-Blackwell.

[57] Espelage (2021), supra.

[58] Campbell, E.M. & Smalling, S.E. (2013) American Indians and Bullying in Schools. *Journal of Indigenous Social Development.* Volume 2, Issue 1 http://www.hawaii.edu/sswork/jisd http://scholarspace.manoa.hawaii.edu/handle/10125/29811 E-ISSN 2164-9170 pp. 1-15.

[59] Southern Poverty Law Center. (2011). Violence crimes hit Native Americans hardest. *Intelligence Report.* http://www.splcenter.org/get-informed/intelligence-report/browse-all-issues/1999/spring/crime-study.

[60] Allam, L. (2018) Indigenous children more likely to fear lack of safety, bullying and discrimination. *The Guardian.* https://www.theguardian.com/australia-news/2018/oct/11/indigenous-children-more-likely-to-fear-lack-of-safety-bullying-and-discrimination.

[61] Act To Change, ADMERASIA, and NextShark (2021) *2021 Asian American Bullying Survey Report in Partnership with Act To Change, ADMERASIA, and NextShark.* Available at https://acttochange.org/bullyingreport/.

[62] Mogahed, D. & Chouhoud, Y. (2017) *American Muslim Poll 2017: Muslims at the Crossroads* (Dearborn, MI: Institute for Social Policy and Understanding, 2017). https://www.ispu.org/american-muslim-poll-2017/.

[63] Hinduja, S., & Patchin, J. W. (2022). Bias-Based Cyberbullying Among Early Adolescents: Associations With Cognitive and Affective Empathy. *The Journal of Early Adolescence,* 02724316221088757.

[64] United Nations Educational, Scientific and Cultural Organization (UNESCO) (2019) *Violence and bullying in educational settings: the experience of children and young people with disabilities.* https://unesdoc.unesco.org/ark:/48223/pf0000378061. See also: O'Moore, M. & McGuire, L. (2021) Disablist Bullying. *Wiley Blackwell Handbook of Bullying: A Comprehensive and International Review of Research and Intervention.* Wiley-Blackwell.

[65] Blaya, C. (2021) Bias Bullying Problems Among School Children: Sexual and Gender-Based Bullying, and Intersectional Considerations. *Wiley Blackwell Handbook of Bullying: A Comprehensive and International Review of Research and Intervention.*

[66] Jones, D. & Franklin, J. (2022) *Not just Florida. More than a dozen states propose so-called 'Don't Say Gay' bills.* National Public Radio. https://www.npr.org/2022/04/10/1091543359/15-states-dont-say-gay-anti-transgender-bills.

[67] Flentje (2020) supra.

[68] There is, unfortunately, not sufficient research on the common identity focused basis upon which students are treated badly in addition to protected classes. The recent report by National Academies of Sciences, Engineering, and Medicine, did have an extensive section on concerns of students with obesity who experience bullying.

[69] Waasdorp, T. E., Mehari, K., & Bradshaw, C. P. (2018). Obese and Overweight Youth: Risk for Experiencing Bullying Victimization and Internalizing Symptoms. *American Journal of Orthopsychiatry.* Advance online publication. http://dx.doi.org/10.1037/ort0000294.

[70] Gray, W.N., Kahhan, N.A., & Janicke, D.M. (2009) Peer victimization and pediatric obesity: A review of the literature. *Psychology in the Schools.* https://doi.org/10.1002/pits.20410.

[71] Lee, J (2011). *President Obama & the First Lady at the White House Conference on Bullying Prevention.* https://obamawhitehouse.archives.gov/blog/2011/03/10/president-obama-first-lady-white-house-conference-bullying-prevention.

[72] UNESCO (2019, supra.

[73] https://www.who.int/teams/noncommunicable-diseases/surveillance/systems-tools/global-school-based-student-health-survey; https://www.who.int/europe/initiatives/health-behaviour-in-school-aged-children-(hbsc)-study.

[74] Id.

[75] US Centers for Disease Control (CDC), *Youth Risk Behavior Survey,* (CDC YRBS) https://www.cdc.gov/healthyyouth/data/yrbs/index.htm.

[76] CDC YRBS. Questionnaires. https://www.cdc.gov/healthyyouth/data/yrbs/questionnaires.htm

[77] CDC (2015) *Youth Risk Behavior Survey: Data Summary and Trends Report 2007-2019.* https://www.cdc.gov/healthyyouth/data/yrbs/pdf/YRBSDataSummaryTrendsReport2019-508.pdf.

[78] Irwin, V., Wang, K. Cui, J. Zhang, K. & Thompson, A. (2020) *Report on Indicators of School Crime and Safety, 2020.* US Department of Justice. https://bjs.ojp.gov/library/publications/report-indicators-school-crime-and-safety-2020.

[79] Id.

[80] https://nces.ed.gov/programs/coe/indicator/a10.

[81] https://nces.ed.gov/pubs2015/2015056.pdf.

[82] https://nces.ed.gov/fastfacts/display.asp?id=719.

[83] https://nces.ed.gov/fastfacts/display.asp?id=719.

[84] Organization for Economic Cooperation and Development (OECD). *2018 Program for International Student Assessment* (PISA). https://unesdoc.unesco.org/ark:/48223/pf0000378061.

[85] Schleicher, A. (2019). *PISA 2018 Results What School Life Means for Student Lives.* Organization for Economic Cooperation and Development. https://www.oecd-ilibrary.org/sites/cd52fb72-en/index.html?itemId=/content/component/cd52fb72-en#fig10.

[86] Gini, G., Card, N.A. & Pozzoli T. (2018). A meta-analysis of the differential relations of traditional and cyber-victimization with internalizing problems. *Aggressive Behavior* 44(2), 185–198.

[87] Bacher-Hicks, A., Goodman, J. Greif Green, J. and Holt, M.K. (2021). *The COVID-19 Pandemic Disrupted Both School Bullying and Cyberbullying.* (Ed WorkingPaper: 21-436). Annenberg Institute at Brown University: https://doi.org/10.26300/7jy7-x816

[88] See generally, https://cyberbullying.org

[89] Patchin, J.W. (2021) *Bullying During the Covid-19 Pandemic.* https://cyberbullying.org/bullying-during-the-covid-19-pandemic.

[90] Belsha, K. (Sep 27, 2021) Stress and short tempers: Schools struggle with behavior as students return. *Chalkbeat.* https://www.chalkbeat.org/2021/9/27/22691601/student-behavior-stress-trauma-return; Meckler, & Strauss, V. (Oct 26, 2021) Back to school has brought guns, fighting and acting out. *The Washington Post.* https://www.washingtonpost.com/education/2021/10/26/schools-violence-teachers-guns-fights/; Chavez, N. (Dec 5, 2021) Students are fed up with racist slurs and bullying. Now they're walking out of class. *CNN.* https://www.cnn.com/2021/12/05/us/racist-bullying-school-incidents/index.html?fbclid=IwAR3NfBFh_E6QaF3DFKOrUp0Z.nu0BoRSJcPhsrJyNdlv8U9oL1BBUbgumSFU; Stubbs, R. (Dec 18, 2021) As fans return to high school sports, officials say student behavior has never been worse. *The Washington Post.* https://www.washingtonpost.com/sports/2021/12/18/high-school-sports-student-fan-behavior/; Pierce, E. (Nov. 17, 2021) As Students Return to School, So Does School Violence. *US News and World Report.* https://www.usnews.com/education/k12/articles/as-students-return-to-school-so-does-school-violence.

[91] Natanson H. (Nov 9, 2021) Death threats, online abuse, police protection: School board members face dark new reality. *The Washington Post.* https://www.washingtonpost.com/local/education/death-threats-online-abuse-police-protection-school-board-members-face-dark-new-reality/2021/11/09/db007706-37fe-11ec-9bc4-86107e7b0ab1_story.html; Atterbury, A & Perez, J. (Oct 27, 2021) 'Threats of violence': School boards curb public comments to calm raucous meetings. *Politico* https://www.politico.com/news/2021/10/27/school-boards-covid-restrictions-violence-517326; Kamenetz, A. (Sept 30, 2021) School boards are asking for federal help as they face threats and violence. *NPR.* https://www.npr.org/sections/back-to-school-live-updates/2021/09/30/1041870027/school-boards-federal-help-threats-violence; Talbot, A. (Oct 8, 2021) The Increasingly Wild World of School-Board Meetings. *The New Yorker.* https://www.newyorker.com/news/daily-comment/the-increasingly-wild-world-of-school-board-meetings; Saul, S. (Oct. 21, 2021) Energizing Conservative Voters, One School Board Election at a Time. *The New York Times.* https://www.nytimes.com/2021/10/21/us/republicans-schools-critical-race-theory.html.

[92] Schwartz, B. (Nov 10, 2021) Business executives and wealthy Republican donors helped fund attacks on critical race theory during campaigns. *CNBC* https://www.cnbc.com/2021/11/10/critical-race-theory-executives-rich-gop-donors-funded-attacks-during-elections.html; Aviles, G. (Nov 15, 2021) Conservatives used critical race theory to influence voters and win elections. Critics warn the propaganda is working. *Insider.* https://www.insider.com/conservatives-won-elections-with-critical-race-theory-propaganda-2021-11.

[93] Rotella, S. (Jan. 22, 2021) Global Right-Wing Extremism Networks Are Growing. The US Is Just Now Catching Up. *ProPublica.* https://www.propublica.org/article/global-right-wing-extremism-networks-are-growing-the-u-s-is-just-now-catching-up; Beckett, L & Wilson, J. Aug 5, 'White power ideology': why El Paso is part of a growing global threat. *The Guardian.* https://www.theguardian.com/us-news/2019/aug/04/el-paso-shooting-white-nationalist-supremacy-violence-christchurch.

[94] Schuster MA, & Bogart LM. (2013) Did the ugly duckling have PTSD? Bullying, its effects, and the role of pediatricians. *Pediatrics.* 2013 Jan;131(1):e288-91.

[95] American Educational Research Association. (2013). *Prevention of Bullying in Schools, Colleges, and Universities: Research Report and Recommendations.* Washington, DC: http://www.aera.net/newsroom/news/preventionofbullyingresearchreportandrecomm/tabid/14865/default.aspx. pp. 9-10.

[96] Sainio, M., Veenstra, R., Huitsing, G., & Salmivalli, C. (2011). Victims and their defenders: A dyadic approach. *International Journal of Behavioral Development*, 35(2), 144–151. doi:10.1177/0165025410378068.

[97] Schacter, H. L. & Juvonen, J. (2019). Dynamic changes in peer victimization and adjustment across middle school: Does friends' victimization alleviate distress? *Child Development.* 90, 1738–1753. doi:10.1111/cdev.13038.

[98] Huitsing, G., Veenstra, R., Sainio, M., & Salmivalli, C. (2012). "It must be me" or "It could be them?": The impact of the social network position of bullies and victims on victims' adjustment. *Social Networks*, 34, 379–386. doi:10.1016/j.socnet.2010.07.002

[99] Garandeau, C. F., & Salmivalli, C. (2019). Can healthier contexts be harmful? A new perspective on the plight of victims of bullying. *Child Development Perspectives*, 13, 147–152.; Huitsing, G., Van Duijn, M. A. J., Snijders, T. A. B., Perren, S., Alsaker, F. D., & Veenstra, R. (2019). Self, peer, and teacher reports of victim-aggressor networks in kindergartens. *Aggressive Behavior*, 45, 275–286. doi:10.1002/ab.21817)

[100] Felitti V.J., Anda R.F., Nordenberg D., Williamson D.F., Spitz A.M., Edwards V., Koss M.P., & Marks J.S. (1998) Relationship of childhood abuse and household dysfunction to many of the leading causes of death in adults. The Adverse Childhood Experiences (ACE) Study *Am J Prev Med.* 1998 May;14(4):245-58. doi: 10.1016/s0749-3797(98)00017-8.

[101] Bhushan et. al. (2020) supra.

[102] Idsoe, T., Dyregrov, A. & Idsoe, E.C. (2012) Bullying and PTSD Symptoms. *J Abnorm Child Psychol* 40:901–911. http://www.uis.no/news/being- bullied-can-cause-trauma-symptoms-article62673-8865.html

[103] Id. at 902.

[104] Vaillancourt, T., Hymel, S., & McDougall, P., (2013). The biological underpinnings of peer victimization: Understanding why and how the effects of bullying can last a lifetime. *Theory into Practice*, 52, 241-248.

[105] National Child Traumatic Stress Network. *Defining Trauma and Child Traumatic Stress.* http://www.nctsnet.org/content/defining-trauma-and- child-traumatic- stress.

[106] American Psychiatric Publishing (2013) *Posttraumatic Stress Disorder.* http://www.dsm5.org/Documents/PTSDpercent20Factpercent20Sheet.pdf.

[107] Id.

[108] Huang, F. L., Eklund, K., & Cornell, D. G. (2017). Authoritative school climate, number of parents at home, and academic achievement. *School Psychology Quarterly*, 32(4), 480–496; O'Brien, N. (2021) School Factors with a Focus on Boarding Schools. *Wiley Blackwell Handbook of Bullying: A Comprehensive and International Review of Research and Intervention.* Wiley Blackwell.

[109] Lacey, A., & Cornell, D. (2013). The impact of teasing and bullying on schoolwide academic performance. *Journal of Applied School Psychology*, 29, 262–283. p. 364)

[110] Havik, T., Bru, E., & Ertesvag, S. K. (2015). School factors associated with school refusal-and truancy-related reasons for school non-attendance. *Social Psychology of Education*, 18(2), 221–240.

[111] Id.

[112] Vidourek, R. A., King, K. A., & Merianos, A. L. (2016). School bullying and student trauma: Fear and avoidance associated with victimization. *Journal of Prevention & Intervention in the Community*, 44(2), 121–129.

[113] Suicide Prevention Resource Center (2011) *Suicide and bullying: Issue Brief.* http://www.sprc.org/library_resources/items/suicide-and- bullying-issue-brief.

[114] Plemmons, G., Hall, M., Doupnik, S., Gay, J., Brown, C., Browning,W., Casey, R., Freundlich, K., Johnson, D.P., Lind, C., Rehm, K., Thomas, S., & Williams, D. (2018) Hospitalization for Suicide Ideation or Attempt: 2008–2015. *Pediatrics.* http://pediatrics.aappublications.org/content/early/2018/05/14/peds.2017-2426.

[115] Newman, K. (2018) For Kids, Suicide-Related Hospital Visits Increase During School Months. *US News and World Report.* https://www.usnews.com/news/healthiest-communities/articles/2018-05-16/study-suicide-related-hospital-visits-double-among-youth-increase-during-school-months.

[116] Hinduja, S, Patchin, JW. Connecting adolescent suicide to the severity of bullying and cyberbullying. *J Sch Violence.* 2019;18:333-346.

[117] https://cyberbullying.org/bullying-cyberbullying-suicide-among-us-youth.

[118] Holt, M. K., Vivolo-Kantor, A. M., Polanin, J. R., Holland, K. M., DeGue, S., Matjasko, J. L., & Reid, G. (2015). Bullying and suicidal ideation and behaviors: A meta-analysis. *Pediatrics*, 135, e496–e509. doi:10.1542/peds.2014-1864.

[119] Nock, M. K., Joiner, T. E., Jr., Gordon, K. H., Lloyd-Richardson, E., & Prinstein, M. J. (2006). Non-suicidal self-injury among adolescents: Diagnostic correlates and relation to suicide attempts. *Psychiatry Research*, 144, 65–72. doi:10.1016/j.psychres.2006.05.010.

[120] Boxer, P. (2010). Variations in risk and treatment factors among adolescents engaging in different types of deliberate self-harm in an inpatient sample. *Journal of Clinical Child and Adolescent Psychology*, 39(4), 470–480.; Kiekens, G., Hasking, P., Boyes, M., Claes, L., Mortier, P., Auerbach, R. P., & Bruffaerts, R. (2018). The associations between non-suicidal self-injury and first onset suicidal thoughts and behaviors. *Journal of Affective Disorders*, 239, 171–179.

[121] Heerde, J. A., & Hemphill, S. A. (2018). Are bullying perpetration and victimization associated with adolescent deliberate self-harm? A meta-analysis. *Archives of Suicide Research*, 23, 353–381. doi:10.1080/13811118.2018.1472690.

[122] Robinson, I. (2018) I Tried to Befriend Nikolas Cruz. He Still Killed My Friends. *The New York Times.* https://www.nytimes.com/2018/03/27/opinion/nikolas-cruz-shooting-florida.html.

[123] Cox, J.W. & Rich, S. (Dec, 31, 2021) 'Please help me': Kids with guns fueled a record number of school shootings in 2021. *The Washington Post.* https://www.washingtonpost.com/dc-md-va/2021/12/31/2021-school-shootings-record/.

[124] Id.

[125] Diaz, J. (2022) 27 school shootings have taken place so far this year. NPR. https://www.npr.org/2022/05/24/1101050970/2022-school-shootings-so-far.

[126] Strauss, V. (2019) Study: There's no evidence that hardening schools to make kids safer from gun violence actually works. *The Washington Post.* https://www.washingtonpost.com/education/2019/04/16/study-theres-no-evidence-that-hardening-schools-make-kids-safer-gun-violence-actually-works/.

[127] Mccullough J. & Mcgee, K. (2022) Texas already "hardened" schools. It didn't save Uvalde. *The Texas Tribune.* https://www.texastribune.org/2022/05/26/texas-uvalde-shooting-harden-schools/.

[128] Vossekuil, B., Fein, R.A., Reddy, M., Borum, R., & Modzeleski, W. (2004) *The Final Report and Findings of the Safe School Initiative: Implications for the Prevention of School Attacks in the United States.* US Secret Service and US Department of Education. https://www2.ed.gov/admins/lead/safety/preventingattacksreport.pdf

[129] Id.

[130] National Threat Assessment Center (2018) *Enhancing School Safety Using a Threat Assessment Model: An Operational Guide for Preventing Targeted School Violence.* US Department of Homeland Security. Secret Service https://www.secretservice.gov/data/protection/ntac/USSS_NTAC_Enhancing_School_Safety_Guide_7.11.18.pdf.

[131] Langman, P. (2017) A Bio-Psycho-Social Model of School Schooters. *The Journal of Campus Behavioral Intervention.* https://schoolshooters.info/sites/default/files/bio_psycho_social_1.0.pdf.

[132] US Secret Service. (2018) *Enhancing School Safety Using a Threat Assessment Model: An Operational Guide for Preventing Targeted School Violence.* National Threat Assessment Center. https://www.cisa.gov/enhancing-school-safety-using-threat-assessment-model.

[133] Id. at 12.

[134] Pham, T.B., Shcapiro, L.E., John, M. & Adesman, A. (2017) Weapon Carrying Among Victims of Bullying. *Pediatrics.* https://publications.aap.org/pediatrics/article/140/6/e20170353/38167/Weapon-Carrying-Among-Victims-of-Bullying.

[135] Vossekuil, et. al. (2004) supra.

[136] Amman, M. Bowlin, A.S., Burton, K.C. Burton, K.F. Brunell, K.A. Gibson, ..., C.J. Robins. *Making prevention a reality: Identifying, assessing, and managing the threat of targeted attacks.* US. Department of Justice, Federal Bureau of Investigation (2017) https://www.fbi.gov/file-repository/making-prevention-a-reality.pdf/view

[137] Planty, M., Banks, D., Lindquist, C., Cartwright, J., & Witwer, A. (2020). *Tip Lines for School Safety: A National Portrait of Tip Line Use.* Research Triangle Park, NC: RTI International

[138] Id.

[139] Id.

[140] Stein-Seroussi, A., Hanley, S., Grabarek, M. & Woodliff, T. (2021) Evaluating a statewide anonymous reporting system for students and multidisciplinary response teams: Methods for a randomized trial. *International Journal of Educational Research*, Volume 110, 101862, ISSN 0883-0355. https://doi.org/10.1016/j.ijer.2021.101862.

[141] Southern Poverty Law Clinic (2022) *The Year in Hate & Extremism Report 2021*. https://www.splcenter.org/20220309/year-hate-extremism-report-2021; Alliance Defending Freedom. (2022) *US White Supremacist Propaganda Remained at Historic Levels in 2021, With 27 Percent Rise in Antisemitic Messaging.* https://www.adl.org/resources/report/us-white-supremacist-propaganda-remained-historic-levels-2021-27-percent-rise.

[142] Southern Poverty Law Center and American University's Polarization and Extremism Research and Innovation Lab (undated) *Building Resilience & Confronting Risk: A Parents and Caregivers Guide to Online Youth Radicalization.* https://www.splcenter.org/peril-guide-online-youth-radicalization; Alliance Defending Freedom. (2021) *US White Supremacist Propaganda Remained at Historic Levels in 2021, With 27 Percent Rise in Antisemitic Messaging.* https://www.adl.org/resources/tools-and-strategies/extreme-measures-how-help-young-people-counter-extremist-recruitment.

[143] Greenblatt, J (December 9, 2021) *Congressional Testimony Holding Big Tech Accountable: Legislation to Build a Safer Internet.* House Committee on Energy and Commerce: Subcommittee on Consumer Protection and Commerce.

[144] Southern Poverty Law Center and American University's Polarization and Extremism Research and Innovation Lab, supra.

[145] Rodkin, P.C., Espelage, D.L & Hanish, L.D. (2015) A Relational Framework for Understanding Bullying Developmental Antecedents and Outcomes. *American Psychologist.* Vol. 70, No. 4, 311–321; Rodkin, P.C. (2012) Bullying and Children's Peer Relationships. Colleagues Volume 8 Issue 2 *Education Matters,* Article 4, pp 5-10. Rodkin, P. C., Farmer, T. W., Pearl, R., & Van Acker, R. (2006). They're cool: Social status and peer group supports for aggressive boys and girls. *Social Development*, 15, 175-204. Farmer, T. W., Petrin, R. A., Robertson, D. L., Fraser, M. W., Hall, C. M., Day. S. H., & Dadisman, K. (2010). Peer relations of bullies, bully-victims, and victims: The two social worlds of bullying in second-grade classrooms. *Elementary Youth Organization Journal*, 110, 364-392.

[146] Rodkin, et. al. (2015), supra.

[147] National Academies of Sciences, Engineering, and Medicine. 2016. *Preventing Bullying Through Science, Policy, and Practice.* Washington, DC: The National Academies Press. https://doi.org/10.17226/23482.

[148] Id. at 133.

[149] https://www.stopbullying.gov/bullying/at-risk. (Accessed June 2022.)

[150] https://www.stopbullying.gov/bullying/why-some-youth-bully. (Accessed June 2022.)

[151] https://www.stopbullying.gov/about-us.

[152] Faris, R. & Felmlee, D. (2014) Casualties of Social Combat: School Networks of Peer Victimization and Their Consequences *American Sociological Review* 2014, Vol. 79(2) 228–257 (citations omitted).

[153] Juvonen, J. Wang, Y. & Espinoza, G. (2013) Physical Aggression, Spreading of Rumors, and Social Prominence in Early Adolescence: Reciprocal Effects Supporting Gender Similarities? *J Youth Adolescence.* 42:1801–1810.

[154] Id. at 1804.

[155] Al-Jbouri, E. & Volk, A.A. (2021) Evolutionary Perspectives on Bullying. *Wiley Blackwell Handbook of Bullying: A Comprehensive and International Review of Research and Intervention.*

[156] Griskevicius, V., Tybur, J. M., Gangestead, S. W., Perea, E. F., Shapiro, J. R., & Kenrick, D. T. (2009). Aggress to impress: Hostility as an evolved context-dependent strategy. *Journal of Personality and Social Psychology*, 96(5), 980–994.

[157] UNESCO, (2017) and (2019) supra.

[158] Volk, A.A., Dane, A.V., Marini, Z.A., & Vaillancourt, T. (2015). Adolescent bullying, dating, and mating: Testing an evolutionary hypothesis. *Evolutionary Psychology*, 13(4), 1–11.

[159] Wohlleben, P. (2016). *The hidden life of trees.* Vancouver, BC: Greystone Books.

[160] Sanders, J.B.P., Malamut, S. & Cillessen, A.H.N. (2021) Why Do Bullies Bully? Motives for Bullying. *The Wiley Blackwell Handbook of Bullying: A Comprehensive and International Review of Research and Intervention.* Wiley Blackwell.

[161] Volk, A. A., Veenstra, R., & Espelage, D. L. (2017). So you want to study bullying? Recommendations to enhance the validity, transparency, and compatibility of bullying research. *Aggression and Violent Behavior*, 36, 34–43. doi:10.1016/j.avb.2017.07.003

[162] Sanders, et. al. (2021) supra.

[163] Thornberg, R., & Knutsen, S. (2011). Teenagers' explanations of bullying. Child Youth Care Forum, 40, 177–192. doi:10.1007/s10566-010-9129-z; Thornberg, R., Rosenqvist, R., & Johansson, P. (2012). Older teenagers' explanations of bullying. *Child Youth Care Forum*, 41, 327–342. doi:10.1007/s10566-012-9171-0

[164] Salmivalli, C. (2010). Bullying and the peer group: A review. *Aggression and Violent Behavior*, 15(2), 112–120. doi:10.1016/j.avb.2009.08.007

[165] LaFontana, K. M., & Cillessen, A. H. N. (2010). Developmental changes in the priority of perceived status in childhood and adolescence. *Social Development*, 19, 130–147. doi:10.1111/j.1467-9507.2008.00522.x

[166] Sanders, et. al. (2021) supra.

[167] Runions, K. C., Salmivalli, C., Shaw, T., Burns, S., & Cross, D. (2018). Beyond the reactive proactive dichotomy: Rage, revenge, reward, and recreational aggression predict early high school bully and bully/victim status. *Aggressive Behavior*, 44, 501–510. doi:10.1002/ab.21770

[168] Fluck, J. (2014). Why do students bully? An analysis of motives behind violence in schools. *Youth & Society*, 1–21. doi:10.1177/0044118X14547876

[169] Juvonen, J., & Galvan, A. (2009). Bullying as a means to foster compliance. In M. J. Harris (Ed.), *Bullying, rejection, and peer victimization: A social cognitive neuroscience perspective.* (pp. 299–318). New York: Springer.

[170] Thornberg, R. (2010). School children's social representations on bullying causes. *Psychology in the Schools,* 47, 311–327. doi:10.1002/pits.20472

[171] Ellis, B. J., Volk, A., Gonzalez, J. M., & Embry, D. D. (2016). The Meaningful Roles intervention: An evolutionary approach to reducing bullying and increasing prosocial behavior. *Journal of Research on Adolescence,* 26, 622–637. doi:10.1111/jora.12243

[172] Vaillancourt, T. (2013). Do human females use indirect aggression as an intrasexual competition strategy? Philosophical Transactions of the Royal Society B: *Biological Sciences,* 368. doi:10.1098/rstb.2013.0080

[173] Salmivalli, C., Kaukiainen, A., Kaistaniemi, L., & Lagerspetz, K. (1999). Self-evaluated selfesteem, peer-evaluated self-esteem, and defensive egotism as predictors of adolescents' participation in bullying situations. *Personality and Social Psychology Bulletin,* 25, 1268–1278. doi:10.1177/0146167299258008

[174] Fluck (2014) supra; Thornberg & Knutse (2011) supra; Thornberg et. al. (2012) supra.

[175] Id.

[176] Connolly, J., Pepler, D., Craig, W., & Taradash, A. (2000). Dating experiences of bullies in early adolescence. *Child Maltreatment,* 5(4), 299–310; Faris & Femlee (2014) supra.

[177] Al-Jbouri & Volk (2021) supra; Sijtsema, J. J., Veenstra, R., Lindenberg, S., & Salmivalli, C. (2009). Empirical test of bullies' status goals: Assessing direct goals, aggression, and prestige. *Aggressive Behavior,* 35, 57–67; Reijntjes, A., Vermande, M., Olthof, T., Goossens, F. A., van de Schoot, R., Aleva, L., & van der Meulen, M. (2013). Costs and benefits of bullying in the context of the peer group: A three wave longitudinal analysis. *Journal of Abnormal Child Psychology,* 41, 1–13.

[178] Al-Jbouri & Volk (2021) supra; Rodkin, et. al. (2015) supra; Faris & Felmlee (2014) supra; Juvonen, et. al, (2013), supra.

[179] Stoltz S, Cillessen AH, van den Berg YH, & Gommans R. Popularity differentially predicts reactive and Proactive Aggression in early adolescence. *Aggress Behav.* 2016 Jan-Feb;42(1):29-40. doi: 10.1002/ab.21603. Epub 2015 Aug 24. PMID: 26299476.

[180] Sidanimus, J. & Pratto, F. (1999). *Social Dominance: An Intergroup Theory of Social Hierarchy and Oppression.* Cambridge: Cambridge University Press

[181] Pratto, F. Sidanius, J., Stallworth, L. & Malle, B. (1994). "Social Dominance Orientation: A Personality Variable Predicting Social and Political Attitudes" *Journal of Personality and Social Psychology.* 67 (4): 741–763.

[182] Goodboy, A.K., Martin M.M. & Rittenour C.E.(2016) Bullying as a Display of Social Dominance Orientation, *Communication Research Reports,* 33:2,159-165

[183] Sanders, et. al. (2021) supra.

[184] Pouwels & Garandeau, (2021), supra.

[185] Garandeau, C. F., Lee, I. A., & Salmivalli, C. (2014). Inequality matters: Classroom status hierarchy and adolescents' bullying. *Journal of Youth and Adolescence,* 43, 1123–1133.

[186] Cheng, J. T., Tracy, J. L., Foulsham, T., Kingstone, A., & Henrich, J. (2013). Two ways to the top: Evidence that dominance and prestige are distinct yet viable avenues to social rank and influence. *Journal of Personality and Social Psychology,* 104, 103-125.

[187] Maner, J.K. (2017) Dominance and Prestige: A Tale of Two Hierarchies. *Current Directions in Psychological Science* 26(6):096372141771432 DOI: 10.1177/0963721417714323.

[188] National Center on Response to Intervention. (2010, April). *Essential components of RTI – A closer look at response to intervention.* https://mtss4success.org/resource/essential-components-rti-closer-look-response-intervention.

[189] Runions, et. al. (2018), supra; Mahady Wilton, M. M., Craig, W. M., & Pepler, D. J. (2000). Emotional regulation and display in classroom victims of bullying: Characteristic expressions of affect, coping styles and relevant contextual factors. *Social Development,* 9, 226–245; Tapper, K., & Boulton, M. J. (2005). Victims and peer group responses to different forms of aggression among primary school children. *Aggressive Behavior.*

[190] Kochenderfer–Ladd, B. (2004). Peer victimization: The role of emotions in adaptive and maladaptive coping. *Social Development,* 13, 329–349.

[191] McEvoy, A. (2005). *Teachers who bully students: Patterns and policy implications.* Paper presented at the Hamilton Fish Institute's Persistently Safe Schools Conference, Philadelphia, PA.

[192] Cherry, K. (2020) Social Cognition in Psychology: The Way We Think About Others. *Very Well Mind.* https://www.verywellmind.com/social-cognition-2795912

[193] Bandura, A., Ross, D. & Ross, S.A. (1961). Transmission of aggression through imitation of aggressive models. *Journal of Abnormal and Social Psychology,* 63, 575-82; Bandura, A., Ross, D., & Ross, S. A. (1963). Imitation of film-mediated aggressive models. *The Journal of Abnormal and Social Psychology,* 66(1), 3; Bandura, A. (1965). Influence of models' reinforcement contingencies on the acquisition of imitative responses. *Journal of personality and social psychology,* 1(6), 589; Bandura, A. (1977). *Social Learning Theory.* Englewood Cliffs, NJ: Prentice Hall.

[194] Simon, P. & Olson, S. (2014) *Building Capacity to Reduce Bullying Workshop Summary. Institute of Medicine and National Research Council.* The National Academies Press. Page 111. http://iom.nationalacademies. org/Home/Reports/2014/Building-Capacity-to-Reduce-Bullying.aspx.

[195] Id.

[196] National Academies of Sciences, Engineering, and Medicine, (2016) supra.

[197] http://stopbullying.gov.

[198] UNESCO (2019) supra.

[199] Id. at 5.

[200] Twemlow, S.W., Fonagy P., Sacco F., and Brethour J. (2006) Teachers who bully students: a hidden trauma. *Int J Soc Psychiatry.* Vol 52(3) 187-198.

[201] McEvoy (2005) supra.

[202] Id, at 2-3.

[203] Whitted, K., & Dupper, D. (2008). Do Teachers Bully Students?: Findings From a Survey of Students in an Alternative Education Setting. *Education and Urban Society.* 40:3.329-341. Corwin Press, Inc.

[204] Sylvester, R. (2011). *Teacher as Bully: Knowingly or Unintentionally Harming Students. Morality in Education.* The Delta Kappa Gamma Bulletin.

[205] Wilson, K. S. (2006). *Teacher Perceptions of Classroom Management Practices in Public Elementary Schools.* Doctoral Dissertation. University of Southern California.

[206] Ki. S.J. (2015) *Elementary Principal Perspectives of Teacher to Student Bullying Within Classroom Management Practices.* A Dissertation Presented to the Faculty of the USC Rossier School of Education, University of Southern California. https://www.academia.edu/23707742/ Elementary_Principal_Perceptions_of_Teacher_to_Student_Bullying.

[207] McEvoy, A. & Smith, M. (2018) Statistically Speaking: Teacher bullying is a real phenomenon, but it's always been hard to quantify—until now. *Learning for Justice.* https://www.learningforjustice.org/magazine/ spring-2018/statistically-speaking.

[208] The article did not provide the actual numbers. These were provided to me by Dr. McEvoy. Personal communication July 2022.

[209] Datta, P., Cornell, D. & Huang, F. (2017) The Toxicity of Bullying by Teachers and Other School Staff. *School Psychology Review,* Volume 46, No. 4, pp. 335–348.

[210] Greytak, E.A., Kosciw, J.G., Villenas, C. & Giga, N.M. (2016). *From Teasing to Torment: School Climate Revisited, A Survey of US Secondary School Students and Teachers.* New York: GLSEN.

[211] Id.

[212] UNESCO (2021) supra.

[213] Butler, J. (2009) *Unsafe in the Schoolhouse: Abuse of Children with Disabilities.* The Council of Parent Attorneys and Advocates, Inc. http://c.ymcdn.com/sites/www.copaa.org/resource/collection/662B1866-952D-41FA-B7F3-D3CF68639918/UnsafeCOPAAMay_27_2009.pdf.

[214] https://www.wrightslaw.com/info/abuse.school.staff.htm.

[215] Perry, D.M. (2017) *When Teachers Abuse Disabled Students.* Pacific Standard. https://psmag.com/social-justice/ teachers-abusing-disabled-children.

[216] Puhl, R.M., Peterson, J.L. & Luedicke, J. (2013) Weight-Based Victimization: Bullying Experiences of Weight Loss Treatment–Seeking Youth. *Pediatrics* 131:e1-e9.

[217] Mogahed & Chouhoud (2017) supra.

[218] http://supportiveschooldiscipline.org/connect/discipline-disparities.

[219] Gilliam, W.S., Angela N. Maupin, A.N., Reyes, C.R., Maria Accavitti, M., & Shic, F. (2018) *Do Early Educators' Implicit Biases Regarding Sex and Race Relate to Behavior Expectations and Recommendations of Preschool Expulsions and Suspensions?* Yale Child Study Center. https://medicine.yale.edu/childstudy/zigler/publications/ Preschool%20Implicit%20Bias%20Policy%20Brief_final_9_26_276766_5379_v1.pdf.

[220] The Chi-square test of independence was used to determine how witnessing staff maltreatment of students related to student responses to these questions.

[221] Chi-square (3) = 223.94, p<.001.

[222] Chi-square (3) = 241.14, p<.001.

[223] Chi-square (3) = 259.75, p<.001.

[224] Kleinhekse, C.J. & Geisel, R.T. (2019) An Examination of Adult Bullying in the K-12 Workplace: Implications for School Leaders. *School Leadership Review.* Volume 14 Issue 1 Article 7.

[225] https://www.stopbullying.gov.

[226] https://www.stopbullying.gov/prevention/at-school

[227] Hall W. The Effectiveness of Policy Interventions for School Bullying: A Systematic Review. *J Soc Social Work Res.* 2017 Spring;8(1):45-69. doi: 10.1086/690565. Epub 2017 Jan 26. PMID: 28344750; PMCID: PMC5363950.

[228] Id.

[229] Gaffney, H, Ttofti, M.M. & Farrington, D.P. (2021) Effectiveness of school-based programs to reduce bullying perpetration and victimization: An updated systematic review and meta-analysis. *Campbell Systemic Reviews.* https://doi.org/10.1002/cl2.1143

[230] National Academies of Sciences, Engineering, and Medicine. 2016. *Preventing Bullying Through Science, Policy, and Practice.* Washington, DC: The National Academies Press. https://doi.org/10.17226/23482.

[231] Id.

[232] Yeager, D.S., Fong, C.J., Lee, H.Y., & Espelage, D. (2015). Declines in Efficacy of Anti-Bullying Programs Among Older Adolescents: A Developmental Theory and a Three-Level Meta-Analysis. *Journal of Applied Developmental Psychology.* Volume 37, Pages 36–51.

[233] Kärnä, A., Voeten, M., Little, T.D., Alanen, E., Poskiparta, E. & Salmivalli, C. (2013) Effectiveness of the KiVa Antibullying Program: Grades 1–3 and 7–9. *Journal of Educational Psychology,* Vol. 105, No. 2, 535–551 DOI: 10.1037/a0030417535.

[234] Bradshaw, C.P., Sawyer, A.L. & O'Brennan, L.M. (2007) Bullying and Peer Victimization at School: Perceptual Differences Between Students and School Staff. *School Psychology Review,* Volume 36, No. 3, pp. 361-382.

[235] Thomson P. and Gunter H. 2008. Researching bullying with students: a lens on everyday life in an 'innovative school'. *International Journal of Inclusive Education* 12: 185–200.

236 Perkins H.W., Perkins J.M., & Craig D.W. (2014) No safe haven: locations of harassment and bullying victimization in middle youth organizations. *J Sch Health*. 84: 810-818.

237 Bjereld, Y. (2018). The challenging process of disclosing bullying victimisation: A grounded theory study from the victim's point of view. *Journal of Health Psychology*, 23, 1110–1118. doi:10.1177/1359105316644973

238 Rigby, K., & Bagshaw, D. (2006). Using educational drama and bystander training to counteract bullying. In H. McGrath & T. Noble (Eds.), *Bullying solutions: Evidence-based approaches to bullying in Australian schools* (pp. 133–145). Melbourne: Pearson Education.

239 USDOJ NCVS-SCS, supra.

240 Bradshaw, C. P., Sawyer, A. L., & O' Brennan, L. M. (2007). Bullying and peer victimization at school: Perceptual differences between students and school staff. *School Psychology Review*, 36, 361–382; Ging, D., & O'Higgins Norman, J. (2016). Cyberbullying, conflict management or just messing? Teenage girls' understandings and experiences of gender, friendship, and conflict on Facebook in an Irish second-level school. *Feminist Media Studies*, 16, 805–821. doi:10.1080/14680777.2015.1137959

241 MacDonald H & Swart E. (2004). The culture of bullying at a primary school. *Education as Change* 8: 33–55.

242 Garpelin A. (2004). Accepted or rejected in school. *European Educational Research Journal* 3: 729–742.

243 Oliver C, and Candappa M. 2007. Bullying and the politics of 'telling'. *Oxford Review of Education* 33: 71–86.

244 Risanger Sjursø, I., Fandrem, H., O'Higgins Norman, J., & Roland, E. (2019). Teacher authority in long lasting cases of bullying: A qualitative study from Norway and Ireland. *International Journal of Environmental Research and Public Health*, 16, 1163–1171. doi:10.3390/ijerph16071163.

245 Spears, B., Taddeo, C., Ey, L. A., Stretton, A., Carslake, T., Langos, C., & Sundaram, S. (2018). Pre-service teachers' understanding of bullying in Australia and India. Implications for practice. In P. K. Smith, S. Sundaram, B. Spears, C. Blaya, M. Schäfer, & D. Sandhu (Eds.), *Bullying, cyberbullying and pupil well-being in schools: Comparing European, Australian and Indian Perspectives* (pp. 208–236). Cambridge: Cambridge University Press; Ramya, S. G., & Kulkarni, M. L. (2011). Bullying among schoolchildren: Prevalence and association with common symptoms in childhood. *Indian Journal of Pediatrics*, 78, 307–310. doi:10.1007/s12098-010-0219-6.

246 Id.

247 Lai, T., & Kao, G. (2018). Hit, robbed, and put down (but not bullied): underreporting of bullying by minority and male students. *Journal Of Youth and Adolescence*, 47(3), 619-635. https://doi.org/10.1007/s10964-017-0748-7

248 Shaw, T., Campbell, M. A., Eastham, J., Runions, K. C., Salmivalli, C., & Cross, D. (2019). Telling an adult at school about bullying: Subsequent victimization and internalising problems. *Journal of Child and Family Studies*. doi:10.1007/s10826-019-01507-4; Bradshaw et al., supra; Mishna, F., Pepler, D., & Wiener, J. (2006). Factors associated with perceptions and responses to bullying situations by children, parents, teachers and principals. *Victims and Offenders*, 1, 255–258. doi:10.1080/15564880600626163

249 Bradshaw, et. al. (2007) supra.

250 Davis, S. & Nixon, C. (2013) *Youth Voice Project: Student Insights into Bullying and Peer Mistreatment*. Research Press: Illinois; Davis S. and Nixon, C. (2011) *Youth Voice Project, National Data Set*. Youth Voice Project. http://www.youthvoiceproject.com.

251 Fekkes, M., Pijpers, F. I. M., & Verloove-Vanhorick, S. P. (2005). Bullying: Who does what, when and where? Involvement of children, teachers and parents in bullying behavior. *Health Education Research: Theory and Practice*, 20(1),81–91.

252 Rigby, K., & Johnson, K. (2016). *The prevalence and effectiveness of anti-bullying strategies employed in Australian schools*. Adelaide: University of South Australia. https://www.unisa.edu.au/siteassets/episerver-6-files/global/eass/eds/184856-anti-bullying-report-final-3large.pdf

253 Act To Change, et. al. (2021), supra.

254 In the US, Title IX of the Education Amendments of 1972. 20 USC. §§ 1681-1688. Title VI of the Civil Rights Act of 1964. 42 USC. §§ 2000d-2000d-7. Section 504 of the Rehabilitation Act of 1973. 29 USC § 794. The Americans with Disabilities Act of 1990. 42 USC. §§ 12131-12134.

255 Duncan, A. (December 16, 2010) *Key Policy Letters from the Education Secretary and Deputy Secretary. US Department of Education*. https://www2.ed.gov/policy/gen/guid/secletter/101215.html. See also: *Federal Partners in Bullying Prevention. Key Components in State Anti-Bullying Laws*. http://www.stopbullying.gov/laws/key-components/index.html.

256 http://supportiveschooldiscipline.org/connect/discipline-disparities.

257 Cornell, D. & Huang, F.L. (2016) Authoritative School Climate and High School Student Risk Behavior: A Cross-sectional Multi-level Analysis of Student Self-Reports. *Journal of Youth and Adolescence*; Konstantina, K. and Pilos-Dimitris, S. (2010) School Characteristics as Predictors of Bullying Among Greek Middle School Students. *International Journal of Violence and School*, 11 Septembra 2010. 93-113.

258 Yoneyama, S & Naito, A. (2003). Problems with the paradigm: The school as a factor in understanding bullying (with special reference to Japan). *British Journal of Sociology of Education*, 24: 315-330.

259 Swearer, S. M., Espelage, D. L., Love, K. B., & Kingsbury, W. (2008). School-wide approaches to intervention for school aggression and bullying. In B. Doll & J. A. Cummings (Eds.), *Transforming school mental health services* (pp. 187–212). Thousand Oaks, CA: Corwin Press.

260 The Family Educational Rights and Privacy Act (FERPA) contains provisions restricting release of information pertaining to disciplinary actions taken against students. (20 USC. § 1232g; 34 CFR Part 99)

261 This term initially emerged in the context of *Tinker V Des Moines*, 393 US 503, a student free speech case that is discussed in Chapter 9.

262 USDOE, OCR. (2010) *Dear Colleague Letter*. https://www2.ed.gov/about/offices/list/ocr/letters/colleague-201401-title-vi.pdf.

263 USDOJ & USDOE (2015) *Dear Colleague Letter.* https://www2.ed.gov/about/offices/list/ocr/letters/colleague-201401-title-vi.htm; USDOE (2015), *Rethink School Discipline: School District Leader Summit on Improving School Climate and Discipline, Resource Guide for Superintendent Action,* Washington, D.C. http://www.ed.gov/school-discipline.

264 Id.; See also, American Psychological Association (APA) Zero Tolerance Task Force. (2008) Are Zero Tolerance Policies Effective in the Schools? An Evidentiary Review and Recommendations. *American Psychologist*

265 USDOE, OCR. (2010) *Dear Colleague Letter.* https://www2.ed.gov/about/offices/list/ocr/letters/colleague-201812.pdf,

266 Pub.L. 114–95; https://www.ed.gov/essa?src=rn.

267 Section 1111. "State Plans"

268 Section 1112. "Local Educational Agency Plans.

269 http://www.p12.nysed.gov/dignityact/.

270 https://www.osc.state.ny.us/press/releases/2017/10/some-ny-schools-not-reporting-bullying-or-harassment

271 https://ag.ny.gov/press-release/2016/ag-schneiderman-and-state-education-commissioner-elia-release-guidance-and-model.

272 Youth Risk Behavior data for New York state. https://nccd.cdc.gov/youthonline/app/Results.aspx?LID=NY.

273 https://vtdigger.org/2018/05/06/data-indicates-schools-may-underreporting-bullying/.

274 http://www.sun-sentinel.com/news/education/fl-bullying-statistics-20161230-story.html.

275 https://www.theindychannel.com/longform/despite-law-indiana-schools-are-misreporting-their-bullying-data-call-6-investigation-finds.

276 For example: https://locker.txssc.txstate.edu/3942be0c6bbe569ed1417377e6c1d2a9/Bullying-Checklist-BW.pdf.

277 ESEA section 1111(h)(1) and (h)(2)).

278 https://ocrdata.ed.gov/profile/9/district/31194/harassment/reportedallegationsofharassmentorbullying; https://ocrdata.ed.gov/profile/9/district/31194/harassment/studentsdisciplinedforharassmentorbullying.

279 https://ocrdata.ed.gov/profile/9/district/30388/harassment/reportedallegationsofharassmentorbullying; https://ocrdata.ed.gov/profile/9/district/30388/harassment/studentsdisciplinedforharassmentorbullying.

280 US Departments of Education and Justice, (2014) *Supportive School Discipline Initiative, School Discipline Guidance Package.* http://www2.ed.gov/policy/gen/guid/ school-discipline/index.html?exp=1. Helpful references on this include https://www.schoolcounselor.org/asca/media/asca/PositionStatements/PS_Discipline.pdf.

281 https://www.pbis.org

282 Individuals with Disabilities Act (IDEA. 20 USC. § 1400 et seq.

283 McIntosh, K., Filter, K. J., Bennett, J., Ryan, C., & Sugai, G. (2010). Principles of sustainable prevention: Designing scale-up of school-wide positive behavior support to promote durable systems. *Psychology in the Schools,* 47, 5-21.

284 PBISApps (2018) *Motive, Motivate, Motivation: Why Are My Students Doing That?!* https://www.pbisapps.org/community/Pages/Motivation-of-Problem-Behavior.aspx.

285 Pollastri, A.R, Epstein, L.D., Heath, G.H. & Ablon, J.S. (2013) The Collaborative Problem Solving Approach: Outcomes Across Settings. *Harvard Review of Psychology.* Volume 21, Number 4 at 189.

286 Cohen, J., Espelage, D., Twemlow, S. W, Berkowitz, M. W. & Comer, J. P. (2015) Rethinking Effective Bully and Violence Prevention Efforts: Promoting Healthy School Climates, Positive Youth Development, and Preventing Bully-Victim-Bystander Behavior. *International Journal of Violence and Schools.*

287 287 Pollastri, et. al., supra.

288 Deci E.L. Koestner R, & Ryan R.M. .(1999) Effects of reward on intrinsic motivation—negative, neutral and positive. *Psychol Bull.*

289 Yale Center for Teaching and Learning. (undated) *Awareness of Implicit Biases.* https://ctl.yale.edu/ImplicitBiasAwareness.

290 The author also bases this statement on witnessing this in action time and time again in schools in the University of Oregon region, where her children attended schools and where she has been a substitute teacher.

291 Simmons, Rachel (2002). *Odd Girl Out: The Hidden Culture of Aggression in Girls.* New York, New York: Mariner Books; McGrath, Mary Zabolio (2006). *School Bullying: Tools for Avoiding Harm and Liability.* Thousand Oaks, Calif: Corwin Press; Marion K. Underwood (2003). *Social Aggression among Girls* (Guilford Series On Social And Emotional Development). New York: The Guilford Press.

292 Steinberg, L. (2008). *Adolescence, 8th ed.* 101. New York, NY: McGraw-Hill.

293 PBIS (2020) *Ditch the Clip! Why Clip Charts Are Not a PBIS Practice and What to Do Instead.* https://www.pbis.org/resource/ditch-the-clip-why-clip-charts-are-not-a-pbis-practice-and-what-to-do-instead

294 These are situations I became aware of: 1. A 3rd grade student who in my assessment had mild autism had significant challenges in his classroom. Two girls, who always got reward tickets, had discovered that they could pick on him at recess until he blew up. He would then get in trouble. They had great fun with this. Whenever this student tried to explain what was happening, the principal indicated that he did not believe him. 2. A girl in middle school, who had ADHD, tried very hard to stay focused and do her work. Her grades were lower. This school always took their PRIDE students on incredible field trips once a term. To go on these trips students had to have no absences, no incident reports, and decent grades. If one went to the school on a day when the PRIDE students were away it was quite clearly evident that the non-PRIDE students were those of lower income, students of color, and students with disabilities. This girl was bullied throughout middle school—by the students who always got to go on the field trips. 3. I was at a school board meeting at Springfield Public Schools. A middle school principal was making a presentation. Much of what this school was doing was great. But after the principal described the behavior management plan, he turned to the student members of the school choir and asked them, "How many of you are in the green zone?" Most of the students gleefully raised their hands. The audience applauded. My jaw dropped. This school had clearly created a PBIS caste system. How are these "green zone" students treating the "yellow zone" and "red zone" students in their school? Note that SPS has a rate of student reported bullying that is higher than the state level. 4. Once I spoke at a small parent gathering about the concerns of PBIS. A mom told me her daughter's school gave all of the compliant students "Self Manager" buttons. I suggested some concerns about this approach. This woman's daughter was close by—and apparently listening. The next day she told her mom that she was going to give her "Self Manager" button back. She said, "This is discriminatory (not a term I had used). I really hate seeing the faces of the students who did not get these buttons at the awards ceremony." I concluded that this 8 year old girl was vastly more intelligent than her principal and the UO PBIS consultants who were working with the district. However, her principal did get rid of the Self Manager buttons approach the following school year.

295 Sugai, G., & Horner, R. H. (2009). Defining and describing schoolwide positive behavior support. In W. Sailor, G. Dunlop, G. Sugai, & R. Horner (Eds.), *Handbook of positive behavior support* (pp. 307–326). Springer Publishing Company. https://doi.org/10.1007/978-0-387-09632-2_13.

296 https://www.iirp.edu.

297 https://www.wested.org/resources/restorative-justice-in-u-s-schools-an-updated-research-review/.

298 Id.; Fronius, T., Persson, H., Guckenburg, S., Hurley, N., Petrosino, A. (2016) *Restorative Justice in US Schools: A Research Review.* WestEd. https://www.wested.org/resources/restorative-justice-research-review/

299 Wong, D. S. W., Cheng, C. H. K., Ngan, R. M. H., & Ma, S. K. (2011). Program effectiveness of a Restorative Whole-school Approach for tackling school bullying in Hong Kong. *International Journal of Offender Therapy and Comparative Criminology,* 55(6), 846–862.

300 StopBullying.gov. *Misdirections in Bullying Prevention and Intervention.* https://www.stopbullying.gov/sites/default/files/2017-10/misdirections-in-prevention.pdf.

301 Ttofi, M. M., & Farrington, D. P. (2011). Effectiveness of school-based programs to reduce bullying: A systematic and meta-analytic review. *Journal of Experimental Criminology,* 7, 27–56. doi:10.1007/s11292-010-9109-1

302 Amstutz, L. S., & Mullet, J. H. (2005). *The little book of restorative discipline for schools: Teaching responsibility, creating caring climates.* Intercourse, PA: Good Books.

303 Dreikurs, R. & Grey, L. (1968). *Logical Consequences: A New Approach to Discipline.* Meredith Press Dreikurs, R. & Stolz, V. (1964). Children: The Challenge. New York: Meridith Press.

304 Zehr, H. (2005) *Changing Lenses – A New Focus for Crime and Justice.* Scottdale PA: 268–69.

305 Id., at 268–69.

306 Smith, C.P. & Freyd, J.J. (2014). Institutional betrayal. *American Psychologist,* 69, 575-587.

307 Smith, C. P., & Freyd, J.J. (2017). Insult, then injury: Interpersonal and institutional betrayal linked to health and dissociation. *Journal of Aggression, Maltreatment, & Trauma,* 26, 1117-1131https://dynamic.uoregon.edu/jjf/institutionalbetrayal/ibq.html.

308 https://dynamic.uoregon.edu/jjf/defineDARVO.html.

309 Swearer, S. M., & Espelage, D. L. (2011). Expanding the Social-Ecological Framework of bullying among youth: Lessons learned from the past and directions for the future. In D. L. Espelage & S. M. Swearer (Eds.), *Bullying in North American Schools* (pp. 3–9). New York: Routledge; Thornberg, R. (2015). The social dynamics of school bullying: The necessary dialogue between the blind men around the elephant and the possible meeting point at the social-ecological square. *Confero: Essays on Education, Philosophy and Politics,* 3, 161–203.

310 Lee, J. (2011). *President Obama & the First Lady at the White House Conference on Bullying Prevention.* https://obamawhitehouse.archives.gov/blog/2011/03/10/president-obama-first-lady-white-house-conference-bullying-prevention.

311 UNESCO (2019), supra.

312 Cowan, K. C., Vaillancourt, K., Rossen, E., & Pollitt, K. (2013). *A Framework for Safe and Successful Schools.* Bethesda, MD: National Association of School Psychologists. Participants included: National Association of Elementary School Principals, American School Counselors Association, National Association of School Resource Officers, National Association of Secondary School Principals, and School Social Work Association of America.

313 Id., at 1.

314 Id., at 1.

315 Id, at 12.

316 Section 8101(21)(A) of the ESEA.

317 USDOE (2016) *Non-Regulatory Guidance: Using Evidence to Strengthen Education Investments.* https://www2.ed.gov/policy/elsec/leg/essa/guidanceuseseinvestment.pdf.

[318] West, M. R. (2016) *From evidence-based programs to an evidence-based system: Opportunities under the Every Student Succeeds Act.* Brookings Institute. https://www.brookings.edu/research/from-evidence-based-programs-to-an-evidence-based-system-opportunities-under-the-every-student-succeeds-act/.

[319] Id. (Emphasis added.)

[320] Safe and Drug-Free Schools and Communities Act (SDFSCA) Title IV, Part A, Subpart 1, Elementary and Secondary Education Act, as amended by the No Child Left Behind Act of 2001 Section 4155(a)(1).

[321] §4115(a)(3) WAIVER-A local educational agency may apply to the State for a waiver of the scientifically based requirement to allow innovative activities or programs that demonstrate substantial Likelihood of Success. §4115(a)(1)(C)- Programs or activities funded under Title IVA (SDFSC) must be based on scientifically based research that provides evidence that the program to be used will reduce violence and illegal drug use. §4114(d)(8)-A waiver request will be available for public review.

[322] Id.

[323] Panorama: https://www.panoramaed.com. Specifically this page provides insight on teacher use of student data: https://academy.panoramaed.com/article/645-sharing-sel-survey-data-with-students

[324] Thornberg, R., Wänström, L., & Jungert, T. (2018). Authoritative classroom climate and its relations to bullying victimization and bystander behaviors. *School Psychology International,* 39(6), 663–680. https://doi.org/10.1177/0143034318809762.

[325] Baumrind, D. (1971). Current patterns of parental authority. *Developmental Psychology Monographs,* 4, 1–103. doi:10.1037/h0030372.

[326] Gregory, A., & Weinstein, R. S. (2004). Connection and regulation at home and in school: Predicting growth in achievement for adolescents. *Journal of Adolescent Research,* 19, 405–427.

[327] Gregory, A., Cornell, D., Fan, X., Sheras, P., Shih, T.-H., & Huang, F. (2010). Authoritative school discipline: High school practices associated with lower bullying and victimization. *Journal of Educational Psychology,* 102(2), 483–496. doi:10.1037/a0018562; Gregory, A., & Cornell, D. (2009). "Tolerating" adolescent needs: Moving away from zero tolerance policies in high school. *Theory into Practice,* 48, 106–113; Green, V.A. (2021) The Role of Teachers. *Wiley Blackwell Handbook of Bullying: A Comprehensive and International Review of Research and Intervention.* Wiley Blackwell.

[328] Wubbels, T., Brekelmans, J. M. G., den Brok, P. J., & van Tartwijk, J. W. F. (2006). An international perspective on classroom management in secondary classrooms in the Netherlands. In C. Evertson & C. S. Weinstein (Eds.), *Handbook of classroom management: Research, practice and contemporary issues* (pp. 1161–1191). New York: Lawrence Erlbaum.

[329] Harber, C. (2015). Violence in schools: The role of authoritarian learning. In D. Scott & E. Hargreaves (Eds.) *The Sage Handbook of Learning* (pp. 243–253). Thousand Oaks, CA: Sage.

[330] Green (2021) supra.

[331] Gregory, et. al. (2010) supra.

[332] https://education.virginia.edu/sites/default/files/images/YVP Authoritative%20School%20Climate%20Survey%20Research%20Summary%2010-13-19.pdf.

[333] Cornell, D. (2016) *School Climate and Bullying.* https://www.bu.edu/bullying/files/2015/06/School-Climate-and-Bullying.pdf

[334] Anda, R.F.,Butchart, A., Felitti, V.J., & Brown, D.W. (2010). Building a Framework for Global Surveillance of the Public Health Implications of Adverse Childhood Experiences. *American Journal of Preventive Medicine,* 39(1): 93–98; Tishelman, A.C., Haney, P., Greenwald O'Brien, J. & Blaustein, M. (2010). A framework for schoolbased psychological evaluations: Utilizing a 'trauma lens.' *Journal of Child and Adolescent Trauma,* 3(4): 279-302; Helping Traumatized Children Learn – Volume 2; Fairbank, J.A. (2008). Epidemiology of Trauma and Trauma Related Disorders in Children and Youth. *PTSD Research Quarterly,* 19(1): 1-8.

[335] Idsoe, T., Dyregrov, A. & Idsoe, E.C. (2012) Bullying and PTSD Symptoms. *Child Psychol* 40:901– 911. http://www.uis.no/news/being- bullied-can-cause-trauma-symptoms-article62673-8865.html; See also, Penning, S., Bhagwanjee, L., Anil, & Kaymarlin, G. (2010). Bullying boys: the traumatic effects of bullying in male adolescent learners. *Journal of Child and Adolescent Mental Health,* 22(2), 131-143; Vaillancourt, T., Hymel, S., & McDougall, P., (2013). The biological underpinnings of peer victimization: Understanding why and how the effects of bullying can last a lifetime. *Theory into Practice,* 52, 241-248.

336 Guarino, K. & Chagnon, E. (2018). *Trauma-sensitive schools training package.* Washington, DC: National Center on Safe Supportive Learning Environments. https://safesupportivelearning.ed.gov/trauma-sensitive-schools-training-package This resource provides four training programs. These training packages support school and district administrators and staff to do the following: Understand trauma in a broad and inclusive way. Recognize the effects of trauma on students, families, school administrators and staff, and communities. Learn a process for implementing a schoolwide trauma-sensitive approach. Integrate trauma-sensitive practices into their daily operations. The *Building Trauma-Sensitive Schools Handout Packet* provides insight into implementing these seven core practices Building Trauma-Sensitive Schools Handout Packet: *Handout 2 Pages 2-6.* https://safesupportivelearning.ed.gov/sites/default/files/TSS_Building_Handout_Packet_ALL.pdf.: 1. Understand trauma and its impact. In a trauma-sensitive school, all staff share a common understanding of trauma and its impact on students, families, and staff and a joint mission to create learning environments that acknowledge and address the effects of trauma on school success. 2. Believe that healing happens in relationships. Trauma-sensitive schools believe that establishing safe, authentic, and positive relationships can be corrective and restorative to survivors of trauma and can be resilience-building for all. This principle encompasses relationships among and between school staff, students, and families. 3. Ensure emotional and physical safety. Trauma-sensitive schools are committed to establishing a safe physical and emotional learning environment where basic needs are met; safety measures are in place; and staff responses are consistent, predictable, and respectful. 4. View students holistically. Schools invested in taking a trauma-sensitive approach understand the interrelated nature of emotional and physical health and academic success and the need to view students holistically and build skills in all areas. 5. Support choice, control, and empowerment for students, staff, and families. Trauma-sensitive schools operate in a way that supports choice, control, and empowerment for students, families, and staff and empowers all by building skills that enhance sense of mastery. 6. Strive for cultural competence. Trauma-sensitive schools strive for cultural competence by acknowledging and respecting diversity within the school; considering the relationship between culture, traumatic experiences, safety, healing, and resilience; and using approaches that align with the cultural and linguistic backgrounds of students, families, and the broader community. 7. Use a collaborative approach. Trauma-sensitive schools use a collaborative approach with students, families, and staff. This approach includes sharing power and decision making across all levels of the school and seeing students and families as partners.

337 Cole, S.F., Jessica Greenwald O'Brien, J.G., Gadd, M.G., Ristuccia,J., Wallace, D.L. & Gregory, M. (2009) *Helping Traumatized Children Learn: Supportive school environments. for children traumatized by family violence.* Massachusetts Advocates for Children. Trauma and Learning Policy Initiative. https://traumasensitiveschools.org/trauma-and-learning/the-solution-trauma-sensitive-schools/ The Trauma and Learning Policy Initiative provides this guidance on the core attributes of a trauma sensitive school: Share an understanding of how trauma impacts learning and why a school-wide approach is needed for creating a trauma-sensitive school. Support all students to feel safe—physically, socially, emotionally and academically. Address students' needs in holistic ways, taking into account their relationships, self-regulation, academic competence, and physical and emotional well-being explicitly connect students to the school community, providing them with multiple opportunities to practice newly developing skills. Embrace teamwork with a sense of a shared responsibility for every student. Anticipate and adapt to the ever-changing needs of students and the surrounding community.

[338] NCTSN (2017) *National Child Traumatic Stress Network, Schools Committee. Creating, supporting, and sustaining trauma-informed schools: A system framework.* Los Angeles, CA, and Durham, NC: National Center for Child Traumatic Stress. https://www.nctsn.org/sites/default/files/resources//creating_supporting_sustaining_trauma_informed_schools_a_systems_framework.pdf indicates the following approaches defines all trauma-informed child- and family-service systems as: "(O)ne in which all parties involved recognize and respond to the impact of traumatic stress on those who have contact with the system including children, caregivers, staff, and service providers. Programs and agencies within such a system infuse and sustain trauma awareness, knowledge, and skills into their organizational cultures, practices, and policies. They act in collaboration with all those who are involved with the child, using the best available science, to maximize physical and psychological safety, facilitate the recovery or adjustment of the child and family, and support their ability to thrive. SAMHSA's Concept of Trauma and Guidance for a Trauma-Informed Approach notes that the need to address trauma is increasingly viewed as an important component of effective behavioral health service delivery and that with appropriate supports and intervention, people can overcome traumatic experiences. NCTSM indicates that trauma-informed approaches within any system should aim to adhere to the "4 Rs:" Realizing the widespread impact of trauma and pathways to recovery. Recognizing traumas signs and symptoms. Responding by integrating knowledge about trauma into all facets of the system. Resisting re-traumatization of trauma-impacted individuals by decreasing the occurrence of unnecessary triggers (i.e., trauma and loss reminders) and by implementing trauma-informed policies, procedures, and practices. NCTSM's recommended core areas of focus for trauma informed schools include these activities: Identifying and Assessing Traumatic Stress. Addressing and Treating Traumatic Stress. Trauma Education and Awareness. Partnerships with Students and Families. Creating a Trauma-Informed Learning Environment. Cultural Responsiveness. Emergency Management/Crisis Response. Staff Self-Care and Secondary Traumatic Stress. School Discipline Policies and Practices. Cross System Collaboration and Community Partnerships. In this excellent document, each of these Core Areas receive further elaboration. NCTSN recommends addressing bullying concerns. The most significant and helpful reference is this: Teaching Social Skills. The school provides training for staff and curriculum implementation for students on creating, sustaining, and promoting a positive and safe learning environment. Content includes conflict resolution, problem-solving skills, social communication, emotional/behavioral literacy, bullying prevention, and suicide prevention. The school recognizes that unhealthy social conflict between peers can have serious developmental consequences and negatively impact the mental health of all youth involved. Consequently, the school proactively addresses bullying/cyberbullying by educating staff, students, and families in bullying awareness, relevant social skills (empathy, friendship, assertiveness) and effective response and repair strategies. Providing targeted supports for youth at risk of displaying behaviors that adversely impact the psychological and physical safety of others is an important supplement to universal supports.

[339] Substance Abuse and Mental Health Services Administration. (2014) *Concept of Trauma and Guidance for a Trauma-Informed Approach.* HHS Publication No. (SMA) 14-4884. Rockville, MD: Substance Abuse and Mental Health Services Administration. https://ncsacw.samhsa.gov/userfiles/files/SAMHSA_Trauma.pdf.. SAMHSA's key assumptions and principles are framed with this understanding: A program, organization, or system that is trauma-informed realizes the widespread impact of trauma and understands potential paths for recovery; recognizes the signs and symptoms of trauma in clients, families, staff, and others involved with the system; and responds by fully integrating knowledge about trauma into policies, procedures, and practices, and seeks to actively resist re-traumatization. SAMHSA's six key principles fundamental to a trauma-informed approach include: 1. Safety: Throughout the organization, staff and the people they serve, whether children or adults, feel physically and psychologically safe; the physical setting is safe and interpersonal interactions promote a sense of safety. Understanding safety as defined by those served is a high priority. 2. Trustworthiness and Transparency: Organizational operations and decisions are conducted with transparency with the goal of building and maintaining trust with clients and family members, among staff, and others involved in the organization. 3. Peer Support: Peer support and mutual self-help are key vehicles for establishing safety and hope, building trust, enhancing collaboration, and utilizing their stories and lived experience to promote recovery and healing. The term "Peers" refers to individuals with lived experiences of trauma, or in the case of children this may be family members of children who have experienced traumatic events and are key caregivers in their recovery. Peers have also been referred to as "trauma survivors." 4. Collaboration and Mutuality: Importance is placed on partnering and the leveling of power differences between staff and clients and among organizational staff from clerical and housekeeping personnel, to professional staff to administrators, demonstrating that healing happens in relationships and in the meaningful sharing of power and decision-making. The organization recognizes that everyone has a role to play in a trauma-informed approach. As one expert stated: "one does not have to be a therapist to be therapeutic." 5. Empowerment, Voice and Choice: Throughout the organization and among the clients served, individuals' strengths and experiences are recognized and built upon. The organization fosters a belief in the primacy of the people served, in resilience, and in the ability of individuals, organizations, and communities to heal and promote recovery from trauma. The organization understands that the experience of trauma maybe a unifying aspect in the lives of those who run the organization, who provide the services, and/or who come to the organization for assistance and support. As such, operations, workforce development and services are organized to foster empowerment for staff and clients alike. Organizations understand the importance of power differentials and ways in which clients, historically, have been diminished in voice and choice and are often recipients of coercive treatment. Clients are supported in shared decision-making, choice, and goal setting to determine the plan of action they need to heal and move forward. They are supported in cultivating self-advocacy skills. Staff are facilitators of recovery rather than controllers of recovery.34 Staff are empowered to do their work as well as possible by adequate organizational support. This is a parallel process as staff need to feel safe, as much as people receiving services. 6. Cultural, Historical, and Gender Issues: The organization actively moves past cultural stereotypes and biases (e.g. based on race, ethnicity, sexual orientation, age, religion, gender- identity, geography, etc.); offers, access to gender responsive services; leverages the healing value of traditional cultural connections; incorporates policies, protocols, and processes that are responsive to the racial, ethnic and cultural needs of individuals served; and recognizes and addresses historical trauma. (Unfortunately, as excellent as the SAMHSA resources are, the term "bullying" does not occur within the document.)

[340] Goetz, J.L., Keltner, D. & Simon-Thomas, E. (2010) Compassion: An Evolutionary Analysis and Empirical Review. *Psychol. Bull.* 136(6):351-374. https://www.ncbi.nlm.nih.gov/pmc/articles/PMC2864937/#%21po=9.74026.

[341] Ryan, R. M. & Deci, E. L. (Eds.), (2002). Self-determination theory and the facilitation of intrinsic motivation, social development, and well-being. *American Psychologist,* 55, 68-78; http://selfdeterminationtheory.org/.

[342] Deci, E. L., Koestner, R., & Ryan, R. M. (1999). A meta-analytic review of experiments examining the effects of extrinsic rewards on intrinsic motivation. *Psychological Bulletin,* 125(6), 627–668. https://doi.org/10.1037/0033-2909.125.6.627; http://selfdeterminationtheory.org

[343] Id, at 68.

[344] Fletcher, A. (2005) *Meaningful Student Involvement Meaningful Student Involvement Guide to Students as Partners in School Change.* Soundout.org. Page 5. https://soundout.org/wp-content/uploads/2015/06/MSIGuide.pdf.

[345] https://soundout.org/.

[346] https://www.wested.org/resources/speak-out-listen-up-tools-for-using-student-perspectives-and-local-data-for-school-improvement/.

[347] Qualgia, R.J. & Corso, M.J. (2014) *Student Voice: The Instrument of Change.* Corwin Press.

[348] https://www.gse.harvard.edu/news/uk/16/08/giving-students-voice.

[349] https://www.stuvoice.org/.

[350] Maner, J. K., & Case, C. R. (2016). Dominance and prestige: Dual strategies for navigating social hierarchies. In J. M. Olson & M. P. Zanna (Eds.), *Advances in experimental social psychology* (pp. 129–180). Elsevier Academic Press; Cheng, J. T., Tracy, J. L., Foulsham, T., Kingstone, A., & Henrich, J. (2013). Two ways to the top: Evidence that dominance and prestige are distinct yet viable avenues to social rank and influence. *Journal of Personality and Social Psychology,* 104, 103-125.

[351] Henrich, J., & Gil-White, F. J. (2001). The evolution of prestige: Freely conferred deference as a mechanism for enhancing the benefits of cultural transmission. *Evolution and Human Behavior,* 22, 165–196.

[352] Maner & Case (2016) supra.

[353] Id.

[354] Id. at 163.

355 Id.

356 356 Van Vugt, M. (2006). Evolutionary origins of leadership and followership. *Personality and Social Psychology Review*, 10, 354–371.

357 https://www.nationalgeographic.co.uk/animals/2020/10/how-animals-choose-their-leaders-from-brute-force-to-democracy.

358 Maner & Case (2016) supra; Cheng, J. T., Tracy, J. L., & Henrich, J. (2010). Pride, personality, and the evolutionary foundations of human social status. *Evolution and Human Behavior*, 31, 334-347

359 Chang et. al. (2013) supra.

360 Id.; Maner and Case (2016) supra

361 Weidman A.C., Cheng J.T., Tracy J.L. (2016) The psychological structure of humility. *J Pers Soc Psychol.* 2018 Jan;114(1):153-178. doi: 10.1037/pspp0000112..

362 Cheng, et. al. (2010) supra.

363 Nery, M. Ventura, C. & Stirling, A. (2021) Bullying in Sports. *Wiley Blackwell Handbook of Bullying: A Comprehensive and International Review of Research and Intervention.* Wiley-Blackwell; Evans, B., Adler, A., MacDonald, D., & Côté, J. (2016). Bullying victimization and perpetration among adolescent sport teammates. *Pediatric Exercise Science*, 28, 296–303. doi:10.1123/pes.2015-0088.

364 MacDonald, C. A. (2014). Masculinity and sport revisited. A review of literature of hegemonic masculinity and men´s Ice Hockey in Canada. *Canadian Graduate Journal of Sociology and Criminology*, 3(1), 95–112; Chalabaev, A., Sarrazin, P., Fontayne, P., Boiché, J., & Clément-Guillotin, C. (2013). The influence of gender stereotypes and gender roles on participation and performance in sport and exercise: Review and future directions. *Psychology of Sport and Exercise*, 14, 136–144. doi:10.1016/j.psychsport.2012.10.005

365 Volk, A., & Lagzdins, L. (2009). Bullying and victimization among adolescent girl athletes. *Athletic Insight*, 1(1), 15–25.

366 Nery, et.al. (2021) supra.

367 Stirling, A. E., Bridges, E., Cruz, L., & Mountjoy, M. (2011). Canadian Academy of Sport and Exercise Medicine position paper: Abuse, harassment and bullying in sport. *Clinical Journal of Sport Medicine*, 21, 385–391.

368 Nery, et. al. (2021) supra; Evans, B., Adler, A., MacDonald, D., & Côté, J. (2016). Bullying victimization and perpetration among adolescent sport teammates. *Pediatric Exercise Science*, 28, 296–303. doi:10.1123/pes.2015-0088

369 Mendez-Baldwin, M., Fontaine A., & Consiglio, J. (2017) An Examination of High School Athletes' Attitudes about Bullying and Hazing. *Journal of Bullying and Social Aggression,* Volume 2, Number 2

370 Id.

371 Id.

372 Thornburg, et. al. (2018) supra; Cornell, D., & Shukla, K. (2018). Bullying and school climate in the United States and India. In P. K. Smith, S. Sundaram, B. Spears, C. Blaya, M. Schafer, & D. Sandhu (Eds.), *Bullying, cyberbullying and student well-being in schools: Comparing European, Australian and Indian perspectives* (pp. 336–351). Cambridge: Cambridge University Press.

373 Fisher, L. A., & Dzikus, L. (2017). Bullying in sport and performance psychology. *Oxford Research Encyclopedia of Psychology*, 1–24. doi:10.1093/acrefore/9780190236557.013.169

374 Nery, et.al., supra (2021).

375 US Center for SafeSport. (2019) *Preventing Bullying What Great Coaches Need to Know.* https://uscenterforsafesport.org/wp-content/uploads/2019/11/US-Center-for-SafeSport-Preventing-Bullying-What-Great-Coaches-Need-to-Know.pdf

376 https://itgetsbetter.org/get-help/.

377 Dweck, C. S. (2006). *Mindset: The new psychology of success.* New York: Random House.

378 Mueller, C. M. & Dweck, C. S. (1998). Intelligence praise can undermine motivation and performance. *Journal of Personality and Social Psychology*, 75, 33–52. See also, Kamins, M., & Dweck, C. S. (1999). Person vs. process praise and criticism: Implications for contingent self-worth and coping. *Developmental Psychology*, 35, 835–847; Yousefi, H., & Khalkhali, V. (2020). The Effects of Mastery Versus Social-Comparison Praise on Students' Persistence: A Role of Fixed Versus Growth Mindset. *Education Sciences & Psychology*, 55(1), 3–9.

379 Yeager, D.S., Trzesniewski, K.H. and Dweck, C.S. (2013) An Implicit Theories of Personality Intervention Reduces Adolescent Aggression in Response to Victimization and Exclusion. *Child Development*, Volume 84, Number 3, pp 970-988.

380 Id. at 970.

381 Id.

382 https://www.mindsetworks.com.

383 Positive Psychology Center at the University of Pennsylvania. http://www.ppc.sas.upenn.edu/.

384 Greater Good Science Center at UC Berkley. https://greatergood.berkeley.edu/.

385 Center on the Developing Child at Harvard University. https://developingchild.harvard.edu/science/key-concepts/

386 Id. See also. Bethell, C.D., Newacheck,P. Hawes, E. and Halfon, N (2014) Adverse Childhood Experiences: Assessing The Impact On Health And Youth Organization Engagement And The Mitigating Role Of Resilience. *Health Affairs*, 33, no.12 :2106-2115.

387 Seeley, K., Tombari, M., Bennett, L.J. & Dunkle, J.B. (2009) *Peer Victimization in Schools: A Set of Quantitative and Qualitative Studies of the Connections Among Peer Victimization, School Engagement, Truancy, School Achievement, and Other Outcomes.* National Center for School Engagement. https://www.ncjrs.gov/app/ publications/abstract.aspx?ID=256074.

388 Hinduja, S. & Patchin, J. (2017) Cultivating youth resilience to prevent bullying and cyberbullying victimization. *Child Abuse & Neglect.* Nov. 73:51-62.

389 https://greatergood.berkeley.edu/.
390 Peterson, C. & Seligman, M.E.P. (2004) *Character Strengths and Virtues: A Handbook and Classification*. New York: Oxford University Press and Washington, DC: American Psychological Association. More information here: https://www.viacharacter.org/character-strengths-and-virtues.
391 https://www.viacharacter.org/research/findings/selection-of-full-text-articles
392 http://viacharacter.org.
393 Palmer, S.B., Mulvey, K.L. & Rutland, A. (2021) Developmental Differences in Evaluations of, and Reactions to, Bullying Among Children and Adolescents: A Social Reasoning Developmental Approach. *Wiley Blackwell Handbook of Bullying: A Comprehensive and International Review of Research and Intervention*. Wiley Blackwell.
394 Salmivalli, C. & Voeten, M. (2004). Connections between attitudes, group norms, and behaviors associated with bullying in schools. *International Journal of Behavioral Development*, 28, 246–258. doi:10.1111/1467-9450.00040
395 Berkowitz, A.D. (2010) Fostering Healthy Norms to Prevent Violence and Abuse: The Social Norms Approach. In Kaufman, K. Ed, *The Prevention of Sexual Violence: A Practitioner's Sourcebook*. NEARI Press.
396 National Social Norms Center http://socialnorms.org/.
397 Perkins, H.W. , Craig, D.W. & Perkins. J.M. 2011. Using Social Norms to Reduce Bullying: A Research Intervention in Five Middle Youth Organizations. *Group Processes and Intergroup Relations*, Vol. 14, No. 5, pp. 703-722. DOI: 10.1177/1368430210398004; http://www.youthhealthsafety.org/bullying.htm.
398 Gini, G. Pozzoli, T, Jenkins, L. & Demaray, M. (2021) Participant Roles in Bullying. *Wiley Blackwell Handbook of Bullying: A Comprehensive and International Review of Research and Intervention*. Wiley Blackwell; Pozzoli, T. and Gini, G. (2010) Active defending and passive bystanding behavior in bullying: the role of personal characteristics and perceived peer pressure, *Journal of Abnormal Child Psychology*, Aug; 38(6):815-27; Rigby, K., and Johnson, B. (2006). Expressed readiness of Australian youth organization children to act as bystanders in support of children who are being bullied. *Educational Psychology*, 26, 425-440; Salmivalli (2010) supra.
399 Berkowitz (2010) supra.
400 Id. page 3.
401 Perkins, J.M., Perkins, H.W. & Craig, D.W. (2020) Norms and Attitudes about Being an Active Bystander: Support for Telling Adults about Seeing Knives or Guns at School among Greater London Youth. *J Youth Adolescence*, 49, 849–868. https://doi.org/10.1007/s10964-019-01127-7.
402 Pöyhönen, V., Juvonen, J., and Salmivalli, C. (2010). What does it take to stand up for the victim of bullying? The interplay between personal and social factors. *Merrill-Palmer Quarterly*, Vol. 56: Iss. 2, Article 4.
403 Schleicher, A. (2019) PISA 2018, supra.
404 Cialdini, R.B. (2006) *Influence: The Psychology of Persuasion: Revised Edition*. Harper Business
405 Katz, N. & McNulty, K. (1994) *Reflective Listening*. https://www.maxwell.syr.edu/docs/default-source/ektron-files/reflective-listening-nk.pdf?sfvrsn=f1fa6672_5.
406 Id. at 1.
407 Id. at 2.
408 Yeager, D.S., Fong, C.J., Lee, H.Y., & Espelage, D. (2015). Declines in Efficacy of Anti-Bullying Programs Among Older Adolescents: A Developmental Theory and a Three-Level Meta-Analysis. *Journal of Applied Developmental Psychology*. Volume 37, Pages 36–51.
409 Id., citations omitted.
410 This following section on the teen brain was initially written in a book for teens, where I decided not to use citations. There are many articles online that discuss the teen brain. I pulled from many of them. I will not cite each point in this chapter. These are three very excellent resources: Steinberg, L. (2015) *Age Of Opportunity: Lessons from the New Science of Adolescence*. Harper Paperbacks; Armstrong, T. (2016) *The Power of the Adolescent Brain: Strategies for Teaching Middle and High School Students*. Alexandria, VA: ASCD; Jensen, F.E. & Nutt, A.E. (2015) *The Teenage Brain: A Neuroscientist's Survival Guide to Raising Adolescents and Young Adults*. Harper.
411 As I indicated earlier, this following section on the teen brain was initially written in my book for teens, where I decided not to use citations. There are many articles online that discuss the teen brain. I pulled from many of them. I will not cite individual point in this section.
412 Erikson, E.H. (1968) *Youth, Identity and Crisis*. Norton, New York.
413 Schwartz, S. J., Beyers, W., Luyckx, K., Soenens, B., Zamboanga, B. L., Forthun, L.F., ...Waterman, A. S. (2011). Examining the light and dark sides of emerging adults' identity: A study of identity status differences in positive and negative psychosocial functioning. *Journal of Youth and Adolescence*, 40, 839-859.
414 Erikson, (1968) supra.
415 Schwartz, S. J., Zamboanga, B. L., Weisskirch, R. S., & Rodriguez, L. (2009). The relationships of personal and ethnic identity exploration to indices of adaptive and maladaptive psychosocial functioning. *International Journal of Behavioral Development*, 33, 131-144.
416 Erikson (1968) supra.
417 Marcia, J. E. (1966). Development and validation of ego-identity status. *Journal of Personality and Social Psychology*, 3, 551–558.
418 McAdams, D. P., & McLean, K. C. (2013). Narrative identity. *Current Directions in Psychological Science, 22*(3), 233–238. https://doi.org/10.1177/0963721413475622.
419 Grotevant, H. D. (1987). Toward a process model of identity formation. *Journal of Adolescent Research, 2*(3), 203–222. https://doi.org/10.1177/074355488723003
420 Tatum, B.D. (2017) *Why Are All The Black Kids Sitting Together in the Cafeteria*. Basic Books, Hachette Book Group.
421 Id.
422 Cross Jr., WE (1971). The negro-to-black conver- sion experience. *Black World, 20*(9), 13–27.

[423] Ghavami, N, Letitia A. Peplau, L.A. Fingerhut, A. Grant, S.K. & Wittig, M.A. (2011) Testing a Model of Minority Identity Achievement, Identity Affirmation, and Psychological Well-Being Among Ethnic Minority and Sexual Minority Individuals. *Cultural Diversity and Ethnic Minority Psychology*, Vol. 17, No. 1, 79–88 1099-9809/11/DOI: 10.1037/a0022532.

[424] Id.

[425] Id.

[426] Birman, D., & Simon, C.D. (2013). Acculturation research: Challenges, complexities, and possibilities. In J. Trimble, F. Leong, L. Comas-Diaz, & G. Nagayama Hall (Eds.), *APA handbook of multicultural psychology*. American Psychological Association; Burnett-Zeigler, I., Bohnert, K. M., & Ilgen, M. A. (2013). Ethnic identity, acculturation and the prevalence of lifetime psychiatric disorders among Black, Hispanic, and Asian adults in the US. *Journal of psychiatric research, 47*(1), 56-63. https://doi.org/10.1016/j.jpsychires.2012.08.029.

[427] Tajfel, H., & Turner, J. C. (1979). An integrative theory of intergroup conflict. In W. G. Austin & S. Worchel (Eds.), *The social psychology of intergroup relations* (pp. 33–47). Monterey, CA: Brooks-Cole.

[428] Anderson, R. E., Jones, S. C., Navarro, C. C., McKenny, M. C., Mehta, T. J., & Stevenson, H. C. (2018). Addressing the mental health needs of Black American youth and families: A case study from the EMBRace intervention. *International journal of environmental research and public health, 15*(5), 898. https://doi.org/10.3390/ijerph15050898; Morris, S. L., Hospital, M. M., Wagner, E. F., Lowe, J., Thompson, M. G., Clarke, R., & Riggs, C. (2021). SACRED connections: a university-tribal clinical research partnership for school-based screening and brief intervention for substance use problems among Native American Youth. *Journal of Ethnic & Cultural Diversity in Social Work, 30*(1), 149-162. https://doi.org/10.1080/15313204.2020.1770654; Morris et al. 2021) Chandler, M. J., & Lalonde, C. E. (2009). Cultural continuity as a moderator of suicide risk among Canada's first nations. In L. J. Kirmay- er & G. G. Valaskakis (Eds.), *Healing traditions: The mental health of Aboriginal peoples in Canada*. UBC press. Edwards & Romero, 2008; Sellers et al., 2006

[429] Ghavami, N., Fingerhut, A., Peplau, L. A., Grant, S. K., & Wittig, M. A. (2011). Testing a model of minority identity achievement, identity affirmation, and psychological well-being among ethnic minority and sexual minority individuals. *Cultural Diversity and Ethnic Minority Psychology, 17*(1), 79–88. https://doi.org/10.1037/a0022532.

[430] Id. at 87.

[431] Fordham, S., Ogbu, J.U. (1986) Black students' school success: Coping with the "burden of 'acting white'". *Urban Rev* **18**, 176–206. https://doi.org/10.1007/BF01112192.

[432] Bothaa, M. & Gillespie-Lynch, K. (2022) Come as You Are: Examining Autistic Identity Development and the Neurodiversity Movement through an Intersectional Lens. *Human Development*, 2022;66:93–112 DOI: 10.1159/000524123

[433] Meyer, I. H. (2003). Prejudice, social stress, and mental health in lesbian, gay, and bisexual populations: Conceptual issues and research evidence. *Psychological Bulletin*, 129(5), 674– 697.

[434] Chau, A. (2018) *Political Tribes: Group Instinct and the Fate of Nations*. Penguin Press.

[435] Bell, M.K. (2015) Making Space: Affinity groups offer a platform for voices often relegated to the margins. Issue 50. *Learning for Justice*. https://www.learningforjustice.org/magazine/summer-2015/making-space

[436] Anderson, T & Martin, N. (February 8, 2022) Wellesley schools reach settlement with parents group over federal lawsuit. *Boston Globe*. https://www.bostonglobe.com/2022/02/08/metro/wellesley-schools-reach-settlement-with-parents-group-over-federal-lawsuit-alleging-violation-white-students-civil-rights/; Tietz K (December 5, 2021) Parents Defending Education Files Civil Rights Complaint over Middle School's Plans for Racially Segregated 'Affinity Groups.' *The Tennessee Star*. https://tennesseestar.com/2021/12/05/parents-defending-education-files-civil-rights-complaint-over-middle-schools-plans-for-racially-segregated-affinity-groups/; Chasmar, J. (July 14, 2022) Education Dept. to investigate racial affinity groups at New York City middle school: Racial segregation 'has no place in America's schools,' parents' group says. *Fox News*. https://www.foxnews.com/politics/education-dept-investigate-racial-affinity-groups-new-york-city-middle-school

[437] Bandura, A. (1997). *Self-efficacy: The exercise of control*. W H Freeman/Times Books/ Henry Holt & Co; Maddux, J. E., & Gosselin, J. T. (2012). Self-efficacy. In M. R. Leary & J. P. Tangney (Eds.), *Handbook of self and identity* (pp. 198–224). The Guilford Press.

[438] Vecchio, G. M., Gerbino, M., Pastorelli, C., Del Bove, G., & Caprara, G. V. (2007). Multi-faceted self-efficacy beliefs as predictors of life satisfaction in late adolescence. *Personality and Individual Differences, 43*(7), 1807–1818. https://doi.org/10.1016/j.paid.2007.05.018.

[439] Bandura, (1997) supra.

[440] Maddux, J. E., & Volkmann, J. (2010). Self-efficacy. In R. H. Hoyle (Ed.), *Handbook of personality and self-regulation* (pp. 315–331). Wiley-Blackwell. https://doi.org/10.1002/9781444318111.ch14; Bandura, A., & Locke, E. A. (2003). Negative self-efficacy and goal effects revisited. *Journal of Applied Psychology, 88*(1), 87–99. https://doi.org/10.1037/0021-9010.88.1.87; Vancouver, J. B., More, K. M., & Yoder, R. J. (2008). Self-efficacy and resource allocation: Support for a nonmonotonic, discontinuous model. *Journal of Applied Psychology, 93*(1), 35–47. https://doi.org/10.1037/0021-9010.93.1.35.

[441] Seeley, K., Tombari, M., Bennett, L.J. & Dunkle, J.B. (2009) *Peer Victimization in Schools: A Set of Quantitative and Qualitative Studies of the Connections Among Peer Victimization, School Engagement, Truancy, School Achievement, and Other Outcomes*. National Center for School Engagement. https://www.ncjrs.gov/app/ publications/ abstract.aspx?ID=256074.

[442] Gross, J.J. (1998(The Emerging Field of Emotion Regulation: An Integrative Review. *Review of General Psychology*. https://doi.org/10.1037/1089-2680.2.3.271.

443 Mischel, W., Shoda, Y., & Peake, P. K. (1988). The nature of adolescent competencies predicted by preschool delay of gratification. *Journal of Personality and Social Psychology, 54*(4), 687–696. https://doi.org/ 10.1037/0022-3514.54.4.687; Shoda, Y., Mischel, W., & Peake, P. K. (1990). Predicting adolescent cognitive and self-regulatory competencies from preschool delay of gratification: Identifying diagnostic conditions. *Developmental Psychology, 26*(6), 978–986. https://doi.org/10.1037/0012-1649.26.6.978.

444 Kurtines, W.M. Gewirtz, J. & Lamb, J.L. (1991) *Handbook of Moral Behavior and Development. Volumes 1, 2 and 3.* Psychology Press

445 Kohlberg, L. (1984). *The psychology of moral development: The nature and validity of moral stages.* San Francisco: Harper & Row.

446 Vera-Estay, E., Dooley, J.J. & Beauchamp, M.H. (2014). Cognitive underpinnings of moral reasoning in adolescence: The contribution of executive functions. *Journal of Moral Education,* 44 (1), 17-33.

447 https://www.nctsn.org.

448 Tedeschi RG, Calhoun LG. The Posttraumatic Growth Inventory: measuring the positive legacy of trauma. *J Trauma Stress.* 1996 Jul;9(3):455-71. doi: 10.1007/BF02103658. PMID: 8827649.

449 Kaufman, S.B. (2020) *Transcend.* Tarcher Perigee, Penguin Random House. LLC Copyright (c) 2020 by Scott Barry Kaufman

450 https://developingchild.harvard.edu.

451 National Scientific Council on the Developing Child (2015). *Supportive Relationships and Active Skill-Building Strengthen the Foundations of Resilience: Working Paper No. 13.* https://developingchild.harvard.edu/resources/ supportive-relationships-and-active-skill-building-strengthen-the-foundations-of-resilience/

452 Id.

453 https://www.gottman.com/about/research/; https://www.johngottman.net/research/

454 Benson, K. (undated) *The Magic Relationship Ratio, According to Science.* The Gottman Institute. https:// www.gottman.com/blog/the-magic-relationship-ratio-according-science/.

455 Salmivalli (2010) supra.

456 Lu., P., Oh, J., Leahy, K. & Chopic, W.J. (2021) Friendship Importance Around the World: Links to Cultural Factors, Health, and Well-Being. *Front Psychol.,* 18 January 2021 | https://doi.org/10.3389/fpsyg.2020.570839. (citations omitted)

457 National Scientific Council on the Developing Child (2015) supra.

458 Id. at 1.

459 Whitlock, J. Wyman P.A., Moore. S.R. (in press) Connectedness and Suicide Prevention in Adolescents: Pathways and Implications. Suicide and Life-Threatening Behavior. *The American Association of Suicidology.* http://onlinelibrary.wiley.com/doi/10.1111/sltb.12071/abstract.

460 https://mcc.gse.harvard.edu/resources-for-educators/relationship-mapping-strategy.

461 Buchanan, K. E. & Bardi, A. (2010) Acts of Kindness and Acts of Novelty Affect Life Satisfaction. *The Journal of Social Psychology,* Vol. 150, Issue 3; Aknin, L.B., Dunn, E.W. & Norton, M.I. (2012) Happiness Runs in a Circular Motion: Evidence for a Positive Feedback Loop between P, Issue Prosocial Spending and Happiness. *Journal of Happiness Studies.* Vol 13, Issue 2, pp. 347-355.

462 https://www.randomactsofkindness.org/.

463 Random Acts of Kindness, Kindness Health Facts http://downloads.randomactsofkindness.org/ RAK_kindness_health_facts.pdf

464 Caprara C.V., Barabaranelli C., Pastorelli C., Bandura A., & Zimbardo P.G. (2000) Prosocial foundations of children's academic achievement. *Psychol Sci* 11: 302–306.

465 Layous K, Nelson S.K., Oberle E., Schonert-Reichl K.A., Lyubomirsky S. (2012) Kindness Counts: Prompting Prosocial Behavior in Preadolescents Boosts Peer Acceptance and Well-Being. *PLoS ONE* 7(12).

466 Id.

467 http://rak-materials.s3.amazonaws.com/cde/en/RAK_educator_guide.pdf

468 Seeley, et. al. (2009) supra.

469 http://futuredirectedtherapy.com/.

470 Vilhauer J., Young S., & Kealoha C. (2011) Treating major depression by creating positive expectations for the future: a pilot study for the effectiveness of future directed therapy (FDT) on symptom severity and quality of life. *CNS Neurosci Therapeut.* 2011:1–8. http://futuredirectedtherapy.com/wp-content/uploads/2011/05/ FDT-and-MDD-CNS-published-version.pdf.

471 Hildrew, C. (2018). Becoming a growth mindset school: The power of mindset to transform teaching, leadership and learning. Routledge; Gerstein, J. (2014). The educator with a growth mindset: A staff workshop. *User Generated Education.* https://usergeneratededucation.wordpress.com/2014/08/29/the-educator-with-a-growth-mindset-a-staff-workshop/; Brock, A., & Hundley, H. (2017). *The growth mindset playbook: A teacher's guide to promoting student success.* Ulysses Press.

472 Allen, S. (2019) *The Science of Gratitude.* A white paper prepared for the John Templeton Foundation by the Greater Good Science Center at UC Berkeley. https://ggsc.berkeley.edu/images/uploads/GGSC-JTF_White_Paper-Gratitude-FINAL.pdf _ga=2.132158348.385669189.1654547242-1849723812.1654547242

473 Hanson, R. (2013). *Hardwiring happiness: The new brain science of contentment, calm, and confidence. Harmony.* Please also watch the TedTalk by Dr. Hanson: https://www.youtube.com/watch?v=jpuDyGgIeh0

474 Hanson, R., Shapiro, S., Hutton-Thamm, E. Hagerty, M.R. & Sullivan, K.P. (2021) Learning to learn from positive experiences. *The Journal of Positive Psychology,* https://www.tandfonline.com/doi/full/ 10.1080/17439760.2021.2006759

475 The "L" in Hanson's HEAL approach is this: **Step 4. Link Positive and Negative Material Together.** This step is considered optional by Hanson. The idea is to strongly feel this positive experience, briefly bring to mind a negative thought, and then let go of the negative thought and just focus on the positive experience. It is my perception that this approach would be challenging to convey to students.

476 https://greatergood.berkeley.edu/topic/gratitude/definition.

477 Smith, J.A., Newman, K.M., Marsh, J. & and Keltner, D (editors) (2020) *The Gratitude Project: How the Science of Thankfulness Can Rewire Our Brains for Resilience, Optimism, and the Greater Good.* New Harbinger Publications: New Harbinger Publications.

478 http://www.umassmed.edu/cfm/.

479 https://www.uclahealth.org/marc/research

480 Zenner, C., Herrnleben-Kurz, S., & Walach, H. (2014). Mindfulness-based interventions in youth organizations – A systematic review and meta-analysis. *Frontiers in Psychology,* 5, 603. See also research noted at: http://www.mindful.org/the-mindful-society/mindfulness-in-education-research-highlights.

481 Belsha, K. (Sept 27, 2021) Stress and short tempers: Schools struggle with behavior as students return. *Chalkbeat.* https://www.chalkbeat.org/2021/9/27/22691601/student-behavior-stress-trauma-return.

482 Colvin, G. (2004). *Managing the cycle of acting-out behavior in the classroom.* Eugene, OR: Behavior Associates; Document noted from: https://k12engagement.unl.edu/AppropriateResponsestoEscalation.pdf. Colvin, G. & Scott, T.M. (2004) *Managing the Cycle of Acting-Out Behavior In the Classroom.* Corwin. https://us.corwin.com/en-us/nam/managing-the-cycle-of-acting-out-behavior-in-the-classroom/book243522.

483 https://mindfulnessinschools.org

484 https://www.mindful.org/mindfulness-in-education/

485 https://www.mindfulschools.org

486 Siegel, D.J. & Bryson, T.P. (2012) *The Whole-Brain Child 12 Revolutionary Strategies to Nurture Your Child's Developing Mind, Survive Everyday Parenting Struggles, and Help Your Family Thrive.* Random House Publishing Group.

487 Cuddy, A. (2012) *Your Body Language May Shape Who You Are.* TedTalk. https://www.ted.com/talks/amy_cuddy_your_body_language_may_shape_who_you_are?language=en; Cuddy, A. (2016) Presence: Bringing Your Boldest Self to Your Biggest Challenges. Little, Brown & Company.

488 A Greek philosopher. https://plato.stanford.edu/entries/epictetus/.

489 Ellis, A. (1994) *Reason and Emotion in Psychotherapy: Comprehensive Method of Treating Human Disturbances: Revised and Updated.* New York, NY: Citadel Press; Ellis, Albert (2003). Early theories and practices of rational emotive behavior theory and how they have been augmented and revised during the last three decades. *Journal of Rational-Emotive & Cognitive-Behavior Therapy,* 21(3/4).

490 https://www.ted.com/talks/amy_cuddy_your_body_language_shapes_who_you_are?language=en# and https://www.ted.com/talks/amy_cuddy_your_body_language_shapes_who_you_are?language=en#.

491 https://www.youtube.com/watch?v=L0MK7qz13bU.

492 Dr. Shure's books include: Shure, M. B. (1992). *I Can Problem Solve (ICPS): An Interpersonal Cognitive Problem Solving program.* Champaign, IL: Research Press. Shure, M B. (1992). *I Can Problem Solve (ICPS): An Interpersonal Cognitive Problem Solving program.* Champaign, IL: Research Press. Shure, M. B. (1992). *I Can Problem Solve (ICPS): An Interpersonal Cognitive Problem Solving program.* Champaign, IL: Research Press. Shure, M. B. (1996). *Raising A Thinking Child Workbook.* New York, Holt (Republished, Champaign, IL: Research Press, 2000).

493 https://thinkkids.org; https://livesinthebalance.org.

494 Sanders, et. al. (2021) supra.

495 Ahmed, E. (2001). Shame management: Regulating bullying. In E. Ahmed, N. Harris, J. Braithwaite, and V. Braithwaite (Eds.), *Shame Management Through Reintegration* (pp. 211–314). Cambridge, UK: Cambridge University Press.

496 Nathanson, D. (1992). *Shame and Pride: Affect, Sex, and the Birth of the Self.* New York: Norton. See also the International Institute for Restorative Practices at http://iirp.edu.

497 Zehr, H. *The Little Book of Restorative Justice.* Good Books: Intercourse PA.

498 Id.

499 International Institute for Restorative Practices. http://www.iirp.edu/.

500 http://education.state.mn.us/MDE/StuSuc/SafeSch/RestorMeas/. See also: Riestenberg, N. (2012) *Circle in the Square Building Community and Repairing Harm in School.* St Paul: Living Justice Press.

501 The Collaborative Problem Solving process was specifically developed to be used with those students who have greater challenges. It includes both an assessment of those challenges and joint problem solving to develop strategies. Thus, a decision was made to identify the problem solving practice necessary to support a remedy of harm Accountability Problem Solving.

502 Cialdini, supra; See also: https://www.influenceatwork.com.

503 Thornberg, R. Gini, G., Malti, T. & Galarneau, E. (2021) Personality Factors, Empathy, and Moral Disengagement in Bullying *Wiley Blackwell Handbook of Bullying: A Comprehensive and International Review of Research and Intervention.* Wiley-Blackwell; Gini, et. al. supra (2021); Caravita, et. al., supra (2012); Gini, et. al. supra (2011); Pozzoli, et. al., supra 2016; Thornberg, et, al, (2015). Thornberg, R. (2010). School children's social representations on bullying causes. *Psychology in the Schools,* 47, 311–327. doi:10.1002/pits.20472; Gini, G., Thornberg, R., & Pozzoli, T. (2018). Individual moral disengagement and bystander behavior in bullying: The role of moral distress and collective moral disengagement. *Psychology of Violence.* doi:10.1037/vio0000223

504 Bandura, A. (1991). Social cognition theory of moral thought and action. In W. M.Kurtines and J. L. Gewirtz (Eds.), *Handbook of moral behavior and development* (Vol. 1, pp. 45-96). Hillsdale, NJ:Lawrence Erlbaum.

505 Killer, B., Bussey, K., Hawes, D., & Hunt, C. (2019). A meta-analysis of the relationship between moral disengagement and bullying roles in youth. *Aggressive Behavior,* 45, 450–462. Advance online publication. doi:10.1002/ab.21833.

[506] Thornberg, et. al. (2021) supra; Gini, et. al. (2021) supra.

[507] Thornberg, R., & Jungert, T. (2014). School bullying and the mechanisms of moral disengagement. *Aggressive Behavior*, 40, 99–108.

[508] Thornberg, et. al. (2021) supra.

[509] Pozzoli, T., Gini, G., & Vieno, A. (2012). Individual and class moral disengagement in bullying among elementary school children. *Aggressive Behavior*, 38, 378–388. Thornberg, R., Wänström, L., & Pozzoli, T. (2017). Peer victimisation and its relation to class relational climate and class moral disengagement among school children. *Educational Psychology*, 37, 524–536.

[510] Thornberg, et. al. (2021) supra; Gini, et. al. (2021) supra.

[511] Bjärehed, M., Thornberg, R., Wänström, L., & Gini, G. (2020). Mechanisms of moral disengagement and their associations with indirect bullying, direct bullying, and pro-aggressive bystander behavior. *Journal of Early Adolescence*, 40, 28–55.

[512] Thornberg, R., Wänström, L., Pozzoli, T. & Hong, J.S. (2019) Moral Disengagement and School Bullying Perpetration in Middle Childhood: A Short-Term Longitudinal Study in Sweden. *Journal of School Violence*, 18:4, 585-596, DOI: 10.1080/15388220.2019.1636383

[513] Id.

[514] Wang, C., & Goldberg, T. S. (2017). Using children's literature to decrease moral disengagement and victimization among elementary school students. *Psychology in the Schools*, 54, 918–931. https://doi.org/10.1002/pits.22042 Barkoukis, V., Lazuras, L., Ourda, D., & Tsorbatzoudis, H. (2016). Tackling psychosocial risk factors for adolescent cyberbullying: Evidence from a school–based intervention. *Aggressive Behavior*, 42, 114–122. https://doi.org/10.1002/ab.21625;

[515] Greene, R. W. (2008). *Lost at school: Why our kids with behavioral challenges are falling through the cracks and how we can help them.* New York: Scribner.

[516] https://livesinthebalance.org.

[517] https://thinkkids.org

[518] Id.

[519] Pollastri, A.R, Epstein, L.D., Heath, G.H. & Ablon, J.S. (2013) The Collaborative Problem Solving Approach: Outcomes Across Settings. *Harvard Review of Psychology*. Volume 21, Number 4. 196.

[520] Id. at 189- 190.

[521] http://thinkkids.org/wp-content/uploads/2013/01/TSI_clinical-9-12.pdf

[522] Pollastri, et. al. (2013) supra at 196.

[523] Id. at 190.

[524] Yeager, D.S., Trzesniewski, K.H. & Dweck, C.S. (2013) An Implicit Theories of Personality Intervention Reduces Adolescent Aggression in Response to Victimization and Exclusion. *Child Development*, Volume 84, Number 3, pp 970-988.

[525] Craig, W. M., & Pepler, D. J. (1997). Observations of bullying and victimization in the school yard. *Canadian Journal of School Psychology*, 13(2), 41–60; Gini, et. al. (2021) supra; Salmivalli, (2010) supra.

[526] Rigby, K., and Slee, P. T. (1991). Bullying among Australian youth organization children: Reported behavior and attitudes toward victims. *Journal of Social Psychology*, 131, 615–627; Rigby, K., and Johnson, B. (2006). Expressed readiness of Australian youth organization children to act as bystanders in support of children who are being bullied. *Educational Psychology*, 26, 425-440.

[527] Hawkins, D. L., Pepler, D. J., & Craig, W. (2001). Naturalistic Observations of Peer Interventions in Bullying. *Social Development*, 10(4): 512-527; Henderson, N. R., and Hymel, S. (2002). *Peer contributions to bullying in youth organizations: Examining student response categories.* Poster presented at the National Association of Youth Organization Psychologists Annual Convention, Chicago, February; O'Connell, P., Pepler, D., and Craig, W. (1999). Peer involvement in bullying: Insights and challenges for intervention. *Journal of Adolescence*, 22(4), 437-452.

[528] Sainio, M., Veenstra, R., Huitsing, G., & Salmivalli, C. (2011). Victims and their defenders: A dyadic approach. *International Journal of Behavioral Development*, vol. 35 no. 2 144-151.

[529] Schleicher, A. (2019) PISA 2018, supra.

[530] Salmivalli, C., Lappalainen, M., & Lagerspetz, K. (1998). Stability and change of behavior in connection with bullying in youth organizations: A two-year follow-up. *Aggressive Behavior*, 24, 205–218; Rigby & Johnson, (2006) supra; Henderson & Hymel, (2002) supra; O'Connell, et. al. (1999) supra; Salmivalli (2010) supra.

[531] Gini, et. a. (2021) supra.

[532] Schleicher, A. (2019) PISA 2018, supra.

[533] Wachs S., Görzig A., Wright M.F., Schubarth W., & Bilz L. Associations among Adolescents' Relationships with Parents, Peers, and Teachers, Self-Efficacy, and Willingness to Intervene in Bullying: A Social Cognitive Approach. *Int J Environ Res Public Health*. 2020 Jan 8;17(2):420. doi: 10.3390/ijerph17020420.

[534] Darley, J. M., & Latane, B. (1968). Bystander intervention in emergencies: Diffusion of responsibility. *Journal of Personality and Social Psychology*, 8, 377–383. doi:10.1037/h0025589

[535] Latane, B., & Darley, J. M. (1970). *The unresponsive bystander: Why doesn't he help?* Englewood Cliffs, NJ: Prentice Hall.

[536] Dovidio, J. F., Piliavin, J. A., Schroeder, D. A., & Penner, L. A. (2006). *The social psychology of prosocial behavior.* Mahwah, NJ: Lawrence Erlbaum.

[537] Darley & Latane, (1968) supra.

[538] Pozzoli, T., & Gini, G. (2010). Active defending and passive bystanding behavior in bullying: The role of personal characteristics and perceived peer pressure. *Journal of Abnormal Child Psychology*, 38, 815–827. doi:10.1007/s10802-010-9399-9; Pozzoli, T., & Gini, G. (2013). Why do bystanders of bullying help or not? A multidimensional model. *Journal of Early Adolescence*, 33, 315–340. doi:10.1177/0272431612440172.

[339] Anker, A. E., & Feeley, T. H. (2011). Are non-participants in prosocial behavior merely innocent bystanders? *Health Communication*, 26, 13–24. doi:10.1080/10410236.2011.527618

[340] Lodge, J., & Frydenberg, E. (2005). The role of peer bystanders in school bullying: Positive steps toward promoting peaceful schools. *Theory into Practice*, 44, 329–336. doi:10.1207/s15430421tip4404_6; Jenkins, L. N., & Nickerson, A. B. (2017). Bullying participant roles and gender as predictors of bystander intervention. *Aggressive Behavior*, 43, 281–290. doi:10.1002/ab.21688.

[341] Craig, W. M., & Pepler, D. J. (1997). Observations of bullying and victimization in the school yard. *Canadian Journal of School Psychology*, 13(2), 41–60.

[342] Hawkins, Pepler, & Craig, (2001) supra.

[343] O'Connell, P., Pepler, D., & Craig, W. (1999). Peer involvement in bullying: Insights and challenges for intervention. *Journal of Adolescence*, 22, 437–452. doi:10.1006/jado.1999.0238.

[344] Hawkins, Pepler, & Craig, (2001) supra.

[345] Sainio et. al., (2011) supra.

[346] Id.

[347] Rivers, I., Poteat, V.P., Noret, N. & Ashurst, N. (2009) Observing bullying at school: The mental health implications of witness status. *Sch. Psychol. Q.* 24, 211.

[348] Jenkins, L. N., & Fredrick, S. S. (2017). Social capital and bystander behavior in bullying: Internalizing problems as a barrier to prosocial intervention. *Journal of Youth and Adolescence*, 46, 757–771. doi:10.1007/s10964-017-0637-0

[349] Gini, et. al. (2021) supra.

[350] Salmivalli. et. al. (2011) supra.

[351] Bjarehed, M., Thornberg, R., Wanstram, L. & Gini, G. (2019). Individual moral disengagement and bullying among Swedish fifth graders: The role of collective moral disengagement and probullying behavior within classrooms. *Journal of Interpersonal Violence*. doi:10.1177/0886260519860889.

[352] Salmivalli, C., Lagerspetz, K., Bjorkqvist, K., Osterman, K. & Kaukiainen, A. (1996). Bullying as a group process: Participant roles and their relations to social status within the group. *Aggressive Behavior*, 22, 1–15. doi:10.1002/(SICI)1098-2337.

[353] Gini, et. al. (2021) supra.

[354] Gini, et. al. (2021) supra.

[355] Plamer, S.B., Mulvey, K.L. & Rutland, A. (2021) Developmental Differences in Evaluations of, and Reactions to, Bullying Among Children and Adolescents: A Social Reasoning Developmental Approach. *Wiley Blackwell Handbook of Bullying: A Comprehensive and International Review of Research and Intervention*.

[356] Juvonen, J., & Galvan, A. (2008). Peer influence in involuntary social groups: Lessons from research on bullying. In M. Prinstein & K. Dodge (Eds.), *Peer influence processes among youth* (pp. 225–244). Guilford Press.

[357] Pouwels, J.L. & Garandeau C.F. (2021) The Role of the Peer Group and Classroom Factors in Bullying Behavior. *Wiley Blackwell Handbook of Bullying: A Comprehensive and International Review of Research and Intervention*. Wiley Blackwell.

[358] Juvonen & Galvin, (2008) supra.

[359] https://www.kivaprogram.net/what-is-kiva/.

[360] Salmivalli. et. al. (2011) supra.

[361] Saarento, S., Boulton, A. J., & Salmivalli, C. (2015). Reducing bullying and victimization: Student-and classroom-level mechanisms of change. *Journal of Abnormal Child Psychology*, 43, 61–76. doi:10.1007/s10802-013-9841-x

[362] Kärnä, A., Voeten, M., Little, T.D., Alanen, E., Poskiparta, E. & Salmivalli, C. (2013) Effectiveness of the KiVa Antibullying Program: Grades 1–3 and 7–9. *Journal of Educational Psychology*, Vol. 105, No. 2, 535–551 DOI: 10.1037/a0030417535.

[363] Edwards, K.M., Banyard, V.L., Sessarego, S.N., Waterman, E.A., Mitchell, K. & Chang, H. (2019) Evaluation of a Bystander-Focused Interpersonal Violence Prevention Program with High School Students. *Prevention Science* (2019) 20:488–498 https://doi.org/10.1007/s11121-019-01000-w

[364] Maner & Case (2016) supra.

[365] Pouwels, & Garandeau (2021) supra.

[366] Juvonen & Galván (2008) supra; Sentse, et. al. (2014) supra.

[367] Thornberg, R., & Jungert, T. (2013). Bystander behavior in bullying situations: Basic moral sensitivity, moral disengagement and defender self-efficacy. *Journal of Adolescence*, 36, 475–483.

[368] Thornberg et al. (2012) supra.

[369] Huitsing, G., Lodder, G., Oldenburg, B., Schacter, H., Salmivalli, C., Juvonen, J., & Veenstra, R. (2019). The healthy context paradox: Victims' adjustment during an anti-bullying intervention. *Journal of Child and Family Studies*, (28), 2499–2509.

[370] Ma, T. L., Meter, D. J., Chen, W. T., & Lee, Y. (2019). Defending behavior of peer victimization in school and cyber context during childhood and adolescence: A meta-analytic review of individual and peer-relational characteristics. *Psychological Bulletin*, 145, 891–928. doi:10.1037/bul0000205.

[371] Peets, K., Poyhonen, V., Juvonen, J., & Salmivalli, C. (2015). Classroom norms of bullying alter the degree to which children defend in response to their affective empathy and power. *Developmental Psychology*, 51, 913–920. doi:10.1037/a0039287.

[372] Caravita, S. C., Sijtsema, J. J., Rambaran, J. A., & Gini, G. (2014). Peer influences on moral disengagement in late childhood and early adolescence. *Journal of Youth and Adolescence*, 43, 193–207. doi:10.1007/s10964-013-9953-1

573 Gini, et. al. (2021) supra; Poyhonen, V., Juvonen, J., & Salmivalli, C. (2012). Standing up for the victim, siding with the bully or standing by? Bystander responses in bullying situations. *Social Development*, 21, 722–741. doi:10.1111/j.1467-9507.2012.00662.x.

574 Gini, et. al. (2021) supra.

575 Ma, et. al. (2019) supra.

576 Id.; Poyhonen, et. al. (2012) supra; Lambe, L. J., Hudson, C. C., Craig, W. M., & Pepler, D. J. (2017). Does defending come with a cost? Examining the psychosocial correlates of defending behaviour among bystanders of bullying in a Canadian sample. *Child Abuse & Neglect*, 65, 112–123. doi:10.1016/j.chiabu.2017.01.012.

577 Gini, et. al. (2021) supra; Pouwels & Garandeau, (2021) supra.

578 Pouwels & Garandeau, (2021) supra; Reijntjes, A., Vermande, M. M., Olthof, T., Goossens, F. A., Aleva, L., & van der Meulen, M. (2016). Defending victimized peers: Opposing the bully, supporting the victim, or both? *Aggressive Behavior*, 42, 585–597. doi:10.1002/ab.21653

579 Pouwels & Garandeau, (2021) supra.

580 Pronk, J., Olthof, T., Goossens, F., & Krabbendam, L. (2019). Differences in adolescents' motivations for indirect, direct, and hybrid peer defending. *Social Development*, 28, 414–429. doi:10.1111/sode.12348; Reijntjes et al., supra (2016)

581 Reijntjes, et al. (2016) supra.

582 Pronk, et al. (2019) supra; Reijntjes, et al. (2016) supra.

583 Salmivalli, C., & Voeten, M. (2004). Connections between attitudes, group norms, and behaviors associated with bullying in youth organizations. *International Journal of Behavioral Development*, 28, 246–258; Gini, G., Albiero, P., Benelli, B., and Altoe, G. (2007). Does empathy predict adolescents' bullying and defending behavior? *Aggressive Behavior*, 33, 467–476; Pöyhönen, V., Juvonen, J. & Salmivalli, C. (2010). What does it take to stand up for the victim of bullying? The interplay between personal and social factors. *Merrill-Palmer Quarterly*, Vol. 56: Iss. 2, Article 4; Menesini, E., Codecasa, E., & Benelli, B. (2003). Enhancing children's responsibility to take action against bullying: Evaluation of a befriending intervention in Italian middle youth organizations. *Aggressive Behavior*, 29, 10–14; Simona, C.S., Caravits, P.D. & Silmivalli C. (2008) Unique and Interactive Effects of Empathy and Social Status on Involvement in Bullying. *Social Development*, Vol. 18, No. 1., pp. 140-163.

584 Ma, et. al. (2019) supra.

585 Jenkins, L. N., & Fredrick, S. S. (2017). Social capital and bystander behavior in bullying: Internalizing problems as a barrier to prosocial intervention. *Journal of Youth and Adolescence*, 46, 757–771. doi:10.1007/s10964-017-0637-0; Mazzone, A., Camodeca, M., & Salmivalli, C. (2016). Interactive effects of guilt and moral disengagement on bullying, defending and outsider behavior. *Journal of Moral Education*, 45, 419–432. doi:10.1080/03057240.2016.1216399.

586 Pronk, J., Olthof, T., Aleva, E. A., van der Meulen, M., Vermande, M. M. & Goossens, F. A. (2018). Longitudinal associations between adolescents' bullying–related indirect defending, outsider behavior, and peer–group status. *Journal of Research on Adolescence*. doi:10.1111/jora.12450.

587 Salmivalli (2010) supra; Faris & Femlee (2014) supra.

588 Bandura, A. (1997). *Self-efficacy: The exercise of control*. New York: Freeman.

589 Gini, et. al. (2021) supra.

590 Ferrans, S.D., Selman, R.L. & Feinberg, L.F. (2012) Rules of the Culture and Personal Needs: Witnesses' Decision-Making Processes to Deal with Situations of Bullying in Middle Youth Organization. *Harvard Educational Review*, Vol. 82 No. 4 Winter.

591 Pronk, J., Goossens, F. A., Olthof, T., de Mey, L., & Willemen, A. M. (2013). Children's intervention strategies in situations of victimization by bullying: Social cognitions of outsiders versus defenders. *Journal of School Psychology*, 51, 669–682. doi:10.1016/j.jsp.2013.09.002.

592 Gini, et. al. (2021) supra; Casey, E. A., Lindhorst, T., & Storer, H. L. (2017). The situational-cognitive model of adolescent bystander behavior: Modeling bystander decision-making in the context of bullying and teen dating violence. *Psychology of Violence*, 7, 33–44. doi:10.1037/vio0000033

593 Palmer, et. al. (2021) supra.

594 Thornberg, R, (2007) A classmate in distress: youth organization children as bystanders and their reasons for how they act. *Social Psychology of Education*, Vol. 10; Goldammer L., Swahn M.H., Strasser S.M., Ashby J.S. & Meyers J. (2013) An examination of bullying in Georgia youth organizations: demographic and youth organization climate factors associated with willingness to intervene in bullying situations., *West J Emerg Med*; 2013 Aug;14(4):324-8; Bandura (1997) supra.

595 Ahmed, E. (2008). "Stop it, that's enough": Bystander intervention and its relationship to school connectedness and shame management. *Vulnerable Children and Youth Studies*, 3, 203–213. doi:10.1080/17450120802002548

596 Mazzone, A. Kollerová, L. & Norman, J.O. (2021) Teachers' Attitudes Toward Bullying: What Do We Know, and Where Do We Go from Here? *Wiley Blackwell Handbook of Bullying: A Comprehensive and International Review of Research and Intervention*. Wiley Blackwell.

597 Bradshaw, et. al. (2007) supra.

598 Gini, et. al. (2021) supra; Pozzoli & Gini (2013), supra; Rigby & Johnson, (2006) supra.; Salmivalli (2010) supra.

599 Gini, et. al. (2021) supra; Berkowitz (2010) supra.

600 Thornberg, & Jungert (2013) supra.

601 Latane & Darley, (1968) supra.

602 Thornberg, et. al. (2021) supra; Gini, et. al. (2021) supra; Caravita, et. al. (2012) supra; Thornberg, & Jungert (2013) supra.

[603] Patrick, R. B., Rote, W. M., Gibbs, J. C., & Basinger, K. S. (2019). Defend, stand by, or join in?: The relative influence of moral identity, moral judgment, and social self-efficacy on adolescents' bystander behaviors in bullying situations. *Journal of Youth and Adolescence*, 48, 2051–2064. doi:10.1007/s10964-019-01089-w; Pozzoli, T., Gini, G., & Thornberg, R. (2016). Bullying and defending behavior: The role of explicit and implicit moral cognition. *Journal of School Psychology*, 59, 67–81. doi:10.1016/j. jsp.2016.09.005.

[604] Forsberg, C., Thornberg, R., & Samuelsson, M. (2014). Bystanders to bullying: Fourth-to seventh grade students' perspectives on their reactions. *Research Papers in Education*, 29, 557–576. doi:10.1080/02671522.2013.878375

[605] Gini, G., Thornberg, R., & Pozzoli, T. (2018). Individual moral disengagement and bystander behavior in bullying: The role of moral distress and collective moral disengagement. *Psychology of Violence*. doi:10.1037/vio0000223

[606] Obermann, M.-L. (2011). Moral disengagement among bystanders to school bullying. *Journal of School Violence*, 10, 239–257; Thornberg, et. al. supra (2021); Gini, et. al. supra (2021)

[607] Thornberg, R., & Jungert, T. (2013). Bystander behavior in bullying situations: Basic moral sensitivity, moral disengagement and defender self-efficacy. *Journal of Adolescence*, 36, 475–483.

[608] Bandura (1997) supra.

[609] Fogelman, E. (1994) *Conscience and Courage: Rescuers of Jews during the Holocaust,* New York, Anchor Books

[610] http://www2.ed.gov/about/offices/list/ocr/index.html.

[611] Title IX of the Education Amendments of 1972. 20 USC. §§ 1681-1688.

[612] https://www2.ed.gov/about/offices/list/ocr/lgbt.html.

[613] Title VI of the Civil Rights Act of 1964. 42 USC. §§ 2000d-2000d-7.

[614]. USDOE OCR (2004) *Dear Colleague Letter on Title VI and Title IX Religious Discrimination in Schools and Colleges.*

[615] Section 504 of the Rehabilitation Act of 1973. 29 USC § 794.

[616] The Americans with Disabilities Act of 1990. 42 USC. §§ 12131-12134.

[617] USDOE OCR (October 26, 2010) *Dear Colleague Letter on Harassment and Bullying.* https://www2.ed.gov/about/offices/list/ocr/letters/colleague-201010.html

[618] USDOE OCR *Dear Colleague Letter* (2010) supra (emphasis added).

[619] Id. at 1.

[620] Id. at 3-4.

[621] *Davis v Monroe County Board of Education* 526 US 629, 633, 650 (1999).

[622] *Vance v. Spencer Cnty. Pub. Sch. Dist.* 231 F.3d 253, 261 (6th Cir. 2000).

[623] Id.

[624] *Zeno v. Pine Plains,* 702 F.3d 655, 664 (2nd Cir 2012).

[625] *S.B. v. Harford County, No. 15-1474* (4th Circuit, April 8, 2016); *Stiles v. Grainger County, No. 01-91360* (6th Circuit, March 25, 2016).

[626] Section 504, supra.

[627] ADA, supra.

[628] Individuals with Disabilities Act. 20 USC. § 1400 et seq.

[629] USDOE, Office of Special Education and Rehabilitation Services (OSERS) (August 20, 2013) *Dear Colleague Letter Keeping Students with Disabilities Safe from Bullying.* http://www.ed.gov/policy/speced/guid/idea/memosdcltrs/bullyingdcl-8-20-13.doc.

[630] USDOE OCR (2014) *Dear Colleague Letter* on Bullying of Students under Section 504. https://www2.ed.gov/about/offices/list/ocr/docs/disabharassltr.html.

[631] USDOE-OCR, 2010 *Dear Colleague Letter,* supra.

[632] USDOE OSCRS, 2013 *Dear Colleague Letter,* supra.

[633] Id. at 2.

[634] Id. at 3.

[635] Id. at 4.

[636] 34 C.F.R. § 104.35(a) (504) and 34 C.F.R. §§ 300.536(a), 300.530 (IDEA).

[637] USDOE OCR (2016) *Parent and Educator Resource Guide to Section 504 in Public Elementary and Secondary Schools.* https://www2.ed.gov/about/offices/list/ocr/docs/504-resource-guide-201612.pdf.

[638] Id., p. 32 - 34.

[639] 34 C.F.R. § 104.35(a) (504) and 34 C.F.R. §§ 300.536(a), 300.530 (IDEA).

[640] USDOE OCR (2014) *Dear Colleague Letter* supra.

[641] Rozsa, M. (2021) "Why can't you be normal?": How the neurodivergent are mocked for being different. *Salon.* https://www.salon.com/2021/02/15/why-cant-you-be-normal-how-the-neurodivergent-are-mocked-for-being-different/.

[642] 34 C.F.R. §300.320(a)(4).

[643] 34 CFR §104.32(a).

[644] 34 CFR §104.32(b).

[645] 34 C.F.R. §104.3(j)(2)(i).

[646] 42 USC. § 12102(2).

[647] 34 C.F.R. §§ 104.4(b), 104.21-23, 104.37, 104.61 (incorporating 34 C.F.R. § 100.7(e)).

648 Anderson, T. & Martin, N. (February 8, 2022) Wellesley schools reach settlement with parents group over federal lawsuit. *Boston Globe*. https://www.bostonglobe.com/2022/02/08/metro/wellesley-schools-reach-settlement-with-parents-group-over-federal-lawsuit-alleging-violation-white-students-civil-rights/; Tietz K. (December 5, 2021) Parents Defending Education Files Civil Rights Complaint over Middle School's Plans for Racially Segregated 'Affinity Groups.' *The Tennessee Star*. https://tennesseestar.com/2021/12/05/parents-defending-education-files-civil-rights-complaint-over-middle-schools-plans-for-racially-segregated-affinity-groups/; Chasmar, J. (July 14, 2022) Education Dept. to investigate racial affinity groups at New York City middle school: Racial segregation 'has no place in America's schools,' parents' group says. *Fox News*. https://www.foxnews.com/politics/education-dept-investigate-racial-affinity-groups-new-york-city-middle-school.

649 Gay Straight Alliance Network.

650 Gay Straight Alliance (2018) *GSA Advisor Handbook*. https://gsanetwork.org/wp-content/uploads/2018/09/GSA_Advisor_Handbook-web.pdf.

651 Id. at 6.

652 Wachtel, T., Costello, B. & Wachtel, J. (2019) *Restorative Circles in Schools: A Practical Guide for Educators - Second Edition*. IIRP.

653 Levy, L. (1985) *The Emergence of Free Press*. New York: Oxford University Press.

654 Trenchard & Gordon, *No. 15, Feb 4, 1720, in Cato's Letters* (6th ed., 1755), 1:96. (emphasis added).

655 American Jewish Committee and Religious Freedom Education Project/First Amendment Center. (2012) *Harassment, Bullying and Free Expression: Guidelines for Free and Safe Public Schools*. http://www.firstamendmentcenter.org/madison/wp-content/uploads/2012/05/FAC-Harassment-Free-Expression-BROCHURE.pdf. (emphasis added).

656 *Hazelwood School District v. Kuhlmeier*, 484 US (1988), related to student speech in school publications and is therefore not discussed.

657 *Tinker v. Des Moines Ind. Comm. Sch. Dist*, 393 US 503 (1969).

658 *Bethel School District v. Fraser*, 478 US 675 (1986).

659 *Morse v. Frederick*, 551 US 393 (2007).

660 *Mahanoy Area School District v. B.L.*, 141 S. Ct. 2038 (2021).

661 Willard, N. (2012) Student Off-Campus Online Speech: Assessing Substantial Disruption. *Albany Journal of Law and Technology*. http://www.albanylawjournal.org/documents/articles/22.3.611-willard.pdf.

662 *Saxe v. State College*, 240 F.3d 200 (3d Cir. 2001).

663 *Kowalski v. Berkeley County Sch.*, 652 F. 3d 565 (4th Cir. July 27, 2011, cert. denied 132 S. Ct. 1095 (2012).

664 American Educational Research Association, supra.

665 USDOE OCR 2010 *Dear Colleague Letter* supra.

666 The Federal Partners' website is at http://StopBullying.gov.

667 Stuart-Cassel, et. al., supra.

668 *Fraser*, supra.

669 *Davis*, supra.

670 See example, *Boroff v. Van Wert City Bd. of Educ.*, 220 F.3d 465, 466 (6th Cir. 2000), cert. denied, 149 L. Ed. 2d 286, 121 S. Ct. 1355 (2001).

671 *Melton v. Young*,465 F.2d 1332 (6th Cir. 1972).

672 *West v. Derby Unified Sch. Dist.*, 206 F.3d 1358 (10th Cir. 2000).

673 *Scott v. Sch. Bd. of Alachua County*,324 F.3d 1246 (11th Cir. 2003), cert. denied, 540 US 824 (2003).

674 *Castorina ex rel. Rewt v. Madison County School Board*, 246 F.3d 536 (6th Cir.2001).

675 *Nixon v. Northern Local School District Board of Education*, 83 F. Supp. 2d 956 (S.D. Ohio 2005).

676 *Zamecnik v. Indian Prairie School Dist.* #204, 636 F.3d 874 (7th Cir. 2011).

677 *Harper*, supra.

678 *Sapp*, supra.

679 *Tinker*, supra.

680 *Saxe*, supra.

681 *Morse*, supra.

682 *Castorina*, supra.

683 *Nixon*, supra.

684 *Zamecnik*, supra

685 *Zamecnik*, supra.

686 *Harper*, supra.

687 *Sapp*, supra.

688 KVAL (January 27th 2017) High school administrators resign in wake of text messages mocking former students. *KVAL* https://kval.com/news/local/creswell-administrators-resign-in-wake-of-text-messages-mocking-former-students.

689 https://sourcesofstrength.org.

690 https://www.randomactsofkindness.org.

691 https://www.beyonddifferences.org.

692 https://www.glsen.org/no-name-calling-week.

693 https://www.viacharacter.org

694 https://greatergood.berkeley.edu.

695 https://www.learningforjustice.org.

696 https://www.noplaceforhate.org.

697 https://www.gse.harvard.edu/news/uk/17/02/one-and-all.

698 https://www.viacharacter.org.

[699] https://www.unh.edu/research/prevention-innovations-research-center/evidence-based-initiatives/know-your-powerr-bystander-social-marketing-campaign

[700] Potter, S. J. (2012). Using a multi-media social marketing campaign to increase active bystanders on the college campus. *Journal of American College Health*, 60, 282-29; Potter S. J., Moynihan, M. M., Stapleton, J. G. & Banyard, V. L. (2009). Empowering bystanders to prevent campus violence against women. *Violence Against Women*, 15, 106-121; Potter, S. J., Stapleton, J. G. & Moynihan, M. M. (2008). Designing, implementing, and evaluating a media campaign illustrating the bystander role. *Journal of Prevention & Intervention in the Community*, 36, 39-55

[701] Potter S. J., and Stapleton J. G., (2013). Assessing the efficacy of a bystander social marketing campaign four weeks following the campaign administration. *Sexual Assault Report*, 16(5), 65-80.

[702] https://www.cdc.gov/healthyyouth/hecat/

[703] https://www.cdc.gov/healthyyouth/hecat/pdf/hecat_module_v.pdf.

[704] Id.

[705] Sugai, G., Horner, R., Algozzine, B. (2011) Reducing Effectiveness of Bullying Behavior in Schools. *PBIS*. http://www.pbis.org/common/cms/files/pbisresources/PBIS_Bullying_Behavior_Apr19_2011.pdf.

[706] Id.

[707] Id. at p. 3.

[708] Id. at p. 3.

[709] Id. at p. 3.

[710] See full discussion on legal standards in Chapter 9.

[711] ThinkKids. (2016) *Collaborative Problem Solving Thinking Skills Inventory.* http://www.thinkkids.org/wp-content/uploads/2016/05/Electronic-CPS-Assessment-and-Planning-Tool-LIKERT-05-2016.pdf.

[712] See full discussion on legal standards in Chapter 9.

[713] Id.

[714] Williams, J. (2021) *Peacekeepers: An Implementation Manual for Empowering Youth Using Restorative Practices.* Jen Williams, publisher.

[715] https://www.samhsa.gov/brss-tacs/recovery-support-tools/peers

[716] Suresh, R., Karkossa, Z., & Richard,. Program evaluation of a student-led peer support service at a Canadian university. *Int J Ment Health Syst* **15**, 54 (2021). https://doi.org/10.1186/s13033-021-00479-7

[717] Id.

[718] American School Counselor Association (Adopted 1978; Revised 1984, 1993, 1999, 2002, 2008, 2015, 2021) The School Counselor and Peer Support Programs. https://www.schoolcounselor.org/Standards-Positions/Position-Statements/ASCA-Position-Statements/The-School-Counselor-and-Peer-Support-Programs. (Citations omitted)

[719] https://www.adolescentpeersupport.org

Made in the USA
Middletown, DE
25 January 2023

21758084R00239